COLOUR LIBRARY BOOKS

TRADITIONAL BRITISH CRAFTS

COLOUR LIBRARY BOOKS

TRADITIONAL BRITISH CRAFTS

Colour Library Books

CLB 2314
This edition published 1989 by Colour Library Books Ltd
Godalming Business Centre, Catteshall Lane,
Godalming, Surrey GU7 1XW

Original material © 1985–87 Marshall Cavendish Ltd
This arrangement © 1989 Marshall Cavendish Ltd

Prepared by Marshall Cavendish Books Ltd
58 Old Compton Street, London W1V 5PA

Printed and bound in Italy

ISBN 0 86283 753 7

This material was previously published in the Marshall
Cavendish partwork *Country Companion*.

CONTENTS

FOREWORD

It is a real pleasure to recommend this book. It is such an enjoyable book, a happy celebration.

The sharp fact is that we all of us have a hankering for the 'good old days', even though they surely lacked much of what we ourselves take for granted. There was nothing in the way of today's health service for the sick, pensions for the old, or even the power of the vote for many citizens. Life was hard for most people. So why do we find those olden times so deeply nostalgic?

I think that a large part of the reason is our innate respect for craftsmanship. We find pleasure in a job well done, personally seen through from start to finish. Not many modern employments offer that satisfaction, but it was once commonplace. Every community relied on its pool of skilled and reliable craftsmen – the makers of straw baskets (they'd soon be out of business if their bottoms fell through), the thatcher, the local potter.

Moreover, such skills enabled people to live closely off the land. The farm provided work and reason for the most people, and here the dry-stone waller was as canny a craftsman as the blacksmith, cattle droving kept as many secrets as thatching. For those communities facing the sea, there were the matching survival skills of boatbuilding, smoking fish to see the village through the winter, net making.

The skill of those past masters has been matched by the devotion and care with which this book has been assembled. It is meticulously researched and superbly presented. There are nuggets here for any and all magpie minds. Who can resist returning to the secrets of the coracle makers, or of the flint knappers whose skills originated in prehistoric times?

And what could be more evocative than the superb selection of old photographs in these pages? Those poachers (for people living so close to the land, poaching was only different in that it was illegal); the weary harvesters resting sweat-stained but happy, surrounded by the proud sheaves, their wives and daughters standing to their rakes (all the family helped to bring in the corn in those days); the merry fishwives whose smiles still warm us down the years.

However, there is additional importance in all this. Today our society is taking stock, querying where we're at, becoming uneasy about our treatment of the countryside, of wildlife, of the environment as a whole. Old skills are being examined anew, old ways brought forward for fresh appraisal. There is now a healthy market for organic food; and Shetland knitting, cheese making and traditional pottery are amongst the many skills experiencing a revival. Many are now even arguing that the crofting way of life can point us towards the long-term solution of agricultural over-production – those grain and butter mountains that we hear so much about.

This book can't but encourage such welcome developments.

Geoffrey Young

LIVING OFF
THE LAND

Following the Plough

Through the long dark days of winter, lashed by driving rain and chilled to the marrow by icy blasts, the ploughman, trailed by fluttering clouds of scavenging birds, carved the stubbled land into a rich ribbed seedbed ready for the new crop.

The plough is the most basic farming implement, and has been used by farmers since ancient times. Throughout the centuries its function has remained the same: to prepare the earth for a crop by turning the compacted soil, thus exposing it to the elements which will help to break down the earth into a crumbly well-structured tilth. At the same time the soil is aerated and any stubble or weeds are buried beneath the furrow where they will compost and help to replace the vital nutrients removed from the soil by the previous crop. Ploughing also promotes effective drainage: the rains that sweep across the winter landscape drain down the sides of the furrows into the subsoil where the moisture is stored to give life to the new seed.

The principle of ploughing is unchanged but the structure of the plough itself has developed through a series of refinements and adaptations designed to further increase its efficiency.

The soft, alluvial floodplains of Mesopotamia (in the Middle East) worked by the first farmers were so nourishing and friable that they had only to scratch the surface of the ground with a V-shaped piece of wood to bury the remains of the previous crop. Similar methods, sometimes using a deer's antler were common in Europe, as is evidenced by the small size and irregular shape of ancient fields.

THE FIRST PLOUGH

Such primitive picks were superseded some 3500 years ago by the first ploughs. The earliest plough, or 'ard', was like a long-handled wooden spade with an iron tip which was angled into the ground. It was hauled by oxen and guided by a ploughman. A second and even third man kept the oxen moving in the right direction. The iron tip scored crude furrows but did not entirely bury the weeds, so the field had to be ploughed across as well as up and down. This need to cross-plough a field led to the demarcation of square-fields – much easier for cross-ploughing. The existence of such fields has been detected in the subsoil near Avebury, Wiltshire, and from this and other archaeological investigations it seems that the simple ard may have been the

A LONG TRADITION *The medieval ploughman (far right) would find much familiar in the work of his early-20th-century counterpart (above), though his plough was of wood not iron, and was drawn by oxen rather than horses. Now the modern tractor has replaced both horse and ox, and much reduced the arduous nature of the ploughman's labours.*

tool responsible for extensive clearing and cultivation of lowland Britain thousands of years ago.

The heavy, wheeled plough, introduced around 100 BC, incorporated the three principal parts common to all ploughs from then on: the *coulter* which cut the furrow slice, the *share* which lifted it and the *mouldboard* which turned it over. The wheels – the larger one running in the furrow and the smaller one on land – lessened the drag on man and beast, and helped keep the furrows even. In some places a heavy, wheelless plough was used and many experts scorned the use of wheels for centuries.

Now that the furrow could be cut and inverted, cross-ploughing was no longer necessary and a further change in field shape took place. The heavy plough needed sometimes as many as eight oxen to draw it and turning the team at the headland – the end of the ploughing run – became a cumbersome manoeuvre. Fields be-

came long and narrow to reduce the number of turns that were necessary.

The plough was central to medieval life. Its vital role as the bread-giver was reflected in ritual and folklore, in the tax system and in the language itself. The word 'furlong' (220 yards) originated in the 'furrow long' of the heavy plough. A 'hide' was the area a team of oxen could plough in a year and became the unit on which tax assessments were calculated. An 'acre' was the area which could be ploughed in a day.

PLOUGH MONDAY

When most crops were spring-sown, the ploughing season began in early January. Plough Monday was the first Monday after Twelfth Night and on this day, the village ploughmen and boys would call at each homestead with their plough, expecting contributions for their evening festivities. Anyone reluctant to give

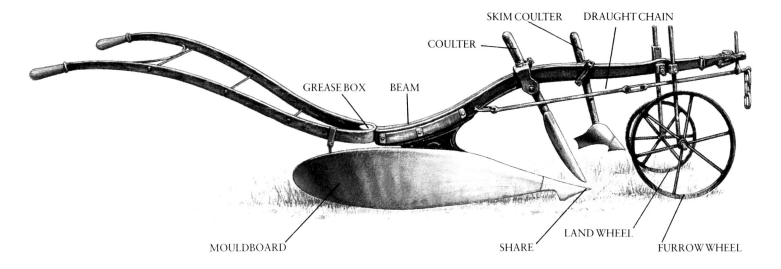

SKIM COULTER   DRAUGHT CHAIN

COULTER

GREASE BOX   BEAM

MOULDBOARD

SHARE   LAND WHEEL   FURROW WHEEL

THE COMMON PLOUGH
Variations in plough design proliferated throughout the 19th century, but the basic parts of the plough remained the same. This early-20th-century version shows the coulter, which sliced down the sides of the furrow, the share which cut beneath it, and the mouldboard, which turned it over.

PRIMITIVE METHODS
In some remote areas, such as the Orkneys (below), primitive farming tools and methods persisted long after most other places had joined the march of progress. This 19th-century photograph shows a crude, ox-drawn plough with coulter and share but no mouldboard. The medieval plough (far right) is more sophisticated.

would find a rough furrow driven outside their door for all to see.

The medieval open-field system was a co-operative enterprise. The ploughs, like the ram and the bull, were usually the property of the parish. They were made by the ploughwright who doubled as the village carpenter, while the iron ploughshares were forged and sharpened by the blacksmith. A well crafted plough could last for generations. The ploughman would plough his neighbours' field strips as well as his own receiving some other service in return.

REVOLUTION ON THE FARM

This system bound the community together in mutual dependence and kept everybody gainfully employed, but it was not highly productive. The invention of the four-coulter plough and mechanical seed drills by Jethro Tull in the early 18th century heralded an agricultural revolution that was to sweep all the old practices away. The enclosure movement led to the dispossession of many smallholders, and the ploughman became a hired hand.

Improvements to the plough continued. In the 1790s the Ransome family firm, pioneers of plough design, produced chilled iron shares,

which, unlike the old wrought iron ones, were made of hardened cast iron and tempered to be self-sharpening. Gradually cast-iron parts replaced wood for everything but the handles, though wooden ploughs remained in use in remote areas until the 20th century.

The 19th century also saw the transition from oxen to horses as the principal draft animals. The most popular breeds for farmwork were the Shire, the Clydesdale and the Suffolk Punch, all large, heavy and immensely strong. Usually two or three would be yoked to a single plough, sometimes in a line so they trod in the furrow bottom. In each team there was always a line horse who knew the ropes and could be relied on to steer a steady course and

THE PERFECT FURROW *The dimensions of the furrow slice were subjects of hot debate. The ideal was said to be 7" deep, 10" broad and laid against the next one at a 45-degree angle.*

FACTORY PRODUCTION *(right) The use of cast-iron for ploughs made it possible to make large numbers of parts from one mould. The old local ploughwrights became redundant, and firms like Ransome's sold their wares throughout the country.*

HORSE POWER *(below) Most ploughs could be drawn by two good horses – Shires were the favourites. For breaking up stubble, or ploughing old rough lea ground, three or four horses might be necessary.*

give a lead to the younger horses. Compatibility between the horses, and between team and ploughman, was essential.

Ploughing was always a strenuous task. Before dawn the ploughman would harness his animals and yoke them to the plough. All day long, often in freezing, windy weather, he would tramp up and down with one leg in the furrow and the other on the land, guiding the plough as it pitched and rolled, and shouting encouragement to his beasts. On the lea, where the land had lain fallow for several years, the ploughing would be even more arduous than on the stubble fields. Not until way past dark, after he had fed and groomed his team, would he have time to examine his calloused hands and rest his aching legs and arms, and the next morning he would be hard at work again before most other folk had risen from their beds.

STEAM PLOUGHING

By 1850 steam engines were being used instead of horses as a source of power to pull the plough. The apparatus involved was expensive and complicated and, in most cases, special steam contractors were engaged. One or two engines would be positioned at the headlands and the plough would be winched up and down the field by a series of cables, sometimes wrapped around drums, rotated by steam. Now that the power to pull a seven-furrow plough was available, claims that twelve acres a day could be covered were no exaggeration.

Steam ploughing was especially effective in heavy soils and it could be carried out at any time of year when the horses were otherwise occupied. The horses could be helping with harvesting in one field while the engines ploughed in the next ready for autumn sowing. Yields and profitability increased and steam

11

up into areas, known as 'lands', which would be ploughed alternately.

THE REVERSIBLE PLOUGH

The time-consuming process of travelling across the headlands from one land to another was eventually eradicated in the 20th century by the invention of the reversible plough. This has plough bodies mounted on the left-hand and right-hand sides of the main beam, which is pivoted on turning, enabling a single strip to be worked successively from one side to the other and back again.

By 1920 both horse- and steam-power had been replaced by the tractor. At first it was a two-man operation. As one drove the tractor the other steered the plough and controlled the depth of the furrow. But by the 1930s Ferguson had invented the hydraulic lift system which gave the tractor driver sufficient control to work the plough alone.

Ploughing today can still be a tedious business, especially on some of the huge, prairie-like fields of East Anglia, but the tractor has removed much of the sweat and toil of earlier days. The modern ploughman may sit in his air-conditioned cab with a console of lights and gauges before him to indicate the depth and accuracy of his plough, and levers and switches to make the adjustments.

In some places, ploughing has been abandoned altogether in favour of direct seed drilling. Modern spraying methods and the enormous range of light tillage implements available mean that minimum cultivation methods can now be effective. Even so, most British farmers still plough their fields at least once a year, usually after the harvest. It is an ancient tradition, and one that, in spite of modern theories, will not easily be relinquished.

PLOUGHING MATCHES *Ploughing competitions began in the 1790s and are still held in many places today. They provided a forum for debate, a showcase for new inventions and a chance for expert ploughmen to display their skills.*

THE AGE OF STEAM *The speed and efficiency of steam ploughs meant that much more of the land could be prepared for a winter crop immediately after the harvest.*

ploughs continued to be used in England right up until the 1940s.

The common plough had a fixed mouldboard which was 'handed', usually to the right. This meant that if the plough was worked successively up and down the field, it would create a series of deep troughs prone to waterlogging. The furrow seams had to be laid consistently in one direction. Various systems were employed. In medieval strips they would begin with a central ridge and plough on either side of it laying the furrow slices towards the middle on each side. Another practice was to plough in a circular course, beginning at the middle of a field and working to the perimeter. For most fields however it was necessary to divide them

Agricultural Gangs

**Victorian artists romanticized the life of the agricultural worker
with pictures of rosy-cheeked peasants working in sunny fields,
but the reality was somewhat different.**

The fields of Victorian England, in contrast to the countryside of today, bustled with activity – whatever the weather. Gangs of agricultural workers, mostly women and children, had a hard life, suffering bad weather, hard physical labour and sometimes the brutality of a drunken gang-master.

By the mid-19th century many farmers in East Anglia and the East Midlands relied on itinerant gangs of women and children to do routine jobs on their farms all the year round. Most of these farmers were working new land which they had recently reclaimed from wasteland. Some had cleared gorse and scrub from light upland soils to take advantage of high grain prices. Other farmers in the fenlands used steam pumps to drain huge areas of marsh and make them fit for cultivation. Farmers needed more help to cope with this extra workload, but they were reluctant to employ labourers on a permanent basis. They feared that if grain prices fell, they might be forced to abandon the land and dismiss their labourers. If they did this, and the labourers were housed in the parish, the

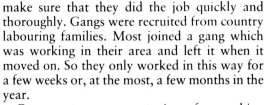

COUNTRY COMMUTERS
(above) Although some gang-workers had to walk for miles to the fields before starting work, many were provided with transport by the farmer or gang-master.

GANG AND MASTER
(left) Young men, women and children were recruited from the nearest village by the travelling gang-master, seen here far left. Gang-masters could be unsavoury characters, brutal and often drunk (below). There were also complaints that they 'took liberties' with the girls.

make sure that they did the job quickly and thoroughly. Gangs were recruited from country labouring families. Most joined a gang which was working in their area and left it when it moved on. So they only worked in this way for a few weeks or, at the most, a few months in the year.

Gang-masters were notorious for working their charges hard. As a rule the farmer paid the agreed price for the job no matter how long it took, while the gang-master paid the members of his gang a wage of anything up to a shilling (5p) a day each, depending on their strength and skill. So the harder a gang worked, the more money the gang-master made, while, if they worked slowly or inefficiently, he could end up with little or nothing. It is not surprising, therefore, that there were many complaints that masters bullied their gangs to make them work harder – shouting, swearing and even striking them if they seemed to be slacking. There were also complaints that some gang-masters 'took liberties' with girls under their charge, and one or two were actually prosecuted for indecent assault.

The number of people working in gangs and the kind of work they did varied according to the time of year. In 1866 a government enquiry reckoned that in all about 6500 people had worked in gangs in the Midlands and East Anglia at some time during the previous year. In winter, only a few were at work and the ones that were had strenuous jobs to do – clearing stones from arable land and sorting potatoes. In spring they dug up couch grass, spread muck, hoed and planted potatoes. In early summer, when the demand for their services was at its height, they helped with the hay harvest, cleared fallow land and hand-weeded grain and root crops. In late summer the gangs usually disbanded for the main grain harvest, when whole communities traditionally worked in the fields. In the autumn some gangs re-formed to harvest potatoes and mangolds.

Some jobs undertaken by gangs involved hard physical labour. Stone-clearing, turnip-pulling and potato-picking were particularly strenuous and were certainly more physically demanding than the alternative employment in the mills and factories. A particularly uncomfortable task was weeding a field of wet corn, where the women's long skirts and petticoats would quickly become saturated.

Most healthy children soon grew accustomed to the outdoor life of the agricultural gang. The work was more varied than at a factory and the air was certainly cleaner. By modern standards, the gang worked a long day – between ten and twelve hours – depending on the season. In the long warm days of early summer, when work was plentiful, the gangs worked even longer hours. A 16-year-old Norfolk girl described a typical autumn day: 'We topped and tailed this morning for one farmer, and forked docks this afternoon for another. We left the ground the

farmers, as ratepayers, would still be responsible for maintaining them and their families.

Some of these farmers recruited women and children from the nearest village and formed their own 'private gangs' of field workers who would work on their land for a few days or weeks at a time. Often they would provide horses and carts to take them to and from the fields. When the work on the farm was finished, the workers would be paid off.

PUBLIC GANGS

Farmers who did not want the bother of recruiting and supervizing gangs of workers, used 'public gangs'. These were under the control of a gang-master, who was usually an unemployed farm labourer. He toured the local farms, found out what jobs needed to be done, and agreed a price for them with the farmers concerned. He then recruited a gang of between 10 and 40 women and children, often transporting them to the farms to work and supervising them to

STEAM POWER
(right) The increasing use of heavy, steam-powered machinery slowly squeezed out the need for agricultural gangs. Although manual workers were often more thorough than the machines, they were much slower – one machine could do the work of many children.

CROWDED CONDITIONS
'Respectable' middle class country folk accused gang workers of being immodest and bawdy and viewed the gangs as a corrupting influence. But most of the gang-workers lived in appallingly overcrowded living conditions (left). Whole families, including grown-up children, had to share the same bedroom – with several to a bed – and had little chance of privacy. Many felt that it was this and not the gangwork which accounted for their lack of propriety.

afternoon at 5. Tomorrow morning we shall start at 7. I take dinner with me to work, bread, or bread with cheese or butter'.

Occasionally a gang would stay overnight at a farm, sleeping in a barn or outhouse, but as a rule gang workers travelled to and from their homes every day, either on foot or in a cart provided by the gang-master. A Huntingdon-shire mother complained that her two daughters, aged 11 and 13, had to walk eight miles, work in the fields for eight hours and then walk back home again – all for the pitiful reward of 3p per day each. But a journey of this length was exceptional, most gang workers walked only two or three miles to work.

NURSERIES OF VICE

Some gang workers were very young. Joseph Smith, a 10-year-old Lincolnshire boy who worked in a gang for 12 hours a day in early summer weeding corn, mangolds and carrots, said that some boys in his gang were even younger than he was. He remarked that though they were hit sometimes when they were idle, he 'would not mind going again. It was good fun'.

Like many children in rural areas at that time, Joseph Smith had taken time off school to join his gang, which probably accounts for his description of the work as 'good fun'. Certainly, many gang workers seem to have been very high-spirited, particularly on their way to and from work. Their shouts and screams shattered the peace of the countryside as they made their way to the fields, laughing and joking and trying to trip each other into muddy ditches and thorn hedges.

Their lack of propriety shocked many staid middle-class country dwellers who complained about their bad language. They were horrified when they saw the girls take off their wet skirts and petticoats and hang them up to dry after spending a morning weeding a field of wet corn, or witnessed boys bathing naked in the farm pond, while girls sat watching on the banks. These and other such scenes convinced many respectable observers that gangs were corrupt-ing the youth of the countryside.

In 1865, concern about the bad influence of the gangs reached such a height that the Children's Employment Commission was asked

EAST-ENDERS
Every September, until fairly recently, the hop fields of Kent would bustle with families from the East End of London. Travelling from London by train, they treated hop-picking as a kind of paid holiday – a wonderful opportunity to get away from smoggy London and into the clean country air. The farmers gave them a roof over their head, and many families returned year after year to the same farm. Some would even extend their holiday and stay to pick apples, plums and other fruit.

HOP HARVESTING
Today, manual workers are still used to harvest the hops (below), although machines also do their share of the work. Manual workers on foot and on tractor-driven platforms cut the hop strings and then feed them one at a time into a machine which strips off the hop cones.

to investigate them. One Norfolk clergyman interviewed by the commission did not agree that the gangs were the corrupting influence. He pointed out that labouring families usually lived in cottages with no more than one or two rooms, so that whole families, including growing and even grown-up children, had to share the same bedroom. So the lack of modesty among labourers was more likely to be as a result of their living conditions than the influence of working in gangs. But his contemporaries remained convinced that gang work damaged both the physical and moral health of young people. Critics were particularly concerned about the welfare of young girls tempted away from school and placed under the charge of a rough, sometimes brutal and occasionally drunken labourer to do hard, dirty outdoor work in all weathers in the company of ne'er-do-well boys and older women who were probably far from respectable. A possible underlying cause of this middle-class indignation was hinted at by the Rector of Stilton in Cambridgeshire, he told the commission that he thought gang work was unsuitable for girls as it made them

'rude, rough and lawless, and consequently unfits them for domestic servants and domestic duties'. Previously, most girls from poor country families had been expected to go into domestic service for the local landowner or rector. Once they had tasted the freedom and independence of open field work, they did not relish the prospect of subservience to, and respect for, their 'betters', and so gangs were also blamed for a shortage of domestic servants.

THE GANGS ACT

Though the witnesses interviewed by the Children's Employment Commission were far from unanimous in their condemnation of agricultural gangs, the commissioners decided that gang work did damage the health of the children who worked in them, and recommended that they should be controlled.

In 1867 Parliament passed an Act which set up a licensing system for gang-masters. It also prohibited the employment of all children under the age of eight, and made it illegal for males and females to work together in the same gang.

The Gangs Act marked the beginning of the

PERSONAL HARVEST
(above) In spring and summer women and children can still be seen working the fields, picking soft fruit which is difficult to harvest mechanically. But unlike Victorian workers (below) they pay to 'Pick-Your-Own'.

end for agricultural gangs. The increasing use of machinery hastened their decline – a pair of horses pulling a chain harrow to clear couch grass could do as much work as fifty children. The other development which undermined both public and private gangs was the growth of compulsory schooling. This was introduced in some areas in 1870, and became universal in 1880. The new law was enthusiastically enforced by teachers because their income depended partly on the number of pupils regularly attending school. Compulsory education was the final blow to the gangs system. Inevitably, some farmland suffered. In 1889 Earl Fortescue told the House of Lords that 'the fields of Norfolk, which had been kept like a garden by gangs of labouring children, now sprouted with weeds'.

Farmers throughout the country still relied on short-term casual labour to help harvest their crops. Fortunately, in most areas school holidays coincided with harvest time, so that for a brief period of the year gangs of women and children still picked fruit, stooked corn and, later in the season, picked potatoes.

Gangs of hop-pickers were among the most highly organized. Every September hundreds of East-Enders travelled to Kent to work in the hop-fields. They treated it as a kind of paid holiday. Hop-growers provided them with places to stay, and many families went back to the same farm year after year.

Today, machines pick crops such as hops, peas and potatoes. But some crops still need to be harvested by hand and on warm summer days elderly men, women and children can still be seen working long and hard in the fields. Now they arrive in the family car to pick their own personal harvest – more strawberries than they can possibly eat – seduced by the invitation to Pick-Your-Own.

Bringing the Harvest Home

Harvest time was once a busy, boisterous occasion. Now, instead of the rhythmic swish of scythes and the chatter of the reapers, only the steady chugging of the combine harvester, and the rattle of the tractors which serve it, disturb the silence.

The grain harvest is the climax of the farming year. The moment when the wheat, barley, oats or rye is safely gathered in is the culmination of an annual ritual which began the previous winter with ploughing the land and sowing the seed. Even today, when it is difficult to associate the sliced loaf in the supermarket with its wheatfield origins, there is still a sense of summer ending when the smoke of burning stubble clouds out the late summer sun.

Harvesting techniques remained virtually unchanged from time immemorial until well into the 19th century. The crop was cut with scythes and sickles; the sheaves were bound and stooked by hand; the dried harvest was carted to rick and barn. The changes that did occur were slow and subtle; crop yields improved and over the years the tools of the job were gradually refined.

The first sickles, from the tiny seven-inch blade of Bronze Age farmers to the reaping hooks of the Middle Ages, were narrow-bladed, deeply curved implements designed to be drawn smoothly across a bunch of stems held firm in the left hand. Some early sickles had small saw-teeth, as did the larger 'hewk' used in the north of England until the end of the 19th century. In an age when every last grain was precious, smaller sickles were used to cut relatively sparse crops so that there would be the least wastage. Later, as yields improved, the need for faster mowing saw the development of larger sickles and the more widespread use of scythes which had previously been used mainly for hay-making.

RIGS OF REAPERS

In contrast to today's one-man operated machines, harvesting used to be a labour-intensive activity. The well-being of the entire community during the coming year would depend on a successful harvest and, when the time and weather were right, everyone in the village would strive to bring the harvest home. In some places the harvest fields were worked by 'rigs', or teams of reapers, often women, using sickles. There were four reapers to a rig, plus a couple of children. The breadth of corn cut by two rigs was sufficient to provide sheaves for one bindster working between the rigs. He would bind the sheaves with twisted corn-stalk bands left on the ground by the reapers.

Hand-mowing continued to be common until the second half of the 19th century with the scythe replacing the sickle in all but the most remote areas. A double rig of sickles was hard pushed to cut one acre a day, but the scytheman could cut at least an acre a day single-handed. The scythe was a beautifully balanced tool that worked best to a steady rhythm. Led by the 'lord', usually the tallest and most expert mower, up to a score or more scythemen would progress in a staggered line up the cornfield. The corn fell to the left of each man, forming a neat row for gatherers and bindsters following behind. Everyone had to work at the same pace, set by the lord, pausing only to sharpen their blades. Sharpening was itself a major skill, performed with a strickle, a short length of oak with a pitted surface, into which was smeared a mixture of mutton fat and sand. In the late 19th century, the horse-drawn reaper and the reaper-binder were introduced, rapidly replacing the

PRECIOUS GRAIN
Women still worked in the fields well into the 20th century. They would follow the scythemen and binders and rake up the 'leazings' – loose cornstalks left on the ground – with a stubble rake.

THE SOLITARY COMBINE
The combine harvester in a modern harvest field not only cuts the corn, but threshes it at the same time, leaving the straw and chaff on the ground for baling or burning.

women with the sickles, the men with the scythes, the gatherers and the bindsters. With the reaper-binder one man and a couple of horses could accomplish in one hour what a good hardworking scytheman and his following wife could manage in a whole day.

But the sheaves still had to be stooked by hand. The corn was always mown when only half-ripe. Stooking gave time for weeds and grasses to wither away, and hastened the drying and ripening of the corn itself. Sheaves were usually stooked, a dozen or so at a time, in a tent-like shape, with space in the middle for air circulation. To gain maximum sun the stooks were lined up north-east to south-west. In wet weather they might be covered with two further sheaves.

When the stooked harvest had been dried by the sun and wind for as long as possible, the farmer, with one eye on the weather, would summon all hands to transport it to the barn or the rick-yard.

The 'pitchers' with their pitch forks would hoist the sheaves aloft on to horse-drawn carts, and 'loaders' would lay the sheaves methodically according to a well-established pattern. When the corn reached the top of the wagon's sides, harvest ladders were fitted at either end, and the load could be doubled.

In the yard another team unloaded the sheaves and stored them in the barn or built the ricks. Ricks had to be rat-proof and rain-proof. They were built either on a base of 'staddle-stones', consisting of conical pillars with domed capstones – later they were made of iron – or else on a raised stone or wooden platform with an overhanging lip to deter rodents. On completion the ricks were thatched against the weather.

The corn continued ripening in store over the next few months and was threshed – to separate the ears of corn from the stalk – in winter under cover of the barn. The threshing barn – the name

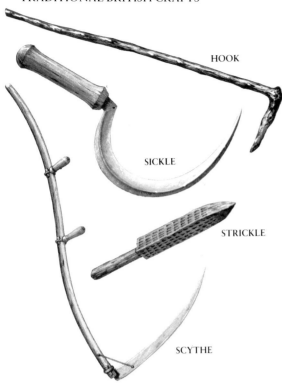

HOOK

SICKLE

STRICKLE

SCYTHE

AGE-OLD TOOLS
Harvesting tools have a long tradition. Where crop yields were low and women did the reaping, the sickle was used, often with a hooked stick to hold back the corn for the cut. Elsewhere the scythe reigned supreme. The corn was threshed with a flail and winnowed to separate the grain from the husk.

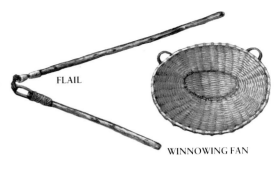

FLAIL

WINNOWING FAN

MEDIEVAL HARVEST
The harvest remained unchanged for centuries. The tools which were still being used in the early 20th century can be clearly seen in this medieval harvest panel (left). The entire village depended on the harvest so everyone lent a hand.

comes from an Old English word meaning 'barley house' – was a workplace, and not just a store-room. Built of different materials and with some variations in layout and size, the same basic design can be found all over the country. At its simplest it consists of two storage bays with a threshing floor between them. Centrally positioned doorways were usually at both sides of the threshing floor, and were high enough to allow passage of a well stacked cart. The double sets of doors enabled teams of oxen, which cannot be made to back up, to enter, unload and pass on through the other side. These facing doors were also partially opened during threshing, creating a through draught which aided the winnowing process – by which the grain was separated from the husk.

Most of the earliest barns still surviving are stone-built. Of these the largest are the great medieval ecclesiastical barns, built on a grand scale to accommodate the tithes, or church taxes, which were levied on local landowners and tenants of church lands, and paid in kind, particularly in grain. Yet despite their great size they are of the same design and function as the much smaller barns used by farmers. The harvested sheaves were stored at one end, threshed in the middlestead, or central area, and the residue of straw stored at the other end for animal feed, bedding and thatching.

SEPARATING THE GRAIN

The threshing floor was carefully constructed. Richer farmsteads used smooth, pegged oak, elm or poplar boards; others used flags of granite or other hard stone. Some were prepared by digging out, then layering gravel or sand, followed by a mortar-like mixture of clay, sand, crushed shells, chaff, cow dung and bullock's blood. This was laid at least an inch thick, allowed to dry, and then the entire process was repeated several times, finishing

off with a heavy pounding.

The corn was threshed on this surface by pairs of men using flails. The flail was basically two rods joined by a loose knot which allowed the implement to be swung in a circular action. The rod that struck the corn, the swingel, was shorter than the smoothed ash handle and was usually a thorn stick cut from a convenient hedge.

After threshing the grain was gathered up in wickerwork winnowing fans, or with wide wooden casting shovels, and thrown up into the air in a draught or breeze, so that the husks were blown to one side, and the heavier grain fell to the ground. The winnowed grain was either taken straight to the miller for grinding, or stored in a specially built granary. Like the ricks, this was raised on staddle stones or pillars to deter rats and mice.

There were many variations in the structure of the threshing barn. Sometimes the doors were porched to extend the threshing floor and give protection to laden carts waiting their turn in bad weather. Pitching holes were built into the gable

THRESHING BARNS
Most barns are similar in layout. There is a threshing floor with facing doors at either end, and a storage space for unthreshed corn on one side and one for straw on the other (below). Larger barns may have several threshing floors.

DOVECOTE

OWL HOLE

PORCH

PITCHING HOLE

THRESHOLD LEADING TO THRESHING FLOOR

AIR VENTS

PLAN VIEW OF BARN

end of some barns. These are like high windows with wooden shutters, and were used for throwing down sheaves into the barn from carts on the outside. Air vents – holes or slits in the walls – helped prevent the stored sheaves becoming mouldy. Sometimes these were formed by removing single bricks from the wall in various patterned formations. Others resembled the arrow slits in a medieval castle, where the outer edge of the opening is narrower than the inner edge. This allowed plenty of light and fresh air into the barn while keeping out damaging strong winds and rain. Another common feature is the owl hole let into the apex of the gable; barn owls helped keep down mice and rats.

By the end of the 19th century the traditional function of the barn had been taken over by mechanical threshing. However, the old barns were often adapted to house the new machines. Mechanical threshers had to be fed from above so lofts were built into the barns. Octagonal and circular housings for horse-powered units, known as 'gin-gangs', were added to the outside, and gear wheels, rods and belts transferred the horse-power to threshers, elevators and other machines. Manpower had given way to horsepower, but that in turn succumbed to steam and then to the internal combustion engine. The hustle and bustle of the traditional harvest has been replaced by the solitary splutter of the combine harvester.

Even so, the magic of harvest-time lingers on and in many parts of the country its traditions and rituals persist. In earlier times a successful harvest was, literally a matter of life and death. If the crop failed, the price of grain would soar which could mean hardship, and even starvation, for many families. So bringing the harvest home was the occasion for a great feast of rejoicing and thanksgiving, at the farmer's expense, in which the whole community would take part.

Tables would be set out in the open air or in the

THE MIDDLESTEAD
A typical three-bay, cruck-framed barn at Weston Court, Pembridge in Herefordshire, has now been adapted mainly for storage, and one of the huge doors has been partly boarded up.

shade of the barn if it rained. They would be laden with all manner of festive foods – ribs of beef, decorated hams or sucking pigs, great dishes of steaming vegetables, plus puddings and jugs of ale. The harvest workers would, on this occasion, be served by their masters and afterwards there would be music and dancing until far beyond nightfall in the light of the fat harvest moon. The harvest festivals still celebrated in many churches to this day are a more sedate legacy of this age-old practice.

CORN DOLLIES

The making of corn dollies is a relic of an ancient, pre-Christian ritual which aimed to preserve the Corn Spirit through the long dark days of winter. The twisted spiral or 'neck', fans, knots and charmers are some of the traditional shapes still made. Corn dollies had other names – 'kern baby', 'mare' and in Wales, 'the hag'.

PRESERVING THE CORN SPIRIT

As well as giving thanks for the year's harvest, it was important to ensure the success of the next. The Corn Spirit, a relic of pre-Christian beliefs, was thought to occupy the last sheaf of corn and there was often great reluctance to cut it. Several men would throw their sickles at it, thus sharing the responsibility. Once cut it would be decorated with ribbons, flowers and oak or ash boughs – or in some areas, women's clothes – and then it would be carried home on the cart or in procession and hung up in the farmhouse until the following year. Remnants of these traditions persisted well into the 20th century – until World War 2 boys in the East Midlands and East Anglia wore little button-hole emblems of twisted straw in their jackets at harvest-time.

Another widespread harvest custom – hundreds, possibly thousands of years old – was the fashioning of the last stalks to be harvested into one of the many 'corn dolly' shapes, in which the Corn Spirit could safely reside. Now commercialized for the tourist trade, with its significance largely forgotten, the making of corn dollies is yet a living fragment of our rural past.

DEVON NECK

STAFFORDSHIRE KNOT

CHARMER

HEREFORD FAN

Harnessing the Wind

Throughout history, the harnessing of wind-power has captured man's imagination, inspiring majestic windmills – marvels of early engineering – which were used to grind cereals or pump water.

Windmills were once characteristic of Fenland, their tarred towers and white sweeps prominent against huge East Anglian skies, often filled with scudding clouds. On a breezy day, vistas of racing sails animated the monotonous landscape: close to, the urgent swish and swift shadow of descending canvas and, in the background, a rhythmic splash of water scoops discharging into ditch and dyke. Yet these Fenland drainage mills – as many as two thousand in the 1700s – represented a minority use of wind-power: most of England's windmills, throughout their seven hundred year history, were built specifically for grinding corn.

The windmill has uncertain origins. Traditionally it was invented in the Middle East and, according to popular legend, introduced into Europe by returning Crusaders. But whatever its beginnings, the windmill emerged in England during the 12th century. Previously, mills were worked either by water or – more primitively –

by animals: almost certainly, none of the five thousand structures recorded in Domesday (1086) was wind-driven. However, although water-power was cheap and reliable, it was not uniformly plentiful. The dry eastern counties, in particular, lacked fast-flowing streams and it was here – across the flatlands of East Anglia and on the southern downs – that windmilling first developed.

The earliest type of windmill was the timber-framed post mill: the rectangular body, or buck, which housed the machinery and supported the canvas sails, was mounted on a giant centre post – some 20 feet high, two feet thick and normally made of oak. By means of the tail-pole, a long beam sticking out from the back, the carefully balanced mill could be turned – pivoting on its post – to face the wind.

By the late 1200s, post mills – their weather boards either painted white or coated with tar – were commonplace in waterless villages and

THE MILLER'S SHARE
(left) In times gone by, hundreds of windmills lined the ridges and hilltops of the English countryside, grinding cereals into flour for the local population. The miller worked hard to meet the demand, and in return took a toll of grain as payment for his labours. Since millers were allowed to sell their toll grain, some inevitably appropriated more than their official share. Chaucer's pilgrim miller 'was a master-hand at stealing grain./ He felt it with his thumb and thus he knew/ Its quality and took three times his due.'

of up to two months), it was vital to take advantage of the slightest breeze. The miller's first task was to luff the mill into the wind. Having first raised the sturdy step ladder – which not only gave access but also counter-balanced the sails – he either set his shoulder to the tailpole and pushed or, especially on bigger mills, harnessed a horse to the beam. The sails then had to be set: each sail was brought to the 'six o'clock' position so that the miller could easily climb up and thread the canvas lengthwise around crossbars attached to the stock. At this juncture, he had to decide how much canvas to use; for a light wind he would spread the whole cloth but in blustery weather he reefed the sails, drawing their outer edge inwards, like curtains. Inside, sacks of grain were hoisted up to the bin floor and the hopper (a cone through which the grain was passed) filled in readiness. Finally, when the infinitesimal gap between the mill-stones had been checked, the brake lever was released and the mill shuddered into life.

Above all, the miller had to be alert as to what was happening both inside the mill and out. If the hopper became empty, the stones, deprived of corn, might touch and throw out sparks to start a devastating blaze. The stones themselves were in constant need of attention as the gap between them, regulated according to wind speed, also determined the type of flour produced. Close-set stones gave a fine meal but, in a light breeze, could choke and cease turning altogether; stones set well apart yielded a coarser meal but, driven by a strong wind, could race and cause the mill to 'run away'.

In his traditional pose, standing at the mill door, the miller was not just enjoying a breath of fresh air away from the hot, dusty interior;

hamlets throughout the country. At that time all mills, whether driven by oxen, horses, water or wind, belonged to the lord of the manor on whose land they stood; furthermore, tenants were obliged to grind their corn at the manor mill. These rights, called soke laws, gave the lord a profitable monopoly over milling but they also safeguarded the people's interests: the lord was obliged to maintain enough mills to meet demand (in practice, one mill per 1000-1500 population) and keep them in good repair.

THE MILLER'S WORK

The soke also regulated grinding tolls: the amount of grist a miller could retain as payment for his work. Normally, this amounted to one sixteenth and was measured out in a toll-dish then stored in a special bin or ark.

The medieval miller worked a long, hard day – wind permitting. Since mills could be becalmed for several weeks on end (records show stoppages

THE POST MILL
The earliest and simplest type of windmill was the post mill – a sturdy, timber-framed mill constructed around a massive central post upon which the body (or buck) revolves. A 16th-century post mill can be seen among the stained-glass decoration of Stoke-by-Clare church, in Suffolk (right), while an unusually large post mill at Aythorpe Roding in Essex (above) has survived from the mid-18th century. This carefully restored windmill has a fantail built up around the ladder, which automatically turns the mill to face the wind.

rather, he was intuitively reading the wind, watching for any change in strength and direction. Variation in wind speed meant stopping the mill to increase or decrease sail area; in squally conditions this could be a hazardous operation, for if the brake slipped the miller, clinging to a sail, hurtled round and round. A sudden gale was particularly dangerous: the sails would be turning too quickly for the brake to be used (the immense friction caused by the brake would generate a hail of lethal sparks); so instead, the miller tried to calm the frenzied motion by choking the stones with grain and then by turning the mill at right-angles to the wind. In this new position, once the sails had slowed, the brake could be applied and the canvas reefed. An unexpected change in wind direction, through 180°, could be even more disastrous: when a mill was tailwinded the sails spun backwards, twisted out of shape and smashed into the back or were torn off completely; in extreme cases, the mill itself toppled over.

After five hundred years, mill design took a

WINDMILL DESIGN
(below) This cross-section of a post mill reveals the ingenuity of windmill design. The central post, about which the body revolves, leads to a central platform which supports the weight of the millstones. Outside, at the top, are two stocks; set at right angles onto the windshaft, these carry the sails. Inside, also on the windshaft, is a large cogged brake wheel which engages with the wallower (a horizontal gear wheel) to drive the millstones. A long tailpole projects from below the rear of the mill; the mill's position could be adjusted by moving the beam, using, for example, horse or man power (right).

major step forward with the invention of the cap – a revolving unit mounted at the top of the mill to which the sails were attached. Instead of having to luff, or wind, the whole mill, it was now only necessary to turn the cap and, as a result, the mill itself became a solid, immobile structure. Two types developed, both during the late 1600s: the smock mill and tower mill. The smock mill, so named because of its resemblance to a worker's smock, was a tapering wooden structure standing on a brick base; it was normally octagonal in plan, although some had as many as twelve sloping sides or as few as four.

The tower mill was very similar in design, except that it was usually round in plan and was built either of brick or stone; like the

THE SMOCK MILL
(right) In the 1600s, a new type of mill was developed, which did away with the inconvenience of turning the entire body of the mill to face the wind. The smock mill, so-called because it looked like a man in a smock, was fitted with a revolving cap to which the sails were fixed, together with a fantail mechanism: the fan automatically turned the cap so that the sails faced into the wind.

smock, it was tapered to lessen wind-resistance behind the sails. Initially, both types were winded manually, either with a tailpole extending down from the cap or by an endless-rope pulley system, but in the mid-1700s the fantail was introduced. Mounted at the rear of the cap and set at right angles to the sails, the fan automatically kept the sails facing the wind at all times. Fantails were also fitted to many post mills that were still in use – either attached to a wheeled carriage at the end of the tailpole or built up round the ladder.

IMPROVED SAIL DESIGN

Around this time sail design, too, improved considerably. First came the spring sail where the canvas was replaced by a row of hinged shutters – arranged like a Venetian blind – which were opened and closed by means of a spring loaded bar on each sail. The shutters themselves were normally made of either wood or canvas fixed to a frame. Although spring sails still had to be set individually in the six o'clock position, the operation was a lot simpler and safer than perching precariously on the sweep itself. The next invention, dating from 1807, was even more significant: patent sails which could be adjusted without stopping the mill. The shutters, controlled by a suspended weight, were self-reefing but could also be altered by the miller from inside the mill.

Windmills reached their zenith in England during the 18th century when, in their thousands, they stood sentry-like across exposed ridges, hilltops and open fields. The majority ground cereals into flour, or peas and beans into animal feed, but a few processed other materials such as snuff, tanning-bark, bonemeal, linseed oil and flint (for china). There were also wind-powered sawmills, fulling mills and, in the eastern counties, drainage mills – predominantly smocks in the Fens and brick towers on the Broads.

Whatever their function, all mills required regular attention from the millwright – the craftsman who built them (except for brick and stone sections) and who was responsible for their maintenance. Storm-smashed sails and other emergencies apart, repairs were normally carried out in winter when the mill was least busy, but the weather at its worst: balanced hazardously on a sailstock or crouched against the cap ridge, millwrights often endured icy cold, biting wind and drenching rain as they removed rotted or broken members and

THE TOWER MILL
(above) Whereas the smock mill is timber-framed, the tower mill is built of brick or stone. Both have a similar tapering shape – designed to provide the least wind resistance – but the tower mill is usually round in plan, rather than octagonal. The majority of tower mills are equipped with a fantail mechanism and a gallery. In general, tower mills are more durable structures than post or smock mills, because their thick walls are easier to weatherproof.

DRAINAGE MILLS
(left) While the majority of windmills were used for grinding cereals, there were also 'wonderful engines for throwing up water... one in particular threw up twelve hundred ton of water in half an hour; and goes by wind sails' (Daniel Defoe, 1724). Hundreds of these mills were used to drain the fenland of East Anglia; they were fitted with a bevel gear connected to a pit wheel, which was mounted on the same axle as a revolving paddle wheel. The largest could drain five hundred acres, lifting some eight tons of water a minute. (Defoe's claim was somewhat exaggerated!)

29

installed new ones.

If he was local, the millwright would prepare replacement parts in his shop, otherwise he worked on site. Using an adze, an axe-like tool known to the ancient Egyptians, he fashioned well-seasoned timber into shaft, whip, cap curb, fantail stage ... and, especially, cant or corner posts for smocks; in this type of mill the angled corners were very vulnerable to water and consequently, tended to rot. The millwright's choice of wood varied according to the task in hand: oak was preferred for the centre post and wind shaft; pitch pine for the sails; poplar for the cap rafters; elm for the brake wheel rim but apple (or beech) for its cogs.

The millwright also supervised removals. As settlements grew, wooden windmills were often re-located: in some cases, the encroachment of new buildings created turbulence and a better wind-catching position was required; in others, the mill – perhaps having become part of a built-up environment – constituted a danger to passing traffic. The sails, machinery and, where applicable, the cap were dismantled and transported separately. The mill itself followed on rollers or a special trolley, drawn by up to 40 horses or oxen.

Another essential craftsman was the stone-dresser. Often, he was an itinerant, travelling from mill to mill after harvest to renew the working surfaces of the two stones. Before this could happen, the runner, or upper stone, weighing around a ton, had to be lifted off. The dressing process itself – which took four or five days for a pair of stones – consisted first of smoothing the face by chipping away high spots and rubbing down, and then of recutting the fine furrows that served both to mill the flour and guide it outwards into sacks or bins.

The decline of windmilling began in the late 1700s with the advent of steam which had the dual advantage of being more reliable and more powerful: in the Fens, a steam pump soon proved itself to be 15 to 20 times more efficient than a windmill. Gradually, throughout the country, steam began to supplement, then replace the wayward wind. A century later, wind-milling's future was further eroded by the introduction of roller milling which produced whiter-than-white flour – greatly to the public's liking and quickly endorsed through government regulation. By the end of World War 2, most windmills had gone out of business.

Today, some old mills have been restored as evocative reminders of our industrial heritage; others have been renovated and turned into picturesque dwellings. And, on the horizon, wind-power is making a comeback. Not to grind corn or pump water, but to generate electricity. These new hi-tech structures – sleek wind turbines – are currently being tested in Scotland and could ultimately produce 20 per cent of Britain's electricity. Nine hundred years on, the sails are still turning and man is still harnessing the wind.

WINDMILL REPAIRS
(above) Because the mill was subject to the most appalling weather conditions, it was in constant need of attention. Repairs were normally carried out in the cold winter months, long after the busy harvesting season. Here, the millwright and his assistants are constructing a new set of sails to replace the old ones, which have rotted away.

THE STONE-DRESSER
(left) After weeks of grinding, the working surface of the great millstones is gradually worn away and the stones have to be restored. This task was traditionally performed by the stone-dresser, who rubbed down the surface and then re-cracked the stone so that the sharp-edged furrows would mill the flour efficiently and guide it into the waiting bins or sacks. The cutting, or cracking, was done with a steel chisel-like tool called a mill-bill; as the dresser worked, splinters of steel would occasionally fly off and embed themselves in his hands – hence a worker could prove his experience by 'showing his metal'.

Making Hay

Haytime – traditionally a vital point in the farming year – brought with it the heady scent of fresh-mown grass, meadows ribbed with drying swathes and the appearance of haystacks in the fields all around.

Ever since Bronze Age cultivators hammered out the first sickle and then learnt how to preserve cut grass, hay has been the staple fodder crop for overwintering livestock and haymaking became an integral part of rural life.

From Celtic times onwards, a plentiful hay harvest insured farmers against a bleak winter and promised a good start to the New Year. By Domesday, all aspects of agriculture came within the feudal system and, as such, were well-organized. Haymaking was no exception. Each parish set aside special meadows for cropping hay. Normally, these were low-lying grasslands outside the village alongside a stream where permanently moist soil guaranteed a strong, rich growth year after year. Rights to graze and mow these water-meadows were granted on an annual basis, usually by drawing lots; the name 'Lot Meadow' persists in various parts of the country to this day. For allocation purposes, the meadows were divided into strips, often one scythe-swath wide and marked out with mere-stones.

Although June and July were the busiest main hay-making months it was possible to take two – or even three – crops during the year, with the last in August. When the grass was ready for cutting (in flower, but not seeding), harvest operations were organized by the hayward, a foreman whose prime responsibility was to supervise the tenants as they mowed and turned the hay, then piled it into cocks and finally, into stacks. After harvest, the same tenants were allowed to graze their animals communally, on the hayfields: this right generally extended from Lammas Day (1 August) to All Saints (1 November) and these meadows were sometimes called Lammas Meads. Not only did the animals benefit from lush grass and nearby water but they, in turn, helped fertilize the meadows for next year's crop with their droppings.

Watermeadows were such a valuable asset

CUT AND DRIED
(right) Modern haymaking is highly mechanized, the whole procedure, from cutting the grass to baling it as hay, performed entirely by tractor-drawn implements.

CUTTING GRASS
(below) The scythe, a tool for cutting grass, probably introduced to Britain by the Romans, was only superseded by mechanical cutting machines in the 1850s.

that many parishes tried to extend their area, sometimes by draining riverside marshes or, more frequently, by damming streams and diverting water along channels into drier pastures.

Throughout the Middle Ages and into Tudor times, the hay cycle continued in its age-old rhythm although, in the background, the feudal system died out. During the period 1550-1650, however, three developments took place which had a significant effect on grass and, by extension, on hay.

AGRICULTURAL CHANGES

First came up-and-down husbandry (farming), an alternating field-use system which was widely adopted during the sixteenth century. Under this system, pasture was ploughed up for corn and cornland was laid down to grass, thus doing away with the ancient problem of having permanent tillage and permanent grazing. Grassland would be broken up and cultivated for three or four years – often with oats, barley, wheat or rye, sown in that order. The field was then laid down – natural grasses sprang up from old roots that had remained undisturbed by surface ploughing – and reverted to pasture for six or seven years. Up-and-down, as this

system was called, brought all-round benefits: grazing animals manured the soil and grass rested it, with the result that crop yields greatly increased – in some cases, by twenty fold. Conversely, the grass itself – growing up young and fresh after a few years' break – was rich in nutrients and often so plentiful that there was enough for a hay crop as well: production of meat, milk, wool and hides escalated.

The second innovation, dating from the 1590s was the extension of the grazing periods in late autumn and early spring. This was done by flooding the water-meadows. A grid of channels, which could be filled by damming the stream, spread over the meads. Water was made to flood out of these channels, so covering the meadows with a shallow, gently-flowing wash. 'Floating' the meadows in this way for a short spell in summer forced an extra crop of hay and made November grazing possible.

Winter floating was even more valuable: sediment from the stream helped fertilize the soil while the water sheet protected it from frosts, so encouraging an earlier, richer growth of grass in spring for longer grazing and a better hay harvest. Within fifty years, floating had become standard farm practice throughout the

THE HAYMAKERS
(above) Up to the mid-19th century haymaking was done by hand. Every able bodied villager took part. The men, organized by a foreman, the hayward, formed mowing teams. At the end of a long day – about 14 hours – a good mower would have cut an acre and a half. Men and women, haymakers, followed the mowers, turning the new-mown hay so that it dried quickly and evenly before it was raked into small heaps or cocks. For two days following, the small heaps were spread again for the hay to dry out and on the third day after cutting it was loaded on to a hay wagon to be taken away and made up into haystacks.

Fig. 11.—Corbett's Combined Hay-Press and Weighing Machine.

Full information on Laying Down Land to Grass gratis and post free.

SUTTON'S GRASS SEEDS FOR ALL SOILS

All Goods of 20s. value, Carriage Free.

5 per Cent. allowed for Cash Payments.

PRODUCE the BEST HAY CROPS and SUPERIOR PASTURAGE.

SUTTON & SONS, The Queen's Seedsmen, READING, BERKS.

TEDDING THE HAY
(above) The drying process was speeded up in the early 20th century by a horse-drawn machine with circulating tines which turned the grass

HAY SEED
(left) This late-19th century seed advertisement reflects the (continuing) search by farmers for grass, which gave a greater and better crop.

HAY PRESS
If the hay harvest was bountiful, farmers sold any surplus at the nearest haymarket. From the late 19th century hay to be sold was baled, tied and weighed using a combined hay press and weighing machine like the one above.

country as is shown by a contemporary saying: 'He that doth drown is a good husband'.

NEW SEEDS

The third innovation, and that which had the greatest effect on haymaking, was the introduction of 'new grasses'. From time immemorial, hay meadows had just grown naturally, containing a range of wild grasses and early-flowering plants, such as cowslips and cuckoo-flowers, which had a chance to seed before the hay-cut. But with the spread of up-and-down husbandry, farmers experimented with planting grass seed to help create even better pastures. At first, they got their seed by threshing grass that had been cut for hay – often simply by beating it against a stone or over a hurdle. Then, in the mid-1600s – following the example of Dutch agriculturalists – they started to sow sainfoin,

clover and rye-grass. Sainfoin (French for 'holy hay') was highly successful: it produced a rich hay-cut, with ample grazing afterwards for at least five years. Italian rye-grass and red clover proved ideal for short-term (one- or two-year) hayfields; while perennial rye-grass withstood repeated grazing and cutting for ten years or more. Ever since, these 'new grasses' have formed the basis of leys – as temporary grass-lands with a maximum life of twelve years were called. Lucerne was also tried but was less popular than sainfoin; ironically, it has now replaced the latter as one of the country's top hay crops, tolerating four cuts a season for several successive years.

In spite of these improvements affecting grass production, haymaking methods themselves scarcely changed. Even by the middle of the 19th century, hay was still being harvested in

BACK TO THE LAND
*During World War 2, the
need for self-sufficiency
resulted in an increase in the
use of manual labour,
recreating the haymaking
scene more typical of
the 19th century than
the 20th.*

USING HAY
*(below) Before the
introduction of mechanized
baling, hay was stacked,
sometimes in a series of small
stacks, from which it was cut
when needed.*

much the same way as it had been, thousands of years previously, by Bronze Age cultivators.

TO MOW A MEADOW

Before the advent of mechanization, haymaking was a village affair: men used to cut, women followed behind turning and raking. As it was all important to take advantage of fine weather, mowing began at dawn – even if dew still moistened the grass – and lasted till dusk. The mowing team – generally three or four men – worked its way across the meadow, swinging long scythes (introduced by the Romans and giving a closer cut than sickles). By the end of the day – probably as long as 14 hours – each mower would have cleared an acre and a half. It was arduous work or, as a contemporary farming

manual states: 'their labour is very severe: they have, however, an allowance of strong beer, which is not usually given to other labourers'. The rest of the workforce would have been issued with a weaker brew, while cider was more common in the West Country and cold tea on teetotal farms.

Behind the mowers, came the haymakers – four or five to each scytheman. Their first task was to ted, or spread out, each swath and then turn the loose grass at intervals of two or three hours so that it dried evenly and quickly. Next, using wide drag rakes, they collected the hay into long, narrow lines called windrows; finally, before nightfall, they forked the hay up into small heaps variously known as cocks, stacklets, pikes or colls.

The following day saw the process repeated: cocks were dismantled and the hay strewn out; raked up again into windrows around noon, and then into cocks by evening. A hay- or drag-rake was a sturdy tool with a span of up to six feet; its handle was made of split willow, the stock of oak and the tines, ash.

STACKING THE HAY

On the third day, hay was normally ready for stacking. Horse-drawn waggons bumped round the meadow, stopping by each cock. Hay was forked up and laid down in sequence – a crossways course followed by a lengthways one – to bind the load together. Children, on top of the cart, trod each forkful down.

The stack itself, constructed either in the field or in the farm rick-yard, stood on a moisture-proof platform of logs, stone, chalk or furze covered with straw. It was built up, carefully, layer by layer; near the top, the sides were made to project outwards slightly, like overhanging eaves, to protect the bulk of the structure from rain. The completed stack, about ten feet high, was thatched with wetted wheat or rye straw; in the 1850s, a thatcher working on an average-sized stack would earn about four shillings.

The ever-present hazard, threatening hay-making at all stages, was damp. Fine weather was essential during the harvest period as hay must dry quickly to maximize its sugar content. For this reason, once cut, it had to be well tedded during the day but cocked before night-

fall to protect it from ground moisture; similarly, on the second day, cocks were not opened until the dew had evaporated. If hay is stacked wet, it ferments too vigorously, overheats and may fire the rick. Also, although slight fermentation is desirable as it makes the hay more nutritious, excessive heating destroys the protein content. But if the weather broke and wet-stacking was unavoidable, farmers would construct smaller ricks, to reduce the heat build-up, and maybe interleave the hay with layers of straw or sift through a sackful of salt.

THE HAYMARKET

A plentiful crop ensured enough hay for the farmer's own use and provided some for market as well. During the 1800s, with the growth of urban centres and the increase in horse-drawn traffic, demand for hay escalated: in summer, convoys of hay barges, called stackies, used to bring loads of fodder up the Thames for London's growing population of horses. And in all parts of the country, most towns and cities had a haymarket where hay was sold in large sheaves.

It was not until the late nineteenth century, when scythe, rake and fork had been in service for some 2000 years, that British haymaking succumbed to mechanization. First came a mowing machine, capable of cutting ten acres a day, but as the mown grass, left in swathes, still had to be tedded, raked and cocked by hand the numbers of haymakers required increased, rather than decreased, to keep up with the faster cutting-rate. By the turn of the century, however, machines had taken over the whole process. Also, towards the end of the 1800s, silage developed as a viable alternative to hay – especially in cooler parts of the country or during a wet summer. Instead of being dried, the cut grass is stored green in silos where, compressed and deprived of air, it converts into rich fodder.

Mechanization has turned haymaking into a one-man-and-his-tractor job. Yet while the weather remains beyond the control of science, haymaking will always be a gamble, even if the odds have improved considerably since the Bronze Age.

MODERN TIMES
(top) Modern baling methods dispense with the need to pitch dried or drying hay from the swathes into small stacks on the field. Instead, as shown above, the hay lies in swathes, where it is turned by a swathe turner, a tractor-pulled machine with rimless wire wheels. When the hay is dry a tractor-driven baling machine (above) moves along the swathes, rolling it in to cylindrical bales. The bales are mechanically lifted on to a cart and transported to barns for storage. When needed, the fodder can be transported to the fields, and unrolled and broken into smaller sections for outwintering stock to eat.

The Lonely Shepherd's Life

Out in all weathers and occupied with his flock from dawn to nightfall,
the good shepherd had to be not only the watchful guardian of his flock but
also a vet and midwife.

Before coal and iron made Britain the first industrial country the wealth of the nation derived principally from wool. The Romans introduced white long-woolled sheep to these islands and over the centuries they displaced the indigenous dark, goatish breeds. Wool manufacture declined during the Dark Ages but with more settled times the industry was quickly re-established and by the 12th century England had become Europe's prime source of fine quality wool.

The largest flocks were owned by the monasteries but there were also secular fortunes to be made. Wool merchants became rich men, and wool money built great houses and churches, endowed colleges and schools, and financed the 100 Years War. By Tudor times there were 10 million sheep in England, producing 8500 tons of wool a year.

Until this century the greatest concentrations of sheep were found in the south and east.

Chalk downlands were particularly suitable and in the 18th and 19th centuries they were covered in sheep. But food shortages in two World Wars saw much of the downs fall to the plough, and the majority of Britain's 33 million sheep are now to be found on the uplands of the north and west.

More than 30 regional breeds and recognized cross-breeds go to make up this population, falling into two major types, hill and lowland. Hill sheep can stand harsh conditions and poor grazing but are not prolific breeders. Whereas a lowland farmer looks for a crop of two lambs per ewe each year, the hill farmer is happy with one.

Lowland sheep on lush pastures form close, dense populations, whereas hill sheep are sparsely scattered across the high rugged ground. But there is nothing random about their roaming. Hill sheep left to their own devices, stay close to the spot where they were

A WINTER GATHER
(below) Hardy upland sheep overwinter on the hills with the shepherd gathering them in only in especially harsh weather or for 'drenching' with medicine.

born – an instinctive bond known as 'hefting'. If they are gathered in by the shepherd, then returned to the hills, they make straight for the familiar surroundings of their heft.

Sheep are reared today more for their meat than their wool and milk, but the shepherd's job has hardly changed for centuries. The life could be a very lonely one. At crucial times like lambing and shearing, the shepherd virtually lived on the job with only his dog for company.

RHYMING SCORE

The ancient, localized and solitary nature of the craft is reflected in the strange and arcane language used by shepherds to describe their charges and, in particular, to count them by what is known as 'rhyming score'. Words redolent of French, German, Norse and Gaelic numbered sheep. In Sussex they began 'one-erum, two-erum, cock-erum, shu-erum . . .'; in Cornwall 'on, dow, tray, pajy, pemp . . .'; in the North and the Scottish Borders, where it remains more common, it was 'yan, tan, tethera, pethera, pimp . . .'.

The outdoor habits of sheep mean that little remains to mark their passing. They were rarely housed in buildings and even shepherds made do with makeshift shelters such as the wheeled shepherd's huts which had windows on all sides so the shepherd could see and hear his flock.

The shepherd listened for the bells of his sheep as well as for their cries. At night they warned him if the sheep were straying or agitated. Bells were used more often on downland than in the hills where the sheep spread out. A more widespread item of the shepherd's equipment were the hurdles – sections of temporary fencing of wood or wattle. In winter hurdles were used to fold the sheep over turnips. The flock would be penned in over a small section of the turnip field until they had cleared all the top growth and manured the ground, then they would be directed to the next section by moving the hurdles.

But the two things that most surely define the shepherd and are indispensable to his job are his crook and his dog. The shepherd's crook has long been the unmistakable hallmark of his profession. At traditional hiring fairs where each man would carry an emblem of his calling – the carter a whipcord, the thatcher a wisp of straw – the shepherd carried his crook. The handle is usually ash or hazel and the hook is iron – in Scotland carved sheepshorn is sometimes used. There are three distinct types which come in a variety of sizes. Most common is the leg crook, designed to hook around the hind leg of the sheep. Neck crooks are the same shape but larger. Dipping crooks have a double curve. One shoves the beast under the water and the other hooks its head out again.

Even more ancient than the crook is the partnership between shepherd and dog. Men and dogs have worked together with sheep for thousands of years.

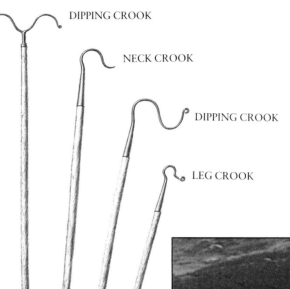

DIPPING CROOK

NECK CROOK

DIPPING CROOK

LEG CROOK

CROOKS *(left) The shepherd's crook probably originated in Britain in the Dark Ages. In the hands of a skilled shepherd it is a cunning tool. Once in its grip the sheep cannot struggle loose, yet it does not bruise or cause the animal any pain.*

WORKING DOG *(right) Managing sheep in the uplands would be an impossible task without the aid of the tireless collie.*

REDDLE MARKS *(below) The red patches on the sheep in 'Sheep Feeding' by Myles Birket Foster is probably 'reddle – a mixture of red ochre and size once used to mark sheep.*

More than 50 breeds of stockherding dogs exist in the world today, but none rival British collies – from the Celtic *coillean*, meaning 'little dog' – in their abilities with sheep. Originally, sheepdogs were essentially guardians of the flock, bred for strength and aggression. In Britain, where ferocious predators like wolves and bears became extinct earlier than in mainland Europe, the emphasis switched to breeding dogs that were smaller, swifter and more intelligent. Collies came to dominate here, whereas in Europe, where wolves survived, alsatians and Pyrenean mountain dogs were more typical.

TRAINING THE COLLIE

Herding ability, limitless patience and a positive relish for work have been bred into collies, and the Border collie, originating in Scotland as recently as last century, now herds more than a third of the world's sheep. A collie's training begins when it is between six months and a year old. In 12-18 months it will learn the basics and it will take another year or two until its training is completed – the best dogs in trials are usually three to five years old. Shepherds prefer to breed and train their own dogs rather than buy them in as, knowing the parents, they can then be sure that the pup's character and temperament are suited to the task.

From very early in its life the collie pup will attempt to herd chickens, cats, or anything else in the farmyard. Training is aimed at bringing out and channelling this natural ability, an adaption of the pack hunting instinct.

When the pup is introduced to sheep, it is usually as a spectator tethered to watch another dog, often its mother, put through her paces by the shepherd. The pup begins to associate the whistles, gestures and shouts of the man with the actions of the dog. Later, the pup is set to work with the older dog and the training is completed with a mixture of encouragement, kinds words and occasional scoldings. Some dogs show special abilities – to find lost sheep, for example – and these are encouraged but all dogs learn to move sheep, to keep them still, and to separate and pick out individuals.

Competitive sheepdog trials are a relatively recent innovation; the first was held in Bala, Wales, in 1873. They were soon recognized as valuable demonstrations of new ideas in the craft of handling sheep and of the merits of individual dogs. Trials have led to great improvements in the breed. For the shepherd they are also a welcome diversion in his working life, which is still very much tied to the annual life-cycle of the sheep.

The shepherd's year begins in the autumn when the rams, or 'tups', are put to the ewes.

SHEEPDOG TRIALS
The trial reflects the everyday tasks of the sheepdog. The 'outrun' (1) sends the dog out behind the sheep without disturbing them. Then he 'lifts' them (2) and 'fetches' them (3) direct to his master. The drive (4-7) is a triangular course taking in two pairs of hurdles. In the 'shed' (8) the dog separates two sheep from the rest. Finally, the dog 'pens' the sheep (9). In some trials there is another stage – the 'single' – in which the dog separates one sheep from the rest.

The gestation period is five months and tupping is timed to produce lambs in the spring. On hill farms this can be as late as December, two or three months after the lowland breeds. The tup carries a patch of dye on his underside so that the shepherd can tell at a glance which ewes have been covered. The pregnant ewes are left to overwinter on the hills.

Hardy upland sheep can survive almost all weathers, foraging beneath the snow for shoots of grass or heather. In very severe weather the shepherd must bring the ewes down from the high ground or, if this is impossible, take extra fodder up to them. Sheep are particularly prone to being swallowed up in snowdrifts owing to their habit of feeding with the wind at their tails. Driven before the wind they stop at an obstruction – a dyke or hedge – and are quickly covered. Fortunately they can survive this for weeks, warm in their wool and sustained by the contents of their ruminant stomachs.

DRENCHING

Six weeks before lambing they are 'drenched' for worms and fed on concentrates and vitamins until they lamb. 'Drenching' is the shepherd's word for dosing with medicine.

In lowland farms, the pregnant ewes are folded together and the new lambs are born into a bedlam of bleating. On the hills they are dropped anywhere that takes the ewe's fancy. In both locations it is the busiest and most important part of the shepherd's year. He assists those ewes with labour problems and seeks out orphaned or abandoned lambs. The orphans are either bottle-fed and hand-reared by the shepherd, or fostered on a 'keb' – a ewe that has lost her lambs.

At four months old the lambs are brought in to be weaned. The ewes are put on to poorer grazing to dry up their milk and the lambs are marked – this used to be done with branding irons, but now ownership is established with ear tags and coloured dyes.

Sometime between May and August shearing takes place. In the warmer weather the fleece 'rises'. The matted inner layer lifts away from the body to cool the sheep, and the whole fleece is then easily removed by cutting through the new wool beneath.

At the end of the summer it is time for the shepherd to take stock; he has to decide which beasts to retain as part of the breeding flock and which to sell. Ewes on the hillside are good for three seasons, after which they are sold to lowland farmers as 'draft ewes'. The better conditions on the lower slopes mean that they can continue lambing for another two years. Hill lambs are rarely large enough to be sold for meat at the end of the summer, and these are also sold to lowland farmers as 'store lambs' to be fattened up. Once the sales are over, it is time for the shepherd to return to the breeding flock on the hills and downs, release the tups and prepare for the new season.

ON THE HILLS
(above) The hefting instinct helps the upland shepherd control the wanderings of his flock, but even so he has to cover many miles of ground.

DIPPING
(right) Periodic dipping in a variety of medicinal concoctions helps protect the sheep from the innumerable diseases and parasites to to which they are prone.

The Wool Clip

For centuries the sheared fleeces of sheep – 'the clip' – have provided work and wealth for Britain. Today, apart from mechanization of some of the activities, the business remains much the same.

'All the world wears it, all the world desires it and all the world almost envies us the glory and advantage of it.' This praise, from Daniel Defoe, referred to 'our English woollen manufacture' which, like the wool trade before it, had been a major source of national prosperity and pride for many centuries.

Britain's long association with wool began about 2000 BC, when Bronze Age peoples developed the arts of spinning and weaving and so invented woollen cloth. These first wool-workers obtained their raw material by 'rooing', plucking it from sheep during the summer moult. But 1000 years later, shearing – cutting off the fleece in one piece – had largely replaced rooing.

The Roman invaders of Britain expanded cloth production and, consequently, sheep-farming: they also introduced new breeds of sheep – the ancestors of today's Romney, Cotswold and Leicester breeds all have Imperial origins. They set up wool workshops in the larger towns and established a weaving mill – Britain's first-ever factory – possibly at Caistor. By the third century, woollen cloth was a major export. During the Dark Ages, however, the industry contracted: sheep being prized more for their manure and meat than for their fleece. Yet most peasants kept a few animals so that their womenfolk might have enough wool to spin and weave into everyday clothing.

WEALTH FROM WOOL

With the Norman Conquest, wool's fortunes revived dramatically. The new landowners – French lords, abbots and bishops – invested in large flocks of sheep, primarily for wool production. Much of the clip was bought by wool merchants for re-sale to weavers in Flanders and Lombardy. In the 1300s, up to two million fleeces were exported annually. Parcelled into huge sacks they were carried to designated ports either by wool train, a convoy of pack-horses, or in wool wains – wagons that were covered against rain but side-ventilated to prevent over-heating of their heat-retaining cargo. They were then shipped to Calais, the official wool port or Staple (exchange), where the Crown levied its export tax – as much as £2 a sack when there were costly wars to finance. Frequently, wool itself served as money: in 1194, the ransom paid to secure the release of

Richard I consisted largely of English fleeces.

From the mid 14th century, however, the trading pattern changed. An influx of refugee Flemish weavers, followed by the trade embargoes imposed during the Hundred Years War, revitalized England's own wool-working industry. Within a century, wool exports fell by three-quarters while overseas sales of cloth increased fourteenfold. For the next four hundred years, woollen manufacturing was Britain's main industry, her leading export and principal source of wealth.

Numerous flock-owners, merchants and clothiers – including Dick Whittington – made vast fortunes out of wool. Some of this wealth from wool went to endow charities, found hospitals and build the magnificent 'wool' churches of East Anglia, the West Country and the Cotswolds. Other enduring reminders of wool's

Baa baa, black sheep, have you any wool.

importance in medieval times include place names such as Ascot (eastern cot or sheep shelter), Sheppey (sheep island), Shipton (sheep farm) and Shiplake (sheep washing-pool). And many traditional sayings, like 'dyed in the wool', 'on tenterhooks' and the nursery rhyme 'Baa, baa black sheep' which recalls the greatly unpopular 1275 export tax on fleeces, date from the time when wool was all-important. Dyer, Fuller, Weaver, Webster and other family names, pub signs advertising The Fleece, The Woolpack, The Pandy (fulling mill) and, most of all,

BAA, BAA BLACK SHEEP *(left) So strong has the influence of wool been at all levels of life in England through the centuries, that it has even percolated into children's nursery rhymes. First written down in 1744, the favourite children's rhyme,* Baa, Baa Black Sheep, *refers in the division of bags, to the export tax of 1275 levied on wool.*

THE ANNUAL WOOL CLIP
(left) Since the Domesday survey, and possibly even before then, sheep shearing has been a specialist and well-organized activity in the countryside. From late May until August, itinerant gangs of up to 30 men would work their way through the sheeplands. In some cases, like that shown left, individual farmers and shepherds performed the annual clip solely on their own flocks. Methods of holding sheep varied from place to place but the general principle was to hold the sheep firmly and then throw it on its back, to immobilize it. It was either sheared on a special wooden trestle or gripped firmly between the shearer's knees on the ground.

SHEARING TODAY
(below) Shearers still operate in groups but the tools they use are more modern. Instead of handshears, today's sheepshearers use electric shears powered from temporarily rigged electric cables.

the House of Commons' woolsack, also confirm the past status of wool.

The 16th and 17th centuries witnessed a further expansion of the wool industry, stimulated partly by the discovery of new markets and partly by the nationwide enclosure movement which made thousands more acres available for grazing. Definite breeds emerged, suited to distinct habitats. Long-wool sheep, like the Teeswater, Lincoln and Romney, belonged to rich lowland pastures. Their long staple (raw wool) – 14 inches long on the Lincoln – was used to manufacture fine worsteds. In contrast, the short-stapled Downland breeds, such as the Ryeland, produced heavier cloths. Hardy mountain sheep, the Herdwick and Scottish Blackface, had coarse wool. The Scottish Blackface, however, currently ranks as a major wool producer, second only to the Mule, a long-wool cross between the Blueface Leicester and the Swaledale.

The Industrial Revolution came as a mixed blessing to the woollen industry. Although mechanization facilitated mass-production of woollen

and worsted cloths, it did the same for wool's upstart, cheaper rival – cotton. The subsequent growth of foreign manufacturers and the introduction of man-made fibres all conspired to diminish Britain's woollen industry. But it did not destroy it. Today's commercial flocks, chiefly concentrated in the Welsh and Scottish uplands, yield some 19 million pounds of wool each year. Over half the clip is exported, mostly to other EEC countries, while the remainder accounts for about 25% of Britain's own raw wool requirements.

SHEEP SHEARING

Traditionally, the sheep year has always reached its climax in early summer, with shearing. But it has always begun with washing the animals: in the words of Thomas Tuser, a 16th-century farmer-poet, 'Wash sheep, for the better, where water doth run, and let him go cleanly, and dry in the sun'. A stream, preferably gravel-bottomed, was dammed to create a pool and the sheep then made to swim from one side to the other; village names like Washbourne, Washbrook, Shipbourne and Sheepwash all derive from this practice. A worker, standing mid-stream (often inside a barrel to keep himself dry) would take hold of each animal and clean it thoroughly. He used water or an alkaline solution leached out from wood ash, lye. After washing, sheep were left for about a week for their fleeces to dry out and the natural grease, or yolk, to spread back to the fibres. They were then ready for shearing.

Shearing was originally undertaken by individual farmers and labourers, but when flocks grew bigger as the woollen trade grew, shearing

MANUFACTURE OF WOOL (above) By the mid 18th century, English woollen manufacture was at its peak. The whole process, from obtaining the fleece, washing it, beating it and combing it to spinning, was labour intensive. A century later, changes caused by the Industrial Revolution had speeded up the process and greatly reduced the number of people involved.

SHEEP DIPPING
Prior to shearing, sheep were washed, usually in a stream dammed to create a pool (right). Today they are herded singly into specially constructed narrow sheep dips (left). After a week, the fleece has dried out and the natural grease spread back into the fibres. Then they are ready for shearing.

PROGRESS
(above) The hand-powered equipment, seen here, was one of the early attempts to mechanize this stage of wool production. (left) Skilled hand shearers working alone could clip a whole sheep in 8 minutes. Today power shears enable shearers to cut 200-300 fleeces per day.

developed into a specialist craft. As long ago as the Norman Invasion, if not earlier, itinerant gangs of shearers used to work their way through the sheeplands from late May to mid August. A gang might contain as many as 30 men, each one of them able to cut 40-50 fleeces a day.

Methods varied. In some places, the sheep's legs were tied, but generally a shearer relied on his own strength and skill to immobilize the animal. He would throw it on its back – the position in which sheep are most helpless – and grip it between his knees to leave both hands free for getting the wool off. With his left hand, he pulled the fleece back, keeping the skin taut; with his right, he held the shears – two scissor-shaped blades, about ten inches long, joined behind the hand-grips by a spring. Working from the underside to the back and from head to tail, he clipped swiftly and, after eight or nine minutes, would have removed the whole fleece.

Any accidental snicks or cuts on the sheep were treated on the spot with broom water (a sulphurous infusion of broom leaves and flowers) or, from the 1500s, with Stockholm tar, which was extracted from pine wood and used principally to waterproof ships' ropes. Tar dried up the wound and sealed it against potentially fatal infections but, although more effective than home-made remedies, it was also more costly since it had to be bought from boatyards and was often used sparingly; hence the expression 'to lose (or spoil) a ship (dialect for sheep) for a ha'porth of tar'.

So as not to interrupt the shearing rhythm, other workers, generally women, were responsible for rolling the fleeces. As each fleece was sheared off it was carried to another part of the

THE WOOLSACK
(right) Today, fleece is often transported loose to the nearest depots of the British Wool Marketing Board, where it is bagged into sacks differing in size and shape according to regional preferences. In the past, the woolsack was such a potent symbol of the importance of England's wool trade, that it was introduced into the House of Lords by Edward III. There it is the official seat of the Lord Chancellor when acting as Speaker of the House of Lords.

CARDING WOOL
(below) Before wool can be spun it has either to be carded, if it is shortwool, or combed, if it is longwool. During the 18th and 19th centuries, both processes were mechanized, but many hand-spinners, like this Shetland Islander, still hand-card wool. The wool is placed between two hand-held boards, backed with teeth – carders. These are pulled in opposite directions to tease open the fibres. The process is repeated several times until the fibres are fully separated.

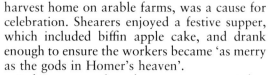

barn, laid out flat on a table and checked over for loose dirt, matted tufts and burrs. It was then wound up – the leg-pieces tucked inside – into a roll and tied round with a strand of neck wool. Stacked at one end of the barn, the fleeces, still warm from the sheep, rustled as they cooled and gave off a misty haze. When cold, they were packed into a large sack. Two men stood inside the woolsack, which was suspended, at floor level, from a beam, and footed down the rolls into compact layers. A full sack, sewn up immediately by the packers, could contain as few as 30 or as many as 100 fleeces.

In sheep country, the end of shearing, like the

harvest home on arable farms, was a cause for celebration. Shearers enjoyed a festive supper, which included biffin apple cake, and drank enough to ensure the workers became 'as merry as the gods in Homer's heaven'.

Before raw wool can be spun into yarn, it has to be sorted, cleaned and, finally, disentangled. Apart from the division into short and long staple, sorting involves assessing fineness, texture, colour and crimp (natural waviness). A good fleece contains as many as ten or twelve grades of wool which the sorter separates out into different baskets. The wool is then cleansed, or scoured, to remove dirt, impurities and natural grease. In the past, scouring commonly meant either dipping the wool in lant, stale urine, or – if the fleece was still whole – coating it with dung which was subsequently beaten off when dry. Thorough rinsing in lime-free water completed the process.

CARDING AND COMBING

The next stage in preparation varied, depending on the staple length – short wool is carded, long wool is combed. Roman and Saxon workers used teasels or thorns to pull short wool apart and straighten it. Not until the 1200s were carders – two hand-held boards backed with wire teeth – introduced. A lump of raw wool was set between the carders which were then pulled in opposite directions to tease open the fibres. These were collected back on to one carder and the process repeated. After four or five brushings the fibres, now smooth and separate, formed a soft fluffy tube or rolag.

According to legend, St Blaise – a 14th-century bishop in Asia Minor – invented the long-wool comb. Ever since, Blaise has been patron of woolcombers. His comb, like a short-handled rake, had several rows of long teeth, or broitches – originally made of wood, later of metal. For centuries combing, like carding, was traditionally done by women. Heated combs, which served to soften the wool's natural lanolin (oil), made the process easier. Thus, charcoal-fuelled pots for warming the broitches became standard combing equipment. However, prolonged exposure to carbon fumes, intense heat from the comb-pot and icy ventilation draughts undermined the combers' health and many died young; not inappropriately, St Blaise is also patron of throats.

During the 18th and 19th centuries, carding and combing – like other stages in wool processing – were mechanized. But it was not until the 20th century that powered shearing became widespread. Today's shearers, four or five to a gang, are usually farm employees. Working with electric clippers, plugged into the mains or a generator, they can each cut 200-300 fleeces in a day. But if they graze the sheep's skin, they might still reach for the Stockholm tar. And, at the end of shearing, they still like to celebrate – though a few rounds at the local are more common than biffen cake or warden pie.

The Crofting Life

Gale-ridden peaks, darkly brooding skies, rugged shores pierced by stark sea-lochs
– from this majestic landscape crofters carve a meagre living, as they have done for years,
sustained by a close-knit culture and a fierce attachment to the land.

F
ew lifestyles have excited as much romantic envy as that of Scottish crofters. At first sight, they are the inheritors of the independent cottage farming life, and they live out this life in a landscape of elemental beauty.

However, this romantic view *is* only a myth. The history of crofting is not yet two centuries old, and its course has been marked by conflict, hardship and an ill-rewarded life of unending labour in winning a living from an unforgiving soil. The features that give the countryside its grandeur make it inimical to the farmer. The climate is wild and bleak, the terrain difficult, and even where there is good land, crofts tend to exist on the fringes of it, where the ground is stony and the soil thin. Some perch on steep craggy slopes; others wallow in quags.

Crofts rarely exist in isolation; most are grouped into townships which hold and manage common grazing lands where each crofter is entitled to keep his stock. The individual holdings vary in size from an acre or two up to 100 acres, though around 10 acres is the norm. Farming such marginal land is hardly ever enough to provide crofters with a decent living – only about five per cent of them live by agriculture alone – and they have always needed another source of income in order to survive.

Crofting is confined to the Celtic fringe of the British Isles: the west of Ireland, the Isle of Man, and, in particular, the Highlands of Scot-

LONELY CROFT
With a few hard-won acres, wrested from the rock-torn land, the crofter battles against impossible odds. The plot is too small and the soil too thin, so he must find work away from the croft in order to keep the farm going.

LAST OF THE CLAN
(above) The destruction of the clan system after Culloden, and the subsequent Clearances led to mass emigration. Between 1780 and 1808 12,000 people left Scotland for America and another 30,000 for the colonies. Many went unwillingly, like those in this contemporary painting by Thomas Faed.

THE BIGGINGS
(above) Traditional 'biggings', or buildings, are still scattered across the Highlands and Islands. This single-storeyed croft in South Uist still bears a straw thatch and is heated by peat cut from the nearby hills, hauled home on peat sledges and stacked outside the house.

wool rocketed, and hordes of Cheviot and Blackface sheep – hardy breeds that could withstand northern winters – invaded the Highlands. The Highland people, now surplus to sheep, were evicted and cleared to the marginal lands that even the sheep did not want.

The infamous Highland Clearances led to new settlements in the narrow fringe of land between the treeless slopes and the coast. There, unable to support themselves on poor plots or pay ever-increasing rents, many people found work in the new kelp industry; cutting, drying and burning seaweed to produce an alkali used in making soap and glass. The population grew and the already small holdings were subdivided. But the collapse of the kelp industry in 1820 led to another wave of clearances. The crofters were redundant again. For many, emigration once more seemed the answer. Some were forcibly deported. Many that remained slipped further into debt with their landlords.

FIGHTING FOR LAND

Inspired by concessions won by land rebellions in Ireland, the Scottish crofting community began to fight back with rent strikes and land occupations – or reoccupations as they saw it, for the emotional tie with the land was still powerful among crofting people: to them land and lineage were indissoluble.

The Crofters Act of 1886 brought them security of tenure and a Commission to fix fair rents but failed to appease the hunger for land. Land raids continued into the 1920s, the last wave fuelled by servicemen returning from the Great War. It was not until 1976 that the crofter, at last, won the right to buy the title to his own land at a fair price.

As an agricultural unit the croft is insignificant, but the total number of crofts in the Highlands and Islands accounts for a quarter of the area's agricultural output and occupies a fifth of the land.

The north-west of Scotland, where crofting is still concentrated, is too cold, wet and windy for most cereal crops. Farming consists mainly of raising sheep and cattle to be sold for fattening on Lowland farms. While the stock are away at the common grazings in the summer, the croft is turned over to growing crops, mainly winter feed for the animals. Oats and potatoes were traditionally the crofters' staple foods. Turnips, kale and maybe a little barley fed man and beast alike, and the rest of the croft land was put down to hay.

In many island crofts the soil was too thin for even the hardiest crops. Often it had to be built up by the crofter from straw, seaweed, turves and manure from the cow byre. The resulting hummocks of soil, called lazybeds, grew a few handfuls of potatoes or a sheaf of oats. Even where the croft could be made to produce a living, it never made a surplus to invest in new methods or machinery to improve the yield. In any case, the small size of holdings and the

land and the Northern and Western Isles. As a system of agriculture, it is largely a creation of the 19th century, the result of the destruction of traditional forms of husbandry by landowners bent on getting better returns from their land.

CONDEMNED TO POVERTY

In Ireland crofting began when the drop in cereal prices at the end of the Napoleonic Wars led landlords to switch from arable to pastoral farming, evicting their tenants and amalgamating their holdings to provide larger areas of grazing for cattle. The dispossessed workers were confined to villages with small plots, and condemned to poverty. Many left for America.

The position was different in Scotland. The Highlands had been in the hands of the clans. Clan chiefs were the protectors, rather than the landlords, of the clan territories, bound to those who worked the land by a sense of kinship and a common obligation to defend clan lands. Large farms were worked by a system called runrig, where the land was divided into strips and these were allocated each year by lot.

Following their suppression of the last Jacobite rebellion and the defeat of the Scots at Culloden in 1745, the English government set about breaking the military power of the clans. The chiefs were made into landlords and the clansmen into rent-paying tenants, and runrig was overturned in one generation owing to the influence of sheep and seaweed.

During the late 18th century the price of

awkwardness of the fields, made most machines useless. The characteristic tools of the crofting farmer were the primitive cas chrom, or foot plough, the harvesting scythe and the hoe.

Livestock was the mainstay of the crofter. The one or two cattle a crofter could raise each year were his main source of income, and the milk, butter and cheese were important additions to the family diet. The hardy sheep could be left to overwinter in the fields of the croft, while the cattle were stalled in the byre and fed on a diet of oats and turnips. It was lonely work for much of the year, but the movement of stock to and from the grazings – which in the Islands could involve a boat trip – and the gatherings of sheep for shearing, dipping and tagging brought the whole community together.

COTTAGE CRAFTS

Much of the work around the croft was done by the womenfolk, the men often being occupied with other jobs. They were in charge of the chickens and bees if they were kept. And they were often accomplished craftswomen: sewing, spinning, weaving and knitting enabled women to bring the necessary outside income into the croft and these skills are still the basis of important cottage industries in the region.

The women would also help to cut and cart the peat which has long been the main fuel of the Islands. It is cut in April or May, stacked to dry in the sun and wind and then stored.

Every crofter had also to construct and maintain the croft buildings – at the least a house, barn and byre. Sometimes all were combined in one building as in the Hebridean Black House. This was constructed of a double dry-stone wall, infilled with sand or rubble, and roofed with a crude thatch tethered against the gales with ropes weighted down with stones.

The Black House sheltered both people and beasts, at either end of a long, low, windowless room. It had no chimney and the smoke from the peat fire escaped the same way as the water got in, through the thatch. With soot-blackened, damp walls, earthen floors, and live-in cows, typhoid and tubercolosis were common.

Earlier this century, Black Houses were replaced by more substantial homes built of mortared stone and roofed with tiles or slates or, in some cases still, the traditional thatch. Most of the new crofts follow the 'but and ben' plan common throughout the Highlands.

The but end of the house was where the fire was kept in. Meals were cooked over the fire and eaten around it. The crofter's diet was dominated by oats and potatoes. Fresh or salted herring, kale, a few eggs and some dairy products made up the rest. The but end was usually barely and functionally furnished but most of the indoor life of the croft went on there. The more comfortable furniture, and whatever personal treasures the family had accumulated, were kept in the ben end, which was where business was transacted.

FOOD FOR MAN AND BEAST *(right) The crofter aims to feed himself and his livestock, but there is rarely sufficient surplus from the land to turn into cash. Potatoes, kale, turnips and, as on this Irish croft, swedes, are all hardy vegetables. The main cereal crop is oats, and hay is grown for winter feed for the precious milk cows.*

Away from the croft, the most consistent source of non-agricultural employment has long been fishing, and whether crofters are farmers who fish or fishermen who farm has always been debatable. The fishing is of various kinds, either for white fish like cod and ling in the Minch, off the West coast, in winter time, or following the herring in the North Sea in the summer. The herring fishing on the East coast attracted a large annual migration of crofters from the Hebrides. Women could also get seasonal employment cleaning and salting the catch. Many crofters also fish successfully for lobster in the coastal waters.

But, like many ways of earning extra money, fishing took the crofter away from his land at the time it needed him most, the harvest. The

FARMER-FISHERMEN *Some of the deficiencies of the land are balanced by the bounty of the sea. Many crofters are also fishermen, either for white fish, or herring, or as here on Barra in the Outer Hebrides, for lobster in the inshore waters.*

tion in English has loosened the hold of their native culture on the crofters' children. The same new roads that bring the tourists, bear the future of crofting away. The close-knit townships find their populations ageing. And with no one to inherit the croft, the connection between land and kin, kept alive by a strong sense of history and succession, is broken.

WOMEN'S WORK
The hardships of the crofting life fell heavily upon the womenfolk. Toiling all hours, they shouldered much of the outdoor work and earned extra cash from spinning and weaving.

same problems were faced by those who were otherwise employed as smiths, masons or carpenters. They would work all day at their trade then work on the crofts by lantern-light.

The need for outside work is just as acute today. Fishing is still important, but in decline. Some jobs are to be had as stalkers or ghillies on the sporting estates, or on the hydro-electric stations that have drowned some of the Highland glens already emptied of people by the Clearances. Forestry and road-building employ some more. There is still a small kelping industry, and knitting, and the weaving of Harris Tweed employs men and women in Lewis, working at home through the winter. Tourism has been encouraged but the benefits of North Sea Oil look to be, at best, short-lived.

THE DRIFT TO THE SOUTH

The underlying problem of crofting as a means of supporting a population is that for so long it has failed to do so adequately. Failure was built into the system at the very beginning. At first the problem expressed itself as not enough security, not enough land; now that the battle for land is more or less over, the problem is that there are not enough people. There has always been a drift to the South in search of work and better standards of living, but it is stronger now.

The crofting communities are among the last refuges of the Gaelic language and culture – a factor which had undoubtedly contributed to the tenacity and, in spite of all the hardships, the extraordinary cohesion of their way of life. But where once the Gaelic language was a bar to moving, the spread of mass media and educa-

HANGING OUT TO DRY
In the Orkneys and Shetlands (above), fish were dried in the summer for winter use. After an initial salting, they were strung along a line like so much fishy laundry, for the wind and sun to finish the job. Whiting, haddock and ling were dried for home consumption, but herrings were salted on a commercial basis (left), providing valuable seasonal employment for the women of the islands.

Shetland Knitting

Although machine-knitting dominates in the modern woollen industry, the remaining hand-knitters on the Shetlands continue to produce distinctive and finely crafted garments using traditional methods.

Knitting was introduced to the Shetlands some time between the late 16th and early 17th centuries, most probably from mainland Scotland. The first Scottish knitters were men – professional bonnet-makers in the Lowland towns, especially Dundee and Kilmarnock. Aberdeen, another bonnet-making centre, was also known for hosiery. Many of the stocking merchants made active attempts to recruit knitters in country areas and, since Aberdeen was the chief mainland link with the islands, it was probably a hosier who first introduced them to knitting.

The uncertainties of agriculture in these bleak windswept islands meant that the income from domestic crafts, however meagre, could be vital. Early travellers to the islands were astonished to find that the women knitted constantly and often at the same time as they did their other chores. Some even knitted as they trudged home from the peat cutting with their straw kishies (baskets) full of peat strapped to their backs, and most of them knitted far into the night.

By the end of the 18th century the export trade in knitting (mostly stockings but also nightcaps, mittens and underwear) was worth more than £17,000 a year. In just over a decade however it had slumped to a third of this amount. One of the reasons was a severe outbreak of sheep scab which decimated the sheep population, but the demand for the islanders' wares had also dwindled. This was due in part to depression on the mainland combined with increasing numbers of sheep there, and also because of competition from the cheap machine-made stockings in the South.

When the kelp industry declined too, thousands of islanders emigrated. In the 1830s those that were left faced starvation. The conscience of the better-off sections of society was stirred leading to organized efforts at relief. Some of these were directed towards revitalizing the knitting industry. The two great traditions of Shetland knitting first appeared around this period: exquisite cobwebby lace and the vibrant geometric patterning of Fair Isle (from the Viking name meaning 'island of sheep').

SHETLAND WOOL

Much of the success of island knitting was, and is, due to the particular qualities of Shetland wool. Harsh conditions bred a resilient type of animal with exceptionally fine soft wool. Unlike mainland sheep, those in the Shetlands ran wild on the hills, or grazed freely on scattalds – common pasture lands. Because of the special nature of their fleece, Shetland sheep moulted frequently, leaving tufts of wool – known in Unst as 'henty leggits' – on bushes and fences to be gathered by women and children. Once a year, usually in summer, the sheep were tracked down with dogs and taken for rooing – the Shetland way of removing wool from the sheep. Instead of shearing or clipping, the wool was simply plucked out, a method which ensured that the fine soft wool came away but left the coarse hairy fibres behind.

Each sheep yielded about 1-1½lb of wool, which might be creamy white, grey, deep dark, brown, a reddish brown known as moorit, or any of several other shades of brown or grey. The wool was used in its natural colours or dyed. Indigo and madder were bought (or bartered) from passing traders, but many dyes could be obtained from heather tops, roots, lichens, peat soot, moss and brambles. Sometimes, the finished article was bleached in the

SHETLAND SHEARING *(below) The fine soft wool of the Shetland sheep comes away so easily that it is simply plucked off by hand, leaving the coarse fibrous hair behind. The process, known as rooing, is carried out in summer when sheep, which range freely all year on the common upland pastures, are rounded up by dogs. The fine and delicate knitting for which the Shetlands are famed stems directly from the particular qualities of the wool from these hardy sheep.*

fumes of a peat-fire strewn with sulphur.

The carding (combing out) and spinning of the wool were done by women, but the carding was also the traditional excuse for a party. When enough wool had been gathered, the invitations to the 'card in' were sent out, and the women gathered at the house in mid-afternoon when they combed out or carded the wool together until late evening. Then the men folk arrived, the work was set aside, and the singing and dancing continued into the early hours.

SHETLAND LACE

Soon after the introduction of lacemaking to the Shetlands the reputation of Shetland wool, the skills of the knitters and the persistent efforts of a number of dedicated publicists, ensured that Shetland lace knitting became a huge commercial success. Eliza Edmondston, a doctor's wife from Unst, and later her daughter Jessie Saxby, introduced stitch patterns, promoted exhibitions all over the country and persuaded merchants to stock the shawls, veils and stockings. In 1837 Albert Anderson presented some fine lace stockings to Queen Victoria and the Duchess of Kent, and in 1851 Edward Standen, who later opened a shop in London, commissioned a superb red and cream wedding

MRS PETRIE AND HER DAUGHTERS
Before the introduction of domestic knitting machines in the 1940s, the scene above would have been commonplace. Many hours were spent knitting companionably with family and friends once the day's chores were done.

SHETLAND LACE SHAWL
(below) Lace shawls from the Shetlands were much in demand in Victorian times. Knitted from as little as 2oz of wool these delicate, feathery shawls were so fine that they could be drawn easily through a wedding ring.

FASHIONABLE FAIR ISLE
*Though promoted in
England in the mid-19th
century, garments from Fair
Isle knitted in exotic patterns
and colours were not
instantly popular with most
Victorians. In 1921 the
popularity of the Fair Isle
sweater was given a dramatic
boost, when a draper from
Lerwick gave one to the
Prince of Wales (above).
He wore it in public at
a golf tournament, and
it was not long before it
became high fashion (above
right).*

ANCIENT FAIR ISLE
*(right) The 100-year old
example of Fair Isle knitting
shows clearly the strong
banded effect typical of this
type of knitting, which is
achieved by varying the
background and motif
colours every few rows. No
more than two colours are
used in any row.*

veil for the Great Exhibition of 1851. Shawls at
that time were selling for £4 to £5 each and by
the 1890s the trade in Shetland lace was worth
£125,000 a year.

Much of the appeal of Shetland shawls came
from the silkiness of the wool spun by hand into
spidery fine two-ply yarn. Exceptionally gifted
spinners could spin enough yarn for a five-foot
square shawl (about 5000 yards of two-ply
yarn twisted from about 6 miles of single thread)
from as little as 2 ounces of wool.

The shawls were knitted on two needles using
a variety of openwork stitch patterns, usually
beginning with a centre square and finishing with
a series of deep borders worked around the edge
of the square. Occasionally, the article would
be worked from the outside in. They were con-

structed in such a way that no seams or joins
were required. Since most of the knitters could
neither read nor write, no written patterns were
used. They simply learned the stitches by heart,
devised new ones and improvised as they worked.

After the knitting, which might take as long
as 500 hours and involve a quarter of a million
stitches, the shawls had to be 'dressed'. Each
shawl was washed gently then stretched either
in a wooden frame or pegged out on the turf. As
it dried the tension in the yarn would tighten,
opening out the stitches and displaying the full
beauty of the patterns. As well as shawls the
lace knitters made caps, veils, stockings, scarves
and gloves. The most sought-after shawls were
from Unst – the famous 'ring' shawls, so gos-
samer fine that they could be drawn smoothly
through a wedding ring.

FAIR ISLE KNITTING

Fair Isle knitting is older than Shetland lace,
though not as old as the Victorians liked to think.
Dazzled by the exoticism of the designs when
they first encountered them in the 1850s, they
accepted the story put out by Eliza Edmondston
that the islanders had been taught the technique
by Spanish sailors from the *El Gran Griffon*,
wrecked on Fair Isle in September 1588 following
the Battle of the Armada. Sadly, relations between the 300 shipwrecked sailors and the 17
families living on Fair Isle at the time were not
so harmonious. The islanders, facing a hard
winter themselves, were not disposed to be

hospitable. Before their rescuers turned up, some 6 weeks later, many of the sailors had died of starvation; others were hurled from the cliffs by unfriendly natives. The invention of Fair Isle knitting had to wait another 200 years.

The oldest fragment of colour-patterned knitting found in the islands came from a 17th-century grave and consisted of a purse with a

STOCKPILE
(above) After the War stocks of hand-knits were sold off by the Woollen Industries Shetland Association.

KNITTING BELT
(below) By anchoring one of the needles to a belt, freeing a hand, knitters could achieve up to 200 stitches a minute.

FRAMED
(below right) When complete, lace garments were, washed, then dried on frames.

row of simple checks. However, none of the travellers in the 17th or 18th centuries mention anything but plain knitting. The first hint of something special comes in 1822 when a traveller writes of knitting 'with variegated and fantastical colours produced by native dyes' – a description which could easily be applied to the oldest examples of Fair Isle knitting in existence, which date from the 1850s.

Fair Isle knitting did not catch on with fashionable Victorians in the same way that lace shawls had. They found the patterns garish and outlandish. It was not until 1921 when Edward VIII accepted a present of a Shetland sweater made to him by James A. Smith, a Lerwick draper, and wore it in public at a golfing tournament at St Andrews, that Fair Isle knitting became popular. The revenue from Fair Isle knitting shot up from the £300-400 a year in 1900 to over £100,000 in the 1920s, and it was still a cottage industry employing part-time labour.

From the very beginning, Fair Isle knits were noted for the brilliance of their colours. On the rest of the Shetlands the patterns were worked mostly in subtle natural shades of grey, brown and cream, but in Fair Isle they often used bright reds, blues, greens and yellows.

Fair Isle knitters made caps and Tam

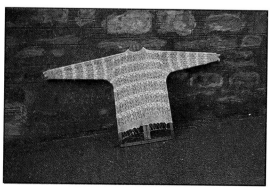

o'Shanters, mittens, gloves, scarves and a type of men's sleeveless sweater based on the traditional gansey (or guernsey) worn by seafaring communities throughout the British Isles. Later, women's sweaters, waistcoats, cardigans and pullovers were added to the list. Like the lace shawls, many of these garments had to be dressed and set over wooden frames to finish them. And like the shawls, the labour involved was immensely time-consuming and badly paid.

The 'trucking' system was virtually the only system of wage payment in the Shetlands both for fishermen and knitters. Goods – fish or knitting – were paid for in cash or kind and the rate of exchange was controlled by the merchants who bought the goods. For knitting, the merchant paid in certain fixed commodities, usually tea, soap or clothing, for all or part of the amount. The balance would be supplied in cash or 'lines', credit notes. If you insisted on cash you would get less than the value of the lines.

However, since the goods exchanged for knitting did not include necessities many knitters had immediately to trade their lines at a loss back to the merchant for food. The inclusion of clothing among the payments meant that knitters might be extravagantly dressed yet go hungry·at the same time. Since the trade was effectively controlled by a handful of Lerwick drapers, many knitters were permanently in thrall to them. The Truck Act of 1887 in theory curbed the worst of the abuses and improvements in postal services meant that individual knitters or groups of knitters could at least attempt to contact their markets direct, but even now Shetland hand-knitters remain poorly paid.

By the late 1800s mechanization was beginning to affect the knitwear industry. Machine-spun wool began to replace handspun wool at least in Lerwick, though the handspun product from rural areas was still highly prized. In 1914 a

steam-driven carding machine was introduced and by the early 1950s there were only half a dozen women left who could spin the fine lace-weight yarn. From the 1940s onwards domestic knitting machines began to replace hand-knitting. Their products could be produced in a matter of hours rather than the weeks or months it would take to hand-knit a shawl or Fair Isle sweater.

In 1969 the knitwear industry in Shetland reached an all-time peak annual turnover of £1.5 million, more than 90 per cent of which came from the machine-made products. Since then the industry has fallen off considerably but, paradoxically, interest in the traditional hand-knitted articles is growing. In an age sated with mass-production, the exceptional artistry of the Shetland knitters is being recognized and eleventh-hour attempts are being made to rescue their extraordinary skills.

A DRESSED SHAWL
(above) The fine cobweb-like filaments of a typical Shetland lace shawl are at their best after the garment has been gently washed and then either pegged out on the grass or stretched across a wooden frame to dry. As the shawl dries the yarn fibres tighten to open out the thousands of stitches. The one above was made by the photographer's mother, Mrs Tulloch, over a two-week period in between other activities.

HAND-KNIT IN SHETLAND
(left) Today Shetland hand-knitting is still practised by many of the island women. Despite the fact that there is a movement towards expanding the use of powered machines, hand-knitted garments with their distinctive and unique patterns and colours, are still highly sought after in markets as far afield as Japan, Europe and America.

Harris Tweed

Today, as in the past, the crofts of Harris and Lewis are alive with the sound of clacking looms, weaving a unique cloth which serves as a reminder of the islands' traditional way of life.

In the same way that the Outer Hebrides are the last major stronghold of the Gaelic language, so Harris tweed, unique to the Hebridean islands of Harris and Lewis, is the natural product both of the land and its people. The beautiful soft colours, the subtle patterns and the closely woven texture of a Harris tweed sports jacket are all clues to its island ancestry.

Today, as an international fashion fabric, Harris tweed is available in three different weights, with a smooth, pressed finish for the lighter weights. But traditional Harris tweed has a hairy surface; like the guard hairs on a cat, it is designed to keep out the elements.

The name 'Hebrides' comes from the Norse 'Havbredey', meaning 'the isles on the edge of the sea', and the west coast of these islands is pounded mercilessly by the unbroken force of the Atlantic. Inland is a harsh, uncompromising landscape, swept in winter by gales and tempests; even in summer, the wind blows three days out of four.

Dr Johnson, visiting the Hebrides in 1773, gives us an idea of the islanders' life: 'The Outer Isles were roadless and stormswept and for the long sea journey only open boats of no great size were available. The natives . . . are still very hospitable but the late years of scarcity brought them very low, and many of the poor people have died of famine.'

No wonder that in this climate and these conditions of hardship the islanders valued their local cloth, which had all the virtues they most needed – it was hard-wearing, warm and water resistant. And although Harris tweed may have been born out of necessity, the weavers also created a fabric which has proved through generations to have a universal appeal.

Weaving is acknowledged as a national industry all over Scotland, but in the Western Isles there is nothing like the strong colours and bold patterning of the Scottish plaids and tartans. The colours of Harris tweed are the colours of nature; indeed, the wool was originally dyed with natural vegetable dyes, crottle (from lichens – rich ochre yellows, greens and browns) and heather.

Unconsciously, the weavers' sense of colour

'WAULKING' IN RHYTHM (left) Once the cloth had been woven, it used to be 'waulked' – a finishing process which shrunk the cloth and firmed up the texture. In the 19th century, the waulking was done by teams of women, who spread out the tweed on a plank between them. Accompanied by the merry rhythm of Gaelic 'waulking songs', they slapped, thumped and squeezed the tweed with their hands. As this was 'women's work', many of the songs (right) poked fun at the men-folk.

and design would have echoed their surroundings of sea, sand, rocks and moorland. For example, one of the most typical colours in a piece of Harris weaving is a rich dark brown, often used to give background depth to a lighter colour. If you were to visit Harris or Lewis, you would recognize this as the colour of peat – the islanders' fuel for their fires and a dominant feature of the landscape. In the centre of both islands are wide stretches of peat moorland, dotted with hundreds of small freshwater lochs and deep fjords stretching back inland from the sea. Centuries of peat-cutting have left the surface of the moors scarred with intricate patterns, each cut laid in a herringbone design.

In autumn, there would be the soft purples and browns of the heather, in summer, the changing blues of the sea and the long, white shell beaches, bare rocks patterned with lichen – the Hebrides is always a land of dramatic contrasts and a weaver would not need to look far for a source of inspiration.

Harris tweed is traditionally a home-based cottage industry, and this continues even today despite attempts to centralize production. The great virtue of weaving the cloth at home is that it allows time to tend the croft, feed the sheep and goats, and cut the peat. In the recent past, the community was totally self-supporting; the islanders grew their own crops of barley, oats and rye, built their own boats and houses, and wove linen and home-spun cloth as well as tweed.

Much of the islanders' work is seasonal, and in the days when Harris tweed was only produced for their own use, every stage was done at home. The women would spin the wool during the long winter evenings round the fireside, while the men repaired the fishing nets and later wove the spun wool into tweed. The

A LIVING TRADITION
(left) Marion Campbell is the only islander who still produces Harris tweed in the traditional way – hand-dyeing, carding, spinning, weaving and finishing the cloth herself in her cottage at Drinishader bay.

I shan't marry an old carle
('S na) hóró laoi leó
Seinn óro nàilibh
'S na hó ró laoi leó
An old man I will definitely not have
He gets up late
Takes a long time to dress
A long, long time to get his clothes on
I shan't have a clumsy old man
He can't go out without a walking-stick
He can't come in without a cough
He mistakes hens for geese
And horses for cows

Refrain after each line

SCOTTISH GROWN WOOL
(right) Harris tweed is made from the wool of the local Blackface sheep, whose coarse, shaggy fleece makes the cloth thick and warm.

NATURE'S COLOURS
The gentle colouring of Harris tweed reflects the subtle hues of the Hebridean landscape. Originally, the cloth was coloured with natural dyes from local plants: heather, for example, was gathered from the moors, while lichens were scraped off the jutting rocks (right). Marion Campbell (below) still uses lichens, 'yellow flowers' and iris roots for her warm browns and yellows, but she has now turned to chemical dyes for the more vibrant colours.

haunting melodies of Gaelic 'labour lilts' and beautiful, descriptive stories of the past helped relieve the tedious and laborious work.

THE RAW MATERIAL

The story of Harris tweed begins with the Scottish Blackface sheep, whose fleece is blended with wool from the other Scottish breeds, the Cross-bred and the Cheviot. These wild-looking, shaggy sheep are reared in the rugged highland and hill pastures, and their wool is coarse and thick. It contains a mixture of three kinds of fibre, one of which (kemp) is brittle and chalky white. This remains lighter than the other fibres when the wool is dyed, giving a distinctive irregularity to the cloth.

In early summer, the island communities gather together for the annual shearing, a great social occasion with women taking part alongside men. After shearing, the wool destined for

Harris tweed arrives, much of it from the mainland, at the three major producers in Harris and Lewis; the main centre of production is the port of Stornoway in Lewis.

The raw wool is scoured in a solution of soap and washing soda, and then dyed. Today, chemical dyes are almost invariably used but in the past the wool would have been dyed with vegetable dyes over peat fires in the crofts.

Once, too, carding and spinning, the next stages in preparing the yarn, would have been done at home, but since the 1930s both these processes have been transferred to the factories. Carding means teasing the wool fibres until they lie consistently and regularly, to produce a controlled yarn. In the factory, the wool fibres are transferred directly from the carding cylinders to the spinning frame, which winds the yarn on to bobbins. In the old days, spinning was done at home, at first using a spindle which was simply a stick with a weight on the end. The embryo yarn has no strength and can easily be pulled apart, so the spinner had to create a twist with the spindle to make the fibres into a continuous thread of yarn. Once the spindle was in motion, the spinner would add a few fibres at a time.

The logical development of this primitive technique was the spinning wheel, which reached the Western Isles in the second half of the 17th century. As with other 'women's crafts', such as knitting, during the Industrial Revolution men adopted the new technology while the women continued to use the spindle. When it first became promoted as a fashion fabric, Harris tweed had to be made from handspun yarn as well as being hand-woven. This was a serious limitation on production, and in 1934 it was

WARPING
(right) Warping is one of the most important processes in the manufacture of Harris tweed as it creates the basic colour pattern. The warp is prepared by winding the threads onto a massive frame of wooden pegs to preserve the tension – a process which is now undertaken by the factory.

WEAVING
(below) Harris tweed is still woven in the islanders' homes on treadle looms, despite recent attempts to introduce power looms. In this way, the Hebridean weavers are free to work as and when they please. The rest of the family help as necessary, and in this way the craft passes naturally from one generation to the next.

decided that the weavers were allowed to use yarn spun by the islands' factories rather than that only spun at home.

The final stage of factory preparation is the warping. Every piece of weaving has two sets of threads – the warp threads, which run vertically on the loom, and the weft threads which cross through the warp, over and under, to create a fabric. To make a warp, the yarn is wound on to a frame of wooden pegs, maintaining an even tension. The colours of the warp and the arrangement of the threads will dictate the basic pattern of the finished weaving. Today, a two-colour herringbone pattern might have a warp of 600-odd threads, but in the old days warping was done with only two threads. It took almost

two days to warp a length of tweed.

The warp, looking like long hanks of yarn, is gathered together with the yarn for the weft, the design instructions and a pattern sample ready to be delivered to the weaver. To make sure that the allocation of work is fair, a tweed distribution centre has now been set up in Stornoway supervising quality standards as well as the difficult task of getting deliveries to and from the remote crofts.

All the preparatory stages may have been modernized and mechanized, but the actual weaving has changed little over the years. Originally, weaving was done on a simple frame loom, a painfully slow business. Today Harris tweed is still woven in the islanders' homes, but on treadle looms. These looms are their own property and are usually housed in sheds adjoining the crofts or houses.

The looms produce cloth 75cm wide, in lengths of about 78 metres. This narrow width reflects the fact that the looms are manually operated, but modern manufacturers increasingly demand 150cm width fabric. Recently, attempts were made to bring the islands in line with the mainland by introducing power looms, but 95 per cent of the weavers voted to retain their traditional methods, partly to safeguard their employment, but also to preserve their quality of life and their independence.

The woven lengths of cloth are left by the roadside, where they are collected by a van from Stornoway which makes the round trip along the winding roads to deliver the tweed back to the factory for the finishing processes.

At this stage, the tweed is still in its 'greasy' state, full of dirt, oil and other impurities. Once again, it is scoured in soapy water and soda, which also shrinks and felts the cloth. Originally this was done by 'waulking' the tweed, tramping it with the feet, or thumping it by hand.

The felting, or milling, process gives the tweed a good 'handle', as well as a closer

COLLECTION
(right) The weaver leaves the completed lengths of tweed by the roadside, where they are picked up by van from Stornoway. As the weavers' crofts are scattered far and wide, the vans often have to climb narrow twisting roads and travel through remote mountain regions to reach them. The van drops off a supply of freshly-spun wool, before delivering the cloth to the factory for finishing.

SPORTING ATTIRE
(top) When Lady Dunmore introduced her aristocratic friends to Harris tweed, she started a fashion for sporting garb. The 'Huntin', shootin' and fishin'' brigade wore the local cloth for their forays into the Scottish hills.

THE ORB MARK
(above) Every three metres of Harris tweed is stamped with the orb mark as a symbol of authenticity.

texture. At this stage, also, the cloth is cropped, a shearing process where rotary cutters remove the loose ends of the fibre. The naturally hairy Harris tweed can be pressed to give a smooth surface, especially the lighter weights, making it more adaptable.

A FASHIONABLE FABRIC

At the time Dr Johnson visited the Hebrides in 1773, the islanders were having a lean time. Bad harvests, extortionate landlords and the terrible 'clearances' of entire villages had driven many Scots to emigrate to the New World on the other side of the Atlantic. In 1886 the Crofters Act restored peace and security to the Hebrides but, in the meantime, in the 1840s, the islanders' plight had attracted the attention of Lady Dunmore, whose husband owned the Harris estate. She introduced Harris tweed to her aristocratic friends, who visited the islands for the excellent salmon and trout fishing, and the deer stalking.

Lady Dunmore persuaded the District Board to help improve the methods of production on the islands. Small carding and spinning plants were introduced, and the weavers were taught to warp with 36 threads instead of two. Instructors paid for by Lady Dunmore also taught them new designs and found them wealthy customers in London.

'Hunting', Shootin' and Fishin'' were the new fashionable pastimes of the Victorian idle rich,

endorsed by royalty. It was a short step for their garb to be adopted by those who had never even seen a Scottish moorland. Soon the cloth which for centuries had been the simple clothing of poverty-stricken crofters was reborn as well-cut sporting jackets and jaunty plus fours.

The islanders were now faced with an expansion of their market and the need for adaptation. In 1909 the Harris Tweed Association was formed to protect and develop the industry, adopting the Orb trademark as its symbol.

The standard weight for sporting clothes is 310 to 340 grammes per metre (g/m) but, in order to make Harris tweed more versatile, a lightweight and a featherweight have been developed – the featherweight being only 210 to 245 g/m. Each year new colours and designs are created for the fashion market and this humble local fabric is exported to countries as diverse in culture and climate as Spain, Japan and Australia.

Most industries adopt new production methods in order to survive. Since the peak year of 1966, the Harris tweed industry has declined again, with the young people attracted to work in the off-shore oil industry. Nevertheless, the islanders choose to remain independent, to weave their tweed at home as they have always done. Wisely, they recognize that mechanization would destroy the image, and hence the appeal, of *Clo Mor* – the Big Cloth.

Droving Days

In an age when it was perilous to take to the road, drovers travelled regularly with vast herds of cattle, from the mountains of Scotland and Wales to the meat-markets of England.

Cattle droves were usually heard long before they were seen, the shouts of the drovers mingling with the barking of dogs, the lowing of cattle and the clatter of hoofs. The sight was no less impressive, with maybe hundreds of beasts – driven by men in full Highland dress or Cambrian smocks – swarming down the lanes. This clamorous cavalcade was a regular summer spectacle in many parts of the country for around four hundred years.

The origin of the great cattle droves from Scotland and Wales to England is lost in time. Regular trade with Wales grew after the accession of the Tudors, and the Scottish trade was formalized after the Act of Union of 1707, with the establishment of customs posts and very high tariffs. The Scots chose to ignore these, crossing the borders in open country, and all restrictions on the trade were later lifted.

Both trades peaked in the late 18th and early 19th centuries and both were practically extinct by the beginning of the 20th, wiped out by new farming methods, increasing restrictions on the freedom of movement across open country and the use of other means of transport, primarily the railways.

The cattle on the droves were hardy store cattle, aged from around six months to three years. Accustomed to living on poor ground in the hills, they soon fattened up on the lusher pastures of England. The Scottish and Welsh farmers ate beef rarely, if at all, their sturdy. small cattle being essentially a cash crop, paying the rent while the farmer and his family lived on oats, a few vegetables, and occasional pieces of pork or mutton. Their fattened cattle went to feed English squires, the navy and the army, as the 'Roast beef of olde England'.,

The Welsh cattle were taken for fattening to

SETTING OUT
(above) In the last few centuries, Scotland's economy depended heavily on the cattle droving trade. Hundreds of mountain cattle would be driven to the meat-markets of England, setting out across moorland and mountainous terrain. The cattle travelled slowly – averaging about two miles an hour – but they were never hurried by the patient men who rode or walked beside them. The aim of the drovers was to get them to their destination in good shape, so that they would soon be ready for the slaughter.

Buckinghamshire valleys or the meadows of Kent and Essex before being sold at Smithfield for slaughter. Some came in early summer to be ready for the Michaelmas fairs, while later arrivals would overwinter in the South. The 250-mile journey from Anglesey to Kent took around three weeks and as many as 60,000 beasts would make the journey from Wales each year. The Scottish cattle, on the other hand, had as their eventual destination the pastures of Norfolk. Their journeys took longer, especially if they came all the way from the remote Western Isles.

It wasn't only cattle that took to the road, though they travelled the greatest distances. Droves of pigs, sheep and geese had their seasons from medieval times, and troops of gobbling turkeys joined them in the 18th century. Sheep were regularly driven from Wiltshire to East Anglia, but rarely undertook longer journeys. Pigs travelled shorter distances still, so as not to wear off their highly desirable fat. They were often muzzled to prevent them browsing, and their trotters were protected by little boots of wool and leather.

Most cattle were shod, though it was not always considered necessary if the majority of their journey was over soft ground. This could prove very expensive, costing between ten pence and a shilling per animal, and on long journeys the animals would often have to be reshod as well. Some smiths on the main routes specialized in the reshoeing of cattle, and the drovers would carry an emergency supply of shoes themselves, with the supply of nails wrapped in bacon fat to stop them rusting.

BUILDING UP NUMBERS

The cattle began their long journeys in relatively small numbers: there were many markets along the lines of the drive (their timings staggered to accommodate the steady migrations of the cattle) where cattle would be bought and sold, and larger droves gradually made up. Most Scottish cattle made for the great markets at Crieff and Falkirk, where still larger droves of hundreds strong were built up.

As much of their business was done on credit, drovers needed to be people of proven probity; they had to be trusted to get the beasts to market and to bring back the proceeds. Laws passed in the reigns of Edward IV and Elizabeth I required drovers to be licensed, so that they could gain exemption from the Vagrancy Laws. They had to register with the Clerk of the Peace for their county and apply annually at the County Quarter Sessions for their licenses, which were awarded only to respectable married householders of over 30 years of age. Unlicensed drovers faced a fine and a term in jail.

Both Welsh and Scottish drovers were distinctively dressed. The Welshmen favoured smocks and heavy trousers covered with knee-length woollen stockings. Leggings of soaped brown paper protected their legs from the hem of their

WELSH DROVERS
(above) These two 19th-century Welsh drovers are dressed for their arduous journey, wearing thick-soled boots, brimmed hats and well-worn overcoats. Despite their shabby appearance, these two gentlemen were probably among the most respected members of their community. Not only were they entrusted with valuable livestock, but they were also often relied upon to carry important documents and arrange financial commissions. Their wages were twice those of the ordinary farm labourer.

MILES TO GO
(left) This weathered milestone lies beside a drovers' road in Shropshire.

65

ABERYSTWITH SOUTH GATES
(CLEAR) ABERYSTWITH NORTH GATES.

Rate of Toll to be taken at this Gate.

For every Horse or other Beast drawing any Coach Chariot £ s d
Berlin, Landau, Landaulet, Barouche, Chaise, Phaeton
Vis-a-Vis, Calash, Curricle, Car, Chair, Gig, Hearse, Caravan
Litter, or any such like Carriage — 0 0 6
For every Horse or other Beast, except Asses drawing
any Waggon, Wain, Cart or other such like Carriage — 0 0 4
For every Ass drawing any Cart, Carriage, or other Vehicle — 0 0 2
For every Horse or Mule laden or unladen, and not drawing — 0 0 1½
For every Ass, laden or unladen and not drawing — 0 0 1
For every Horse or other Animal employed in carrying drawing
or conveying any lime to be used for the purpose of manure — 0 0 2
For every drove of Oxen, Cows, or Neat Cattle, the sum of Ten Pence
per Score, and so in proportion for any greater or less number
For every drove of Calves, Hogs, Sheeps, or Lambs, the sum of Five
Pence per Score, and so in proportion for any greater or less number.

EXEMPTION FROM TOLLS

[small print, partially legible]

TAKING THEIR TOLL

Drovers were prepared to go to almost any lengths – negotiating difficult country and treacherous slopes – to avoid the numerous tollgates on their routes. They were reluctant to pay the high rates charged – 'for every drove of Oxen, Cows or Neat Cattle, the sum of Ten Pence per Score, and so in proportion for any greater or less number' (right) – and begrudged losing valuable time: the tollgates invariably created huge bottlenecks, as the animals had to be counted one by one. Today, many of the tollgates have been converted into cottages. This small turnpike toll cottage (above) is situated on the Denbigh Moors, Clwyd. It is still known as 'Giat y Mynydd' – 'gate to the mountain'.

smocks, invariably wet and muddied. Soap was also applied to the soles of their stockings, to prevent chafing on their clogs. They also wore wide-brimmed hats and sometimes top-coats of Cambrian frieze (heavy woollen cloth). Scots drovers cut a more dashing figure, in slashed waistcoats, trousing, plaid and bonnet; some even wore the kilt, and tartan hose.

As well as cattle, horses and dogs also had a place on the drove. Scottish collies and Welsh corgis helped to herd the cattle – the quick, low-slung collies darting in to nip at the ankles of recalcitrant beasts. Welsh drovers, especially the topsmen, often rode on horseback, using Welsh cobs or the descendants of the Arab pack-horses brought over by the Roman legions. Scotsmen were more likely to use their ponies as pack animals, carrying items for their own use and goods to sell at the markets on the way.

The drovers' party would also include other citizens forced by circumstances to brave the dangers of long-distance travel. Boys going to be apprenticed in London, for instance, would join the Welsh droves for companionship and protection. One brave woman travelled with

the drovers on her way to enlist as a nurse with Florence Nightingale in the Crimea.

Typically, a large drove would contain 400 head of cattle, 12 drovers, half a dozen dogs, a few ponies and one or two fellow travellers. The drove would be divided into 'lots' each with its own attendants. Once assembled the drove set off in double file to an emotional send off. Before leaving, the drovers would take a sprig of rowan as a good luck token for their journey.

The constant noise of a drove was partly an encouragement to the cattle to keep moving, but mainly a warning to local farmers. On hearing the drover's cry, rendered in Welsh as *heiptrw hw*, they would quickly gather and pen their own beasts, because if they joined the passing stream they would be almost impossible to reclaim. Some drovers sounded horns to warn of their approach, or took along a bagpiper for the ride.

The drovers preferred to keep to open country, avoiding roads and towns as far as possible. They followed routes established by ancient custom, spreading out over wild country wherever they could and coming together at passes or other restrictions.

All along the drovers' wild ways, inns grew up to provide them with refreshment and their charges with overnight grazing, or 'stances', in fields which, from the standard charge per beast, came to be known as halfpenny fields. During the last two hundred years of droving the standard charge for people accommodated overnight was fourpence in summer, sixpence in winter. Only the topsman and one or two older drovers would take advantage of this, however, the rest remaining in the field with the beasts. Even though droving was mainly a summer activity, the nights were not always mild, and the drovers had to be hardy men. Highlanders spent many chill nights wrapped in their plaids on exposed moors. It was particularly important to stay with the animals on the

REST AND GOOD CHEER
(above) Once they had crossed the Denbigh Moors, Welsh drovers usually rested at The Drover's Arms, in the small Welsh village of Rhewl. The inn has now been extensively modernized – but the name still survives.

WATER HAZARDS
(below) Drovers often had to cross mountain streams and rivers, which were especially dangerous when in flood. If there was no bridge, the cattle would sometimes swim or be ferried across.

early part of the drove, while their homing instincts remained strong.

Many of the drovers' inns were little more than isolated farmhouses with a surplus of home-brewed ale, and the arrival of the droves was an excuse for general festivities, with music from fiddlers and pipers and boxing and wrestling matches.

The inn also provided a welcome respite from the dangers of the drove. Highwaymen and brigands were a constant threat, especially early in droving history. Indeed, the sums of money involved tempted some drovers themselves into acts of treachery and violence against their fellows. In Scotland, in the 16th and 17th centuries, and particularly in the West, cattle raiding or 'lifting' took on the aspects of a national sport, and drovers went armed with sword and pistol. Because of the prevalence of lifting, drovers were exempted from the 18th-century Disarming Acts – an exemption that helped keep alive the traditions of that proscribed instrument of war, the bagpipe.

Even more of a danger to the drover was the plague. In the years 1745-59, more than half a million cattle died of rinderpest. Fairs were cancelled, and while some small compensations were available for dead beasts, it was much less than half of the price they could have fetched at market. Many drovers were ruined. Some ran off leaving their dying charges in the roads, while others returned home to a lifetime of hard work in an attempt to repay their debts.

The Scottish trail ended at the Falkirk Tryst (a tryst is a non-statutory fair established by the agreement of the participants), which replaced the Crieff Tryst in the 18th century. There were three trysts at Falkirk, in August, September and October (the largest); each lasted several

days and up to 50,000 cattle a day changed hands. Most of the buyers were English, and they would hire some of the drovers to take the cattle on to their destination in Norfolk.

Business was not always over with the selling of cattle. The drovers' position as responsible citizens and long-distance travellers, a rare combination in pre-industrial Britain, meant that they were entrusted with the passing of letters and messages and, especially in Wales, the carrying out of financial commissions. In Cromwellian times they were used as tax collectors, and they also paid rents for estates to big-city landlords. They rarely carried cash, preferring to settle from the proceeds of the sale of the cattle. These financial arrangements were responsible for the foundation of several early banks, among them David Jones Bank of the Black Ox in Llandovery, later to merge with Lloyds, and the Bank of the Black Sheep in Aberystwyth.

Once the drove was over, some drovers would stay on to work on the southern harvest or, longer still, to coat the sheep with the mix of tar and butter then thought essential to their winter survival. The landed drovers returned to their own harvests, selling their ponies at market and either walking back, or, if they had done particularly well, leisurely taking the coach.

Walking or riding, the drovers carried back news from the cities to their isolated communities. It was from drovers that the people of Wales first heard of the Battle of Waterloo, and drovers' tales of the opportunities in America were a major factor in the waves of emigration from Wales in the 19th century. They also brought back news of new farming techniques as well as cuttings and seeds of new crops.

The corgis and collies found their own way home, the collies maybe carrying their masters' saddles on their back. Incredibly, they exactly retraced the steps of the drove, stopping at the same inns to be fed by previous arrangement with their masters. They were often the first to arrive home, and the womenfolk would excitedly begin preparations for the return of their husbands soon after the dogs turned up.

Today, the well-trodden drovers' routes, which even in their heyday were little more than

EARLY BANKERS
(below) The drovers devised a means of transferring cash, which led to the foundation of early banks. The 'Bank of the Black Sheep' issued notes featuring one black sheep for every pound.

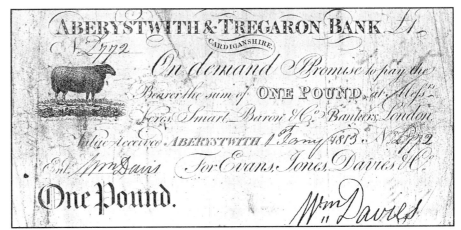

TO THE SLAUGHTER

After their marathon journeys, the Welsh cattle were fattened up in the lush meadows of Essex and Kent, before being sold at London's Smithfield Market (above), or at the Kent markets of Canterbury, Chilham and Maidstone. The Scottish cattle, on the other hand, were usually put out to pasture in Norfolk, where as many as 40,000 were sold each year., The quality of the meat was by no means impaired by the long drove. As Daniel Defoe wrote: 'These Scots runts as they call them, coming out of the cold and barren mountains of the Highlands in Scotland, feed so eagerly on the rich pastures . . . that they thrive in an unusual manner, and grow monstrously fat: and the beef is so delicious for taste, that the inhabitants prefer 'em to the English cattle.'

CATTLE NUISANCE

(above right) Close to the great markets, the summer droves could block the streets for hours at a time. The nuisance they created – holding up traffic and wandering on to the pavements – is graphically illustrated in this 'London Sketch' of 1877.

beaten tracks, have largely returned to the wilderness or have been civilized out of existence. In the high wild places they can sometimes be traced, criss-crossing the lanes that were the local routes to market or, in Scotland, the ways from the home farms to the summer shielings. Signs of the drovers' passing can also be found in stands of trees, buildings or in the names of lanes or fields.

In Wales, farms wishing to attract drove traffic advertised themselves by planting three Scots pines; these quick-growing trees acted as landmarks and signposts. In the chalklands of England, stands of yew, or other more exotic species, served the same purpose. Welsh names – even the adjective 'Welsh' applied to tracks or lanes in England – are another sure sign of droving activity, as are the words 'Drove' and 'Drift'. Halfpenny Lanes or Fields refer to the old charge for overnight stancing, and in Scotland, the ancient pastime of cattle lifting is commemorated in the name 'Thieves' Lane'. Some of the old droving inns still survive, as well, their colourful origins preserved in such evocative names as The Drover's Boy, The Highland Laddie or The Black Ox.

Tanning Hides

When tanning was discovered to improve the durability of animal hide, it soon became a major industry. But some of the processes it once involved made the craft a most unpleasant business.

The use of leather dates back to the very earliest days of civilization in Britain. After the axe and the arrow-head, an ancient Briton's most important tool was the stone scraper, used to convert an animal skin into a multitude of utilitarian objects. These included not only clothes and footwear, but resilient thongs, containers, body armour – even rudimentary water-wings!

The key to these applications of animal skins, though, was the introduction of tanning. In its raw state, an animal skin is of little use: when wet the skin quickly rots; and when dry, it becomes brittle and unyielding. Tanning makes the skin flexible and pliant, insoluble in water, and resistant to decay.

Tanning and the associated finishing processes do not just preserve the leather: they selectively alter the state of the animal skin, to suit it to a wide range of different purposes. Skins and hides are uniquely adaptable: some leathers are tough and hard, other types are diaphanously thin, and as pliant as the finest fabric. A tanned skin can be fashioned into a totally watertight container; yet treated in a different way, the same piece of leather makes a garment that breathes, so that the wearer is warm and protected without feeling sticky and uncomfortable.

The earliest methods of preserving leather did not involve tanning: the skins were just dried in the sun, then treated with a variety of substances to restore suppleness. Oils were a popular choice, but other less pleasant alternatives included animal brains. In time, however, three principal methods of leather preparation evolved, using respectively animal, vegetable and mineral agents. In Britain, the most important process used the tannin present in most vegetable matter to preserve and protect the animal skin.

THE TANNING PROCESS

In principle, this method of tanning is straightforward: it simply means soaking the hide in a bath containing a suspension of ground oak bark – bark which contains a high tannin content. Before soaking, however, the hide must be carefully prepared to remove unwanted materials. Much of the skin is waste: the tanner is interested in preserving only the fibrous central layer, the *corium* or *derma*, that gives the leather its unique properties. Below the derma is a flesh layer that must be scraped away before tanning can start. The outer layer of the hide, the *epidermis*, carries ingrained filth, dead skin and the animal's hairs. All these must be removed to expose the derma. After tanning, the hides had to be carefully dried and then treated to restore some of the suppleness that had been lost, or to alter the properties of the leather to suit a particular application.

These elaborations in the tanning process meant that tanning soon turned from a DIY process into a cottage industry, and then

EMBOSSED AND PAINTED GILT LEATHER *(below) This elaborate wall covering, which dates from the first half of the 19th century, has the natural beauty and rich grain of traditional oak-tanned leather.*

THE TANNERY *(above) The tannery was a notoriously unpleasant place to work: the smell of rotting flesh (most hides were delivered fresh from the slaughterhouse) mingled with the foul stench of excrement, which was used to break down the fibres of the hides.*

FLESHING AND UNHAIRING *(right) Before tanning, the hides had to be fleshed and unhaired by the beamsman. Using a blunt, two-handled knife, he scraped the loosened hair from the follicles, and then used a razor-sharp blade to remove the flesh. Nothing was discarded: the hairs were often sold off to upholsterers, while the flesh was used to make glue.*

developed into a fairly large-scale manufacturing operation.

A tannery was a far from pleasant place to work. Some processes involved the tanner handling rotting flesh; in others, huge mills created clinging dust; tanning chemicals stripped the hairs from the tanner's arms, and dyed his hands brown; razor-sharp knives introduced the constant risk of injury and almost certain infection. The most noticeable characteristic of a tannery, though, was the smell: an overpowering stench of rotting flesh and excrement. In hot weather the odour would become almost unbearable, and in winter, the open-sided tannery sheds would be little better — icy and treacherous. Just to make conditions worse, most tanneries were alive with rats.

Hides arrived at the tannery in various conditions. Those fresh from the slaughter-house might have fair amounts of adhering meat — in some tanneries these skins would be pegged out for the tannery dogs to tear off what they could. Hides which had been preserved by salting would be soaked in a water-pit for several days

to remove the cure. Dried hides were soaked and scrubbed to restore them to their normal state.

All hides were then immersed in a series of lime pits to loosen the flesh and hair adhering to each side of the skin. The pits contained solutions of increasing strength, and of varying age. The first pit was the weakest, but very 'mellow'; the liquor was saturated with bacteria, which softened and digested the leather. The last pit contained a much stronger solution of new lime.

Hides were lifted from the lime pits by beamsmen. These workers took their name from the beam over which they rested the skin. The beamsman slung the hide over the beam with the flesh side down. He would then use a concave, blunt 'unhairing knife' to scrape away the hairs and hair roots: even a trace of the membrane that surrounded the hair-root was sufficient to discolour the leather. Fleshing the hide was a more skilled operation. It was done using a curved two-handled knife with twin blades, both of which were honed to razor sharpness.

Newly fleshed and unhaired hide was still saturated with lime, which had to be removed before tanning. This was done partly by washing in running water and partly by the squeegee action of a blunt tool called a 'scudder'.

Skins – the soft, light hides from the smaller animals such as calves and goats – were too delicate to be scudded in this way. Instead, the residual lime was removed by mastering – a process of bacterial action. This was perhaps the most unpleasant job of all to be found in the tannery, because the most readily available source of bacteria to initiate the neutralization process was excrement. The mastering pits into which the skins were thrown were literally cess pits filled with the diluted dung of hens or pigeons (called 'bates') or with a mixture of dogs' excrement and warm water (called 'pure' or 'drench'). This 18th century description provides a vivid picture of the preparation of the latter solution: 'Put in a large vat, three or four pails of dog's turds...on this they fling a large

STACKING BARK
(above) The tannin solution consisted of ground oak bark leached in cold water. The bark was stored in two-foot cylindrical slabs, which were stacked to dry.

LIMING
(right) In order to loosen the hair and fatty tissue, the tanner immersed the hides in a series of pits, containing lime solution of varying strengths.

MECHANIZED PROCESS
(below) Leather manufacturers today have the benefit of modern machinery – like the dyeing drum, which operates like a huge washing-machine.

pail of water to dilute it; this done, the workman goes into the vat, and with his wooden shoes, tramples it, filling the vat half full of water.' There was certainly no shortage of the raw ingredients: the local hunt kennels provided an ample supply.

The action of the bacteria in the mastering pits not only neutralized the lime; it also reduced the thickness of the skins. One of the tanner's skills lay in knowing when to end the process:

called the 'butt', provided the best leather.

After the complex procedures of preparation, the actual process of tanning was by comparison relatively simple. There were only two active ingredients – water and dry oak bark. The oak bark was milled at the tannery to a carefully-controlled fineness.

Mixed with water, the ground bark was pumped into a succession of pits, and the hides progressed through these in a strict order. The first pits contained the weakest solution, and in these the hides stayed for only a short while – perhaps a day or so in each. From here, the hides were transferred to the 'handlers' or 'floaters', where they were laid flat in the solutions and turned regularly using tanning hooks to ensure even distribution of the tanning liquor. Liberal sprinklings of ground oak bark helped strengthen the last few handling baths.

Handling took some six to eight weeks, after which the hides moved to the final stage of the tanning – the layer pits. The floor of the empty pit was first covered with powdered oak bark, and a hide laid on top. The hide in turn was covered with bark, then another hide, and so on. The layering continued until the pit was full, then tanning liquor from the handling pits was pumped in. Over a period of up to 18 months, the hides were moved from pit to pit, each containing progressively stronger solutions.

After tanning, the hides were washed, possibly

mastering in bates might require a week or more, but drench completed the job in less than a day.

The final preparatory task before tanning could begin was to cut up the hide into several pieces. Different parts of the animal's skin absorb the tanning solution at different rates; each part therefore spent a different period in the solutions. The inferior scraps at the hide edges would be removed first, and the belly section would then be separated from the skin that lay across the animal's back. This central section,

TANNING IN TANKS
(above) Nowadays, the hides are suspended in tanks of tannage, and the treatments are usually mineral rather than vegetable.

THE CURRIER
(above right) The currier's most important task was to shave the hides, to reduce their natural thickness.

tinctive tools and skills: skins were smoothed and stretched, again with a slicker, but of a slightly different design; a stockstone, scouring brush or glass slicker removed the bloom from the skin side of the leather; and the wet currying processes ended with a thorough oiling to protect the hides as they dried.

To protect the leather in future use, there was one further oiling, or 'stuffing', with a mixture of tallow and cod oil when the leather had dried. Subsequent processing was largely cosmetic. Some leathers were rubbed with a cork board; others were blackened with lamp-black and soap, or stained in brown and other colours; sizing with glue made the leather smoother and more lustrous; and various polishing processes employing glass, steel and mahogany tools gave the hides a rich shine or emphasized the grain.

FACTORY METHODS

Mechanization and chemistry slowly but inexorably eroded the craft skills of the tanner and currier. Vegetable tanning declined, as more adaptable – and far quicker – mineral treatments became available. Artificial mastering solutions appeared at the end of the 19th century, removing some of the appalling smells of the tannery. Skiving was virtually eliminated by the introduction of the splitting machine in 1809.

Today's tannery has little in common with the small craft tanneries of the pre-industrial era, but a few remnants of the past survive. Surprisingly, not all are working museums, life like, but essentially lifeless: for a few applications, such as orthopaedic use, there is still no substitute for traditional oak-tanned leather.

brushed or scoured to remove the bloom left by the immersion, then oiled to condition the leather during drying. Drying took place in a cool, well-ventilated room and was punctuated by a series of conditioning stages: the hides were taken down from their racks, damped down and stacked in piles to temper them and make the leather supple and evenly moist. They were then scraped with a three-sided knife, and rolled under great pressure between sheets of zinc to flatten out any creases.

Just as the leather had to be carefully treated prior to tanning, so too a tanned hide was not ready for use until it had undergone further treatment. The tanner passed the finished hides to a currier, who changed the appearance and texture of the leather to suit the end use to which the hide would be put.

Whereas the tanner's task was principally a chemical one, the currier treated the leather in largely mechanical ways. One of his most important jobs was to reduce the thickness of the hide – a process known as 'skiving'.

Before this could begin, the currier had to wash the leather, and soften it using a hot infusion of sumac leaves. Then he set the hide on a sloping table, and removed any bloom left by tanning, using a steel, copper or stone-bladed 'slicker'. This was a blunt blade, measuring about six inches long, and guided by two wooden handles. After drying, the hide passed on to a steeply sloping wooden table for skiving.

This process required more manual dexterity than any other leather-making operation. The currier used a razor-sharp knife of a unique shape to cut small shavings of leather from the flesh side of the skin. Considerable skill was needed to prevent the knife from cutting right through the the hide. Additional currying processes followed, each with their own dis-

AN OLD-FASHIONED FINISH *(above) This photograph shows a Bermondsey firm finishing 'skivers' (thin leather) for 'hat and boot purposes'.*

THE SPLITTING MACHINE *(right) The splitting machine, introduced in 1809, enabled the tanner to easily obtain two hides for the price of one.*

Fruit of the Vine

After success in Roman and medieval times, the burgeoning English wine-making industry was soured by centuries of bad weather. Now, with grapes suited to the climate, English wines are enjoying a revival.

Vineyards, often thought of as out of place in the English landscape, are not alien to these islands. On the contrary, they belong to an agricultural tradition that began – like so much of our heritage – with Julius Caesar and his legions. Having subdued Britain's rebellious tribes, the Romans then introduced their own way of life which included – naturally enough, given their Mediterranean homeland – the wine habit. Since there were no native vines, supplies had to be imported from Italy, as the numerous wine jars discovered in town house and villa excavations prove.

The situation changed after AD 280 when the Emperor Probus, anxious to accelerate Romanization, issued an edict promoting viticulture (cultivation of the vine) in several provinces, among them Britannia. A paucity of imported wine jars after this time indicates that Probus' strategy was successful.

Vine cultivation received a further boost in AD 312 when Christianity became the Empire's official religion (wine was required for the Eucharist). Within a hundred years, however, the Romans' departure and ensuing barbarian attacks had sabotaged British viticulture. Happily, the disruption was short-lived: as the Anglo-Saxons settled and integrated with existing populations, they soon acquired a taste for wine and so developed vine-growing skills.

The Church, once again, provided a timely stimulus. Augustine, sent by Pope Gregory to evangelize the Angles in 597, made thousands of converts. As a result, the demand for altar wine rose considerably. The predominantly white English wine was coloured red, often with elderberries, for communion use. Furthermore, in the wake of Augustine's crusade, monasticism spread to Britain: the monks established themselves in self-sufficient communities living off their own produce which included wine.

By the 8th century, vineyards must have been relatively common – and economically significant – as they merited a mention in 731 by the Venerable Bede in his brief summary of English agriculture: 'This island abounds in grain and trees and is well suited to feeding cattle and beasts of burden. There are vines growing in many places ...' A law passed by King Alfred (849-899), commanding that any person causing damage to another's vineyards should pay full compensation, is further proof of the vine's importance in Dark Age England. Capping all this evidence is the popular theory that the Anglo-Saxons renamed October, Wyn Moneth, in honour of the grape harvest.

Domesday, listing just 45 vineyards, gives an incomplete record but does show how viticulture spread right across the country south of a line from the Wash (tradition has it that Ely was once called 'Isle des Vignes', Island of Vines), to the Welsh borders. According to the survey, the most intensively-planted areas were East Anglia (particularly Essex), present-day Greater London and the West Country. English viticulture thrived under the Normans: the numerous nobles and religious orders who acquired land in William's new kingdom invariably planted part of their estate with vines.

However, a gradual decline of English viticulture happened between the 12th and 16th centuries. It began in 1152, when Henry II married Eleanor of Aquitaine and thus gained the rich wine-growing region of Bordeaux. For the next 300 years, cheap clarets flooded into England, undercutting the native product. Throughout the Middle Ages, however, wine was a popular drink: cheap – around one penny a gallon – and safe, since it contained sufficient alcohol to kill typhoid germs. Consumption was therefore high, and English wines remained in demand.

FAIRWEATHER GRAPES

A far more significant factor in the fortunes of British viticulture was climatic change. From about 1300, summers became progressively cooler and cloudier, winters colder and longer; the deterioration lasted three centuries. During that period, the average August temperature fell from 62°F to 59°F, enough to retard the ripening process, and, with later spring frosts and earlier autumn ones curtailing the growing season, vineyard management became something of a gamble. Around the same time, Britain was ravaged by the plague: in the mid-1300s, the Black Death probably exterminated half the population, thereby decimating the

ENGLISH VINES

Vines and wine-making, first introduced to Britain by the Romans, thrived until about 1300 (left) when three centuries of cooler summers, made vine management in Britain more risky. Although private vineyards and vines under glass were still grown, it was not until 1875 when Lord Bute planted vineyards at Castell Coch (above) that the operation of commercial vineyards became realistic. The 20th century has seen a vigorous revival of interest in English wines. Vines from Hambledon (right) produced the first commercial vintages since Castell Coch.

WINE PIONEER

(below) The late Major-General Sir Guy Salisbury-Jones began the planting of Hambledon Vineyard in 1951. On sale from 1955, Hambledon was the first commercially-made British wine since the closure of Castell Coch 40 years earlier.

WINE MANUAL

(right) Although vines for wine making were not grown on a large scale until the 19th century, many small vineyards flourished over the ages. Two writers, in particular, promoted the planting of vines and praised the character of English wines. Their books – The English Vineyard Vindicated by John Rose and The Compleat Vineyard by William Hughes (title page shown right), still hold good today. Rose, gardener to William III, was one of the first to put forward the view that English wines had to be seen within the context of English soil, weather and topographical conditions.

workforce, and many landowners abandoned labour-intensive viticulture in favour of arable or livestock farming.

A further, and final, reversal of fortune occurred in 1536 when Henry VIII instigated the Dissolution of the Monasteries. In the space of a few years, Britain lost both its prime vineyards and the expert skills of the monks who had tended them, and commercial viticulture dwindled to extinction. Yet the vineyard itself did not disappear altogether.

Throughout the 16th and 17th centuries, vines were planted by the wealthy in their gardens – partly as decoration and partly to provide wine for their own use. The diarist, Samuel Pepys, frequently praises Sir William Batten's vintage '…for joy he did give the company a bottle or two of his own last year's wine, growing at Walthamstow; than which the whole company said they never drank better foreign wine in their lives'. But in spite of a general apathy and scepticism towards 'home-grown' wine – a legacy of the Bordeaux link – private vineyards continued to flourish in the 1700s and there were even two notable attempts at large-scale production. The first happened in 1730 at Westbrook, near Godalming, Surrey, when James Oglethorpe – squire of Westbrook and MP for Haslemere – turned part of his estate into England's largest-ever vineyard.

The other great venture also took place in Surrey, at Painshill near Cobham – home of

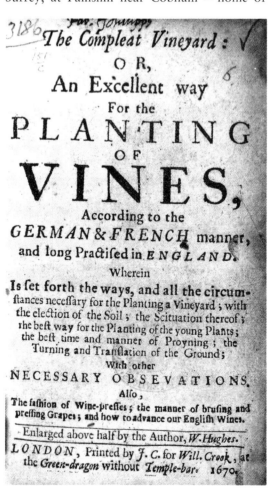

WINNING WAYS

(below) Spraying the vines against mildew, Colin Gillespie, owner of Wootton Vines in Somerset, was the recipient of The English Wine of the Year award for 1986. The award, the Gore-Browne Trophy, was won for Wootton's Seyval 1985.

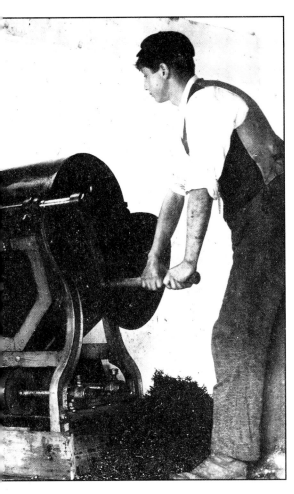

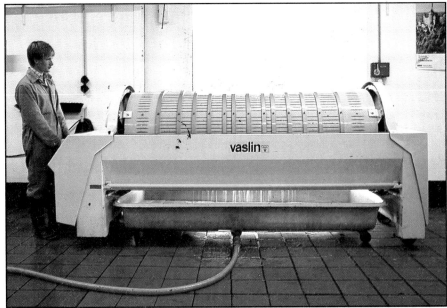

PRESSES OLD AND NEW
Around the turn of the century, grapes from the Marquis of Bute's vineyards at Castell Coch in Wales were pressed in a hand-turned cast iron press in Cardiff Castle (left). The Castell Coch wineries closed down, never to re-open, during World War 1 because of the sugar shortage; it was another 40 years before wine was produced commercially in Britain again. Today, the English vintage is usually pressed in gleaming electric presses (above).

Charles Hamilton, son of the Duke of Abercorn. Around 1740, Hamilton planted five – later ten – acres of vines and eventually engaged a French *vigneron* (vine-grower) to manage them. When Hamilton first tried to sell his wine he inevitably encountered suspicion. But by 1750, he was supplying wine, both white and red, to merchants 'for fifty guineas a hogshead; and one wine merchant, to whom I sold five hundred pounds worth at one time, assured me he sold some of the best of it from 7s 6d to 10s 6d a bottle'.

Hamilton's success, however, did not initiate a vineyard renaissance. The rich, ever biased against English production, preferred imported wine and even managed to obtain it during the Napoleonic blockade. Common folk drank beer which was untaxed and therefore much cheaper.

THE WROTHAM PINOT

The most recent chapter in the story of English viticulture – its current revival – started soon after World War 2 and was pioneered by two gardening enthusiasts: Edward Hyams and Ray Barrington Brock. Hyams put down two new vineyards, in Kent and in Devon and published *The Grape Vine in England*, a comprehensive manual covering the vine's history, cultivation and commercial potential. He discovered that a black grape growing in a cottage garden at Wrotham, Kent, was a Pinot Meunier type (the principal grape used by Hamilton) which had adapted itself to the British climate. Hyams

took cuttings and the Wrotham Pinot is now one of the grape vines recommended by the EEC for use in England.

At the same time, Barrington Brock established the Viticultural Research Station at Oxted, Surrey, to discover which vines were best suited to outdoor cultivation in Britain. In this he was heeding advice given, some three centuries earlier, by William III's gardener, John Rose, who maintained that English viticulture's chequered career was partly the result of using vines and methods inappropriate to England's soil, topography and climate since they came from 'countries of so little affinity with ours'. In his first report, Barrington Brock listed six wine-grapes that were 'likely to be successful under adverse conditions' and added that Riesling-Sylvaner (or Müller Thurgau) may also grow well here. Müller Thurgau is now grown on 96 per cent of vineyards.

Viticulture's comeback advanced significantly in 1952 when the late Sir Guy Salisbury-Jones planted a vineyard at Hambledon, Hampshire.

HARVEST TIME
(above) Grape pickers at Chilsdown Vineyards add their individual bucket-loads of grapes to the central picking trailer during the annual harvest. The Pagets, who planted Chilsdown in 1972, won a Gold Medal in 1984 for their Chilsdown 1983 – a dry wine, made from a blend of Müller Thurgau and Reichensteiner grapes.

WINE REVIVAL
Proof of the successful rebirth of English wine making was the formation in 1967 of the English Vineyards Association. Starting with 20 members it now boasts 550. The vineyards represented below by their labels, all members of the association, produce distinctive and increasingly sought-after wines.

Three years later, he produced Britain's first commercial wine since Castell Coch closed during the First World War. Sir Guy's initiative started a trend: over the next three decades more and more vines were planted and today there are over 300 commercial vineyards in England and Wales, ranging in size from one to 35 acres. Most modern vineyards are located in southern England, inheriting the medieval sites of monastic viticulture – but a few have been put down as far north as Derbyshire and Yorkshire and as far west as the Dyfed coast.

Since vines require maximum exposure to the sun, vineyards are ideally situated on a sheltered south-facing slope; and preferably on sandy gravel or chalk or, as Rose indicated, on ground only fit for brambles. The vine, a hungry plant, responds to poor soil by developing an extensive root system which in turn guarantees steady growth and protection against adverse changes of moisture and temperature near the surface. As for the vines themselves, varieties that do well in countries of similar latitudes, such as Luxembourg and Germany, predominate, especially the Müller Thurgau, Reichensteiner and a hardy French-American hybrid, the Seyval Blanc. They are normally planted, about 3500 to the acre, in symmetrical rows, supported by a trellis of poles and wires; one or two fruiting branches from each vine are trained along a horizontal wire some 18 inches above the earth – high enough to avoid ground frosts, low enough to receive heat reflected off the soil surface. Vines generally start to crop in their third year but do not reach full production until they are least six years old.

On average, an acre of vines yields 2400 bottles of wine; in an outstanding season, like the long hot summer of 1976, that figure can double. Conversely, cool rainy weather can reduce production to as little as 200 bottles per acre. Although quantity fluctuates enormously from year to year, English wines (which officially include output from Welsh vineyards as well) are acquiring a reputation for quality and are now taken seriously by the wine-drinking public. At present almost all English wine is white, but research into suitable vines for red wine production is under way. The English vineyard revival is still gaining momentum but already has become established enough to ensure that this old tradition will continue.

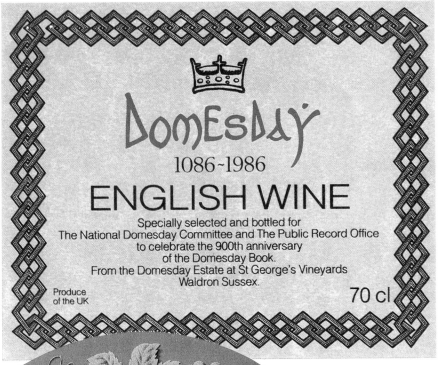

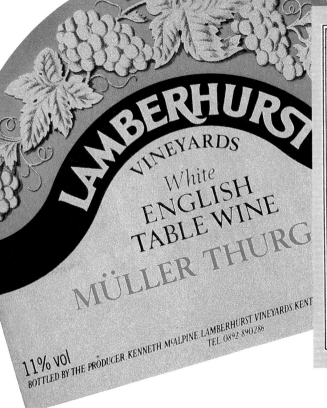

The Brewer

For the brewers of old, the Thames provided both a vital ingredient for their ale and a highway to carry this popular product far afield.

Poets, writers and painters have immortalized the appeal of the Thames, but others see the character of London's waterway in more prosaic terms. Water is the largest single ingredient in beer and the river has just the right combination of dissolved calcium and sodium salts to make a delicious and intoxicating brew.

As with so many things that we now think of as characteristically British, beer was brought here by the Romans. They, in turn, were taught the art of making 'wine from barley' by the Egyptians who had learned the skill as far back as 2000 BC, from, they claimed, Osiris, the god of Agriculture.

The ancient Britons embraced the Roman beverage wholeheartedly, and immediately started to improve on what they had learned. The principal ingredient, barley, grows even in quite northern areas, so unlike wine, beer could be made virtually anywhere in Britain.

Strength was one of the principal aims of the brewer. British drinkers viewed alcoholic potency as a virtue right from the very earliest days of brewing. The tradition of drinking beer recreationally, rather than just to slake a thirst, goes back to Anglo-Saxon times when drinking was part of religious ceremony and accompanied all celebrations: the word 'bridal' is derived from bride-ale, a special brew to celebrate the wedding. Anglo-Saxon feasts were called *beorscopes*, and literature of the period celebrated drinking, as in *Beowulf*: 'A thane attended the service: one who bore in his hand a decorated ale-can. He poured forth the sheer nectar.'

By the time of the Norman conquest, beer had become thoroughly woven into the fabric of British life; if anything, the invading Normans were heavier drinkers than their subjects: accounts in the Domesday Book suggest that good ale of the time was probably stronger than modern barley wine.

Later recipes were even more potent, and people consumed enormous quantities of the stuff: 16th century directions for making 'syngl' ale would produce a brew with an original gravity of 1070°-1100°. Few of today's beers are this strong, and the 'dobl' ale of the time was stronger still. In early legislation governing the size of drinking vessels, the smallest statutory measure for ale was the quart, since nobody would think of drinking just a pint at a time.

Everybody drank beer as a matter of course, and few people – even infants – drank water. Benjamin Franklin outlining the beer consumption of a typical London printer in the early 18th century, reports beer before breakfast, with breakfast, between breakfast and dinner, and at dinner itself; then more beer at six o'clock and a pint at knocking-off time. Franklin did not even go on to write about social drinking in the evening!

The printer would have bought his beer from

an ale-house and brewery combined, and probably from an ale-wife, who might also have been called a brewster or brewess. The tradition of ale-houses making their own beer stemmed from the short shelf-life of ale: until hops were introduced to Britain, beer did not keep well, so brewing was continous. Ale houses identified themselves by hanging out a pole called an ale-stake, and a new brew was indicated with a fir tree or bush. Later, a barrel hoop came to signify that ale could be bought at the place displaying the sign. In 14th-century London, there were such extraordinary numbers of these ale houses – about one for every 12 adults – that the signs became a hazard to traffic and had to be controlled.

Brewing was not just a secular activity: the church too was in the business of brewing. At medieval 'church-ales', church wardens sold beer to raise money for the parish. All monasteries had their own brew-houses, but monks, it seems, were not such expert brewers as church-wardens. In 1224, a writer commented, 'Even in the London Friary, I myself have seen the brethren drink beer so sour that some preferred water.'

Despite the semi-craft nature of brewing, some brewers became quite wealthy and philanthropic. An Elstree Brewer, Richard Platt, established a free school in 1596, but took care to protect his charges from the source of his riches, forbidding 'hauntings of Alehouses and Tavernes.'

THE INGREDIENTS

Beer was not mass-produced until the late 18th century. Until then, most brewing was small-scale. However, the first step in the brewing process, the malting of barley, needs a great amount of space, and so this process was industrialized first.

To make alcohol, yeast must have soluble sugar as a raw material to act on, but barley and other grains consist mainly of starch. Malting is the process of sprouting the barley –

CAKES AND ALE
To make beer, the ancient Egyptians squeezed out cakes of malted barley fermented in water. A similar method is still used in Egypt for a drink called, coincidentally, 'boozah'.

HOPS FOR BEER
(left) Hops were added to ale in the 15th century to make beer. They lent the distinctive bitter taste for the drink and acted as a mild narcotic. Hops grow as high as 30ft with yellow 'flowers' whose petals contain the resins and oils which give the drink its flavour and aroma; the many varieties of hops distinguish various beers.

WORKING HOLIDAYS
(below) Ripe hops must be picked within ten days. Before machinery took over, a large force of casual labour was recruited annually, mostly from the East End of London. Entire families would take off to work a 'busman's holiday'.

letting it germinate briefly – to create the enzymes which will convert the starch into sugar at a later stage of brewing.

Malting begins with the barleycorn soaking in vats of water for up to three days, it is then spread out on the slate or baked-clay floor of the 'maltings' to germinate. The rate of sprouting is carefully controlled, largely by regulating heat and moisture. Careful ventilation and heating keeps the room at 55-60°F, and the sprouting grains are regularly turned over and stirred with wooden rakes. Spreading the barley out slows the sprouting, while piling it in heaps or 'couches' encourages it.

After 10-14 days, drying out the barley grains and heating them to about 80°F arrests the sprouting. Roasting in a furnace follows. Malt destined for pale beers gets a gentle roasting, but for darker brews, the furnace temperature is much higher – up to 400°F. When the grain has cooled and settled, it is ground to make 'grist': cracked malt particles of uniform size, ready for the brewer.

Ales were made principally from malt, water and yeast, but the early 1400s brought a new ingredient: hops. Hops were probably first used just to flavour the drink – not a new idea as other herbs such as bog-myrtle, wild rosemary and milfoil had also been used for the same purpose. However, brewers quickly discovered that hops had special qualities not shared by other flavourings. Hopped beers lasted longer than the traditional unhopped ales, and adding hops made the drink slightly soporific. (Hence, hop pillows for light sleepers, as, in fact, the hop is related to the hemp plant and shares a few of its narcotic qualities although in a much

MASS MANUFACTURE
(right) Traditionally, most beer was brewed by the individual ale houses and taverns, or even at home, but by the mid-18th century, many breweries were set up on a large scale – some of them surviving to this day. British beer was soon introduced to other northern European countries where it fared very successfully with the local brews.

EMPTYING THE
MASH TUN
*The grist – ground
malted barley, is
added to the mash
tun with the liquor to
form a wort. After a
few hours, the wort is
drained into a copper
and the mash tun is
refilled a second or
third time. Beer made
from such subsequent
'mashings' is weaker,
however, and was
once called 'small
beer'. After the
mashing is complete
the spent grain is sold
off as fodder for
livestock.*

milder form.)

Hops are picked over quite a short period and need intensive labour; thus, the traditional East-end Londoner's holiday in Kentish hop fields. The hops are dried over fires for 8-10 days in oast houses before they are ready for beer-making.

THE MASH TUN

The brewer begins work by emptying sacks of the malt grist into the 'mash tun' – usually just an old barrel – and adding hot water or 'liquor'. Steeping the malt in liquor allows the enzymes created in malting to convert the barley starch into soluble carbohydrate. This makes a dark, sugary solution called 'wort', which is drained off and the mash tun refilled to make a second, weaker wort. The process can be repeated, but

beer made from further 'mashings' will be weaker than from the first and second. In practice, the third mashing was the limit, and the weak brew made from it was called 'small beer'. The 'spent-grains' left in the mash tun are shovelled out to be used as animal feed.

Until the 15th century, yeast would not have been added for fermentation to make sweet, strong ale. For beer, though, the brewer adds hops to the wort at this stage in a copper, and brings the mixture to the boil. Boiling sterilizes the wort and extracts from the hops the resins and oils which give the beer its characteristically bitter flavour.

Once the liquid has cooled, it is transferred to a fermenting vessel, and the wort is 'pitched': yeast, sometimes nicknamed 'barm' or 'Godes good', is added. The yeast floats on the top of

THE ALE-WIFE
*From early times, much of
the brewing business was
run by women. Country ale
houses were often run by
brewesses, or brewsters,
who made their own drink.
Brewing was considered a
low calling and the
brewster's and huckster's (a
woman who retailed ale
from the manufacturer)
produce was regularly
inspected by agents called
ale-conners.*

the wort forming a foamy head that increases in size as fermentation continues; the brewer scoops off excess yeast and reserves it for starting future brews. Fermentation takes 4-6 days at about 60-70°F, but with less than perfect temperature control it may well take longer.

In traditional brewing, this is almost the end of the process: the beer is drained from the fermenting vessels into barrels, and left to settle; some secondary fermentation also takes place in the barrel. In the past, brewers relied on gravity to remove any particles that clouded the drink, though adding beaten egg-white to the barrel also helped. The bright, crystal clear beers of today are filtered and chemically 'fined' to remove any cloudiness.

Variations in the process allowed the brewer to change the character of the beer. The degree to which the barley was roasted affected the colour of the drink – stouts, for example, were made by adding a small amount of dark-roasted barley. The quantity of soluble carbohydrates in the wort controlled the alcoholic content of the beer, giving the brewer the option of making a weak or strong brew. But intoxication was not the only reason for making strong beer; beers that were very strong had a longer shelf life, and would tide the drinkers over the summer from March to the next malting in October. The strong brews had special names such as Huff-cup, Pharaoh and Nipitatum. Adding different grains to the barley in the mash-tun made possible a wider gamut of flavour; for example, beer brewed with wheat

FROM CRADLE TO . . .
Beer was the staple drink for centuries – even infants and children were reared on it (above). For the majority of the working urban population, drinking was a brief respite from their grim lives. The ale house and tavern flourished and temperance movements fought a losing battle against drunkenness (below).

instead of hops, called Mum ale.

Mixing and blending continued at the bar: warming the ale and adding ginger, the pulp of roasted apples and sugar made 'lambs wool'. Some concoctions would have rivalled today's cocktails. 'Buttered-ale' called for hot strong ale mixed with sugar candy, butter, egg yolk and pepper.

DRINKING AND THE LAW

For centuries, beer was a staple food on a par with bread: the 'Assize of Bread and Ale' was an early attempt around the 12th century to control the price of both commodities. Brewers who charged too much or who sold bad ale could end up in the pillory or on the ducking stool. The purity of beer was tested by the 'ale-conner', whose procedures may seem eccentric by today's standards. He would enter a tavern, pour out a pool of beer onto the seat, and sit in it in his leather breeches for half an hour. Bad, sugary beer, would stick his trousers to the seat, but good beer allowed him to stand freely.

Drunkenness preoccupied legislators as much as the quality of the ales and beers, both for moral reasons and because drunks created a fire risk in the tightly packed and highly inflammable town hovels.

Drunkenness was not the human's prerogative. Parson Woodforde, whose diaries give a vivid glimpse of rural life in the 18th century, fed spent grain to his pigs with disastrous results.

In the early 17th century, regulations to control excessive drinking began to be introduced, and have continued since. From 1643, heavy drinking was discouraged by taxation, which also provided a welcome source of income for the state.

Most of this legislation proved unpopular, and some of it unworkable; for literature, rhyme and fable down the ages have continued to celebrate the joys of beer, drinking – and drunkenness in no uncertain terms.

The Making of Cider

Sharp, strong cider, made from the juice of tart English apples, was for centuries the drink of the rural labourer, and the annual cider-making was as important a date in the country calendar as haymaking or the harvest.

The ancient Celts, who venerated the mistletoe-entwined apple tree and regarded the fruit itself as sacred, were the first British cidermakers, but their drink was a primitive brew made with the fermented juice of bitter wild apples. It was the Norman followers of William the Conqueror who introduced cider made from apples specially grown for the purpose – *sidre*, which is still Normandy's traditional drink. From 1066 onwards cider production spread rapidly: it became the drink of the people and, in the 1300s when the 100 Years' War cut off wine supplies from France, of the nobility as well. Being germ-free, because of its acidity, it was safer to drink than water and was even used for baptisms.

By the 17th century scientific advances had helped create a better fruit and a better drink. As well as ordinary farm cider, with an alcohol content of between four and nine per cent, there was a wine-strength drink containing eleven to twelve per cent alcohol. Fashionable circles adoped the 'English wine', drinking it from specially crafted crystal glasses or flutes. It was also promoted as an aid to health. Diarist John Evelyn wrote in 1664 that 'cider excites and cleanses the stomach, strengthens digestion, and infallibly frees the kidneys and bladder from breeding the gravel stone'. For almost 200 years British ships carried cider to ward off scurvy.

WAGES IN CIDER

In the 1700s cider became a form of currency: it was used to pay part of a farm labourer's weekly wage. The allowance – about half a gallon a day and up to three or four times as much during haymaking or the harvest – was measured into individual wooden casks, known as costrels in some places and firkins in others, which could be taken to the fields to slake the powerful thirst produced by a day's strenuous physical labour. The annual production of this farm cider became a crucial stage in the farming year.

Despite the widespread popularity of cider, with an estimated national consumption of between 5 and 15 million gallons per year, there was no commercial production. Cider-making was a domestic craft, carried out by the farmer using his own fruit to produce a drink for his family and workforce – though he might sell a surplus to the local inns and taverns. Smallholders would have just a few cider apple trees either growing in the hedge or among other

THE CIDER MILL
(far right) Cider apples are very hard so they must be crushed first before pressing to extract the juice. In the old days this was usually done with a horse-powered circular mill.

MECHANICAL SHAKER
(right) Since they are to be milled cider apples do not have to look good, so they have always been harvested by knocking them from the trees – once with long poles and now with a mechanical tree shaker.

fruit trees. On large farms and estates there were cider apple orchards: the trees spaced well apart to allow for undercropping – generally with rye – or for grazing sheep and keeping bees.

Cider apples differ greatly from their dessert and culinary cousins: they are small, hard, blotchy, high in tannin, fibrous and far too bitter to eat. In cider's heyday there were over 350 varieties, many with bizarre names like Foxwhelp, Slack-my-Girdle and Lady's Finger. The most famous apple in cider history was the Redstreak, developed by Lord Scudamore, Charles I's ambassador in France, who retired to his Herefordshire estate and devoted himself to the cultivation and study of cider apples. The Redstreak was the founding father of most modern varieties.

BITTERSHARPS AND BITTERSWEETS

There are two main categories of cider apple: bittersharps and bittersweets. Cider can be made from either of these as well as the ordinary cooking or dessert apples – sharps and sweets – but for centuries bittersharps were the most popular, producing a drink that was both astringent and very dry.

Cider apples mature late, between mid October and the New Year, so they were invariably the last crop to be harvested. They were knocked down from the trees with long poles and then left to mature, either in straw-covered heaps in the orchard or on the upper floor of a barn. During this time – about two or three weeks – the fruit would sweat out excess moisture and concentrate its sugars. When the apples yielded to thumb pressure they were ready for milling.

The poorer country folk milled, or crushed, their apples by hand but more prosperous farmers could afford a horse-powered, circular mill. Made of wood or stone, this type of mill had a vertical grindstone which was pushed around a channel in its outside edge. The cidermakers loaded the fruit in the middle and used a stick to knock the apples systematically into the trough. From time to time a bucket of water was added to stop the pulp, or must, from becoming too sticky. At the end of milling it was thick, dark brown and highly aromatic.

The rotary or scratter mill, first introduced in the 1600s, provided another method of crushing apples. Two toothed rollers inside a wooden frame mashed the fruit as it passed through. Originally turned by hand, scratters were later adapted to take a belt-drive from a water mill or steam engine. They were cheaper and quicker than stone mills, as well as being portable, but the pulp they produced was coarser and they did not break up the pips to release the bitter oils as the stone mills did.

Freshly milled pulp was usually pressed at once. The first stage of the process was building the pulp up into a stable stack, or cheese. In Herefordshire this was done by wrapping it in horsehair cloths. The first cloth was spread over

the press bed, then two buckets of pulp were emptied on to it, and the corners of the cloth folded in like an envelope. On top was laid another cloth with another load of pulp, and envelope followed envelope until the cheese was about three or four feet high. In the south-west the cheese was built up with layers of barley straw which acted as a binder and, according to local tradition, enriched the juice with 'a power of minerals raised up from the soil'.

A heavy board was laid on top of the completed cheese and the press then screwed down. Early presses had a single central screw mounted in a massive oak frame; operating them required great skill and strength. In the late 1800s, however, the more manageable and efficient double-screw press came into widespread use and made light work of pressing the fruit. With each turn of the screw, the juice flowed out – over 100 gallons per ton of fruit – and was collected in wooden or stone vessel positioned below the press.

On many farms the squeezed pulp – the pomace – would be reconstituted with water, left to stand and then pressed a second time. The diluted juice produced a much weaker drink and, often, it was this 'small cider' or 'ciderkin' that servants and labourers received in lieu of wages. Ultimately, the discarded pomace was fed to livestock – provided it had not obviously started to ferment, although tipsy chickens and drunken pigs were a not uncommon sight during the cider-making season.

Generally, the pressed juice was poured straightaway into oak casks to ferment as a result of the action of wild yeasts on the apple

LORD OF THE APPLE
Scudamore's devotion to cider apples greatly boosted their growing. John Evelyn remarked at the time, 'By the noble example of my Lord Scudamore all of Herefordshire . . . is become one entire orchard.'

FIELD CIDER
A daily ration of cider was part of farm workers' wages. When working in the fields harvesting or haymaking, they were supplied with as much as they could drink.

THE MAKING OF CIDER

CIDER APPLES

COWARNE RED

REDSTREAK

skins. If fermentation did not begin within three days – signalled by hissing froth around the bung – a handful of orchard topsoil was added to start the process. During the next few weeks rabbit skins or bacon were sometimes added to feed the yeast; raisins, wheat or barley to increase the alcohol content; and beetroot or burnt sugar to improve the colour.

Fermentation lasted a couple of weeks in warm weather and a couple of months when it was cold. It was not uncommon for casks to go silent during a harsh winter and then start working again in early spring. Eventually, the hissing ceased indicating that fermentation had stopped; the bung was then tightly sealed with lime and clay or mutton fat.

THE TRAVELLING CIDER-MAKER
(above) Towing his scratter mill and screw-press, the cider-maker toured villages, pubs and farms. Growers with no equipment of their own would pay him – a halfpenny a gallon in the late 1800s – to mill and press their fruit. Some travelling cider-makers were still operating as late as 1950.

IN THE CHEESE PRESS
(below) Traditional cider is still made today using methods and equipment broadly similar to those of the old days. Each layer of the cheese may now be separated by a metal grid, but it still takes a prodigious amount of gritty manpower to operate the press.

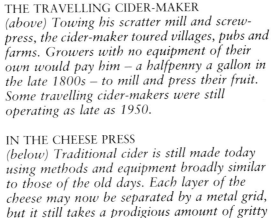

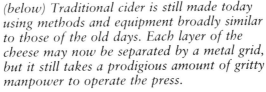

FOXWHELP

KINGSTON BLACK

JOEBY CRAB

91

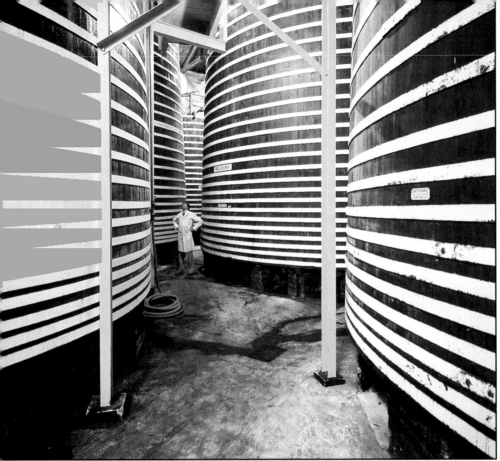

OAK VATS
Oak is the traditional material for cider containers whether they be the old wooden casks or these giant vats in Bulmer's vathouse. Each one holds between 40,000 and 60,000 gallons of cider.

WHERE THE CIDER APPLES GROW
The new commercial cider companies became established in traditional cider-growing areas like Hereford and the West Country. The climate in these parts is especially suitable for apple-growing, with mild winters, frost-free springs and warm wet summers.

Three months later the cider was ready for drinking. Farm cider was never filtered. But it was often clarified, either by racking into a clean cask or by fining – adding egg-white, gelatine or bullock's blood to the cask to carry down suspended solids.

At its best, farm cider was a splendid drink, very dry and strong. But much was badly made, with a sharp, sour taste and a vile afterkick – 'squeal-pig'. Many farmers would also produce

a cask of quality cider for their own family to drink, possibly at Christmas. This was made from selected apples by a special process known as keeving. The apples were milled with little or no water and then left for 24 hours; after pressing, the juice, with lime added, stood in an open-topped cask until a thick brown crust had formed. The liquid was then siphoned off into casks and made to ferment slowly by periodically racking the juice off into another cask, leaving yeast deposits and other impurities behind. The result was a clear, slightly sweet drink with a high alcohol content.

At the end of the 18th century, traditional cider-making began a long period of decline. The Industrial Revolution took workers from farm to factory, and as cities burgeoned, beer production and consumption increased – promoted, in part, by government propaganda advertising beer as a healthy alternative to gin; but also by the food shortages of the Napoleonic wars which had caused farmers to replace orchards with valuable grain crops and cattle feed; then, finally, in 1887, the Truck Act prohibited the payment of wages in cider.

A THRIVING INDUSTRY

However, although farm cider declined, the new cities provided a ready market for commercially made cider, and these urban concentrations were readily accessible by rail and canal to the traditional cider-making areas of the Southwest and Herefordshire. Many cider-making firms, including familiar names like Bulmer (now the world's largest cider-maker), Taunton, Gaymer and Whiteways date from this era.

Today commercial cider-making is a thriving industry, but it has not abandoned its traditional origins. The apples themselves – mostly modern bittersweets, reflecting changing tastes – still rejoice in robust names like Brown Snout, Yarlington Mill and Chisel Jersey, and they are still knocked down from the trees – but by mechanical shakers. Pomace continues to be recycled as animal feed – though the pectin is often extracted and sold to jam manufacturers. Some firms still build up the pulp into cheeses – with synthetic not horsehair cloths – and use oak vats for fermenting the juice. In the final stages, however, commercial cider is blended – to make a consistent product – and has some water added. Factory ciders vary from a safe three or four per cent alcohol to some old-style varieties at eight or nine per cent – quite as potent as Scudamore's best. Even stronger are cider royal and cider brandy: two traditional drinks forgotten for almost 300 years but now being revived.

Alongside the commercial industry, there are still some 300 farm-based producers making cider on a small scale – for their own use, for local pubs and for gate sales – and the equipment and methods employed by these remain substantially the same as those of their forefathers.

BULMER'S CIDER

HEREFORDSHIRE CIDER
CHERRY PEARMAIN
H. P. BULMER & Cº
HEREFORD

MADE ONLY BY H. P. BULMER & Cº HEREFORD.

Coopering

Coopering – barrel making – is a craft once practised in every village and city, and the millions of sturdy casks produced were the standard containers for everyday goods.

Sawn in half and bright with geraniums, yesterday's coopers' casks are today's garden memorials of a craft that once rolled out an Empire's produce. In the photographs of 1920s street life, casks are everywhere. They were stacked on quaysides, lined up before shop fronts or piled in horse-drawn carts. They crowded the decks of cargo boats, the yards of factories and the storage sheds of farms. For centuries, wooden barrels made by coopers were the standard storage containers for almost everything from wine to crockery.

Egyptian wall-paintings of around 2700 BC show barrel-like slatted wooden pails bound with wooden hoops. But it was in northern countries, with their abundance of timber, that the craft of coopering thrived. The Romans may have introduced it to Britain: the word coop comes from the Latin *cupa*, a cask. It is also possible that northern boat-building skills led to the independent development of the cask's special characteristics: tapering ends and watertight seams.

Without casks it is doubtful whether Britain could have been such a successful empire builder.

Casks carried imports and exports safely and unspoiled over thousands of miles of ocean, through all the extremes of heat, cold, damp and storm. Casks of water, salted meat, and vegetables enabled the Royal Navy to stay at sea long enough to achieve the ascendancy it enjoyed throughout centuries of sail-power. The British fishing fleets could never have won herring harvests from the North Sea without casks in which to salt down and store the catch.

ROLL OUT THE BARREL

The secret of the cask's enduring strength and resilience derives from the stressed curve of its hoop-bound staves – the shaped wooden strips from which it is constructed. Held together by dynamic tension rather than fastenings and joints, the cask will long outlive ordinary packing cases. The shape of the cask enables it to be man-handled even though full of liquid, and weighing several times more than a man could lift. It can be rolled and steered with ease, manoeuvred with the help of ropes up and down ramps, on and off carts and boats, in and out of cellars. It can be rocked upright, trundled

MATURED IN THE WOOD
Although many liquids are now stored or transported in metal or plastic kegs, 'wet' coopered oak casks (left) are still vital for the maturation of many spirits, including whisky, brandy and sherry. Scotch whisky is matured in casks varying in size from 33 to 145 gallon capacities. Traditionally casks came in a range of sizes. Smallest was the pin holding 4½ gallons; then came the firkin at 9 gallons; followed by the kilderkin of 18 gallons; the barrel holding 36 gallons; the hogshead of 54 gallons; and the butt of 108 gallons, which weighed in at half-a-ton when full.

HERRING CUTTERS AT WORK. 954. G.W.W.

UNIVERSAL CONTAINERS
For centuries barrel-shaped casks of varying sizes were the standard containers for packing and transporting both dry and wet goods. Dry coopering, the making of casks for dry goods including salted herrings (left), was the least specialized form of coopering. For this purpose barrels did not need to be absolutely water-tight, and as the goods they held were not under great pressure, they did not need to be made with such precision, and machine production replaced hand production quite early. Such 'slack' casks were less tapered than 'tight' casks and their staves were bound with wooden rather than iron hoops. If the contents were a particularly fine powder, like flour or gunpowder, the staves might be tongued-and-grooved for a closer fit.

along on one end on its point of balance. And it can be stowed securely and lashed in groups in a number of tiers.

Playing a vital role in British economic life, the cooper became a man of some status. Coopers' companies, dating from the thirteenth century, insisted on a seven-year apprenticeship before entry into the Cooper's Guild was permitted. In practice a six-year apprenticeship with a seventh year called an 'improver' was usually served. For his initiation a cooper had to build a hogshead (a 54-gallon cask). He was then placed in it and showered with soot, flour, beer, water and wood shavings before being rolled around the workshop floor. At the end of his apprenticeship the cooper received his indentures, and was formally declared a freeman.

Yet, although he was a freeman, he could not work in city or town without the support and approval of the Guild. The Guild ensured that the secrets of the craft were protected, and operated an efficient closed-shop policy, which kept prices up. Any cooper crossing the Guild would be debarred from work and would have to leave town. His only way of carrying on his

TOOLS OF THE TRADE
Coopers' tools and methods of working have changed very little over the years. Just as his modern counterpart would, a Tudor Master Cooper (right) prepares staves before raising and firing them. Other members of the cooperage make then hammer on the willow hoops to hold the barrel staves in place. The long jointer plane and the wood block, probably a converted tree-stump, are permanent tools belonging to the cooperage. All the other cutting and hammering tools, including the large dividers in the foreground (for measuring the capacity of the barrels), belonged to individual coopers.

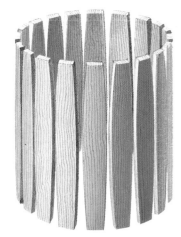

DRESSED STAVES

ASH-WOOD TRUSS

TRUSSING THE BARREL

MAKING A BARREL
(above) The staves are prepared, then raised. Temporary ash-wood trusses hold them together while the barrel is fired into shape. The head (A) is fitted last, after the permanent hoops – (B) chime, (C) quarter and (D) booge – have been hammered into place. The fattest part of the barrel is the pitch (E).

trade would be to gain acceptance elsewhere, set up as a village cooper outside the Guild's jurisdiction, or else join a merchant ship's company. Though working outside the Guild, many village coopers were highly skilled men, turning out a variety of crafted containers from large storage barrels to small tubs for cheese. Some village coopers specialized in 'white coopering' – the making of containers or utensils for dairy and household use.

Another branch of coopering, 'dry coopering', produced casks that did not need to be absolutely waterproof, and which were often used for non-liquid goods. These 'slack' casks were made from a variety of woods including Douglas fir, spruce, poplar, beech and elm. The hoops were usually of twisted willow or hazel, and the tapering of the cask not pronounced. Contents of such casks included herrings, shellfish, crockery, flour, sugar, tobacco, nails, seeds, fruit and vegetables.

But it was 'wet coopering' that really tested the cooper's skill, as this involved the making of casks tough enough to withstand the pressure of liquids such as beer and wine that would continue to ferment 'in the wood'. They were nearly always made of tightly-fitting oak staves and bound with iron hoops.

Oak, preferably Russian memel oak, was used for wet coopering (British oak was too knotty). It bent easily, cracked rarely and was easy to work using sharp tools. Memel oak was very expensive, and became more so as furniture-makers, appreciative of its finely figured grain, started to compete for supplies. Eventually, American oak, which is hard and fibrous, became the most commonly used oak for coopering.

PREPARING THE STAVES

The process begins with the felling of a tree – ideally a two-hundred year old oak, which would be cut up into logs just over a stave's length. These were then halved, quartered and split further by means of driven wedges. In the cross-section of the tree trunk, impermeable ridges radiate out from the centre wood, through the grain to the bark. The planks to be made into staves were split out in such a way that each contained an unbroken ray across its width. This ensured that the wood remained naturally water-tight. After trimming into flat lengths, the

BRINGING OUT THE BARREL
(below) The secret of the success of the barrel was its strength and resilience as well as its design, which enabled it to be pushed, rolled or sometimes carried around relatively easily.

staves were bundled and left to season for up to five years.

At this stage the cooper would select the best wood available for his purpose. Then working with a skilled eye and using a number of tools he would shape the staves according to the size of the cask being made. For casks over nine gallons, the plank was clamped by means of a metal block hook to the working block – usually a hefty section of tree trunk. The first shaping was done with a short-handled broad axe. The sides of a stave were smoothed with a two-handed 'draw knife'. The inside surface of the stave was hollowed with a convex-bladed 'hollowing knife', and the back rounded with a slightly concave 'backing knife'. After the staves were shaped they were finished off on a large inverted box plane or 'jointer'.

RAISING THE STAVES

The finished staves were placed vertically inside a metal 'raising hoop'. An 'over-runner', a thick ash-wood truss hoop, was then pushed about half-way down the staves to hold them in place temporarily. Once raised up, the staves were persuaded into the typical barrel shape by steaming or moistening the wood. When pliable, the wood was bent by the pressure of smaller and smaller truss hoops hammered over the staves. Then the cask was fired over a small brazier of burning shavings. Gradually the splayed bottom ends of the cask were forced closer and the final temporary hoop, the 'dingee' was hammered on flush with the top of the cask. The cask was left over the fire for a final drying out. By this time the staves were so set that they would retain their curved shape even if there were no hoops to hold them together.

After this firing two of the permanent hoops, chimes, made of rivetted iron, were fitted at the top and bottom of the barrel. To make room

TOWN COOPERAGE
Cooperages in the towns (above) were often independently run. They may have produced barrels for breweries but more often than not the breweries employed their own highly skilled wet coopers to produce the large casks and smaller barrels used for the fermentation, storage and transportation of the beer.

for them, the dingee and the raising hoops were knocked off and the cooper then bevelled the inside rims of the cask with a short handled adze and squared off the stave-ends with a 'topping plane'. Then he prepared the ends of the barrel to receive the circular cask heads. At this stage he checked the cask's capacity with a huge pair of dividers, called 'diagonals'.

The trussing hoops were then removed and the cooper smoothed down the outside and inside of the barrel. If the barrel was destined for storage of maturing wines, spirits or certain beers, the inside would be left rough.

The heads were made by dowelling short planks together into panels and cutting out circles from them. These were then bevelled on either side of the edge with a 'heading knife'. To fit the head the chime hoop at one end of the barrel would be removed and the head tapped into place and the chime replaced. The other head was dealt with by screwing a handle or knocking a spike into it so that it could be manoeuvred into its groove.

Finally, the remaining iron hoops were fitted. The cooper drove them into place with a groove-edged 'drift' or 'driver', struck with a three-pound hammer. Last of all a bung-hole was

THE COOPER'S WORKSHOP
Today there are only a few coopers still carrying on this skilled and ancient craft. They work in specialist museums, at whisky and brandy distilleries, and at the more traditional breweries and cider mills. Although there is no longer such a demand for their wares they still work in the same meticulous way to prepare the staves (top right) and finally to hammer on the hoops (right).

bored midway between the bulge hoops with an auger, then burned smooth.

As recently as the mid 19th century, there were over a thousand coopers at work in just three of the London boroughs, with 150 cooperages in London's East End alone. But a basic dependance on expensive imported oak precipitated the decline of this ancient craft. Also contributory was the popularity of imported wines which arrived in well-made reusable casks. Demand for the cooper's wares was further diminished as American bourbon casks, which under US law are usable only once or twice, were imported by Scottish distillers. Coopering's final demise came in the 1950s when difficulties obtaining import licenses for timber, coincided with the development of glass fibre tanks for wine and plastic-lined metal kegs for beer.

Today the craft of cask making is carried on by only a handful of coopers who work in craft museums, distilleries, cider mills and breweries. But while the casks that were once so omnipresent play no part in the modern container industry, the 36-gallon barrel lives on, in name at least, as the unit of measurement of oil – which today is the key to the fortunes of the world's economies.

REAL ALE
With the advent in the mid 20th century of the metal keg (below) as a vessel for storage, the fate of the wooden barrel (above) was sealed. However, a recent revival in interest in real ale has brought with it a new demand for the traditional flavour.

Dry-stone Walling

Centuries old, the craft of dry-stone walling – the construction of unmortared walls of local stone – is alive and well in Britain's upland areas, where new walls are still being built and age-old ones repaired.

If you stand on a hillside in the Lake District, in Derbyshire or Yorkshire – indeed, on most upland hillsides – you can see grey stone walls, rather than hedges, meandering for miles, threading their way around the contours of the land marking fields and boundaries. One careless push, seemingly, would start a domino run that would unstitch the valley like a snagged sweater. Dry-stone walling ('drystane dyking', as such walling is known in Scotland) – the unmortared stacking of gathered rocks, held together by gravity and friction – is the oldest known form of masonry work. Yet, like most apparently simple crafts, centuries of experience lie behind the technique.

Dry-stone walls are usually found in upland areas as high ground is often unsuitable for the bushes and trees required for hedging. Here, too, usable stone is most likely to be found as outcroppings, or as rock strata close enough to the surface to make quarrying easy.

A well made dry-stone wall can last indefinitely – properly maintained it will outlive its original builder and patron many times over. A mortared wall, on the other hand, gradually loses its strength as rain, damp, frost and wind break down the mortar bond. The dry-stone wall's only requirement is that those who look after it understand the way it was originally constructed. Nothing shows up more clearly than an inexpert patching-up job of an old, well-built wall.

ANCIENT WALLS

The earliest examples of British dry-walling techniques are up to 4000 years old, and can be seen in the ancient chambered burial mounds known as long barrows. The hilltop site at Belas Knap, at Charlton Abbas in the Cotswolds, is a dramatic example. Full dry-walling has been excavated at village sites from this period in Orkney, at Skara Brae and Rinyon, and at Jorishof in Shetland.

Some of the finest early dry-walled structures are Scottish 'brochs'. These massive round, open-topped towers built between about AD 100 and 400, rose up to 40 feet in height,

sometimes with an inner wall, and enclosed a yard some 40 feet across. The brochs were built as fortified shelters against the depredations of sea-borne raiders and pirates.

FIELD WALLS

The earliest field walls probably started off as marker stones and cairns placed at intervals to mark off territorial boundaries. Later the spaces between the markers were filled up to stop livestock straying. Some walls may have arisen more from a need to clear potentially arable land of surface boulders than from a desire to demarcate property limits. The first small enclosures were homestead structures for holding animals overnight, and maybe also for the protection of domestic grain or flax crops.

Over the centuries the techniques of walling improved as demand for them grew. Most of the walls visible in Britain today are no earlier than the 15th century, with the majority having been built much later. The walls of the Lake District are among the oldest, and a consider-

STONE WALLING
In the high, bare sheep country of Lakeland (below and left), Scotland, Yorkshire and Derbyshire, the upland landscape is criss-crossed by dry-stone walls. These walls are life-savers to lambing ewes, and to the flocks when the snow is driven on the wind and shelter is at a premium. Men, too, are glad of their strength and protection.

able mileage is over four hundred years old. The Enclosure Acts of Elizabeth I had more effect in the north than the south of the country, and much of Northumberland and Wales was walled by the end of the 1580s as local landowners established their holdings. Further south, the main period of enclosure occurred half-way through the 18th century. The modern dry-stone wall, with its regular construction and straight lines stems from this later era.

Most of the walls built during the main enclosure period, from 1760 to 1840, were built with gang labour. The period coincided with a long recession in the Lancashire and Yorkshire mining industry, and many walling gangs consisted of miners who worked on the walls in spring and summer, returning to mining in the worst of the winter weather. Many of the Pennine walls visible today were built by these miners, working long hours for little pay and often sleeping rough at the work-site. One man's work for one day was considered to be a 'rood' of six or seven feet of finished wall,

ENDURING CRAFT
(above) Deceptively simple to the eye, a dry-stone wall is, in fact, a complicated structure – the result of centuries of skill and experience. Dry-stone wallers are still in demand, building new walls and repairing old ones. Unlike a brick and mortar wall, a dry-stone wall can be renewed indefinitely, using nothing but its own substance.

according to the type of stone being used.

The dry-stone wall is generally between four and six feet in height, though much higher walls can be made – such as the 'march' or boundary walls between great estates. There is no standard wall for the whole country, but in the most common design there is a shallow foundation supporting two outside walls or 'facings' built with a 'batter' or taper from bottom to top. The space between the two facings is filled with a 'hearting' of smaller stones. 'Through-stones', also known as 'through-bands', 'throughs', and 'tie-bands', are laid right through the double wall's thickness at intervals to help hold the structure together. The wall top is finished with a 'cover band' linking both sides, which is stopped off in turn with a 'coping' of large regular stones.

The waller uses few tools beyond a spade to dig the 'footings', and, in some parts, a walling

CORNISH VARIATION
Many distinct regional styles of dry-stone walls exist including the Cornish herring-bone pattern (above).

A GAP IN THE WALL
The tapered gap in this overgrown Cornish wall (top right) once allowed the carriage of coffins across the fields.

ROCKING STONES
To deter over-ambitious sheep scrambling over walls, the top courses of a stone are sometimes left deliberately gappy, often with a layer of loose, rocking stones on top.

hammer with a boat-shaped head, weighing between one and four pounds. The first job of the waller is to mark out the trench for the foundation with pegs and string. This is slightly wider than the base of the wall. The 'batter' or sloping pitch of the 'double' – the section of double construction – brings the wall to a top width of about 14 inches from a base width of about 26 inches. Some wallers worked by eye alone, but many, including highly skilled professionals, used, and still use, a 'batter frame'. This is a template made of four slats of wood with a cross-brace, nailed together to give the correct profile or cross-section for the wall under construction.

BUILDING A WALL

Having marked out the foundation stretch the waller cuts out the turf with his spade, levelling the footings down to firm subsoil or rockbed. Six inches is usually a sufficient depth, though it is sometimes made deeper in softer, lowland soils. Foundation material varies. Some specifications called for the trench to be carefully packed with small flat stones, others for very large footing stones. Once the foundation is laid, the double, or facing, is built on top of it. If a pair of batter frames is used, strings are fastened between them, and the stones of the double are placed with their faces touching the string, and their length projecting inwards into the wall. Laying long stones laterally along the wall's length is a weak technique that results in sagging and cracking. The two facings of the double are raised up simultaneously and evenly, and the hearting is carefully packed between them as they rise. The hearting is of good quality stone carefully placed. Where possible, the facing stones are laid so that they slope slightly from the centre towards the outside, aiding the run-off of rain water.

At specified heights and spacings the through-stones, are fitted into the wall. There are between one and three levels of through-stones, depending on the height and style of the wall. Where they are fitted on more than one level they are staggered. They are usually about a yard apart, and often long enough to project slightly on either side of the wall. When the wall

is built up to its designated height, flat, even, cover-bands are positioned to seal off the top, and also act as a base for the coping. The coping is a crest of large, evenly shaped stones set close together on edge.

Where a public footpath crosses the line of a wall, the waller may build in extra-long through-stones, slightly staggered, to form a crossing stair. Other variations may include a 'squeeze gap' – a V-shaped gap which allows people through but defeats sheep and cattle, or a separate wooden ladder-stile that completely straddles the wall.

Often a gap is built into the foot of a wall, beneath a strong stone lintel. These gaps have a variety of names, including smoot, creep-hole, hogg-hole and lunkie. Their main purpose is to allow storm water to pass through, or to provide a passage-way for animals.

A 'gatehead-cheek' or 'wallhead' is constructed where a dry-stone wall comes to an end, or joins another at a land boundary. A solid, self-supporting end is made by building alternating layers of through-stones and long

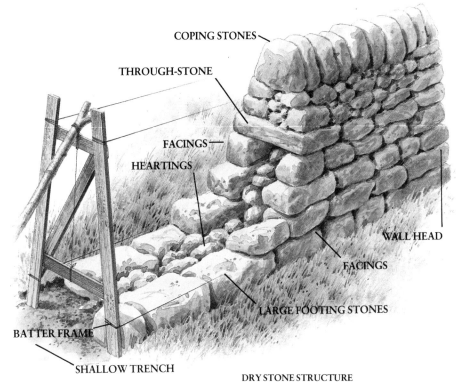

DRY STONE STRUCTURE

stones set across the facings.

A number of different wall designs can be found throughout Britain varying according to local stone and traditions. In parts of Scotland and Ireland single-dyking consists of single-stacked layers of large stones in place of the twin-facings found elsewhere. These are especially difficult to build well, but are good enclosures for more agile sheep breeds, such as the Black-face. Some walls found in Devon and Cornwall, are topped with a planted hedge – called a 'Galloway hedge'. These are made by using a

mix of small stones and earth for the hearting, and planting the hedge along the crown. Sometimes planting is done behind the wall, and the hedge trained through both sides, to rise above it. In this case the coping is retained.

Another Cornish variation uses thinly split Cornish stone in a distinct herring-bone pattern, topped with a tightly packed vertical coping like a row of thin books. More frequently, the herring-bone pattern is built into conventional walls as a decorative course. Often the patterned walls are used as retaining walls for banks.

Cotswold limestone is an ideal walling material, splitting with great regularity and predictability, and allowing an exactness of style not possible with the harder and bulkier fragments and boulders of granite country. Some Devon walls include quite massive granite boulders lifted into position by means of a thick four-foot board, counter weights and a central

DRY-STONE PROFILE
(above) In construction or repair two tapering facing walls, filled with hearting stones are laid. Large through-stones hold the wall together and heavy coping stones cap the wall.

ORKNEY WALLING
(right) Local stone is tightly packed in a slanting pattern.

EARLY DRY-STONE
(left and below) The Broch of Mousa, built between AD 100 and 400, was a fortified shelter. The outer wall, twenty feet thick at the base, was built on an inward sloping batter for about 25 feet of its 43 feet. Entry for villagers and their animals was through a low tunnel that could be blocked off with boulders. It is estimated that 10,000 tons of stone were used to build the broch.

pivoting stone.

Northumberland limestone can be cut and split into very precise blocks to produce a tight-seamed and regular wall. The effect is heightened by the regular overlapping of stones in adjacent courses, in the manner of brick-laying. This is essential in a stone wall, as vertical spaces in the heavy facing soon lead to slips and collapses.

Pennine walls are made to very strict Enclosure specifications, and are beautiful structures. Taller than most walls – at six feet – they have three rows of staggered through-stones. Frequently built on steep terrain, their coping stones lean slightly uphill, as if avoiding a 'knock on' effect should one be dislodged.

COMPETITION WALLING
(below left) Enthusiasm for an ancient skilled craft is tempting increasingly more people into dry-stone walling competitions. These are regularly held in many areas where these walls are found.

FLAGSTONE WALL
A regional variation taken to an idiosyncratic extreme, the drystone wall in Caithness (below); is made from overlapping flagstones.

Much dry-stone walling has been allowed to collapse, but many hundreds of miles still exist, and are still carefully serviced by countrymen. The trade, which still has a training period of at least two years, has not died out, and a skilled waller can earn good money on landscaping work as well as wall maintenance. One factor in the craft's survival has been the enthusiasm of organizations such as the Dry Stone Walling Association, formed in 1968 by the Stewartry Drystane Dyking Committee. Walling competitions are held at a growing number of agricultural shows, and a new generation of young wallers is being trained under a number of voluntary schemes.

The Hedge-layer's Art

Hedgerows have long played a special part in rural life. Their construction and maintenance provided valuable winter employment for farm workers, while the rich harvest of fruits and herbs was a vital source of free foods and medicines the whole year round.

Hedgerows form such a typical part of the British countryside that it is easy to forget that they are not natural, but artificial barriers planted for a specific purpose – to act as a windbreak for crops, to prevent sheep or cattle straying, and to provide shelter for the animals from sun and storm.

In the past, all hedgerows were regularly maintained, for left to itself a hedge will shoot ever upwards and outwards, straggling at the top and becoming thin and gappy at the bottom. To grow thick, strong and stockproof the hedge must be carefully pruned or 'laid' by a skilled hedger every 20 or 30 years depending on local soil and climatic conditions. The art of hedge laying, known since Roman times, is a dwindling craft, as most hedges are now roughly trimmed by chainsaws and mechanical cutters – a process which is more economical in time and labour. But formerly, when the autumn leaves had fallen and most other work on the farm had ceased, it was a common sight to see hedgers at work in the countryside.

THE HEDGER'S TASK

Hedge laying is a slow and laborious business and one or two large fields could keep the hedger busy throughout a whole winter. The task involves a considerable number and variety of skills – traditionally these were passed on from father to son as were so many rural crafts. The hedger must have an expert knowledge of hedgerow trees and shrubs, plus a fine eye to judge which are the best stems to lay, which are the best timbers to use for staking and how to make the willow or hazel 'ethers', used to bind the hedge. He must also be able to handle his tools expertly; their efficiency lies as much in the way they are wielded as in the way they are wrought. The hedger also needs protective clothing, for hedging can be a painfully prickly business – thick leather mittens to protect his hands from thorns and spikes, and sometimes leather trousers too.

A skilled hedger can lay up to 30 yards of hedge in a day. First he removes dead leaves and the undergrowth of bramble, briar and elder from the base of the hedge. Then he will select out of the hedge long hazel, willow or wych elm stems and trim the side growth off them, putting them aside to use later as binders or ethers. Likewise he will cut and trim stronger stems of hazel, ash or elm to use as stakes. As he continues cutting out the wood, the skill is to decide which of the old stems to leave. It is surprising how much of the wood he does remove – virtually nothing is left of the original hedge. Then he trims the sides of the remaining bushes, using his billhook with upward strokes to avoid tearing and splintering the wood.

The actual laying can now begin. Usually he works from left to right, although if the hedge is on a slope the stems are laid running uphill. With a downward stroke of the billhook he cuts the first of the main stems (the pleachers) as close to the ground as possible, cutting through just enough to bend it – but sufficient bark must be left intact so that the sap can travel upwards and keep the stem alive. He then bends the cut stem over at an angle of 60 degrees or more and repeats this process along

THE HEDGE LAYER
(above) Using his billhook and wearing stout leather mittens, the hedger binds the top of a hedge with 'ethers' – flexible stems of hazel or willow.

A LAID HEDGE
(left) Newly pruned and layered, this hedge will grow strong and stockproof. Mature trees provide shelter for cattle.

the length of the hedge so that all the main stems slope to the left at the same angle. If possible the stems are laid towards the sunlight in order to give them the best chance of regrowth.

To keep the stems in place he drives in vertical stakes every two feet or so. These must be driven in hard and deep to prevent cattle knocking them out. If there are living saplings in the hedge he may use these as stakes and lop them off to the finished height. The stems of bushes are then woven in and out of the stakes, the brush being laid so that it faces the field side of the hedge, and the stakes trimmed to the final height. Finally, the hedger

binds the hedge: long rods of willow, hazel or wych elm are twined in and out between the stakes, making a continuous strip of basketry along the crown of the hedge. He finishes the job by trimming the brush side of the hedge, burning the unwanted growth cut out of it and clearing the ditch, if there is one.

There are many regional styles of hedge laying and these depend in part on whether the hedge is designed to enclose cattle or sheep. The typical Midlands technique, known as 'bullock fencing', is intended to contain cattle and must be strong enough to withstand their heavy leaning and

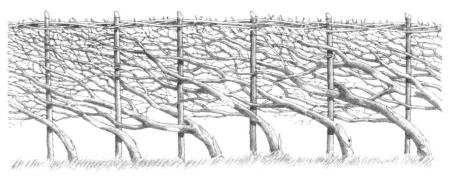

MIDLANDS HEDGE
(above) To contain cattle, this style of hedge is taller than other types and has vertical stakes.

WELSH HEDGE
(below) The base of this hedge is packed with dead wood to fill the gaps and make it sheep-proof.

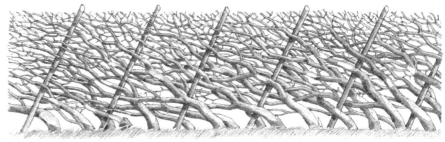

SETTING THE STAKES
(above) The hedge stems are bent and layered, then held firmly in place with strong stakes.

HEDGING TOOLS

SINGLE-EDGED BILLHOOK

DOUBLE-EDGED BILLHOOK

AXE

LEATHER MITTENS

SLASHER

shoving. A Welsh hedge, on the other hand, is designed to be sheep-proof: it will have its pleachers laid in from both sides of the hedge and the base will be packed with dead wood to stop sheep squeezing through, since they can scramble through quite tiny gaps – it is a common saying among farmers that 'what sheep can see through they'll go through'. In gale-swept Pembrokeshire, hedges are made strong and squat on top of earth banks. They are often wider than they are tall and are angled towards the prevailing wind. Another style, the 'arable,' consists of laying branches directly over cut 'stools' (where the stems have been cut right down to the base) so that the new growth comes up through the old.

The painstaking – and backbreaking – labour involved in hedge laying is made easier by certain specialized tools, once forged by the village blacksmith but nowadays the preserve of the local ironmonger. A large axe is needed for the heavy work of cutting back large stems or saplings, while a slasher, or long-handled knife, is required for trimming the bushy undergrowth. But the most important hedging tool is the billhook, a heavy chopper with a curved end. This ancient tool was originally related to the battle axe or halberd, and has been modified into a short-handled single- or double-edged tool used to cut all but the very thickest branches. Billhooks vary in design from county to county. Welsh sheep hedges, for example, are usually cut with a single-edged billhook, while the Midlands bullock hedges are cut with a double-edged blade.

The time and labour required for traditional hedge laying are the main factors which have led to its decline in the age of mechanized farming. But the craft is nurtured by competitions in some parts of the country. Hedgers from all over Britain are attracted to the national competition, which is held in a different place each year on the last weekend in October. This is a fascinating event, for the speed and skill with which these craftsmen work is wonderful to watch.

THE HEDGEROW HARVEST

When the hedge-layer has finished his work, the once-glorious profusion of the overgrown hedge will have disappeared into a huge pile of discarded cuttings. But despite the apparent butchery, the hedgerow shrubs and climbers – the blackthorn, hawthorn and elder, the tenacious bramble and the

Elderberries

Crab apples

Sloes

Rosehips

Blackberries

wild rose – soon grow back, more compactly now, but as fruitful as ever. In a very short time it will be not only a dense green barrier, but a valuable economic resource. Indeed, for country folk the hedgerow was once both a wild larder and a medicine chest. Country women knew their hedge plants very thoroughly – which ones were good to eat, which ones were poisonous, and which provided useful remedies.

The hedgerow harvest continued throughout the growing year. From early spring, when the first green shoots appeared, succulent young leaves were used to supplement the tedious winter fare. Tender shoots of nettle were made into soups, chickweed was eaten like cress in salads, garlic mustard was used to flavour sauces, and the first hawthorn leaves, chewed raw, were called 'bread and cheese'.

As the year progressed towards high summer wild herbs appeared in the hedgebanks – thyme, borage, fennel, chives and marjoram. Garlic and mint grew in shady places by the ditches. Dandelion was used in salads, elderflowers for making cordials and puddings, hops and plantain cooked like spinach and mallow chopped into soups. Sharp sorrel made a good sauce for meat or fish and the pretty yellow-flowered tansy spiced up cakes with its strong, characteristic flavour.

As the days grew shorter and autumn chills brought mists to the fields, the country housewife would be out with her basket, mushrooming and collecting berries. The elderberry, a highly nutritious fruit, found its way into pies and ketchups, the blackberry into the puddings and jams so loved by her children, crab apples into jellies and rosehips into syrup. The harvest of cob nuts was eagerly gathered in competition with squirrels and

PICKING BLACKBERRIES
A watercolour by Miles Birket Foster (1825-99) shows a typical autumn scene in the countryside. Village children pick blackberries in the bountiful hedgerow – once an invaluable source of food.

other rodents, and sloes and bullaces (a type of wild plum) were picked for wines and preserves.

Throughout the year the hedgerow harvest supplied country folk with nutrients they would otherwise have lacked, for many of these foods are rich in vitamins, iron and other minerals. Many of them could also be preserved to last through the long winter months; in a community which relied more on barter than money, this source of food was a necessity rather than a luxury.

COUNTRY CURES

The medicinal value of the hedgerow plants was vitally important to village communities where every woman had to be both doctor and nurse to her own family and relied on her inherited knowledge of folk remedies for any minor – and sometimes major – ailments. Many a bruise or broken bone would be healed with a poultice of comfrey. To cure a headache or bring down a fever an infusion of willow leaves – which contain aspirin – would be taken, while foxglove tea was considered a cure for dropsy. Through the trial and error of ages these plants and many others had proved their worth, and most 'old wives' knew of at least one plant remedy for almost any complaint. And their faith in this traditional lore is being vindicated today as modern research into plant drugs leads steadily to the conclusion that many of these country cures were no mere placebos, but were indeed effective medicines.

Men of the Forest

Although modern power tools make his work simpler and quicker, today's forester works in harmony with the forest just as his predecessors did many centuries ago.

Like many others whose life and work is bound up with the countryside, the forester is intimate with the environment in which he works. At certain seasons he teams up with other workers in the forest to perform some of the tasks of forest management, but often he spends days on end alone among the trees. Tree felling – associated most in the public imagination with the forester – is but a small part of his life in the forest. It is in fact the end of a long cycle that may stretch back decades, through the working lives of successive generations of foresters who tend, nurture and then harvest the forest.

Neolithic immigrants who came to Britain from the European mainland from about 300 BC onwards first began to work the massive primeval forests which had formed in the wake of the last Ice Age some 5000 years previously.

By the time of the Roman invasion much of the old primeval forest had been cleared to make way for wheatlands. But the Romans, too, felled many trees in creating great 1000 acre agricultural estates. When they left Britain,

around the mid 5th century, the forests may have regenerated slightly as regular systematic forest management declined during the early Dark Ages.

By the 7th century the regenerated forest was once more being worked, this time by the Saxons who introduced professional foresters called 'woodwards'. They organized and supervized timber-felling, undergrowth cutting and animal grazing in the forest. From this time on forests became commercial concerns. Forest dwellers paid for the rights they enjoyed, from firewood collection to pig grazing. These forest lease-holders were usually the people who carried out the maintenance which today is the work of the modern forester.

Coppicing, carried out scientifically from before the Norman invasion in the 11th century AD, provided poles and branches for fencing, hurdles, and walls. The 'underwood' used in coppicing provided income for landowners and eventually, in the 15th and 16th centuries, acts were passed to protect recently cut areas with fences, giving the trees time to restore them-

POWER FELLING
(left) With the advantage of power tools, like the chain saw, today's forester working alone can fell a huge tree in a matter of minutes. However, even with the benefits of modern technology, forestry work still demands the age-old knowledge of trees and timber management, as well as the skills of fit, strong men.

AXED
(above) Until the mid 20th century, the traditional tool of the forester, the felling axe, was in everyday use in many parts of the country. It was either used on its own to fell a tree, or in conjunction with a cross-cut saw, operated by two men, after the initial axe cuts had been made. Axe and cross-cut saw were superseded by mechanical chain saws and then by tree harvesters – huge machines which can fell, debranch and cut up big trees in seconds.

selves. Areas which were hunted were also left to renew themselves.

As the protection of forests for hunting gave way to tree-based industries, the basic forestry work of clearing, planting, thinning, and felling, became more important than the policing of the forest for poachers.

Some of the first tree nurseries were the result of the horticultural experiments carried out in the monasteries throughout the Middle Ages and later. It became the forester's job to plant and tend especially raised young trees, and far sighted landowers began to import useful species to supplement the native stock. Beech, Norway spruce, and European larch were all planted on Scottish estates from the 18th century onwards, and cultivated in addition to the traditional

species of English oak and Scots pine.

The first recorded plantation (1580) in England was a 13-acre site in Windsor Park, planted with acorns and fenced to protect it from deer. By 1625 it had become a flourishing oak wood. The growing enthusiasm for timber management received an added boost from the enclosures, which resulted in the fencing in of six million acres between 1702 and 1844. Wealthy landowners designed their own landscapes, introduced new trees, and contributed to the spread of conifers. The Scots pine reintroduced into England by the diarist John Evelyn, was used as a nurse tree. Fast growing and thick domed, it conveniently sheltered the oaks and beeches among which the pine was interplanted.

Modern foresters still use existing mixed

woodland as an early protection for strip-planted seedlings. Only a narrow row is cleared for planting the seedlings. The protective undergrowth and existing trees can then be gradually thinned out as the seedlings grow.

Planting is usually carried out in the spring, though only after careful preparation. Access roads and 'rides' have to be dug, laid, or bulldozed in advance, so that eventually, in decades to come, the timber harvest can be extracted without having to damage mature crops. One man can plant up to 2000 trees in a day, working on foot, with traditional tools such as a spade and mattock. Apart from weeding in early years, and the occasional clearing of invading climbers, such as honeysuckle and ivy, the trees are left to themselves until the first major thinning after twenty years or so. Whole rows are removed in early thinnings,

FUTURE FOREST
(below) In good planting conditions a forest worker can plant up to 2000 seedlings per day. The Sitka spruce being planted here will take from 60 to 80 years to mature.

and, at later stages, the best trees are left, while others are transplanted to give them growing space. The thinnings are not a loss, as at this age they provide usable wood for stakes and fence posts. At between 50 and 60 years a conifer is at its optimum commercial size. Deciduous trees need from 80 to 150 years to reach equivalent economic maturity. After felling and clearing,

FELLING A TREE
(below) Using axes, two foresters prepare the face – and felling-cuts. A third forester cuts away bark from a branch to send to local tanneries.

the cycle is begun again with planting.

The most basic of the forester's jobs is tree felling. For centuries the felling axe was his primary tool. The introduction of the cross-cut saw, a long-bladed double-handled saw wielded by two men, greatly speeded up the process. The modern power saw enables one man to do the work in a fraction of the time, bringing down and trimming off a mature tree in a matter of minutes. However, over the ages, the cutting sequence has remained exactly the same.

Firstly, the forester looks at the lie of the land, deciding on the direction he wants the tree to fall. Factors in his mental equation include land-slope, the shape, size and lean of the tree, the distribution of its branches and general weight, the disposition of other trees – which might be damaged by a falling tree – and wind direction. The tree should fall, ideally, into a relatively clear channel in the undergrowth, and

CROSS-CUT SAW
(left) The steel cross-cut saw is between four and six feet long, with large teeth set at an angle to each other along a convex cutting edge.

HORSE POWER
(left) Before the advent of mechanical equipment, wood was dragged to a loading point by horses and then loaded on to horse-drawn waggons to be transported out of the forest. Forest dwellers or the family of the forester himself took part in the associated task of stacking the bark to season it, before chipping it into small pieces and bagging it up.

TRAVELLING SAW MILL
(below) Most large forest estates had permanent saw mills to suit the needs of the landowner and his tenants, but the forester was not required to operate them on a large scale. If a major timber sale was agreed, the wood merchant concerned would erect portable sawing machinery near the woods.

in making the first cut, the forester has to decide whether it will be a clear fall, or whether it will be necessary to nudge the tree in the right direction by means of extra wedges, supplementary cuts, or by the use of ropes and chains.

The first cut is a V-shaped notch on the side of the tree facing the direction in which it is to fall. This is known as the face-, sink-, or under-cut. A horizontal cut is then made into the tree, for maybe a quarter of its diameter, and a sloping cut brought down on to it to form a wedge-shaped notch. This can be done with a chain or cross-cut saw. With an axe it takes longer, and will not be quite so neat, but the effect is the same. The felling-cut, or back-cut which will fell the tree, is made on the side of the trunk opposite to the face-cut.

The felling-cut is made horizontally, at a point a little higher than the bottom surface of the face-cut. As the blade bites into the trunk, a point is reached when the tree 'sits' back on the saw-blade immobilizing it. Wedges are then driven by sledgehammer into the cut behind the saw, freeing it to continue the back-cut. Care must be taken to prevent 'pulling', which, after

EXTRACTING TIMBER
(right) Tough machinery is needed to cope with the rough ground within the forest. Purpose-built vehicles, forwarders, take the felled timber from the forest to the roadside for loading on to huge transport lorries.

WINCHED AWAY
(below) Although parts of the hillside are left bleak and bare, most foresters have a felling plan, designed to suit the landscape. Where the terrain is too steep for vehicles, an overhead cable winch is used to drag logs to more accessible collection points. Connected to a specially modified tractor, the winch is operated by two men, who communicate by radio. One, the chokerman, attaches the logs to the haul line and the other, the winchman, offloads them at a stacking point.

the tree has been felled, leaves a long spike of ragged tree-core standing from the stump. Pulling can distort the densest and most valuable part of the trunk.

Inferior wood, or wood grown specifically to a narrow dimension over a short period as a quick harvest, may eventually be made into pulp. The forester cuts pulpwood into four-foot lengths between four and eight inches in diameter, stacking it in standard piles, called

cords. Whether cutting trees for timber or pulp, the forester clears up as he goes, burning waste branches and foliage on bonfires that are sometimes kept alight for many days.

The timber is then cut and tagged with the cutter's personal number and taken out of the forest. Traditionally, timber was dragged by horses into clearings and rides and then transported by wagon. Nowadays, specially designed tractor-trailers, fitted with mechanical grabs, or cable-winches are generally used. Even so, there may be occasions when the old methods have to be called on.

THE FORESTER TODAY

The modern forester, has the benefit of modern equipment, yet the overall character of his job, and the life he leads, have changed surprisingly little. Wood production, coupled with an intimate relationship with the flora and fauna around him, still links the forester of today to his predecessors. In the felling season, in summer and autumn, he rises with the sun, to get well into the work before heat and insects make the woods a sweaty torment, sometimes working a day that begins at 4.30 or 5 a.m. He must still protect his nurseries and saplings from the depredations of deer, squirrels and rabbits. He must still be skilful with the ancient hand-tools of his trade, hand-axe, billhook, wedges and maul. Most important of all, he must have the quiet, patient temperament that has always marked the true forester, who can lovingly plant a seed and nurture a sapling to grow into a tree that he will never see mature.

Coppice Craft

In an age when almost every craft depended on wood, the management or coppicing of woodland was a prized skill. Coppicing ensured a reliable supply of all types of timber from ash hop poles to oak pit props.

When a broadleafed tree is felled it does not usually die but undergoes a remarkable regeneration. Bereft of its branching boughs, the massive root system channels all of its energy into regrowth. New shoots quickly sprout and, nourished by the deep roots, grow straight and true towards the sunlight. This type of growth results in a crop of many useful poles from a single stump. Coppicing is the way in which this natural process is harnessed to produce a regular supply of certain types of timber in particular forms. In Britain the trees that coppice readily include oak, ash, sycamore, lime, alder, hazel, birch, willow and sweet chestnut. With the exception of the American Redwood, conifers cannot be coppiced because when cut to a stump their shallow root system dies.

The earliest evidence indicates that alder trees may have been coppiced in Britain as early as 3174 BC, to provide the straight poles for the 'corduroy' roads laid across the peat bogs of the Somerset Levels. Much later, the Romans in Britain probably practised deliberate coppicing to provide wood for burning to make charcoal. The Saxons after them, with their traditions of wooden house building, developed the technique to produce an even greater range of timber, leaving only the sturdier house frame beams to be cut from uncoppiced forest land.

In the Middle Ages the science of coppicing became still more sophisticated, and the practice of interspersing coppice trees with 'standards' was established. Standards such as oak or elm were allowed to mature alongside the coppiced wood to provide the timbers for larger structures, such as bridges, ships and houses. A greater number of species was also encouraged

WATTLE HURDLES
(left) Many craftsmen work in the coppice itself, amid their source of supply. This hurdle maker is splitting the uprights and fitting them into a split log, or mould, which will hold the framework steady while he weaves into it the riven hazel strips.

BASKETS AND BESOMS
Coppiced timber provided materials for hundreds of objects in everyday use in the countryside, including these spale baskets woven from oak laths, and sweeping besoms – bound bunches of birch twigs with ash handles.

at this time to meet the huge demand for wood and in one Suffolk wood with a long unbroken record of use for coppicing with standards, over 40 different species can be found.

MANAGING COPPICES

A properly coppiced wood is self-replenishing and while the first coppices almost certainly occurred naturally (from the stumps of trees felled in the course of land clearance) once the technique became established the need to institute some sort of rotation based on the time taken for a particular type of tree to reach the required size was recognized. Areas were planted out or layered to create patches where all the stumps or 'stools' were of the same species. The rotation times varied from as little as three years for slim willow rods, to as much as 24 years for the stout oak poles used for propping the shafts in coal pits. Charcoal (the residue of

partly burnt wood) used for smelting iron was made from coppiced wood up to 21 years old. Ash being grown for long hop poles was cut every 15 years. Hazel might be cut every 9 to 12 years if it was to be used for hurdles.

In order to maintain continuity of production, the forester would aim to have as many plots of a particular tree as it took years for the wood to reach the required dimensions. In this way a dozen hazel plots, for example, would provide a hurdle maker with a never-ending supply of materials as one plot was cut per year.

Other rotations might be five years for walking sticks with natural crooks, though only two years' growth was needed if the handle was to be steam curved. The commonest walking stick woods were ash and sweet chestnut.

Each year the woodsman would cut the plots in his charge in strict sequence. It would take a week to cut an acre of hazel coppice and could take another six weeks to cut, sort and bundle the rods from the acre into crate rods, pea sticks, and bean rods. The cutting season ran from autumn to spring or early summer – when there was the least sap in the wood. The summer would be used to make up the final product.

Often the men who harvested the coppices also made the finished article. Living locally to the woods, they would buy the product of the mature coppice plots, cutting all harvestable wood, selecting what they themselves needed for the year, and selling off any surplus.

A MULTITUDE OF USES

Not all of a crop would be used for the same purpose. An acre of hazel coppice, for example, harvested after 10 years' growth, could provide 3500 hedge stakes, 188 bundles of pea sticks, 127 bundles of bean rods, 148 barbed-wire stakes, 70 faggots for burning, 27 clothes-line props and a ton of kindling.

Fast-growing hazel sprouts fibrous rods that can be easily split, and are flexible enough to be twisted, bent over, and even tied into knots,

HARVESTING COPPICE-WOOD (left) The trees are cropped in rotation depending on the uses of the timber. The stems are cut close to the stump, on a slant to deflect rainwater, sorted according to size, then transported by wagon (above) to the craftsman's workshop or to a nearby village.

without breaking across the grain. The torsional strength of hazel makes it ideal for use in binding and weaving and apart from the straight support and firewood uses, hazel is also used for thatching spars, besom binders, barrel hoops, fodder cribs, wattle hurdles and crates.

The wattle hurdle is a portable fence panel used to enclose sheep. Made from woven hazel, it is about six feet long by three feet high. The wattle maker secures the ten uprights or 'sails' in holes based in a split log, called a mould. The first six inches of weaving is done with whole hazel, while most of the horizontally woven strips are of 'riven' or split hazel. The wattle

maker's only tool is a billhook, which is used to rive the rods and sharpen the bottom ends of the sails. The hurdle is finished off at the top with another course of unriven hazel, and a hole is left near the centre to allow the shepherd to thread several hurdles on to a pole and carry them off on his shoulder.

Straight-grained ash is the most versatile of the coppice woods, valued for its strength and natural springiness. It is easily split along the grain, and can be easily bent by steaming. Uses include many sorts of tool handle, including hay rakes, curved scythe sneads, and axe handles. Its length and strength made it ideal for ladders, and cart shafts. It is also favoured for gate hurdles, thatcher's bows, 'lazy back' shovels, tent pegs and besom sticks.

The traditional hay rake, with all its local variants, could be made entirely of ash, though some makers preferred to use elm or sycamore for the head – the cross-piece into which the tines were fitted. The tines and shaft were always of ash. The tines would be riven from an ash pole of six inches diameter, using a mallet and metal wedge called a froe. The pole was split, first one way, and then the other at 90 degrees. This produced a bunch of square sectioned tines which could then be straightened and rounded off by hammering them through a sharp-edged metal pipe set in a bench. Some shafts were fastened to the head directly, and braced with a semicircular hoop of hazel. Others were first split a little way along their length, and the two halves separated, and fitted into holes drilled in the head. If necessary the haft would be straightened by first steaming it and then pulling it through the rake maker's brake, a massive frame of timber with a weighted and pivoted beam used to grip the wood being worked. The brake was also used to hold the head while it was shaped and drilled for the tines. The tines would be wetted before being hammered into place. A sort of giant homemade pencil sharpener called a stail engine was used to smooth down the haft after straightening.

The most prized of all British woods, oak is valued for its hardness, great strength, and resistance to the elements. It was originally cultivated particularly for ship and house building, but it became the major raw material for

the charcoal industry until it was ousted by coke and coal. Oak bark was also stripped from sapling poles for use in the leather tanning industry. The bark was stripped in the spring, while the sap was rising, and the saplings themselves were not harvested until later in the year. Heart of oak was used for wheel spokes and ladder rungs and coppice poles were used in the making of oak spale baskets.

SPALE BASKETS

The spale or spelk basket was made from interwoven laths of oak, had a diameter of up to three feet and was bowl-shaped. The rim or 'bool' was of hazel, boiled to make it pliable. Six-inch diameter oak poles between twenty-five and thirty years old were selected for spale making. The poles were cut into five-foot lengths after seasoning, and then boiled for a number of hours, before being riven into quarters with a heavy mallet, called a beetle, and the wedge was usually a froe. A smaller wedge or a billhook was then used to split the quarters into strips a sixteenth of an inch thick. In either case the strips were properly riven – with the blade edge being carefully inserted into the end grain, and the tool then being worked and rocked along the length of the wood. A spokeshave was then used to smooth the 'spelks' which after soaking in water were woven and fastened to the frame. Spale basket making was considered so skilled as to require a seven-year apprenticeship.

Waterproof alder was used for clog soles and milking pails, after an ancient history which had seen it used for the piles of lake villages. Chestnut was used for palings (fencing stakes), trug (a type of basket) frames, handles and some gate hurdles, as well as hop poles. Sycamore was the carvers' and turners' wood, ideal for making bowls, butter moulds, and loving spoons. Elm, which will neither splinter nor split, was sawn into boards for weather-boarding

THE BROOM SQUIRE *(below left) The besom maker sits astride a broom horse and using a strong clamp with a circular mouth – known as a besom-grip – he binds birch twigs into a tight round bundle, securing it with hazel wands or willow rods or, nowadays, soft galvanized wire.*

COPPICING WITH STANDARDS *(below) Sometimes coppice woods were scattered with other trees which were allowed to mature fully. Oak was the favourite tree for this treatment, the timber being used, among other things, to build the British fleet of earlier centuries.*

weight back against the grip of the clamp to pull the binding tight. The broom handles of ash, lime or hazel were sharpened with a hand axe at one end which was driven into the wired end of the head and tapped home. A skilled worker could complete a besom head every ninety seconds.

After a long and steady decline, coppicing is currently enjoying a revival. With timber becoming an increasingly valuable resource the managing of deciduous woodland has, once again, become profitable. A growing number of farmers and landowners have discovered that money can be made by thinning out previously neglected and unproductive woods and supplying the wood pulp and fire-log trades. Encouraged by organizations such as the Woodland Trust, the ancient coppicing skills, using traditional tools and methods are being practised once more. The benefits are not purely economic, however. Coppicing can also improve the quality of the woods themselves. Thinning out old or diseased trees creates light and space for the healthy trees to flourish in. Furthermore, by offering a potentially viable means of management, coppicing may save acres of deciduous woodland from destruction or replacement by stands of dull, uniform conifers.

PICKS AND SHOVELS
The handles of innumerable tools were made from coppiced ash. The handles of spades and picks (left) would be cut from straight saplings, but scythe sneads (below) had to be bent and steamed into the correct shape.

and partitioning. Chair seats, table tops, floor boards, wagon wheel hubs, chocks and wedges, were all made from elm.

The craft of the 'broom squire', the besom (or witches' broom) maker largely depended (and still does) on the birch tree. Cuttings from the crowns of seven-year-old birch trees were stacked in bundles in autumn, to weather and season over winter under a ridged roof, also of birch. In spring the bundles were sold to the besom maker, who opened the bundles, trimmed them with a billhook, and sorted the twigs, cutting away brittle material with a stripping billhook. The long, rough twigs were separated out for the core of the besom, while the shorter, smoother twigs would be reserved for the outside layer. Sitting astride a broom horse, with a foot-operated clamp, and a coil of wire, the broom squire formed the head and secured it with two wire loops, leaning his

Basketry

As recently as a century ago, over 200 different types of basket were being made in Britain by craftsmen practising skills which have survived largely unaltered for over nine thousand years.

The interlacing of twigs and grasses to make baskets is one of the very oldest of crafts – predating even weaving and pottery. Yet while most traditional crafts have either been mechanized or have died out, basketry has remained a true handicraft and continues to thrive – the willow baskets produced today in the West Country providing a living link with those craftsmen who cut and wove the willow many millenia ago.

The value of basketry to early man is not easily exaggerated. Basketry is a relatively easily acquired skill, requires virtually no tools and uses materials which, quite literally, grow on trees. Yet wicker baskets offer a combination of strength and lightness rarely surpassed even today. And so baskets were developed for every purpose from carrying logs and peat, to transporting poultry and eggs.

Basketwork was also commonly used for making furniture, and hurdles for fencing in livestock have been made of basketwork for at least 3000 years. Neolithic panels have recently been found at Walton Heath on the Somerset Levels, laid down flat to make a track across the marshy ground.

In County Antrim, in Northern Ireland, archaeologists have also very recently discovered the remains of thirty houses dating from 650-1100 AD built entirely of basketwork. It has been estimated that each building contains around five miles of intricately woven hazel branches, arranged as two five-feet high concentric walls with a one-foot space between them insulated with chopped straw. The two walls were tightly woven in opposite directions to provide a draught-proof structure, and all the sharp ends were pushed into the cavity so that both outer and inner walls are neat and smooth. On top of the outer wall stood a 10-feet tall conical basketwork roof. Other evidence found on the site shows that these were the homes of wealthy people, but in later centuries basketwork as a building material was more often associated with poor people who could not afford timber or the tools to work it with. Apart from the supporting posts, they built their houses of willow-work and clay, mixed with goat's hair or straw-wattle and daub.

THE WICKER SEX
(below) Baskets on the head did not always bear loads. Fashionable 15th-century women wore tall basketwork hats covered in linen.

Basketry even found its way into fashion. In the fifteenth century, women wore 'steeple' hats made of light basketwork covered with linen. Later, when elaborate and heavy wigs became fashionable, they were often supported by a basketwork structure.

In Britain there is also a long tradition of making small basketwork coracles. A few can still be seen today on the west coast of Ireland, in Wales, and on the river Severn. *The Universal Magazine* of 1757 describes fishermen rowing such boats with one hand, leaving the other hand free to manage the net.

TRADITIONAL WICKERWORK

But despite the wide application of wickerwork, baskets have always been the chief product of the basketmaker. Basketry can be carried on with almost any material that has the rigidity to be self-supporting and the flexibility to be woven. But in Britain, basketry has traditionally used the willow to produce willow- or wicker-work.

Over the centuries, baskets have been made for every purpose imaginable, and even at the turn of the century it was estimated that over 200 different designs were in production throughout the country.

As with other traditional crafts, most wickerwork was originally produced locally to meet local needs – hop baskets for Kent, potato baskets for Lincolnshire, cheesebaskets in Leicestershire. For while wickerwork did not suffer the transportational difficulties of heavy

BIRTH OF A BASKET
(left) To accommodate the long spokes of a large emergent basket, David Drew, a modern-day basketmaker, works outdoors using traditional tools and techniques.

CONTAINER TRANSPORT
(below) Until modern packing materials took over, baskets in all shapes and sizes were used for packing and transporting goods.

WOVEN HOUSES
(left) Excavations at Glanarm in Co. Antrim have revealed a settlement of 30 houses 'woven' between the seventh and twelfth centuries. The round houses had double walls, one foot (30 cm) apart, of hazelwood branches intertwined in a unique pattern which gave the wattling a spiralling effect; the space in between the walls was filled with straw for insulation, while the outer wall supported a conical basketwork roof.

and fragile wares such as pottery, it was bulky, but more importantly, its raw materials were widely distributed and so baskets could be made almost anywhere.

In the days before cardboard and plastic, almost everything from hats to carboys was packaged in baskets. An idea of the once commonplace nature of basketry can be gained from the small baskets in which bakers' yeast was supplied from breweries. A skilled basket-weaver could knock out around 40 of these baskets a day – each of which would make but one trip to the bakery and end up in the bakehouse fire.

Today the price of labour and materials have, with a few exceptions, made such basketry uneconomic. But the craft itself thrives, and although the range of baskets made today has diminished, those baskets which are still made continue to justify their existence by doing the job they are designed to do, better than any alternative. Even more remarkably, many modern basketmakers still follow a production cycle unchanged for centuries.

WILLOW HUSBANDRY

In common with most rural craftsmen, the traditional basketmaker needs few tools and his raw material – willow – is grown and husbanded with care. In the days when willow was also an important building material, there were osier beds all over the country, wherever there was even a small patch of marshy land. The monks at Westminster grew osiers on the site of what is now Westminster Hall, alongside the river

'THE WICKER GODDESS'
Caesar reported the Druids to have sacrificed humans in large wicker images set on fire, as this much later and historically inaccurate engraving depicts (right).

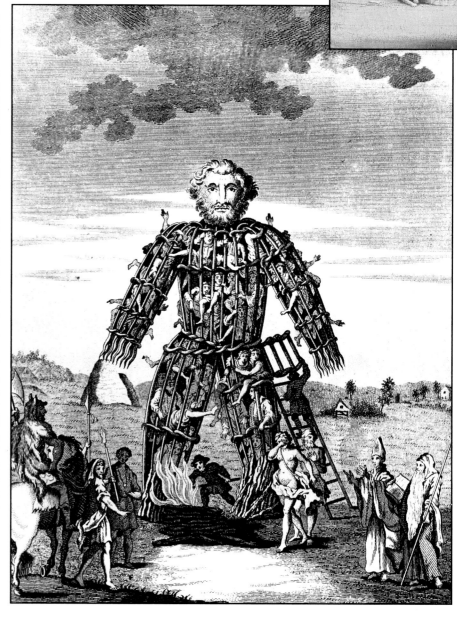

COTTAGE INDUSTRY
(above) Readily available in
different shapes and sizes,
basketware provided light
and durable containers – from
bird cages to sewing baskets.

BACKBREAKING WORK
Formerly, large bands of
seasonal workers were
employed to cut willow –
however, today, basket
makers, such as David Drew,
who grow their own crop,
may undertake the work
themselves (above right).
This can prove backbreaking
work, as the withies are cut
close to the ground.

SIMPLE TOOLS
(right) The tools used for
basketry have hardly
changed. The beating iron
presses down the woven
work; the commander
straightens bent withies.

BASKETRY ART
(far right) Adapting the
traditional technique, Lois
Walpole creates original
designs using dyed natural
cane and painted strips of
cardboard and recycled
synthetic packaging.

Thames. Willow is fast growing and an easy
crop to manage, needing little tending apart
from the annual cutting. A writer in 1607 was
so pleased with his decision to plant an osier
bed that he was led to exclaim: 'I think it yeldeth
me now greater benefit yearly acre for acre than
the best wheat.'

Today, willow-growing is confined mainly to
the Somerset Levels: low-lying ground inter-
sected by drains, or 'rhines'. Commercial willow
growers prefer to concentrate on one good, all-
purpose variety, called Black Maul, although
there are specialists who grow as many as 20
old and new strains of willow; each with specific
qualities suited to different baskets.

The willow-growing cycle begins in early
spring. Cuttings of green willow, known as
'drawn withies', about nine inches long, are
planted in rows about two feet apart. An acre
of good land can thus contain around 15,000
withies. These self-set so easily that it does not

even matter which way up they are planted.
During the best summer days the canes may
grow an inch a day, and by September they have
grown to about six feet. Between the end of
November and spring, when the sap rises, the
shoots, or withies are cut close to the ground
with a sharp knife. Today the withies are usually
transported by tractor but on the flooded parts
of the Somerset Levels, the bundles, or 'bolts'
of withies were traditionally collected in
shallow, double-ended boats which are prop-
elled along the narrow rhines with poles, like
punts. The stumps of the willows – or stools
are left behind in the ground, ready to shoot
again in the spring for the next year's harvest.
Willow beds will produce an annual crop for
up to fifty years.

The withies are then carefully sorted into
groups. If the bark is to be left on ('browns'),
the willow simply needs to be dried and stored.
To produce 'whites' (stripped willow), the green
withies are stood in a pit of shallow water, about
eight inches deep, until late May. This keeps the
willow alive, and when the sap rises and the
bark no longer clings to the wood, it can be
peeled off. Another colour variation, called

BEATING IRONS

COMMANDER

'buffs', are withies that have been boiled for several days until they are thoroughly cooked and have changed colour. This technique was developed in Nottinghamshire in the nineteenth century and not only produces an attractive colour – particularly from osiers grown on heavy clay soils – but also meant stripping, and hence the whole cycle of production, could be extended through the year.

Stripping the whites, was once a seasonal job, like harvesting, with everyone involved taking part. Each rod was pulled through a two-pronged post like a giant clothes peg, called a 'brake'. More recently, a stripping machine has been developed which has a rotating drum on which are mounted banks of small brakes. After stripping, the willow is left to dry in the wind and sun, then bundled according to size.

BASIC TOOLS

Before the basketmaker can use the willow, it first needs to be soaked. Stripped willow only needs an hour or so in water and a few hours under damp sacking; 'browns' need several days in water to make them pliable enough to work with. The withies are then sorted or 'cut over', which involves trimming them to the size required with a 'shop knife'. Other tools used by the basketmaker include a basic awl or bodkin, a 'pick knife' for trimming long ends when the basket is finished, a 'beating iron' for closing up the weave as he works, shears for cutting thick sticks.

Basketmakers still use a 'grease-horn', a hollow cow's horn filled with tallow for greasing the bodkin. Another tool is a special axe, flat on one side and designed to be used with the right hand: baskets are traditionally always made moving upwards to the right. The basket-maker works sitting on a slightly raised wooden platform with the basket standing in front of him on a lapboard.

Baskets are usually begun at the bottom, with the base. For a round or oval basket, a cross made up of two handfuls of withies are placed flat and then opened out like the spokes of a wheel into a circle or oval. Other withies are then woven over and under them until the base is filled in. Next, uprights, or stakes, are added and the sides of the basket are then woven until the top is reached. Various decorative plaiting and twisting techniques are used for 'bordering off', and for handles. Square baskets are often made in a simple screw-block, which acts like a vice to hold the withies in position.

Watching a basketmaker at work is deceptive; it all looks very quick and easy, as he twists and weaves a chaotic collection of sticks neatly and surely into place. Yet, even when prepared and soaked, basket materials are intractable and it takes quite a lot of physical strength as well as skill. Worked by skilful hands, the rods kink and flatten and are beaten tight to build strength and uniformity. The whole process is punctuated by purposeful sleights of hand and illuminated by clean knife cuts which leave flashes of white.

In recent years the supply and demand for wicker-work has stabilized, and despite the impact of cheap foreign imports a thriving wicker industry still exists. With support from the Ministry of Agriculture, increasing acreages are being planted with willows and research is continuing into hybrid 'super willows' with even faster rates of growth. And with the demand still high for baskets for logs, cats and dogs, laundry, letters and parcels, fruit and vegetables, as well as hampers for crockery, food and wine, the tradition of basketry is proving as durable as the baskets themselves.

STRIPPING THE WILLOW
(above left) For white wicker work, the withies are soaked in water for a few months. With the sap rising under the bark, they can be easily stripped either by a traditional hand brake, as shown here, or on a machine with a rotating drum mounted with small brakes.

THE END IN SIGHT
(above right) A nearly finished basket is bordered off. There are many ways of finishing – either by tucking in the uprights or by attaching different thicknesses of plaiting that lock in the top of the basket.

The Walking Stick Maker

Staffs, sticks and canes have given support to countless travellers through the centuries, and while some were simply rough sticks, taken from the hedge, others were skilfully made by rural craftsmen.

From the very earliest days, travellers journeying on foot through wild and inhospitable terrain would have used sticks picked up from wayside hedges to support and protect themselves. In places where wild animals and bandits roamed, a stout stick provided a useful weapon, while on uneven terrain it could provide a strong support. Such a stick did not need to be elaborate, a stout, straightish branch pulled from a tree, or found on the ground often sufficed, but for the traveller it was indispensable.

So valuable was the staff that it soon acquired religious as well as practical significance. In Greek and Roman society the staff became a badge of office, while in the Bible, Christ is often compared to a staff and at one point in St Mark's Gospel, travellers are commanded that 'they take nothing for their journey, save a staff only'.

Staffs used as symbols of authority were often elaborately crafted, and made of anything but wood, but right up until the late Middle Ages the traveller's staff continued to be a simple, rough stick found by the wayside. Only from about the 14th century on did professionally-made sticks, carefully shaped and finished, begin to appear.

Early traveller's sticks were long stout staffs, unlike the short walking sticks common today. Only such a stick could provide adequate protection against assailants along the road. The short stick was only adopted when road travel became relatively safe. Indeed, it is quite likely that the short stick made its first appearances within the confines of the royal court, and was used largely for display rather than protection.

These early court sticks, which probably arrived at the English court from France in about 1500, were elaborately-made hardwood sticks, richly decorated with jewels. Henry VIII,

who had a large collection of over 40 sticks, did much to make them fashionable. Soon, anyone who had the money acquired such sticks, or 'canes', as they were then called. Interestingly, Henry had a number of what are now known as gadget sticks – sticks which have a double purpose. One of his had built in to it a penknife, nail file, tweezers and a bottle of perfume. Later in the 16th century, captains of sailing galleys concealed bottles of perfume in their canes, to quell the foul smells that frequently wafted up from below decks.

SYMBOL OF AUTHORITY
(right) The staff, often elaborately carved and adorned, was, for the Medieval Church, the ultimate symbol of Christ's authority. For pilgrims and travellers, the stick, usually a roadside find, provided support and protection.

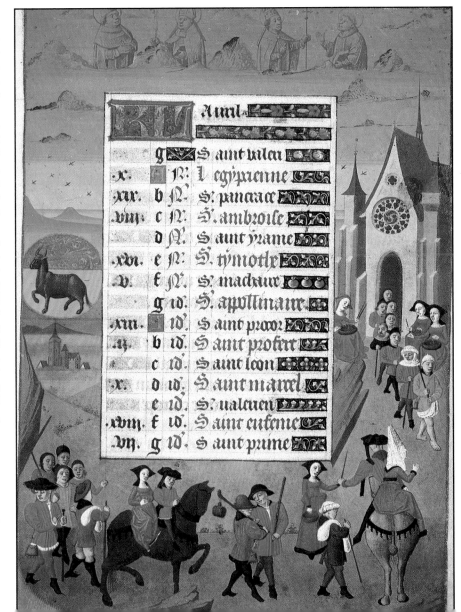

Genuine travellers and country people continued to use rough staffs. But throughout the 17th and 18th centuries, the use of canes began to spread out from the towns and down the social scale. Country people adopted them not for protection but as aids when walking. The canes they used, much simpler and stouter than the court canes, were not made from exotic materials like ebony, but from the native wood – ash, willow, beech, applewood, cherry and blackthorn – found growing freely around in the hedgerows. Many country folk made their own sticks from suitable branches or saplings, but a few were made by craftsmen who began to develop a tradition of fine walking-stick making.

FASHION ACCESSORIES

In the courts and towns, meanwhile, sticks became more and more popular. The 18th century saw the stick in its heyday, and by the end of the century, no lady or gentleman with pretensions to fashionability would walk out without a stick. Although the incredibly fancy sashes and cords which had adorned sticks in the 17th century were now abandoned, the well-to-do demanded increasingly well-crafted sticks, often decorated with extraordinary skill and ingenuity in gold and silver, china, marble and all kinds of exotic materials. Fashionable people vied with each other to commission the most beautifully-made and unusual stick, promoting the simple stick into the category of fashion accessory rather than a practical tool.

Throughout the Victorian era, perhaps inspired by the poet William Wordsworth and his walking tours, more and more townspeople began to venture into the country for long, energetic walks, with, as often as not, a walking stick. It was not that the roads and tracks were so bad that they needed any support, nor did they need much protection from wolves and bears, but a stick could inject a little

HANDLES
Stick handles can be made in a variety of ways. The smoothly curved handles (right) are made by steam-bending the sticks in a bed of damp sand, heated from below. This makes the stick head flexible enough to be bent into shape in a bending jig. It is then tied into place and left to set before being finished, sealed and polished. (below) Some handles are fashioned from the trunk section of the tree, to which the stick shaft-wood is attached. (below right) Non-wooden handles made from horn, were often fitted to wooden shafts. Highly-prized sticks were often dressed to resemble grouse in the heather.

spring into their stride, and help brush the brambles aside.

The range of materials that have been used to make walking sticks, is enormous. There have been glass sticks, whalebone sticks, ivory sticks, and sticks made of almost every conceivable wood. Some of the woods are tropical, such as ebony and malacca and rattan palm; many are homegrown – apple, pear, cherry, oak, cedar, willow, beech, maple, broom. Walking sticks are even made from the giant stalks of 'Jersey cabbage'. But of all the native woods, the most popular are the hedgerow trees: hazel, ash, holly and blackthorn.

CHOOSING THE WOOD

For the individual country stick maker, finding a suitable stick is often the most challenging part of the process. Even in the last century, when hedgerows were abundant, it was far from easy to locate a perfect stick. The stick maker would usually look for a neglected hand-laid hedge where the branches grew upright in tall straight shoots from an almost horizontal main stem. Cutting off a short section of the stem along with a suitable branch made a stick with a good natural handle. Cutting a good straight hazel stem with a part of the root might give an equally good, if knobby, handle to the stick.

Connoisseurs of walking sticks, though, demanded far more than a straight stick and a good natural handle. Sticks were valued for weight, balance, how they tapered towards the tip and the shapeliness of the tip. A good stick must be knot-free, or have knots arranged attractively. With thorn sticks, the spacing of the thorns was considered crucial.

WALKING STICKS *(clockwise) Sticks of all shapes and materials have been popular choices for working sticks and as fashion accessories. Horn handles, often exquisitely carved were sometimes fitted to plain walking sticks. Thumbsticks, usually longer than most sticks, are still popular in the countryside. The V-shaped handle is formed by the fork of two branches. The* knobstick, *about three feet long, has a shaft of rough bark. The bark is removed from the knob, which is polished and varnished. The head of the shepherd's* crook *is carved from a solid block of wood. The* curved head *of an ordinary walking stick is formed by bending the end after steaming it in a bed of hot, damp sand. Canes, once popular and fashionable at court and in society were finished with jewel-encrusted or carved knobs.*

SHEPHERD'S CROOKS *(right) A modern stick maker puts the final touches to a crook head, which he has drilled, carved, and filed from a single block of wood – metal heads (below) were cheaper.*

Stick makers making sticks on a commercial scale could not always afford the time to find sticks in the wild, and many grew their own saplings especially. Chestnut sticks were generally coppiced and cut after two or three years when stems had grown straight and knot-free. Ash sticks, too, might be grown in this way, and in a plantation, young saplings could be trained to grow to give a good natural handle.

STICK PLANTATIONS

In walking stick plantations, ash seedlings were allowed to grow straight up for a year or two and then uprooted. The main stem would then be cut off just above a side bud and the sapling laid down in a trench and buried so that just the side bud appeared above the ground. After the side bud had grown upright for three or four years to good walking stick length, the sapling would be uprooted again – the buried

STICK MEN

The unmistakably sprightly air of the old country gentleman as he leans on his trusty, roughcut walking stick (above) is strikingly similar to the jaunty pose of the 18th century man of fashion with his elegant cane (right) – yet the two are separated by more than a century, and a world of difference in wealth and social standing. The similarity underlines just how effectively walking sticks have transcended all the barriers to become treasured possessions of men from all walks of life.

main stem was now a perfect knobby handle.

All sticks, whether growing wild or on plantations, had to be cut at precisely the right time of year. If cut too early, the sap would still be up, and the stick would crack when drying out; if cut too late, the sapling would have started to grow again. The best time was usually during the last few days of December.

Once cut, the sticks had to be seasoned for one year, sometimes two, by hanging vertically in a dry room. Commercial stick makers had seasoning houses with specially-controlled moisture-free conditions. To ensure the stick did not warp, it would be tied firmly to a straight piece of wood. Some cracking of the handle was inevitable, so stick makers usually cut an over-large handle from which the cracked wood could be trimmed away.

EMBELLISHING THE IMPERFECTIONS

After the stick was seasoned, it would be taken down and fashioned into shape in a vice by sawing, rasping and filing – skilled stick makers would make the most of the wood's knots and natural imperfections. With Irish blackthorn sticks, the bark was left in place, but with most others the bark was removed, and the stick

rubbed down, polished and given up to six coats of varnish. It was finished off with a brass ferrule on the tip.

Besides the knobby natural handles, commercial stick makers could make smoothly-curving crook handles by steam-bending. The end of the stick was dipped in a bed of damp sand heated from underneath, which left the stick so pliable that it could be easily bent into shape in a bending jig.

The elaborate scrolls of shepherd's crooks, however, were not made by bending but by laboriously drilling, sawing and filing away a large block. This made such sticks so expensive that the handles of many crooks were cast from iron and attached to a straight shaft.

Non-wooden handles were often fitted to ordinary walking sticks as well. Ramshorn, bent in to shape after boiling for several hours and rubbed down with rasps, sandpaper and bone, was particularly common. In Scotland, antlers were, and still are, very popular handles.

No longer fashionable accoutrements, nor in so much demand as working sticks, walking sticks and the traditional craftsmen who made them have declined in importance in the 20th century. Nowadays, there are very few commercial walking stick makers making sticks in the traditional way, although factories churn out thousands of sticks a year. Nevertheless, there are still individual stick makers all over the country carrying on the old traditions, scouring the woods for sticks and using age-old skills to fashion them into shape. A few make their sticks to sell, but most make sticks for the sheer pleasure in their craft.

Chapeau de castor Habit de drap à un seul rang de boutons ourlés. Gilet de cassimir

The Poacher

Both a rogue and a romantic hero, the poacher was often seen by ordinary country folk as a resistance fighter against the intrusions of absentee landlords and remote authority.

For well over a hundred thousand years before man took up the plough, he subsisted solely by hunting and gathering, and the urge to hunt and wander freely through the countryside remains strong even today. But ever since man became settled, access to land has been restricted and the right to hunt over it at least partially controlled.

The first game reserves which excluded the common masses appeared in the 8th century, but it was the Norman Conquest, 300 years later, that drew the lines firmly between common and private hunting land, and from this time on the poacher became an established member of the peculiar English rural hierarchy along with the lord, the priest, the blacksmith and others. Men continued to hunt for the pot as they had done since the dawn of history but due to the intervention of greedy landlords, such men were considered poachers and outlaws.

The feudal notion that the king automatically owned all the land and all the creatures living in and on it was imposed by the Norman invaders upon a resentful and unwilling Anglo-Saxon population. All hunting rights were in future to be granted by the king, and were used mostly as a means of rewarding loyal followers and acquiescent local rulers. By the new forest laws, ancient forests were annexed, hunting rights doled out, parks enclosed, and types of game defined in terms of who was allowed to hunt them. Brutal penalties were imposed on those who broke the forest laws, which were fiercely resented by the established population of villagers, many of whom had been made poachers and law-breakers by the stroke of a pen.

HUNTERS AND HUNTED

The main quarry of the hunting nobles were red deer and wild boar. Lesser prizes of the chase included roe deer, hares, foxes and badgers. Lowest on the hunting scale were the creatures of the 'warren' – mainly rabbits. Hunting rights to all these animals were subject to the king's licence, and the peasant had to take what he could, surreptitiously. If the lord's bailiffs caught him, he was punished. The lines of battle between landowner and poacher were drawn, and have not changed since.

At first the poacher's tools were the snare, the net and the dog. The sling, too, was easily concealed and, armed with pebbles, was capable of great power and accuracy. Legal hunting became rigidly formalized in a ritual of expensive hounds and highly bred horses, a complex language of horn signals and great retinues of followers.

The 14th and 15th centuries saw the rise of the country squire, who hunted all forms of game, including birds such as pheasant, partridge, plover and woodcock. He also took water birds such as swans and geese, hawked with his falconers, fished on his private rivers and wielded considerable political power to protect his land rights.

Whereas the squire hunted with the crossbow, the poacher now hunted with the newly evolved longbow. He dressed in forest colours, camouflaged his skin and used specially trained hounds. Having fallen foul of the law, he often became an outlaw in the true sense, living rough in the forest, exercising formidable skills of woodcraft in order to survive, and taking the

FERRETING IT OUT
(left) A ferret fed into the entrance hole of a warren forces the inhabitants to flee, and become trapped in the purse nets set over the exits.

king's deer as and when he could.

On another level, 'cottage' poaching continued, with the taking of snared rabbits and trapped birds for food despite the game laws, which became ever more specific in their provisions. New laws instituted by the gentry in their role as Justices of the Peace forbade those earning below a certain amount even to own hunting dogs, ferrets, nets, snares or other trapping equipment. The use of the sporting crossbow was likewise limited to men of property.

As time went on, increasing restrictions and new game laws combined with large-scale social changes to force the ordinary country dweller more and more to resort to poaching in order to feed his family. Lands were enclosed to facilitate more intensive sheep farming, creating vast numbers of landless labourers without the means to grow their own food. Later still, the fall in corn prices at the end of the Napoleonic wars caused widespread agricultural depression. Landowners were keener than ever to extract the maximum profit from their lands. The hunt became increasingly organized along business

A DAY'S BAG
(above) At one time a much greater variety of wild game was eaten, so the poacher's targets would include birds like the heron as well as mallards, partridges, plovers, pheasants and woodcock.

133

THE KEEPER'S REVENGE
*The war between keepers
and poachers was at its most
violent in the early 19th
century when many brutal
excesses took place on both
sides. Poachers would run
the gamut of man-traps and
trip wires attached to
blunderbusses, and there
would often be all-out
brawls between gangs of
poachers and equal numbers
of keepers and their helpers.
On such occasions, bloodshed
was the norm: men on both
sides would be crippled,
maimed and even killed. The
poacher had little to lose
in these confrontations: if
caught he was likely to be
transported for life to the
penal colonies in Australia.*

lines. Game birds began to be hand-reared and gamekeepers were employed on a large scale to protect the new investment. Game laws became harsher and punishments more severe.

SAVAGE PENALTIES

In medieval times, though some poachers went to the gallows for taking the royal deer, the forest laws became largely a means of raising revenue: the fines went to swell the king's coffers. In Tudor times, deer hunting 'without the License of the Owner' was punishable by three months in prison, and being bound over for seven years. By the late 18th and early 19th centuries, however, poachers were more likely to be 'fourteen years transported unto Van Diemen's land' as happened to the 'three daring poachers' of a contemporary popular song. Poaching counted as stealing, and in those days this could still be punished by hanging. Periods of six months or a year in prison were more common, but a year in an 18th-century jail could kill even the most robust countryman from any number of diseases and privations.

As well as the penalties exacted by the law if he was caught, the 19th-century poacher took other risks. He would have to avoid the perils of vicious man-traps with sprung and toothed jaws that could practically sever a foot, and trip-guns strategically placed around game woods that could kill the unwary with a blast of metal fragments from a blunderbuss barrel.

Eventually, such devices were made illegal, yet the law, and the local assizes in particular, usually favoured the landlord, who would often give his keepers licence to shoot to cripple, or to beat up poachers.

Then, as now, the enormous risks he ran served as much to spur the poacher to refine his skills as to deter him. Among the quarry most carefully guarded by the keeper, and most desired by the poacher were river trout and salmon. For these the poacher needed no equipment beyond a steady hand and an intimate knowledge of the nearest trout stream, for the

POACHED SALMON
*(below) Fresh wild salmon
has long been an expensive
delicacy and, inevitably,
an object of the poacher's
attentions. Here they are
being caught with a special
barbed fishing spear, known
as a 'gaff'. Most will have
found their way on to local
hotel menus by way of the
back door.*

'tickling' of trout must be one of the oldest hunting skills known to man. For all its cunning in avoiding the angler's barbed fly, the trout seems to fall into a trance if skilfully tickled.

TICKLING TROUT

Having found a trout lying in a hollow beneath a bankside overhang, the poacher would slowly slip a hand into the icy water and move it towards the trout from downstream of its hiding place. The tickling that ensued was really a very careful stroking motion with the fingers curled, so that the hand caressed the trout on three sides, working imperceptibly up from the tail towards the head. Suddenly, the poacher would seize the tranquilized trout around the gills, gripping, scooping out and grabbing with the other hand all in one sure movement to deposit the fish on the bank.

Having taken the trout, the poacher still had to get it home undetected. 'Poachers' pockets' were often specially sewn into jackets and could conceal an extraordinary amount of game, though a keeper's dog would soon sniff it out. Sometimes a poacher would hide his catch in a tree, or bush, or beneath a rock, though he risked losing it to wild animals before he could retrieve it. Many trout have travelled home inside the wellington boots of the poacher.

Modern trout farming has made poaching trout from streams a poor prospect, though on occasions greedy poachers have cleaned out streams by pouring in powdered lime, killing everything downstream for hundreds of yards. Many traditional poachers would scorn such methods, and the lack of feeling for the country and its inhabitants that they betray.

The salmon on its upstream runs is another favourite quarry of poacher and licensed fisherman alike. In the shallows below rapids and salmon 'leaps', the poacher can take it with a hooked gaff, or a multi-pronged spear, using a flashlight to pick out the fish's torpedo shape, for salmon poaching is a night-time occupation. On some Welsh rivers poachers use a coracle to lay a net across the salmon stream.

Until the onset of myxamatosis, the rabbit was the staple livelihood of the 20th-century poacher. Many methods were used to take it, including nets, snares, gin traps, guns, dogs and ferrets. Sometimes long nets were staked out across a field, with men and dogs driving their prey towards the net. Gate nets would be set where rabbits and hares were known to bolt beneath a gate. When the animal hit the net, it pulled down from the gate-top the upper edge of the net which was weighted with stones.

THE MOST INFAMOUS POACHERS OF ALL TIME *(right) Albert Ebenezer and Ebenezer Albert Fox, identical twin sons of a Baptist preacher, acquired between them 200 convictions for poaching, but their genial manner and beaming smiles made them favourites with magistrates, and they often got off free.*

One of the most popular methods of catching rabbits was ferreting. The ferret is a domesticated strain of polecat, probably introduced into Britain, by the Romans, who are known to have been keen ferreters. It was put, sometimes muzzled, down rabbit holes to drive the inhabitants out to waiting hunters equipped with nets, guns, or dogs. The main problem with ferrets was that if the poacher was disturbed he had to leave the ferret below ground while he hid. After the danger had passed he would return to the burrow and, if necessary, dig the animal out. This would happen if an unmuzzled ferret had killed and eaten a rabbit while underground. Having feasted it would curl up and sleep for a few hours.

The pheasant has long been a favourite with the poacher for the same reasons that it is with the legal gun: it is large, tasty, slow and stupid. It is most easily taken at night when it is roosting. Pheasants roost in families and their plump forms show up clearly against the sky making them easy prey for the poacher.

Strategies for taking pheasants without shooting them are legion. Poachers have ever been known to lay a bait of grain or dried fruit soaked in alcohol. The greedy birds soon become drunk and are easily caught by hand.

MAN'S BEST FRIEND

The poacher's main accomplice was his dog, the favourites being terriers and lurchers. The terrier was prized for its ability to follow quarry down holes, its courage, and its skill at working through dense undergrowth. The lurcher, which is a cross-bred greyhound, was especially swift – able to catch prey in full flight. Terriers and lurchers were sometimes used together, the terrier driving the prey into the open where the speedier dog could pounce on it or run it down.

The relationship between the keeper and the

TRAPS FOR MAN AND BEAST

SPRING GUN A poacher fouling the trip wires was peppered with shot.

GIN A steel-toothed trap used by poachers to catch rabbits.

MAN-TRAPS (above, below) were set near woodland paths to catch poachers.

THE FOX TWINS

MEASUREMENTS.		1.—R. Ring Finger.
Head Length	18.7	
Head Breadth	15.5	
Left Mid. Finger	11.2	
Left Cubit	43.6	
Left Foot	25.0	
Face Breadth	14.4	
Height	5 ft. 2⅞ in.	

MEASUREMENTS.		1.—R. Ring Finger.
Head Length	18.3	
Head Breadth	15.7	
Left Mid. Finger	11.2	
Left Cubit	43.7	
Left Foot	24.8	
Face Breadth	14.4	
Height		

THE LURCHER
Of great intelligence and cunning, the lurcher would be trained in stealth: it warned its master of the keeper's approach and, if necessary, made its way home undetected. Some lurchers would scamper around the legs of a pursuing keeper, enabling the poacher to make good his escape.

ROUGH SHOOTING
Hunting rabbits, pheasant and woodpigeon for the pot is still a popular pastime for many country dwellers.

traditional local poacher was not always a hostile one. Often they co-existed by unspoken agreement. They had a lot in common: both were skilled and careful countrymen with equal knowledge of the local terrain and its inhabitants. The poacher might be apprehended if he was overtly clumsy in his methods and jeopardized the keeper's credibility. But if he respected certain keeping concerns, such as the breeding of young gamebirds, then a sort of truce might exist. The taking of rabbits where they were plentiful might be tolerated, but a keeper would pursue anyone roaming the pheasant woods after dark.

The village poacher still exists, though his is a rare breed now. Poaching nowadays often involves ruthless slaughtering of animals for commercial gain and bears no resemblance to the skilful hunting of the countryman who worked for his own and his neighbour's table. Deer are blinded by powerful searchlights, dragged down by specially trained dogs and shot indiscriminately. The modern poacher may use a furniture removal van to contain his high-tech equipment and his carcasses, and the kill will have been sold well in advance to commercial dealers maybe hundreds of miles away. All this is very remote from the folk hero who defied the landlord, bested the keeper with stealth and cunning – but drank with him in the local pub of an evening – and, for some symbolized a spirit of independence in a hostile world.

Peat Cutting

The lingering scent of a fresh peat fire is fast becoming a thing of the past. Now peat is mainly used for horticultural purposes and is usually extracted by machine rather than cut by hand.

Smoke seeping through the thatch of a medieval hut or, in later centuries, spiralling out of a cottage chimney, almost certainly came from a fire of turf rather than wood, especially in areas where peat was plentiful and trees were scarce. It would burn steadily throughout the day and, banked up, smoulder overnight – filling the room with welcome warmth, subtle scents and, in a whisper of draught, fine powdery ash.

Peat, probably the first fossil fuel to be exploited, consists of part-decayed vegetation compressed into thick layers. Its formation requires a cool climate – to prevent evaporation of surface moisture – and, most importantly, a high water table: maintained either by heavy rainfall or by local relief. In these conditions, when plants die and sink down into the underlying bog, the water excludes oxygen, bacteria and fungi and so arrests the normal process of decomposition into humus. Instead, the semi-rotted leaves, stems and roots lie in a dense waterlogged mass which gradually, under the weight of subsequent accumulations, subsides and settles into a firm, hard layer. Provided there is no dramatic variation in climate, the peat bed continues to grow, its depth increasing by some six feet every 100 years.

Throughout the British Isles, peat bogs – mostly formed during the last four milennia – occur in two distinct locations. On the one hand, they are prevalent in low-lying coastal areas, like the Cambridgeshire Fens and Somerset Levels, which suffered flooding by the sea some 10,000 years ago at the end of the last Ice Age: when the sea retreated, it left behind brackish swamps that were soon colonized by reeds and sedges – the most common raw materials of peat. On the other hand, peat bogs frequently characterize mountains and moors, such as the Pennines and Scottish Highlands, where contour and climate combine to create the right environment for peat accumulation.

Often, in these upland habitats, the generation of peat has been unwittingly precipitated by human intervention. Five thousand years ago, Dartmoor, for example, was predominantly forested; then, from Neolithic times onwards, farming communities cleared the trees

and burnt the undergrowth, systematically transforming the area into open moor. As a consequence, much of Dartmoor degenerated into a waterlogged waste – aided by high rainfall and poor drainage: optimum conditions for peat formation.

Early man's aim in depleting Britain's forests was two-fold: partly to open up land for cultivation and grazing, partly to obtain wood for fuel. But having felled the trees, he then had to find another source of fuel...and discovered peat. By Roman times, peat-cutting was a well-established activity – not just for domestic use but also to supply industries such as salt-winning (evaporating salt from brine), which the Celts and their successors developed along the east coast.

WINTER FUEL
(above) In regions where woodland had been cleared and peat was in good supply, 'peats' or 'turves' were once widely used as a cheap alternative fuel. Smouldering in the hearth and giving off a distinctive, smoky aroma, a peat fire provided an especially warm welcome. Nowadays, cottagers in Ireland and Scotland – particularly in remote areas – still burn freshly-cut peat.

TRANSPORTING PEAT
(right) *Peat is cut in the spring and summer, when the turf – which acts like a sponge – has lost some of its water. After it has been stacked and left to dry, the family loads the neatly cut turves into special wide-wheeled hand barrows. If the land is boggy, however, alternative transport is used: a sled, a wicker basket strapped across the shoulders, or even a shallow draught boat.*

THE PEAT BOG
(far right) *The dark, spongy peat bogs of the British Isles are formed by layer upon layer of thick, decaying vegetation. The normal process of decomposition has been arrested by the waterlogged soil and by the relatively cool summers which have prevented the growth of soil bacterias. Over the centuries, the peat bed has grown deeper – increasing by a staggering six feet every 100 years.*

Throughout the Middle Ages, peat-cutting took place on a phenomenal scale. It was then that the Norfolk Broads – nothing more nor less than flooded peat diggings – were shaped. When production was at its peak during the 12th and 13th centuries, some ten million cubic feet of peat were gouged out from the Norfolk coastlands. Much of the 'Broads' output went to the populous, prosperous city of Norwich where the cathedral priory alone burnt its way through 200,000 turves each year.

Despite the increasing importance of coal during subsequent centuries, peat remained a significant household fuel right into the Victorian era. This was particularly true in the country areas where, if there were nearby peatlands, or 'turbaries', villagers continued to enjoy medieval rights of turbary: able to rent and work a section of the bog during a specified term – normally 20 years. And, following the example of their Neolithic ancestors, they cut the peat in the traditional way – by hand.

CUT-AND-CATCH

The ideal months for digging were April and May: late enough for winter floods to have drained away, early enough for the new-cut peat to dry out properly through the summer. Among peasants and crofters, cutting was done in pairs – cutter and catcher – often by husband and wife; traditionally the man dug while the woman stacked. Both tasks were equally back-breaking, as fresh peat contains around 90 per cent water and is very heavy.

Starting at the edge of an existing pit, the cutter first stripped off surface vegetation, scored a cutting line and then, using a special long-bladed spade called a scyve or slane, he dug up the peat in blocks – called mumps in the West Country. Each mump measured some twelve inches long by six inches wide and thick and, in its water-logged state, weighed over 20 pounds. Generally, a cutter worked in strips of half-a-dozen mumps and down to a depth of three; given strength, stamina and fair weather, he might clear as many as 5000 mumps in a day and by the end of the week he would hope to have supplied his family's fuel needs for the coming winter.

Meanwhile, his companion sliced each mump into three 'turves' ('peats' in Scotland) and, at the same time, she might differentiate between brown top-layer peat – good for kindling but generating too much ash for day-long use – and the better black peat, from further down. The turves were then lifted into low loose heaps known as 'hiles' or 'windrows'. Exposed to air in this way, the peat began to lose moisture, shrink and, after six weeks or so, was ready to be built up into 'ruckles' – cone-shaped drying mounds about eight feet high. In ruckles, as in hiles, free-flowing air was all important, so a ventilation space was left between each turf, creating an overall lattice-effect.

SOMERSET RUCKLES
The cut blocks are piled into loose heaps, known as 'hiles', and left to dry. After about six weeks, they are built into tall, cone-shaped 'ruckles' (right) – where the drying air, flowing freely between each 'mump', slowly forces out any remaining moisture.

THE LONG JOURNEY HOME
(below) Carrying the peat home has always been heavy work – even though the turves are considerably lighter when dry. This task is usually reserved for the womenfolk.

baskets strapped across the shoulders and, where there were water channels, flat-bottomed boats to carry their winter's warmth across to firm ground and waiting carts. Once home, the peat had to be kept dry for it will not burn wet: turves were stored either under shelter or in a stack, close-built with sloping sides to shed the rain. Surplus production always found a ready market in neighbouring towns with no direct access to woodlands or turbaries: country folk hawking a cartload through the streets could be certain of selling every turf.

Peat's decline as an everyday fuel is relatively recent: during the 1940s it even made a quick come-back as a supplement to war-rationed coal, and in remote or mountainous areas it still heats homes and cooking pots. Nevertheless,

During July and August, the turbaries were void of activity, empty except for 'Jack-o'-lantern' lights, eerily glimpsed in the gloaming (explained as self-igniting bubbles of marsh gas – methane with phosphine traces – that burst up from the bog), and brown-black clusters of ruckles shedding water and weight in the summer sun. By autumn, the turves were significantly lighter – a ton of fresh peat reduces to three hundredweight of fuel – and could now be carried off the bog more easily.

Since conventional wheeled vehicles would straightaway sink into the squelchy morass, peatlanders used alternative transport such as stretcher-like hand barrows, sleds, huge wicker

CUTTING PEAT
(right) The cutter uses special tools and a lot of sheer muscle power to slice through the peat bed. Taking a marking iron, he cuts vertically through the top layer of grass and then strips off the surface vegetation with a paring iron. Finally, he uses a long, narrow-bladed spade – called a 'slane' (right) – to cut the waterlogged blocks, or 'mumps', each of which can weigh over 20 pounds.

serves it; in cottage construction, lining thatched roofs and filling in the cavity between a double skin of dry stone walling; malting, where the germinating barley is dried in a peat kiln; charring barrels for whisky and other spirits; and smelting lead, but not iron – as peat will not support the ore's weight in a blast furnace. More modern applications range from the manufacture of paper – especially blotting and wrapping papers – and plastics, to drug and dye production. From the late 19th century, peat has also served as a good absorbent litter for livestock.

Currently, however, peat's major role is horticultural. The idea of exploiting peat as a compost was developed at the turn of the century but did not really catch on commercially until the 1950s. Today, in a granulated form, it features in a wide range of fertilizers and grass-dressings (top grades are suitable for race courses and golf links), while moist turves are marketed as a general soil-enricher.

The commercialization of peat has inevitably brought about a change in extraction methods. Where large-scale production is concerned, the punishing cut-and-catch teamwork of centuries, now belongs to the past. Instead, machines have taken over. Mechanized digging requires forward planning over several years as the section of bog to be worked must first be drained. Once the water-table has been lowered, plant cover and topsoil are removed – 'unridded' – and the trench lines, or 'heads', marked out. The cutting machine then moves down the head, slicing out blocks and stacking them alongside the trench. When these have partly dried they are turned and eventually built up into ruckles – more severely shaped than the humped mounds of yesteryear but, in their own way, still faithful to the turbary landscape.

MECHANIZATION
(above) The modern commercialization of peat – in horticulture and industry – has seen the introduction of giant turf-cutting machines, which greedily eat into the peat bog. As they are not amphibious, sections of the bog have to be drained well in advance, before the extraction process can begin. Hand-cut peat, however, still fuels the fires of a few local industries, like this small distillery on the Isle of Islay (inset).

the costs of obtaining peat, along with its low heat energy, counted against it. But that does not exclude peat's other uses. Over the centuries, these have included curing fish and meat, practised since prehistoric peoples discovered that peat smoke not only dries flesh but also (because it contains formaldehyde) pre-

PEAT COUNTRY
(right) Traditionally, crofters in the remote Western Isles of Scotland have used peat for winter warmth. And the rich dark colour of the turves, stacked in neat piles outside the crofts, is reflected in the hues and texture of the famous tweed they weave.

The Stone Mason

Little changed since Norman times, the tools and traditions of the stone mason are as enduring as the stone buildings and monuments created by successive generations of craftsmen.

People have built and worked in stone in Britain since time immemorial. The great monument at Stonehenge bears witness to skills in stone-working on a gigantic scale dating from prehistoric days, while the indestructability of stone has preserved dwellings from as long ago as the Iron Age in Cornwall and the Orkneys. But it was with the Norman invasion of the country in 1066 that the great tradition of stone masonry in Britain really began.

The Norman Conquerors demanded vast stone churches and castles to stamp their spiritual and martial authority on the land and brought with them their own skilled masons to erect these edifices. The Norman masons carried to England a tradition already centuries old, and taught their skills to English builders. It was the Normans who gave English stone-masonry many of its methods and much of its terminology. 'Banker' masons, for instance, get their name from the French word (banc), meaning a work bench, while words like 'mallet' and 'chamfer' are also French in origin. In some instances, the Normans even brought their own stone with them. Beautiful creamy-yellow Caen limestone from quarries on the banks of the Orne was shipped to England for inclusion in

ENDURING TRADITIONS
Over the centuries (left), although there have been many refinements and improvements in working practices, the basic traditions, methods and tools of the stone mason have changed very little. In Britain, the heyday of stonemasonry fell in the Middle Ages (above left). Not until the mid 19th-century, when the large-scale production of bricks reduced the demand for stone, did the mason's art decline.

Canterbury and Winchester Cathedrals, and a number of others.

VAST STONE PROJECTS

The great explosion of castle- and, in particular, cathedral-building in the centuries after the Conquest saw the stonemason in his heyday. Literally hundreds of masons were employed on any of the vast building projects that were under way all over the country. At a time when the population of Britain was only a few million, the building of Beaumaris Castle alone employed 400 masons – plus 1000 labourers, 200 carters and 30 smiths and carpenters.

The master mason, who managed all these men, was naturally a very important figure in the Middle Ages. He not only directed the building operations but was usually the 'architect' too, providing detailed drawings and templates and laying out the plan for the building on the ground. Men such as Walter of Hereford, the master mason in charge of building at Vale Royal Abbey, and Henry Yevele, Edward I's master mason at Westminster, were both very eminent men – Yevele, for instance, owned the manor of Langton in Purbeck. But all masons were skilled craftsmen, much in demand, and they could command relatively high wages. Those working on royal buildings, for instance, won the right to be paid for half of the Holy Days when work ceased.

Most medieval masons were journeymen,

MONUMENTAL REPAIRS
(above) Today, much of the work of masons who specialize in architectural sculpture lies in repairing the work of previous generations, which has been damaged by weathering. Here, with chisel and mallet, the traditional tools of trade, the mason is working on new lower halves of the figures of queens from the facade of the Houses of Parliament. The mason's skill will ensure that the new lower halves exactly match the tops.

journeying around the country to work on the big building projects – the only places where stone was used in any quantity. Only a tiny fraction of the masons working on cathedrals and castles were local men; most came from hundreds of miles away. The names of masons recorded as working on the construction of Vale Royal Abbey for example, Hereford, Dore, Furness, Battle, Oxford, indicate just how far they had travelled – on site, these journeyman masons lived and worked in the specially erected wooden 'logges' or lodges, which gave the Freemason's lodges their name.

From the 16th century on, however, the number of vast stone building projects diminished, while the use of stone in building houses – rare in the Middle Ages – began to increase. At first, only manor houses and public buildings were stone built but, over the centuries, stone was adopted for farmhouses, barns and even cottages. The mason no longer needed to travel to find work, but his status diminished with the scale of the buildings and the increasing simplicity of his work. 'Rough' masonry, using rough cut stone, came into its own, especially in the country – though in town, 'free' masonry, using finely cut stone, continued to flourish, as the beautiful 18th-century stone houses of Bath and Stamford bear witness.

CHOOSING THE STONE

To a considerable extent, though, the approach was dictated by the stone available locally (and the wealth of the client) for the cost of moving stone was high. Houses in areas of granite rock, which is hard to cut and has to be hammered and chipped, tend to be rough cut. Houses in areas of freestone have smooth, even facades – freestone is fine-grained stone, such as limestone and sandstone, which can be cut 'freely'

in any direction.

Choosing the right stone for the building was a crucial part of the mason's work, and the master mason would make regular trips to the quarry to point out exactly what stone he wanted and what size blocks it was to be supplied in.

IN THE QUARRY

In the quarry, large blocks of stone were split off from the bedrock by driving a series of wedges, called 'plugs and feathers', into the rock six to twelve inches apart. Before the wedges could be driven in, though, holes had to be drilled by laboriously lifting and turning a bar with a fan-shaped blade at the end, called a 'jumper' bar. Modern pneumatic rock-drills make this task considerably easier.

In soft rock, the quarryman might actually be able to saw the block out, using a thick saw called a frig-bob to make a vertical cut. Hard rock, however, such as granite, would not yield even to plug and feathers, and quarrymen learned to exploit natural weaknesses in the rock. 'Black' gunpowder was used with particularly stubborn sections, but this was extremely wasteful of rock. Nowadays, a flame gun called a thermic lance is used which can cut granite into the thin, polished slabs which are often used to face modern buildings.

Sometimes, the stone would be roughly shaped in the quarry using picks and axes. Often, the stone would be cut exactly to match a template supplied by the mason as well. This was especially valuable with limestone, for it is much more easily worked immediately after digging out from the ground. Fresh limestone contains moisture in the spaces between the grains – as this 'quarry sap' dries out, the calcite in the stone crystallizes and hardens and makes the

FIXER MASONS
(left) Stone for building work is dressed, prepared and numbered by banker masons. At the building site fixer masons, working with diagrams and plans, set the stone in place and then mortar them into position. Sometimes additional carving on the stone is done by these masons once it has been positioned, but more usually this is done by architectural sculptors.

BANKER MASONS
(left) Banker masons (the term was first applied to Norman masons and comes from the French word, banc, a bench), are responsible for cutting, carving and decorating it at the work bench.

NORMAN ARCH
(below) Following the Norman invasion came a revival of the skills of stone-masonry, which were first expressed in Britain by the Romans. The cathedrals, castles and churches built by the Normans were inspiration to masons for the following 500 years.

stone much harder to cut.

Transporting the stone to the building site was a long and costly business, and heavily laden ox-carts would ply to and fro all day. Naturally, stonemasons used local stone where-ever possible and, on major projects, a quarry may have been specially opened up nearby. If there was no suitable stone available locally, it would be floated down river in vast barges or, in a few cases, down specially constructed canals.

DRAWN INSTRUCTIONS

Once on site, the stone had to be cut to shape according to drawings made by the master mason. The master mason often drew these plans on the whitewashed floors and walls of the workshop – or even in a convenient place on site. Some of these drawings still survive from the Middle Ages – a good example can be seen above the porch in Wells Cathedral. After the master mason had completed his drawings, carpenters would make a wooden template from them (modern masons use zinc).

Template, drawings and rough cut stone or 'scant' were then passed to the banker mason whose task was to cut the stone and mouldings and carve any decorative motifs. From Tudor times onward – and especially in the 18th century – one of his most absorbing tasks was to cut the stone into ashlar blocks. These are blocks cut so perfectly square that they can be laid together to form an almost jointless facing for a building. Nowadays, with thermic lances, almost any stone, including granite, can be ashlared, but in the past, masons could ashlar freestones, even with simple tools.

Once the stone was finished, the banker mason cut into the top the code number given it by the

THE STONE, THE TOOLS AND THE MASON
(above, left) An assortment of newly-quarried roughcut stone, including limestone and sandstone (some showing the marks where it was split from the rock), is taken to a stone-sawyer's yard where it is mechanically sawn into basic shapes and sizes. The stone is then stored at the stone mason's yard until required. (centre) The stone is worked on with a range of tools including drags, calipers and saws, which have changed very little over the centuries. The main difference lies in the tungsten or carborundum edges which many modern tools have for extra hardness. Formerly these tools had to be tempered frequently, often by an on-site blacksmith employed specifically to keep the tools sharp. (right) The banker mason uses a template drawn up by the master mason to mark out the tracery he is required to carve out of the stone. He cuts this out using gouges and chisels and a mallet.

of which still exists in the Bell Harry tower of Canterbury Cathedral) – animal power could not be used because of the delicacy of touch required to set several hundredweights of stone to an accuracy of fractions of an inch. The stones would be lifted up the building in a sling, but when actually laying them in place, none of the lifting gear could pass underneath. The solution was to lift the stone into place using a 'lewis', usually a three-legged stand which held the stone suspended by a dovetailed key which slotted into a mortice cut into the top of the block. With perfect precision, the block would be dropped gently into place, and the lewis removed.

MONUMENTAL MASONRY

Stone-carving, which declined steadily after the end of the Middle Ages, received a tremendous fillip from the 18th and 19th century taste for stone monuments to the dead. Stone memorials in the form of engraved slabs and sculpted tombs were installed in churches from before the 12th century, but it was not until Georgian times that they began to appear in churchyards marking virtually every grave. From the mid 18th century on, the demand for carved headstones steadily increased, and more and more masons began to specialize in work on monuments.

The true heyday of the monumental mason came with the creation of the great urban cemeteries in the 19th century. Some of these, like Kensal Green and Highgate in London, or Lawnswood in Leeds became lasting tributes to the mason's art. In these cemeteries, there are not only headstones of all shapes and sizes but coped stones, chest tombs, pedestal tombs, table tombs and vast mausoleums. Some are perfect expressions of refined classical taste, others riots of gothic extravagance; some are figurative, like the great Arab tent that houses the tomb of Sir Richard Burton at Mortlake.

This century, however, has seen a preference for simpler monuments, which can be produced in bulk and the art of monumental masonry has declined. At the same time, the high cost of building in stone meant that more and more houses and public buildings were built of brick and concrete.

MASTERWORK
(above) It took a team of dedicated masons 10 years to restore the West Face of Wells Cathedral to its mid-14th century glory. (left) Here, one of the Cathedral's expert stone masons exhibits all the traditional skills in finishing the turret top.

STONE BILL
(below) Masons traditionally left their marks on stone to identify their work for payment purposes. Few though, gave the details as shown on the stone 'bill' here.

master mason. These code numbers indicated the exact position that the stone was to occupy when the building was assembled.

As well as these location marks, the banker mason would often 'sign' his work with a personal mark called a 'sigil', usually incised in the top bed of a stone where it would be seen once the stone was laid. Individual stones needed to be identified in this way so that it would be clear who was responsible for mistakes and how much work was attributable to each for the purposes of payment.

THE FIXER MASON

After the banker mason came the fixer masons, who set and laid the stone in place. Stones were invariably lifted into place on winches pulled by strong arms or by tread-mills (one

REPAIRS TO A MONUMENT	£	S	D
CORRECTED THE TEN COMMANDMENTS		110	0
EMBELLISHED PONTIUS PILATE AND PUT NEW RIBBON IN HIS BONNET.		20	0
PUT NEW TAIL ON ROOSTER OF ST. PETER AND MENDED HIS COMB.		25	0
REPLUMED AND REGILDED THE WAY OF THE GUARDIAN ANGEL.		155	0
WASHED THE SERVENT OF THE HIGH PRIEST, AND PUT CARMINE ON HIS CHEEKS.		10	0
RENEWED HEAVEN ADJUSTED THE STARS. AND THOROUGHLY CLEANED THE MOON.		65	0
RE-ANIMATED THE FLAMES OF PURGATORY. AND RESTORED SOULS.		27	6
REVIVED FLAMES OF HELL, PUT NEW TAIL ON THE DEVIL. MENDED HIS LEFT HOOF. AND DID SEVERAL ODD JOBS FOR THE DAMMED.		96	6
PUT NEW SPOTTED DASHES ON SON OF TOBIAS AND DRESSING ON HIS BACK.		108	0
CLEANED THE EARS OF BALAAM S ASS. AND SHOD HIM.		14	0
PUT EARINGS IN THE EARS OF SARAH.		26	0
PUT NEW STONE IN DAVID S SLING ENLARGED THE HEAD OF GOLIATH AND EXTENDED HIS LEGS.	45	0
DECORATED NOAH S ARK.		60	0
MENDED THE SHIRT OF THE PRODIGAL SON. AND CLEANED HIS NOSE.		15	6
TOTAL	£ 36	15	6

DECLINE CHECKED

The art of stone masonry seemed fated to die out, but the decline has been halted in recent years by the growing trend towards conserving old buildings. Historic stone towns like Bath or Oxford can now support several mason's yards, ranging from the one-man operation to sizeable subsidiaries of large companies. The cathedrals, where restoration and repair have been continuing ever since they were built, all retain at least one mason. Some, like Chichester and York, keep large yards employing 50 or more people and now, more and more, apprentices are taking up the craft each year.

Flint Knapping

The flint knapper is a living reminder of our prehistoric past. Using timeless skills, he shapes the hard, brittle stone into decorative 'builders' or gun flints for antique firearms.

Flint knapping – the shaping of flints with a hammer – is an extraordinary hang-over from prehistoric times when the only sharp tools were made of flint, and carefully-fashioned axe-heads were used as currency. Early man realized that, as a raw material for tools, flint has considerable advantages over other types of stone. It is harder than steel, has no grain as such, and is so brittle that, when the stone is struck, it flakes off leaving razor sharp edges.

The earliest flint tools were probably made from stone picked up from the ground, but prehistoric flint knappers quickly discovered that nodules dug from the earth were in many ways superior to stones that had been exposed to the elements. Flint nodules are found deposited in strata at intervals in chalk hillsides and occur as irregularly-shaped lumps, coated with a white mantle called a cortex. Stone buried at different depths differs in quality, and Neolithic miners

CHIP OFF THE OLD BLOCK (below) Resting a heavy block of flint on his knee, weighing all of 50lbs, the flint knapper gently breaks it into manageable pieces with 'workable' faces. He uses a soft metal quartering hammer – made by a blacksmith – to split the brittle stone.

Besides providing the raw material for tools, flint played another vital role in prehistoric society – a role that was to endure long after flint tools had been made redundant by the introduction of metals to Britain in about 2000 BC. Struck against the right surface, flint could make fire. In the *Aeneid*, Virgil describes how '...some seek the seeds of flame hidden in the veins of flint', but for once, this was not a technology that the Romans introduced into Britain. Even before the Iron Age, ancient Britons had been striking flint against naturally-occurring pyrites to make fire.

Sparks fly from a piece of flint of almost any shape – but, with time, the shape of flints used to make fire was refined, and even varied according to fashion. Oval flints found favour at one time, but these gave way to square flints. The flint was struck against a piece of steel specially shaped to be easily held in the hand, and these two components (collectively called a strike-a-light) were often carried round in a tinderbox, which also served to keep the kindling material dry.

FLINTLOCK FIREARMS

The first firearms ignited by a flint-on-steel spark appeared in the mid-16th century. Employing the same principle as the flint-on-steel strike-a-lights, these weapons were fitted with a lock in which specially-shaped flint was held in the jaws of a swinging, spring-loaded arm, sometimes called a *snaphaunce* or 'snapping cock'. On pulling the trigger, the cock shot forward, striking sparks from the flash-pan cover and throwing it forward, so that the sparks set light to the priming charge in the pan.

The quality of gun flints was so important that the trade in them flourished. By the 1850s, knappers at just one British site, sent eleven million flints to Turkey alone. The best flint came from France, but English workmanship surpassed that of the French craftsmen, and at

were prepared to burrow many yards into the ground to secure the finest of raw materials for their tools.

Once they had been manhandled to the surface, the largest blocks were broken up into more manageable lumps, and some of the flint tools were manufactured on the spot. There was good reason for this as the atmosphere quickly affects the quality of the stone, making it less easy to work. However, precision work in flint was a rare skill, and quarried stone often travelled many miles before it reached the prehistoric tool manufacturer.

Even in the hands of one of these skilled craftsmen, however, the shaping of flint tools was a rather hit-and-miss affair. One writer points out that a modern Australian aborigine discards 300 flint flakes before he is satisfied with the tool he is creating. The abundance of flakes around Neolithic tool factories confirms that the level of productivity has probably changed little over the last ten millenia or so.

Prehistoric man used several techniques to create flint tools. The roughest and simplest method was to strike a small flint obliquely against the edge of a larger nodule. This technique produced crudely-shaped flake tools with edges as sharp as a razor. Such tools were often awkward to handle, however, and soon lost their edge. To produce more durable and finely crafted core tools, the worker would either use a large stone as an anvil on which to rest the raw material when working it, or else would hold the stone in one hand, and strike it with a shaping stone held in the other. Once the general shape of the tool had been achieved, a smaller shaping stone or hammer made of bone or horn would be used to shape or 'dress' the edges. The finest finishing work was often done not by striking the flint, but by applying consistent heavy pressure, either with a small flint, or a piece of hard wood or bone. By this method, prehistoric man was able to display extraordinary mastery of the most resistant of materials, and to produce tools that were often as beautiful as they were functional.

NEOLITHIC FLINT MINES
(above) Grimes Graves, in Breckland, consists of 366 grass covered hollows, which were once the shafts of Neolithic flint mines. The fine quality 'floorstone' flint was originally gouged out of the chalky soil using stags' antlers and oxen's shoulder blades. The task was not an easy one as the shafts were 40 feet deep.

PREHISTORIC TOOLS
(below) Prehistoric man used flint nodules to make razor-sharp weapons and tools. Flakes struck off the block were used for tools such as scrapers, while a larger instrument like an axe would be made from the core.

one stage the French were exporting flint to Britain for shaping, then importing the finished flints.

The British craftsmen shaped flints in broadly the same way as their Stone-Age predecessors, but they had the advantage of steel tools to work the stone: two heavy hammers, weighing about three and a half and five pounds, were used to 'quarter' or break up large nodules; smaller flaking hammers served to chip the flint flakes from the core; and the tool for the final shaping was a long knapping hammer, which was sometimes made from an old file. The shape of the flaking hammer varied. British craftsmen traditionally used a round-nosed hammer, but in the 19th century an angular, lozenge-shaped hammer, called a French hammer, found favour.

The shaping process began with the craftsman balancing a large block of flint on his knee, and gently tapping the stone, listening carefully to the ring, which provided some indication of the direction in which the stone would break most easily. Then, using a quartering hammer, he would carefully break the stone into pieces with 'workable' fairly flat surfaces: he didn't swing the hammer like a pick-axe, but instead gently raised and dropped it from the elbow, which was held static, close to the hip.

Next the craftsman rested the quarter on his knee, with the flat striking face sloping diagonally downwards. He raised the flaking hammer a couple of inches, and struck the edge of the flat face of the stone, causing tiny splinters and sparks to fly off in all directions. If the stone was struck at the right angle, a long sliver of flint would flake off. A heavy hammer produced flakes about an inch wide, and six times as long; smaller flakes were produced using a lighter hammer. Turning the block a little between blows, the craftsman worked around the stone until he reached the starting point. He would then work round again, displacing his blows a little from the first series. The process continued until all the usable flakes had been chipped off: the core of the stone is of lower quality than the edges, and is more difficult to shape accurately.

REGULAR WORK

To cross-cut the flakes to fit the different sizes of flintlock, the worker moved to an anvil. Typically, this was a tree-stump with a peg of soft iron hammered into it, and covered in leather. The worker sat to one side of the peg, and 'clicked off' neat flint squares, swinging the knapping hammer gently with a flick of the wrist. To watch one of these men in action was a curious sight: he worked very rapidly, yet turned out remarkably regular squares of flint, each with a couple of tiny nicks or 'bulbs' in the back, which could be gripped in the vice of the flintlock's cock.

The unused cores were not usually discarded but were used as building material. With a little extra work, the knappers could flake off

STRIKE-A-LIGHT
(right) Early man's discovery that flint could make fire, when struck against the right surface, developed into the 'strike-a-light', consisting of a piece of flint and steel. Both were usually carried in a simple tinder-box, containing kindling material.

DUELLING MISHAPS
(below) Flintlock pistols were notoriously unreliable and there are numerous historical accounts of farcical duels where the guns misfired. This could be caused by any of the following: the flint might have slipped out of place; the powder may have been blown out of the flash-pan; or the charge could have got wet.

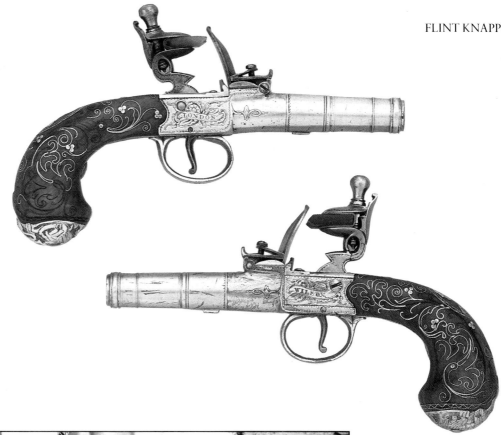

FLINTLOCK PISTOLS
(above) This pair of antique pistols show the flint gripped in the spring-loaded cock. When the trigger was pulled, the flint shot forward, striking sparks from the flash-pan cover and igniting the powder.

KNAPPING GUN FLINTS
(left) Flintlock guns demanded high-quality shaped flints. Using a knapping hammer, the craftsman cut the double-ridged flakes which had been struck off the core.

the cores into rough block-shapes so that the stones fitted together as neatly as possible. Building walls with this technique was known as 'flush-work' and was sometimes taken to extraordinary lengths. A church in Lewes, for example, is built from flints knapped into precise brick shapes, and laid in accurate courses.

BUILDING WITH FLINT

Very precise shaping of flints did not begin, however, until around the 1300s, and for centuries, builders simply used flint like any other stone, as a make-weight in rubble walls. The irregular and rounded shape of flint nodules may have discouraged more creative use of flint, as a great deal of mortar was needed to fill the large voids between the rocks. Also the rounded nodules had a tendency to roll out of the wall until the mortar was set, and this slowed down building work.

By the time of the Norman conquest, British builders were beginning to master the art of making walls primarily of flint. They eliminated the large voids between nodules by roughly shaping the flints into less irregular pieces that fitted together more snugly than unbroken stones. Where there were large areas of mortar showing on the face of the wall, these were often studded with the discarded flakes – an attractive decoration known as garneting or galleting.

But, even with careful shaping, flints were not suitable for every part of the structure. Knapping a flint into a perfect, straight-edged cube is possible, but very time consuming, and for doors and windows straight edges are vital. Consequently, almost all buildings used bricks or timber for columns, arches and lintels.

Many builders chose flint simply for reasons of expediency – it was the local stone, and therefore cheap and easy to get hold of. Often,

FLINT 'BUILDERS'

The rounded cores of flint nodules were often used as building stone. The knapper would flake off the core, creating regular-sized shapes that would fit neatly together. As the rounded nodules tended to roll out of place, they were set in generous amounts of mortar. Although it is possible to shape flint into straight-edged cubes, other materials like red brick were often used around doors and windows, a practice which is handsomely illustrated by this cottage in Glandford, Norfolk (above). Many craftsmen were also attracted by the decorative qualities of the stone: this old wall in Westdean in East Sussex (right) exploits the blacks and greys of the shiny exposed face of the flints, surrounded by the rim of white cortex.

though, flints were used purely for their decorative value. The broken face of a flint nodule has a lovely dark, glassy surface, and flints from different areas vary radically in colour. Some are almost black, while others are paler. Juxtaposition of the various coloured stones gave the medieval builder a palette of tones from which to create masterpieces of pattern and texture.

The different colours of flint are caused by penetration of water from the outside of the stone, and this also creates subtle variations of colour across the broken edge of a nodule. Much flint work exploits these tonal qualities: the builders deliberately split the stones in such a way that they reveal the concentric circles of dark and light flint ringed around with bright white cortex.

Remarkably, flint knapping continues at a few sites today, notably at Brandon in East Anglia. The flints produced are used for building material, and in lovingly restored flintlock muskets and pistols, collected and fired by enthusiasts. There is also a small export trade to countries such as Czechoslovakia and West Africa where flintlocks have not yet been completely replaced by the percussion cap. Ironically, real flints are no longer used as simple fire-makers: in cigarette lighters the hardened steel wheel presses not against stone but instead strikes sparks from an alloy of cerium, iron, and rare metals.

The Thatcher's Craft

Until recently thatching was in decline and many cottages were modernized with unsympathetic slate and tiles, but thatching with reed or straw is once more in demand, and a traditional rural craft is thriving in the modern world.

A green with a pond, encircled by half-timbered cottages drowsing under a golden thatch; brick and rubble walls enclosing gardens crowded with roses and alive with bees; a mellow-stoned church in a leafy yard: this idealized vision of an English village has the timeless quality of a place where the balance between the works of man and those of nature has never been upset. And the gentle contours and warm natural colouring of thatch, fitting harmoniously with different building styles and in most landscapes, are key ingredients in this idyllic picture.

Thatch has other advantages, apart from its appearance. At one time it was the cheapest roofing material: primitive thatches of turves, straw, bracken, heather – whatever was to hand – were used in early settlements as far back as the Iron Age and probably beyond. Nowadays thatch is expensive but it is still exceptionally light and, therefore, for some buildings, like the mud-built cob cottages of Devon, the only roof practicable. It is also an efficient insulator, keeping buildings warm in winter and deliciously cool in summer. Set against this are the need to replace it regularly and its vulnerability to fire – a single spark can set dry thatch ablaze within seconds. This danger can now be partially reduced by steeping the thatching materials in a fire-retardant solution before they are fixed to the roof.

In the Middle Ages and earlier, thatching was the universal roofing method – 'thatch' from the Saxon *thaec*, was originally the term for any kind of roofing material. Most buildings were thatched – barns and mills as well as houses, and even larger buildings, like the 14th-century Pevensey Castle and the knapped flint churches of Norfolk. The largest building presently under thatch in Britain is the huge tithe barn at Tisbury, Wiltshire. Its 1450 square yards of thatch took five men four months to lay in 1971, and used 130,000 bundles of Norfolk reed. Properly maintained, its renewed thatch could last for a century.

LONG-STRAW THATCH
(left) Loose bundles of straw are lashed to the roof, often over the original thatch, giving it a smooth, undulating profile. This golden colour will weather within a year to a dark chestnut brown.

THATCH ON THE FARM

Apart from roofing buildings, the main use of thatch was as coverings for ricks, in which the harvest would be stacked for ripening. Large farms with outbuildings as well as ricks to thatch could provide year-round employment for a skilled man. Large ricks might take up to a week to thatch and were a source of great pride to their makers, who 'signed' their work by decorating the crown with a personal emblem made of straw; birds, keys, bells and sceptres were the most common.

Until quite recently, thatch had experienced a long period of decline. Thatches fell into ruin and were replaced by tiles or slate. The cost of fairly frequent renewal and high insurance premiums were partly responsible for this reversal, but also, in a progressive age, thatch had come to seem old-fashioned and had acquired a faint stigma of poverty. In the late 20th century, however, country villages are being rediscovered by townspeople nostalgic for rural life and fleeing from the congestion, pollution and pressures of the inner city. Few countrymen have benefited from this turnaround in rural fortunes more than the thatcher. Thatch is once again desirable. The new owners of thatched cottages are prepared to pay to keep their thatch in good repair and thatchers are in demand again. There are now around 500,000 buildings under thatch in Britain, providing work for some 800 thatchers.

AGE-OLD METHODS
Thatching is carried out in much the same way today as when this picture was taken earlier in the century. The bundles of straw are held in place by long thin split hazel stems, fixed to the rafters with metal hooks.

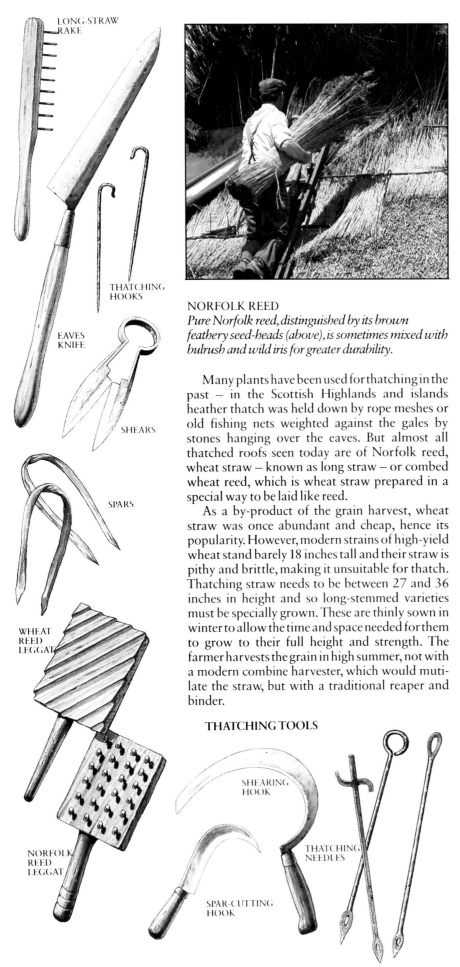

LONG-STRAW RAKE

THATCHING HOOKS

EAVES KNIFE

SHEARS

SPARS

WHEAT REED LEGGAT

NORFOLK REED LEGGAT

NORFOLK REED
Pure Norfolk reed, distinguished by its brown feathery seed-heads (above), is sometimes mixed with bulrush and wild iris for greater durability.

Many plants have been used for thatching in the past – in the Scottish Highlands and islands heather thatch was held down by rope meshes or old fishing nets weighted against the gales by stones hanging over the eaves. But almost all thatched roofs seen today are of Norfolk reed, wheat straw – known as long straw – or combed wheat reed, which is wheat straw prepared in a special way to be laid like reed.

As a by-product of the grain harvest, wheat straw was once abundant and cheap, hence its popularity. However, modern strains of high-yield wheat stand barely 18 inches tall and their straw is pithy and brittle, making it unsuitable for thatch. Thatching straw needs to be between 27 and 36 inches in height and so long-stemmed varieties must be specially grown. These are thinly sown in winter to allow the time and space needed for them to grow to their full height and strength. The farmer harvests the grain in high summer, not with a modern combine harvester, which would mutilate the straw, but with a traditional reaper and binder.

THATCHING TOOLS

SHEARING HOOK

SPAR-CUTTING HOOK

THATCHING NEEDLES

DECORATING THE RIDGE
This reed thatch has a long-straw ridge cut in into scallops and decorated with a cross-hatched arrangement of liggers and spars.

For long straw the wheat may be threshed or used whole. For wheat reed, the sheaves are fed into a comber which removes the ears and 'combs' the stalks so that they emerge intact, disentangled, and all lying in the same direction. It is then tied into bundles, known in Devon, where wheat reed is most commonly used, as 'nitches.'

Norfolk reed *(Phragmites communis)* grows wild in coastal marshes, estuaries and freshwater margins all over Britain and Europe. In the Broadlands of Norfolk, however, it has been regularly cropped for centuries. Regular cutting produces tall straight reeds and, incidentally, helps preserve the habitats of rare birds like the bittern and bearded tit.

A WINTER HARVEST

The reed is harvested in the depths of winter by which time the frost and snow have stripped the spear-shaped leaves and the stems have taken on their golden winter colour. Traditionally, the reed cutting season ran from January to March when the hardiest of labourers, clad in thick coats and waist-high waders would work the icy marshes with scythe and sickle. Once cut, the reed was cleaned, tied in standard-sized bundles with the butts – the root ends – all pointing in the same direction. The bundles were banged on a 'spot-board' to level the ends, then piled in stacks, or 'fathoms' – so-called because a string passed round them would measure 6 feet, and finally carried away, in most cases, on punts known as reedlighters. The tough and unpleasant task of reed cutting has now been largely mechanized. To meet the growing demand for reed, specially adapted tractors have been developed which can cut and bind 40 bundles a minute.

In earlier times, when transport was at horse's pace, thatchers chose materials which were close at hand. Norfolk reed was thus once largely confined to East Anglia, long straw was found

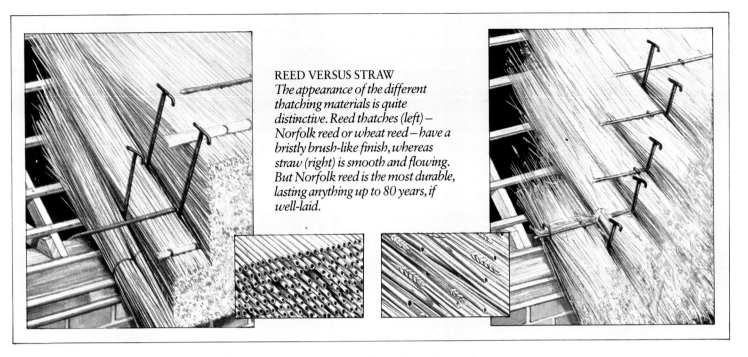

REED VERSUS STRAW
The appearance of the different thatching materials is quite distinctive. Reed thatches (left) – Norfolk reed or wheat reed – have a bristly brush-like finish, whereas straw (right) is smooth and flowing. But Norfolk reed is the most durable, lasting anything up to 80 years, if well-laid.

mainly in the wheat-growing districts of the South and Midlands, while combed wheat reed remained a speciality of the South-west. This overall pattern is still just discernible though the best thatchers travel all over the country whereas once they would have stuck to their own patch. A certain uniformity is the price thatching has paid for its survival as a craft.

As a labour-intensive craft, using relatively scarce materials, thatching is no longer cheap, so the durability of the thatch is nowadays of much greater importance than formerly. Long-straw thatch has a lifespan of 15-20 years, while wheat reed lasts longer – up to 30 years – but the most durable thatch is Norfolk reed which, if well laid and maintained, may last as long as 80 years or more. For this reason it has now become widespread across the country. Some thatchers add

wild iris and bulrush to the reed to increase its durability.

Apart from purely practical considerations, there are marked differences in the appearance of thatching materials, particularly between long-straw thatch and reed thatches, whether Norfolk reed or wheat reed. A long-straw thatch has a distinctive flowing outline, as if it had been poured over the roof like thick cream. Reed thatches are much more crisply sculpted, with a close-cropped, brush-like finish, in contrast to the soft ruffled texture of long straw, where a much greater length of stalk is exposed.

THATCHING METHODS

All thatchers work from the eaves of the roof up to the ridge and usually from right to left. The thatch is laid in courses, each successive course overlap-

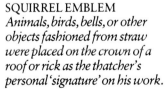

SQUIRREL EMBLEM
Animals, birds, bells, or other objects fashioned from straw were placed on the crown of a roof or rick as the thatcher's personal 'signature' on his work.

THE REED-CUTTERS
Working in the icy depths of winter, the harvesters of Norfolk reed must be the hardiest of men. Mechanical cutters have replaced the old sickles and scythes to make their jobs a little easier.

THE UNIVERSAL ROOF
(above) At one time almost all
buildings were thatched –
houses, castles, mills, churches,
barns, dovecotes and even, as
here, boathouses.

WEATHERED BARN
(far right) Thatch needs regular
renewal. This beautiful old
timber barn is now disused and
the original thatched roof is well
beyond repair.

IRISH CROFT
(right) Both the ricks in the
farmyard, and the croft itself, are
thatched with the crofter's own
straw, which is firmly fixed to the
roof to withstand the Atlantic
gales which ravage the fringes of
Galway Bay.

ping the previous one. Long-straw thatch is laid in
large bundles, or 'yealms,' butted firmly into one
another and held in place by 'sways' – long poles of
split hazel slipped under metal hooks hammered
into the rafters. As new yealms are added they are
combed into their neighbours with a rake and
fixed to them by shorter hazel or willow rods,
sharpened at both ends and twisted into a hairpin
shape, and known variously as 'spars,' 'broaches'
and 'sparrows' among many other local names.

As the long straw lays on the roof almost flat,
the eaves, and often the barges, need to be secured.
This is usually done with a decorative arrangement
of thin split hazel rods called liggers and cross-
rods, which complement the design of the ridge.
Finally, a long eaves knife is used to trim the edges.

REED THATCHING

Norfolk reed and combed wheat reed are laid
quite differently as only the butt ends of the stems
will be exposed in the finished roof. The bundles of
straw or reed which comprise the first course are
lashed to the roof at their thinner top ends with
tarred string. Subsequent courses are secured with

hazel sways. As the courses are built up the stems
become almost horizontal. A tool called a leggat is
then used to level the ends and 'dress' them into the
desired smooth outline, and a light trim from a
shaving hook finishes it off.

Because the spiky reeds are laid end on they can
be decoratively trimmed and the edges may be
sheared into scallops and zigzags or other geometric shapes. The roof ridge, however, requires
special treatment. Norfolk reed is too stiff to bend
over the ridge so sedge or, more often, long straw is
used. Large bundles of straw are bent over the
ridge and held down on each side by liggers,
secured to the thatch by spars. As on long-straw
eaves and ridges, the exposed liggers and cross-
rods make geometric patterns on the surface of the
thatch and scallops and zigzags may be cut into the
edge of the ridge. The ridge work and ornamental
emblems are often damaged by birds particularly
at nesting time; so many ridges are covered by a
fine wire mesh to protect them.

The details of decoration on a thatched roof are
a means by which many thatchers proclaim their
individual craftsmanship. Like rick thatchers,
others make ornaments of twined straw to sit on
the ridge and some have their own particular
method of finishing the edges of the ridge and
dormers. In spite of the general uniformity of
modern thatching practices, the best thatch is
never stereotyped and is clearly marked with the
thatcher's individual style.

Pargetting

Houses throughout Britain – from the humble cottage to great mansion – have been decorated in plaster by the plasterer and pargetter using skills dating back to the Middle Ages.

While styles of houses have changed enormously over the years, from the chocolate box beauty of the traditional timber frame, to the neat utility of the modern house, the art of decorative plasterwork has provided a continuous thread in the history of house decoration. The modern decorative plasterer still uses tools and techniques which were developed by his peers centuries ago.

Plaster itself is an ancient material – the Egyptians used it to finish walls and prepare them for painting over 4000 years ago. The Greeks and Romans took it a stage further, developing *stucco duro* (stucco), a highly refined plaster mixed with marble dust that could be shaped, cut or polished to a silky smooth finish.

Plaster is a mixture of lime, sand and water, but in the past, a variety of materials, such as eggs, beer, cowhair and rye dough, were also added to encourage or retard setting, to strengthen it, or to give a particular finish. Plaster of Paris was introduced into Britain in the mid-13th century and is a soft, white quick-setting plaster made from the mineral gypsum. It was initially used to cover stonework on the interior walls of fine houses.

RELIEF PARGETTING
(above) The spectacular example of relief pargetting pictured here – in Clare, Suffolk – would have been modelled by the craftsman by hand, with only the help of a trowel. The lines of the design were marked out first in rope on the previous layer of plaster.

PLASTER CRAFTSMEN
(left) Craftsmen hard at work at the premises of J. Jackson & Sons, in the early 1900s. The company was founded in 1780 by Jackson and Robert Adam, the famous architect. Although much of the earlier decorative plasterwork was done in situ, as the craft became more sophisticated, plaster mouldings began to be mass produced in workshops.

end tooth was longer than the others and could be stuck into the plaster and the comb turned so that the other teeth cut concentric circles in the plaster. Using this, the pargetter could build up complex designs.

Patterns which were used frequently and repeated across a panel were carved into moulds of deal or oak which were then pressed into the plaster to make the patterns. These durable moulds might last through several generations, accounting for local continuity of styles.

This type of pargetting, where impressing or scratching was used to produce abstract, recessed patterns, was called incised pargetting. It was common up to the 17th century and was usually painted over with several layers of whitewash.

Later, changes in taste and developments in building materials helped to bring about a revolution in the plasterer's art. The art of fine modelling in plaster and stucco had been successfully revived in Renaissance Italy and its effects were soon felt in England. In 1501 Henry VII granted a royal charter to the Worshipful Company of Plasterers, giving the craft recognition and status.

The full impact of the Italian influence was first felt with the commissioning of Nonsuch Palace in 1538. This extraordinary building was decorated with life-size figures moulded by a team of craftsmen under the direction of a Florentine, Toto del Nunziata.

Stucco was used to make high relief models and was a perfect medium for the highly decorative Baroque and Rococo styles. Architects and designers of the great houses tended to use foreign – mainly Italian – craftsmen, who were

PARGETTING

Decorative plasterwork is not confined to the inside of houses. As long as 400 years ago, the external plaster panels of timber-framed houses were inscribed or given moulded designs, by a technique called pargetting.

The walls of timber-framed houses were made by infilling the gaps between the main timber supports with wattle. Vertical hazel stakes were sprung into pre-cut slots in the horizontal timbers and pliable hazel withies, osiers, reeds or oak laths were woven between them. Both sides of these wattle woven panels were then smothered with daub – made from clay mixed with chopped hair, straw, hay, or dung. Once dry, the daub was covered by a coat of plaster to make the building weatherproof and draughtproof. Although the original purpose of plastering was strictly functional, it was quickly realized that the plaster panels had decorative possibilities. At first, the pargetter made simple designs – herringbone and freehand swirls and spirals – by marking the surface of freshly applied plaster with the end of a trowel or with a pointed stick.

Later, more specialized tools were developed including a five-toothed pargetting comb (perhaps the most widely used pargetting tool). One

CLASSICAL INTERIOR
(left) Internal decorative plasterwork reached a peak of perfection and intricacy during the last half of the 18th century with the designs of the Adam brothers. The example here of Robert Adam's work is at Kenwood House, Highgate, London. His Classical interiors set the style of the era and were distinguished by their complicated arrangement of circles, ovals, octagons and lozenge shapes, and their glowing colours.

The fine detail of Adam's plasterwork was achieved by dressing his ceilings with gesso – a mixture of plaster, glue and linseed oil.

Some pargetters attempted representations of birds, animals and people. These would be modelled in situ on the drying plaster using hand and knife and were more notable for their charm and vigour than for their realism. But the effect of a whole building covered in high relief figures, like the Sun Inn at Saffron Walden or Sparrow's House in Ipswich, was very impressive.

More usually, though, the decoration was simpler and set in recessed panels. The pargetter applied three coats of plaster to create the wall panels. The first two – the render and the float – were done in a coarse plaster, while the third coat was of finer plaster. To make the recessed panels a template panel was fixed to the wall

after the second coat and the finishing coat applied around it. When the panel was removed, the decorated and recessed panel was exposed.

The same hair-lime plaster, and basically the same techniques, were used internally for modelling ceilings, friezes and overmantels. In country districts the same workman undertook both types of work.

TOOLS AND MOULDS

The basic tools of the plasterer are trowels and floats for applying the plaster, and chisels, knives and prickers for shaping and finishing it. The decorative plasterer would also have a selection of moulds, templates and dies.

Moulds were made either from beeswax or, more commonly, from plaster which was sealed with a varnish before being used. In use, the mould was filled with a semi-liquid plaster, perhaps mixed, or 'gauged', with plaster of Paris

organized into guilds and schools to carry out the work.

At first the patterns they moulded on to ceilings and walls were simple. Later designs became more ornate and complex and the resulting mouldings were a riot of portrait medallions, fruit, flowers, shells and scrolls. This highly ornate fashion persisted in great houses until the early 17th century. In the countryside it took longer to take hold.

In the early 17th century ornamental plasterwork appeared in the grander farm and merchant houses. Mouldings and decoration on ceilings and beams, decorative friezes and elaborate overmantels, particularly in Devon and Somerset, were quite common. The next century saw simplified forms used in almost every new cottage and town house. The fashion for moulded cornices (decorative plasterwork in the angle between the ceiling and the walls), ceiling bosses and skirtings persisted until Edwardian times.

Fashions in internal relief moulding were paralleled in external pargetting. A shortage of building timber in the 16th century meant that new houses had to be built with less timber. To disguise this, laths were nailed across the timbers and the whole was plastered over, providing larger areas for the pargetter to work on. Developments in the plaster mix – the addition of chopped cowhair to three parts lime and two parts fine washed sand – produced a thicker and tougher plaster and meant that the pargetter could also model in high relief.

HUMBLE DWELLINGS
(above) Pargetting was not only confined to decorating grand houses. In Suffolk and Essex especially, humbler dwellings were also decorated. The method used here was incised pargetting – wooden moulds were pressed into the wet plaster to make the pattern.

A MODERN PARGETTER...
(above right) Plaster mixtures today may be faster setting and easier to work with than the original lime plasters, but the skill involved is just as great as ever.

...AND HIS TOOLS
(right) The tools used in pargetting and decorative plasterwork have changed little over the years. These were made by the craftsman above for his own use. In the past, moulds and presses were often passed down from father to son for many generations.

to speed setting. It was then immediately placed in position, and wedged there so that the back of the cast adhered to the background. Once set, the mould could be removed for cleaning and reuse. Whole designs were built up in this way, with the fine detail added later. The plasterer achieved deeper relief by undercutting the plaster with a knife.

Robert Adam, whose classical interiors set the style for the last half of the 18th century had his ceilings dressed with *gesso*, a mixture of plaster, glue and linseed oil, that could be cut to give a very fine detail.

Mouldings – the ribs on the ceilings, cornices, the edges of panels, and so on – were run in situ using a running mould. This was a piece of iron or zinc, with a profile cut into one or two of its edges, held rigid in a right-angled wooden frame.

RUNNING A CORNICE

To run a cornice, the plasterer first built up a core of plaster in the angle of the wall and ceiling joint that was just a little smaller than the desired moulding. When this was set a thick, creamy plaster was trowelled liberally over the area to be run. A timber batten called a running rule was fixed close to the top of the wall to steady the running mould, which was then passed smoothly back and forth along the whole length of the run of plaster until the basic shape of the moulding was formed. It was then allowed to dry. Finally, a wetter mix was applied to the roughly shaped moulding and repeated several times for a smooth finish.

Circular mouldings for ceiling centrepieces were produced in a similar way, but instead of running the template along a running rule, it was fitted to the end of a tool called a gigstick

HIGH-RELIEF STUCCO
(left) A detail from a series of panels depicting the five senses in the long gallery at Blickling Hall, Norfolk. By the early 17th century, when this panel was made, stucco – a mixture of plaster and marble dust – was being used to make high relief designs.

ELIZABETHAN FRIEZE
(below) A hunting scene from a plaster frieze at Hardwick Hall, Derbyshire. Made for the Countess of Shrewsbury around 1595, it is a fine example of Elizabethan plasterwork.

TIMBER FRAME
Early pargetting was used to decorate the panels between the structural members of timber framed houses. The space between timbers was first infilled with upright hazel stakes, interwoven with pliable withies. This was then covered with a mixture of clay and straw. Because clay is inclined to shrink or expand, according to the weather, it was protected with several coats of plaster. At first this plasterwork was plain, but later intricate patterns were added.

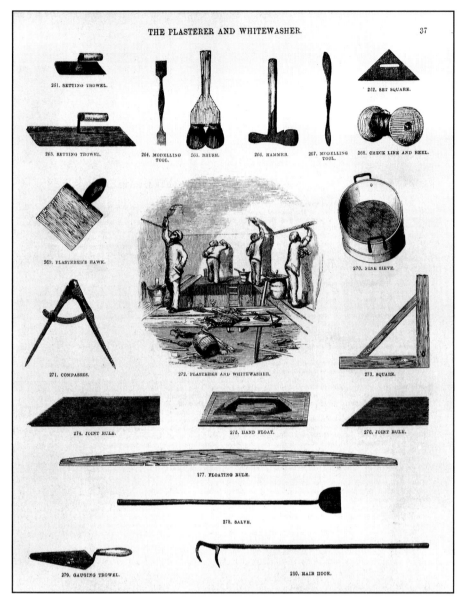

THE PLASTERER AND WHITEWASHER. 37

261. SETTING TROWEL.

263. SETTING TROWEL. 264. MODELLING TOOL. 265. BRUSH. 266. HAMMER. 267. MODELLING TOOL. 268. CHECK LINE AND REEL.

269. PLASTERER'S HAWK. 270. FINE SIEVE.

271. COMPASSES. 272. PLASTERER AND WHITEWASHER. 273. SQUARE.

274. JOINT RULE. 275. HAND FLOAT. 276. JOINT RULE.

277. FLOATING RULE.

278. SALVE.

279. GAUGING TROWEL. 280. HAIR HOOK.

which was fixed into the plaster and pivoted to describe a circle.

In Elizabethan times most mouldings were narrow and plain; in the early 1600s they became wider, with flat surfaces that could take further decoration; small bench-cast foliage and scroll work would be fixed with plaster of Paris or modelled by hand then stamped with a die for surface detail, such as veining on the leaves.

The Classical revival of the late 18th century was the golden age of plastering. – the age of the Adam brothers. But fashions changed, and so did methods and materials.

NEW MATERIAL

Around 1850 moulds of gelatine were gradually introduced. Being pliable, these could be used to cast work with fine, high-relief detail already moulded in. Once the plaster had set, the mould, which had been sealed with alum and oiled, could simply be peeled away. Slow setting lime plaster, which required long and careful preparation, was gradually abandoned in favour of plaster of Paris and other patented preparations that were more fire-resistant and easier to work, even though these gave a less crisp surface for modelling.

Instead of being cast on site in solid plaster, and fixed with the same material, decorations came to be mass produced in workshops using a mix of plaster of Paris and grass fibre. This was built up over a wooden armature (frame) and the completed piece could be nailed into place.

Today, in the restoration of old ceilings, gelatine is packed around the original mouldings, allowed to set and then peeled away to prove a mould for new castings. Very few completely new ceilings requiring elaborate plaster work are now commissioned in Britain. However, many of the old established firms have a thriving export business, especially to the Middle East.

TOOLS OF THE TRADE
(above) An illustration from an 1860 book of trade tools. Many of the plastering tools will be familiar to the DIY enthusiast today.

MODERN WORKSHOP
(right) An intricate plaster cornice being produced at a modern workshop. In the past, decorative plasterwork was usually done on site, but nowadays it is all pre-formed in workshops then transported and screwed or wired in place.

Although there are few new decorative ceilings being commissioned in Britain, craftsmen are still in great demand to undertake the delicate renovation work on existing old ceilings.

Masters of Wood

Wood was once used to make everything, from kitchen utensils to church decorations, and the traditional skills of the woodcarver were vital to the community.

An afternoon stroll led the famous 17th-century diarist, John Evelyn, past a broken-down thatched cottage in Deptford – then in London's countryside. As he walked by, he glanced through the half-open door and glimpsed a young craftsman working on a wonderful piece of carving in wood. The young craftsman's name was Grinling Gibbons, and the carving was *The Crucifixion*, one of the great masterpieces of the carver's art, now in London's Victoria and Albert Museum. Recognizing Gibbons' unique talent, Evelyn helped him gain the patronage of King Charles II, and Gibbons went on to produce exquisite carvings for St Paul's Cathedral, Hampton Court and many other noble buildings.

Gibbons was exceptional, not only in talent, but also in that his name is remembered at all. Woodcarvers, though long among the most respected of craftsmen, were never people to sign their work, and the names of the thousands of woodcarvers who have graced churches and buildings great and small with their work through the centuries are long forgotten. Even one of this century's leading carvers, Robert Thompson of Yorkshire, used a mouse rather than his name as his trademark. Often only the carvings themselves remain to bear witness to the long and distinguished tradition of this still flourishing craft.

A BASIC MATERIAL

Easily worked, readily available, yet tough and durable, wood has been one of Man's basic materials for thousands of years, and wood must have been cut, rubbed and shaped to make crude tools from the Stone Age and even earlier. As Man discovered iron and bronze and other metals, though, he learned to shape wood finely into utensils for everyday living: carved wooden bowls, spoons, tubs and other utensils have been excavated from lake villages near Glastonbury, Somerset, dating back 2000 years.

All but the wealthiest people continued to use carved wood for their basic eating utensils right up until the Middle Ages and beyond. Most of these carved utensils must have been simple and workmanlike, and woodcarvers probably had few opportunities to display their artistry.

Indeed, much wood carving was probably done by ordinary people who fashioned anything from bowls and spoons to furniture and ploughshares for their own use. Nevertheless, there are clear signs of the skill of early woodcarvers in the beautiful wooden boats of the Norse invaders and in early churches (though the oldest surviving example of church carving, at South Cerney in Gloucestershire, dates back only to the 12th century).

It was in the Middle Ages, however, that ornamental carving really flourished, for the

IN THE WORKSHOP *(below) In the Middle Ages, one kind of woodcarving, incised carving, was practised by joiners, rather than specialist carvers. Carved mouldings were used by the joiner to conceal and disguise joints in the furniture or panelling. Shown here is an example of linenfold panelling.*

thousands of churches that were built in the 14th and 15th centuries provided a wealth of opportunities for carvers to show their skill in decoration. While they continued to fashion all the items demanded for everyday life, the medieval craftsmen began to create the beautiful rood-screens, bench-ends and other church furnishings that made the Middle Ages the golden age of carving.

Like stonemasons, medieval woodcarvers worked in teams or 'schools', under a master carver – many woodcarvers were actually stonemasons as well. Some of the carvings they made are simple scrollwork. Some are religious icons. But the medieval church was also a kind of storehouse for the unconscious fantasies of the age and the carvers, like the stonemasons too, chiselled and gouged all kinds of weird and wonderful creatures – severed heads, hermaphrodites, and one legged 'sciapods' who use their limbs as 'sunshades'.

Church patronage, however, which had brought the woodcarvers so much work in the Middle Ages, came to an abrupt halt with the Reformation in England in the 16th century, and with it ended the greatest age of English carving.

At first, it seemed that the new-rich, such as prosperous merchants, yeoman farmers, founders of new-landed dynasties, and the king himself, would replace the traditional ecclesiastical patrons of the arts. John Ripley, for instance, became court carver at the court of

GRINLING GIBBONS
The work of the 17th-century woodcarver, Grinling Gibbons, is regarded as the peak of English woodcarving. These virtuoso pieces (below and below right) are typical of his work.

REVIVING THE TRADITION *(above) The workshops of Robert Thompson Craftsmen Ltd in Kilburn, Yorkshire, have kept alive the finest traditions of English woodcarving. At the beginning of this century, the founder of the company, Robert Thompson (later known as the Mouseman of Yorkshire because of his trademark), was inspired by the wonderful carvings in Ripon cathedral to try and revive the medieval master's skills, and set up the company with this aim. The workshops have maintained the same high standard, producing beautiful work like this carved eagle.*

Henry VIII, and made some exquisite carvings for Henry at Whitehall Palace; it was, of course, aristocratic royal patronage that allowed Grinling Gibbons to create his masterpieces in the following century.

With Gibbons, English ornamental carving reached a brief but glorious zenith, and the carving that the workshops of Gibbons and his contemporaries created is unrivalled in its beauty and skill. But nearly all the work they undertook was in grand projects for the great country houses and cathedrals, and the number of workshops involved was very small. And when the money, and the fashion, for house carving began to fade towards the end of the 17th century, the workshops began to close down. The 18th-century writer R. Campbell commented, 'The carving now used is but the outlines of the art; it consists only in some unmeaning scroll, or a bad representation of some fruit and flowers.'

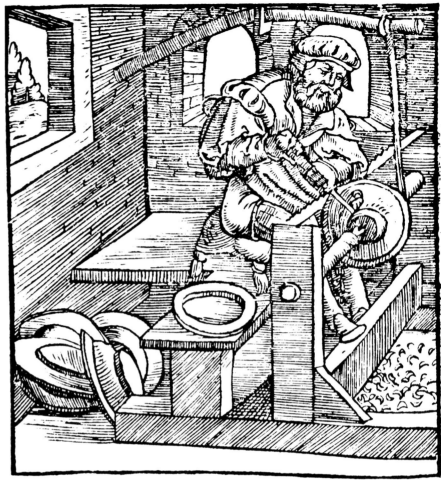

Beyond this limited circle of fine carvers, the status of the woodcarver had continued to decline, since there were few sources of patronage. One contemporary complained that the typical rural journeyman carver was 'an ignorant besotted fellow who would work hard and drink hard… (but) never saved a shilling'.

But there was a growing demand for carved chairs and other furniture, and Thomas Sheraton and Chippendale were just the most famous of the many men trained as both carver and cabinet maker in the 18th century. The shops of Georgian London were full of beautifully carved furniture, 'so richly laid out that they look more like palaces'. And for all the famous craftsmen attached to the city shops, there were hundreds of 'small masters' and journeymen slaving away in back streets and villages to carve and gild furniture for the rising middle classes.

Down in the dockyards, too, there was still plenty of work for the carver in creating the elaborate figureheads and friezes for the great ships that sailed to Britain's colonial empire across the sea. And in the country, carvers competed in the coachyards for work on a basis similar to modern car assembly lines.

Within half a century, though, the demand for the skills of the woodcarver had all but disappeared, as the giant hand of industrialization stretched across the land in the Victorian era. Ornate wooden coaches gave way to the iron of the railroads; the great wooden ships

WOOD TURNING

Many objects made by woodcarvers, like the 17th-century standing cup and cover shown left, are made by turning on a lathe (above). Lathes have been used for thousands of years, and the pole-lathe, with its long springy pole and treadle, was used by the ancient Egyptians.

were superseded by the steel-hulled leviathans pioneered by Isambard Kingdom Brunel; and earthenware and metal replaced wood in the kitchen. Even the dark furniture that filled the Victorian parlours was largely mass-produced.

Only in recent years have the skills of the woodcarver begun to be appreciated once more, as craftsmen like Robert Thompson of Kilburn in Yorkshire and his family try to recapture some of the lost medieval art.

THE CARVER'S CRAFT

There are three basic techniques involved in the craft of woodcarving. In 'incised carving', the design, usually a very simple one, is cut into the wood; in 'relief carving', the ground is cut away to leave the design standing proud; and carving

THE CARVER'S TOOLS
(above) The two basic tools used by woodcarvers are the straight-edged chisel and the curved-edge gouge, but each craftsman builds up a vast collection of each of these, differing usually in width. The tools used today differ from those of the past only in their sharpness and durability.

PAST GLORIES
(left and below) The detail of a bench end from Jesus College Chapel and the delicate tracery of the choir stalls of Peterborough Cathedral, show some of the range and beauty of medieval woodcarving.

'in the round' is effectively sculpting in wood.

In each type of carving, the woodcarver's first task is to select a suitable wood. Oak has long been a favourite with English woodcarvers. Skilled Saxon and medieval woodcarvers, it seems, worked amost exclusively in oak, which is one of the hardest of British timbers. Oak is popularly supposed to be a dark-coloured wood, but the darkening is simply the effect of ageing, weathering and various treatments.

Lime wood, a soft white timber, has also been popular through the ages with British woodcarvers – mainly because it is easily worked, responding readily to the carver's tools. Grinling Gibbons did most of his best work in lime wood. But walnut and box-wood, used extensively in Southern Europe for carving, are little used in Britain, simply because of the limited availability of the wood.

Other woods favoured by carvers include holly, cherry, apple, pear, whitebeam, cedar, maple, yew, laburnum and sycamore. Most of them are rather scarce and available only in small blocks. Yew is very hard and strong and almost as heavy as oak. Cherry is highly decorative. Pear, with a very fine texture which makes it somewhat difficult to work, was much used by Grinling Gibbons – like apple, it is very durable. Maple is excellent for turning and was once much in demand for making the drinking vessels known as mazers.

Most woods can be cut from the tree all the year round – except elm which dries out and splits if felled in early spring or summer. But they need to be well seasoned if they are not to crack. Today, craftsmen season oak for about five years, allowing a year for each inch in thickness of the baulk of wood.

During seasoning, the wood is stacked on a floor, while supports along the length prevent the timber from warping and allow the air to circulate. The stack is usually roofed to protect it from rain and sun. Kiln-drying is now a well developed and satisfactory technique, but master woodcarvers prefer to dry their own.

WORKING THE WOOD

To keep the wood rigid as he works, the woodcarver uses a variety of clamps and vices, which he may have to reinforce with blocks and wedges, to fix the wood exactly into position. An old favourite is the shaping-horse, which the carver sits astride as he shapes the wood. Its movable centre rungs, controlled by the carver's feet, leave his hands completely free.

Numerous tools are used to shape the wood, including no fewer than eight major types of saw. Some, made for cutting along the grain, are known as 'rip-saws'; others for cutting across the grain are called 'cross-saws'. Planes, basically tools for shaping and smoothing

169

WOODCARVING
TODAY
(right) Craftsmen from Robert Thompson Craftsmen Ltd, at work in their studio, display animal figures carved in the round in various stages of progress. The firm is now run by the founders' grandsons, and is renowned for its hand-made domestic, church and boardroom furniture, as well as for its carvings, all made from English oak.

surfaces, also come in many varieties.

Before he begins to cut into or carve the wood, the woodcarver has to mark out the wood from technical drawings or rough sketches. To do this he uses a marking knife, a set-square, gauges and, for round work, compasses and

adjustable calipers. To tap his carving tools he uses a mallet or hammer. Beech seems to have been the standard wood for mallet heads.

There are about 80 different types of cutting tools though most carvers use 20 to 30, mainly gouges and chisels, graded according to width. The heaviest tools are used for the preliminary cutting and the smaller ones for the more refined work. In medieval times, 'parting-tools', gouges which cut a V-shaped incision, were widely used by English woodcarvers, whose work was noted for its bold high-relief, in contrast to the low-relief of southern European craftsmen.

Finishing techniques used by generations of woodcarvers include wax polishing, French polishing, oil polishing, sanding and staining. But some of the most gifted craftsmen prefer to add nothing to their tooled work, leaving a plain natural wood surface. But if the wood is not to be finished, the cuts need to be direct and clean and made with very sharp tools.

Close examination of medieval woodcarving in churches, sometimes reveals that the surface of this lovely matured wood was once covered with paint. A conventional reaction was to deplore such treatment, which was regarded as near-vandalism, but more recently progressive artists have been experimenting in painted carvings and have produced impressive new effects.

Today, wood is recognized as a medium for creative art and more and more people are taking up carving as a hobby. They appreciate that in wood they are working with a living material capable of receiving and reflecting their own energy and inspiration, and at the same time offering them a chance to reveal the hidden beauties of its natural shape and colour.

FIGUREHEAD CARVING
(left) From the 16th to the 18th century, many woodcarvers displayed their skill in creating the magnificent figureheads that graced Britain's vast fleet of wooden ships. With the coming of the iron ships, however, the demand for figureheads slowly died out. This vast carving, being restored by Norman Gaches of the Isle of Wight, is on the world's first iron clad battleship, HMS Warrior, launched in 1860, and acquired in 1979 for the Ships' Preservation Trust.

Bodging

Deep in the beechwoods of Buckinghamshire, many years ago, itinerant craftsmen set up camp in primitive brushwood shelters. These were the 'bodgers' – men who, with their expert skills and simple but ingenious tools, shaped the legs of Windsor chairs.

The beech tree has long been of great use to man. Fast-growing, straight and tall, the timber has a great advantage over many other woods in that it can be split and worked while still unseasoned. The straight close grain resists warping, making it a favourite raw material for makers of furniture, and of numerous other objects requiring the strength offered by wood that splits along the grain. In the past, beechwood objects were in everyday use and included tent-pegs, clothes pegs, shoemakers' lasts, tool handles, piano frames, chopping blocks, frames for coaches, automobiles and aircraft – in fact, an endless list.

Beech, 'the Buckinghamshire weed', grows so profusely in that county that it may even have given it its name, from the Anglo-Saxon word for beech, *boc*. Consequently, the Chiltern beechwoods, particularly around High Wycombe, became the centre of one of the first mass-production rural industries, that of chair-making.

THE BODGERS

Chair-making was a fore-runner of the 'line-assembly' methods developed by later industrialists, though the production 'line' in this case stretched from primitive encampments out in the woods to workshops many miles away. Each stage of the production process was carried out by a different craftsman. The men who were responsible for the first stage, from buying the stands of timber to turning the chair-legs and stretchers, were known as 'bodgers'. Highly skilled craftsmen, these bodgers were in no way associated with the shoddy workmanship that the modern use of the word implies.

The chairs they helped to produce were of the type now called 'Windsor' chairs – distinguished from all other types of chair by the fact that the sub-frame of legs and stretchers (struts) fits into the underside of the seat, and is separate from the upper frame of back and arms, which fits into the seat's top.

The bodger's job began with buying the beech trees – still standing in the woods – at auction. The livelihoods of several men and their families for up to a year could depend on a

successful purchase. Once the trees were bought, the bodgers lost no time in setting up their temporary camps next to the beech stand in the woods.

Some bodgers worked for themselves; others were employed by middle-men such as farmers. Their tools were few. Felling axes began the job, dropping the great trees and lopping off the branches. The felled timber was then cut into lengths called 'butts' with a long two-handled cross-cut saw. Bodgers usually worked in pairs. With a man on either end, the cross-cut saw cut on both strokes. The butts were cut just a little longer than the legs or stretchers of the chair

THE FRAMER'S WORKSHOP
Chairs begun by the bodger were finished by the framer. In contrast to the bodger, he used many tools: to smooth and polish the wood, to bore the holes for legs and stretchers, to cut patterns in the 'splats', and, finally, to glue them all together.

to be made, usually between 16 and 18 inches.

Once cut, the butts were ready for splitting. Because of its straight grain, beech splits readily and predictably, maintaining the full strength of the original branch or trunk. The butts were placed upright on a low block, usually an upturned log, and split into sections called billets by means of wedges and a heavy, short-handled mallet called a beetle.

The billets were finally turned on a lathe to make them smooth and round, but they were first roughly pre-shaped with a side-axe into five- or eight-sided sections, tapering at either end. This part of the process was highly skilful,

and the bodger worked at speed, roughing out the shapes on a high chopping block, and setting the billets aside in stacks for the next stage, which was a further, finer shaping. This was carried out on a low bench called a shave-horse. The bodger sat astride the 'horse' with the billet wedged in a foot-operated clamp. This left his hands free to use the draw-knife, a narrow steel blade fitted with a right-angled handle at both ends.

The smooth and tapering billet was now ready for final shaping on the pole-lathe. This was a home-made device of ancient design going back at least to the Iron Age. It was the

THE BODGER'S CAMP
Thatched with brushwood and with a thick wall of wood-shavings to keep out the draughts, the bodger's hut could be erected in a day. It provided shelter for himself and for his pole-lathe, on which he turned the chair legs. Finished legs were stored in the tall bristling 'hedgehog' stack to season.

bodger's most complex tool, and was set up inside the hovel where it could be used in all weathers. The pole-lathe was operated by a spring treadle beneath the lathe bed. The treadle was originally made from lengths of saplings lashed together. Treadling caused the work to rotate backwards and forwards, and the bodger used his turning chisels to shape the wood while it was rotating towards him.

The stretchers of a Windsor chair are normally plain, but the legs carry a variety of ornamentation applied at the pole-lathe stage. The most common 'bobbin' decoration was achieved with a V-shaped chisel. On average the turning of one chair leg took two minutes, and as the legs came off the lathe, smooth and bright, they were sawn to the exact length required, and stacked in a special shape – known as a 'hedgehog' – that allowed the air to circulate through the stack and dry them out. Eventually chair legs were factory-made but 'village' legs were always considered superior. The reason for this was that legs made by bodgers were always split from the butt, whereas factory legs were often machine-sawn. The splitting axe would always reveal faults and knots, and the billets could be rejected, but sawn billets concealed faults, which only came to light after the chair had been used.

Once made and seasoned, the bodger's wares were sold to a local 'chair-master' by the gross, but the success of the industry did not make the bodgers wealthy. A gross consisted of 144 chair legs plus the 108 stretchers which would eventually help to make up 36 chairs – there were four legs and three stretchers to each chair – but as late as World War 1 the bodgers

BODGING TOOLS
The pole-lathe was a primitive but efficient tool on which a skilled bodger could turn a chair leg in less than two minutes.

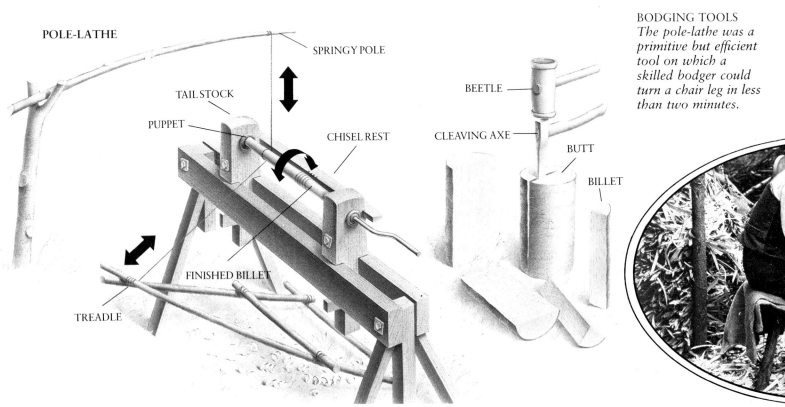

POLE-LATHE

SPRINGY POLE

TAIL STOCK

PUPPET

CHISEL REST

FINISHED BILLET

TREADLE

BEETLE

CLEAVING AXE

BUTT

BILLET

were earning as little as five shillings a gross. Unscrupulous purchasers in furniture towns such as High Wycombe made a point of swindling the bodgers by refusing to buy a load until the price had come down to rock bottom, knowing full well that the bodger could not afford to cart his products back to the woods. To produce two and a half gross, bringing in a subsistence wage of twelve shillings and sixpence a week, the bodger had to work a twelve-hour day for five and a half days. With the legs and stretchers sold, the bodger's involvement in chair-making was at an end, and the remaining processes were completed by other hands.

The seat of a Windsor chair was made from a thick piece of planking, sometimes of beech, but more often of elm. The planks were cut from a log by pit-sawyers, who often worked out in the woods like the bodgers. These planks were supplied to the chair-master's workshop where the 'benchman', who carried out the indoor saw-work, cut them into chair seats. The seats were then carved out and shaped by the 'bottomers', using an adze to sculpt the seat into the elegant saddle form that is one of the hallmarks of the Windsor chair.

The 'bender' was responsible for making the

WINDSOR CHAIRS
Once considered fit only for cottages or the servants' quarters, traditional Windsor chairs are now valuable antiques.

bowed backs typical of some patterns. These were originally split stakes of yew or ash, squared with a draw-knife and then steeped in boiling water or steam until they were pliable enough to be bent around pegs set in the low, bending table. Later, in mass-produced chairs, the cleft stakes were replaced by sawn strips of planking.

The final assembly of the chair was the task of the 'framer', but first he had to smooth and finish all the components coming to him from elsewhere. He might also cut and decorate the splat – the central vertical strut found in many Windsors. Then he bored the numerous holes that would eventually house the tapered ends of legs, stretchers, rails and other parts that comprised the finished chair. Finally the chairs would be sent to a specialist polisher, or they would be stained in the workshop.

By the mid-1800s chair-making had become a flourishing industry. In High Wycombe one factory alone had a weekly output of 9000 chairs.

Old traditions die hard; though the chairs are no longer transported all over the country piled high on horse-and steam-drawn wagons, High Wycombe is still an important centre for making chairs and furniture in general.

As mechanization replaced the old craftsmen, bringing higher profits and lower prices, the chairs lost a great deal of their character. Grained strength gave way to machined symmetry. As late as 1958 chair parts were still being horse-delivered by one Buckinghamshire carrier, but the bodgers had all but disappeared. By 1938 there were only nine Chiltern bodgers left. Now there are none.

SHAVE-HORSE
The roughly hewn billets were further shaved with a draw-knife before being turned on the pole-lathe. The 'horse' was the bench on which the craftsman sat.

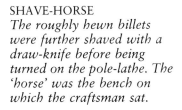

The Country Potter

Using the same materials and tools as his ancient predecessors, the country potter supplied the village community with functional wares like loaf-pots, cream-pans, salt 'kits' and brewing-jars.

Anyone who watches a skilled potter 'throwing' a pot on the wheel, cannot fail to be fascinated and almost mesmerized by the way the spinning lump of clay swells and grows in his hands. This magical experience links us closely to the craftsmen of the past, who used the same methods to produce the everyday wares of long ago.

Little changes in the world of the potter. His materials, tools and equipment remain much the same as they were when the first pottery was made some 9000 years ago. Then, pottery was simple earthenware – raw clay – and was most likely sun-dried, so it could only be used for cereals and dry goods. Soon, however, the ancient potters learned how to bake their pots in a hole in the ground, under a pyre of wood, so that their earthenware vessels became hard enough to withstand the heat of the domestic cooking fire.

Such early pots would not have been made on a wheel but by more primitive methods; by lining a basket with clay, by coiling (building with long rolls of clay), by hollowing and pinching a ball of clay into shape, or by 'slabbing' (rolling lumps of clay flat like pastry, then sticking them together with wet clay) – all techniques which are practised to this day.

No one knows precisely when the potter's wheel was invented, but wheel-made pottery dates back to the middle bronze age (2000-1500 BC). Its invention revolutionized the potter's work, making it much easier to produce good quality domestic ware. The basic potter's wheel is a flat circular slab of wood, metal or stone, mounted to revolve on a vertical axis. It is generally

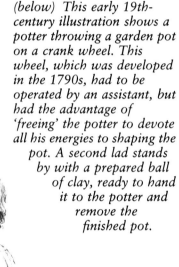

TEAM WORK
(below) This early 19th-century illustration shows a potter throwing a garden pot on a crank wheel. This wheel, which was developed in the 1790s, had to be operated by an assistant, but had the advantage of 'freeing' the potter to devote all his energies to shaping the pot. A second lad stands by with a prepared ball of clay, ready to hand it to the potter and remove the finished pot.

worked by a heavy flywheel which accumulates energy and ensures a good steady movement.

Rural potteries in England were usually family-run affairs and often sited near a local clay pit and water supply. Potters would often farm as well, however, since pottery was not very profitable.

THE RAW MATERIAL

The quality of a rural potter's work depended very much on where he lived. If his local material was fireclay – a poor quality clay – he would only have been able to make coarse pottery, for example, but if he was lucky enough to live in a red sandstone area such as Staffordshire or Nottinghamshire, he would have had access to the rich red-brown earthenware clay of that area. Communications were poor and clay was not exported from one part of the country to another.

Clay is a plastic material – formed from a fine mix of the compounds 'silica' and 'alumina' with water – which hardens into a brittle but virtually indestructible material on firing. Chemical changes take place at about 500°C which preclude a return to the plastic state. Clays vary enormously in character: some are easily manipulated and others are almost unworkable. There are two main types: primary and secondary. Primary clays, which are found in the place where they were originally formed, are not easy to work, but include the whitest and purest of clays, Kaolin, which is the essential ingredient of bone china and porcelain. Secondary clays are those that have been shifted from their natural position – by the action of wind or water, for example. As they have been ground down already, they are very malleable and

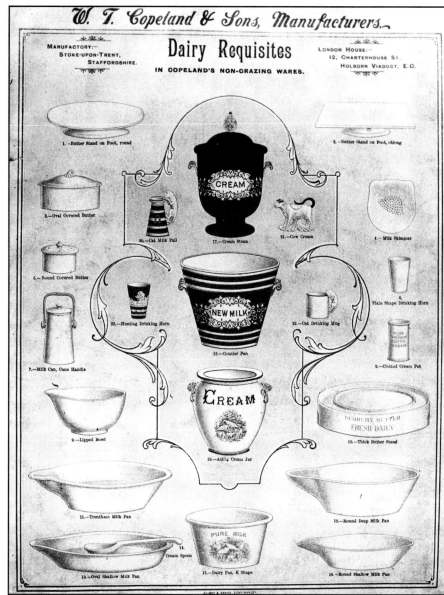

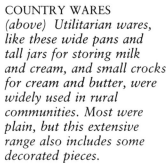

COUNTRY WARES
(above) Utilitarian wares, like these wide pans and tall jars for storing milk and cream, and small crocks for cream and butter, were widely used in rural communities. Most were plain, but this extensive range also includes some decorated pieces.

TRAMPLED UNDERFOOT
(right) Clay in its raw state lacks plasticity and has to be treated before throwing. In the past, it was 'tempered' by being trampled underfoot on the clay-house floor. Boys worked in bare feet, removing any little stones or bits of grit from the mixture.

surplus water evaporated. The clay was then taken out and spread on the floor, where barefoot boys would trample it into a thick dough-like consistency, picking out any stones their feet found. Some village potters had a pug mill which performed this process mechanically.

Now the clay was 'wedged' by hand, that is, cut into slices which were slammed down one on top of the other, to remove all the air bubbles (which cause pottery to explode in the kiln). Then it was weighed and formed into balls by a 'clay boy', who wedged the clay again, keeping the balls the correct shape all the time. If the thrower had any complaints about the size or condition of the balls, it was quite usual for him to throw them at the clay boy, one by one!

The potter's tools have always been simple and every potter would have had his favourites, probably those he had fashioned himself. He

THE GREAT-WHEEL
(above) The 'great-wheel' was introduced in the 18th century and was used right up until the introduction of steam power. A labourer or apprentice slowly turned a large pulley wheel, from which a cord ran under a set of rollers to a small pulley on the shaft of the potter's wheel. When making a large pot, the thrower would shout out various speeds to the turner: fast for centring; medium for raising; and slow for the finishing stages. For smaller ware, however, the turner was expected to maintain a steady rate.

SLIP DECORATION
(above right) The two-handled posset pot was used for drinking 'posset' – a hot milk drink flavoured with ale, wine and spices and sweetened with honey or treacle. This Staffordshire pot of 1696 is trailed in decorative slips – coloured liquid clays.

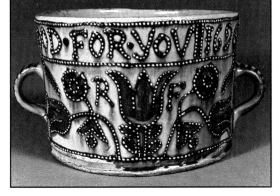

include 'common' earthenware, terra cotta, and stoneware clays. Depending on the type of clay, it will vitrify (that is, turn into a glassy substance) at temperatures of between 1030° and 1450°C. Stoneware and porcelain require particularly high firing temperatures, making them too costly for the average rural potter.

Having found a supply of clay and negotiated for the right to use it, the potter dug it out of the ground from the quarry, river bank or cutting. The clay was usually allowed to weather, to break it up, then flung into pits and well watered for 24 hours and finally put into a blunger – a vat with angled, horizontally revolving paddles, which agitated the clay until it broke down to a creamy consistency. This was run off through a sieve into a sunpan where the

might have had wooden ribs to shape his pots into a specific form; a height gauge, which was probably a stick of wood stuck into a ball of clay at the side of the wheel, so that it leaned forward to almost touch the rim of the pot; a pair of wooden calipers to measure pot lids or neck widths; turning tools to trim the bases of pots; a 'roulette', a small roller into which a pattern was cut, used to impress ornamental borders; and brushes and slip trailers for 'slip' work (decorating the pot with liquid clay). Two essentials were a length of wire, its ends attached to two small toggles of wood, for slicing pots off the wheel, and a sharp, pointed knife.

To make his pots, the potter took a prepared ball of clay and slapped it down firmly on the centre of the wheel. Dipping his hands in water, he centred the moist clay, pressing it down as it spun round until it was exactly at the centre of the wheel – an action easier to describe than perform. Only if the clay is perfectly centred will the pot be symmetrical.

The pot was shaped by forming a hollow in

UP-DRAUGHT KILNS
(far right) These kilns, with their towering chimneys, are 'up-draught' types: the heat from the fires rises through the pots and escapes out of the top. The design of the kiln depended on a number of factors, such as the type of fuel available (coal or wood), and the scale of the country potter's production.

LITTLETHORPE POTTERY
(below) This 1913 photograph shows the staff of Littlethorpe Pottery, Ripon. The boy on the extreme left is George Curtis, who was still producing 'bigware' in 1986.

THROWING A POT
(right) This sequence of photographs illustrates four of the stages involved in 'throwing' a pot. First of all, the potter slaps a ball of clay on to the centre of the wheel as it spins anticlockwise; then, with lubricated hands, perfectly centres the clay and slowly draws it upwards. Next, shaping begins by hollowing out the centre of the clay and drawing up the rim of the pot, using the fingers of one hand inside the pot and the fingers of the other hand outside. When the pot has reached its full height, it is brought to the required finish and then removed with a length of taut wire.

the centre of the ball of clay with the thumbs, drawing up the clay between the fingers of one hand inside the pot and the fingers of the other outside the pot. Every potter had his own style of throwing and used slightly different parts of hand and fingers for this part of the process.

When doing repetitive work (and most of the village potter's work was repetitive), the master potter was assisted by a 'passer' or 'taker off' – usually a young apprentice – whose job it was not only to keep a good supply of clay balls but to remove the pots from the wheel and place them on drying boards.

When the pots were leather hard, that is, firm enough to handle but not brittle enough to break, they had to be dried. In fine weather, they could be dried outside in the sun, but in winter drying was more of a problem. In small family potteries, the owner doubtless brought the pots into the kitchen to dry.

Before the pots were fired, the country potter sometimes applied a simple decoration on the still slightly damp clay: this could be done by incising, by burnishing, by making patterns with coloured liquid slip, by applying patterns of oxide (a compound of an element with oxygen), by scratching, impressing with a patterned roller, carving or piercing, to name just a few of the many techniques.

All pots have to be fired in a kiln to turn the clay into a hard ceramic material. This is a crucial stage of the potter's craft and requires

the finest judgement: if the firing is too fast the water in the pots will expand and shatter them, if the temperature is too low the ware will emerge too soft to use, with an unmelted glaze, and if it is too high the pots will warp.

Very early kilns were basically just bonfires, on which pots were stacked and covered with broken pots to retain heat, or the pots were wrapped in straw and covered with sand. Then the pots were enclosed in bricks covered in mud to achieve a higher temperature. In the simplest kiln, a fire is lit under the floor, the heat rises through the pots and comes out at the top, the kiln acting like a fat chimney. This is known as

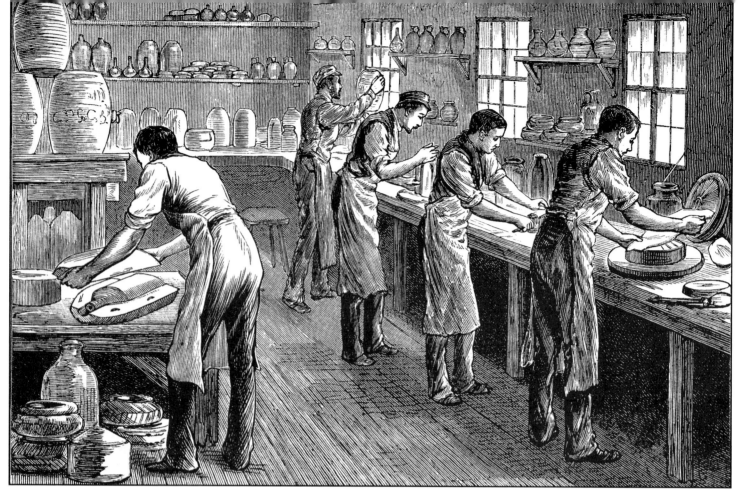

an 'up-draught' kiln. In a 'down-draught' kiln, hot gases from the fire rise first to the roof, then are drawn down through the stacked pots and out into a side chimney through the kiln floor.

The potter's first step is to ensure that the kiln is stacked properly. Unglazed pots can be stacked one on top of the other, but glazed wares have to be separated to stop the molten glaze from gluing them to each other. Large, coarsely thrown vessels called 'saggars' were often used to hold the pots. Alternatively, the pots stood on little pellets of clay called 'bobbs', or small bits of broken pottery to separate them. As firing the kiln was expensive, the main concern was to get as many pots as possible safely in and out of the kiln. The potter's livelihood, and that of his family and employees, was staked on these firings and it is not surprising to find that one potter committed suicide when a huge kiln load was ruined.

At Littlethorpe Pottery, the oldest country pottery still in existence, the ware used to be gradually exposed to a temperature of 400° Centigrade, while cool air was let in through small vents in each of the seven fireplaces. After 12 hours, the vents were blocked with bricks and the fires stoked to reach their fiercest temperature. Before the days when temperature was measured, the heat was judged to be right when the potter singed his eyebrows as he peered through the spy holes, or by the colour of the flames. Small test pieces would be fished out on long iron poles, and if they were right the fireplaces were immediately bricked up and the kiln left to cool.

Flower pots, porous water jugs, butter dishes and the like could be left unglazed, but other ware needed glazing, which means covering a pot with a chemical coating which, when fired, produces a hard, impervious glass-like surface (the 'gloss'). There are four basic types of glaze; feldspathic, lead, tin and salt. All are transparent except tin, which is opaque.

English rural potters produced a variety of utilitarian wares: bread crocks with glazed insides, wide cream-making pans, bread mixing bowls, butter pots, pie dishes, stewpots, fish dishes, ham pans, salt 'kits' (containers), meat dishes, chamber pots, and jelly moulds, to name just a few of them. They were sold mostly at local fairs and markets, since the potter had little time for travel. Soon, however, pot-sellers emerged, travelling round the countryside in horse-drawn carts tempting customers with free gifts of whistles and toys for the children.

Faced with increasing competition from the industrial potteries, whose white cast and moulded pottery was much more popular than traditional red wares, the rural potter was forced to adapt to change as the 19th century progressed. He began to produce pots for the garden and for the Victorian conservatory, and branched out into industry, making pipes, tiles and even sanitary ware.

Nevertheless, the village potter has survived through wars and recessions to emerge triumphant as the artist potter, the art college graduate living in the country and making a good living with his studio pots, and tourist gifts as well as attractive domestic ware. Working on a small, intimate scale, the studio potter has kept alive the traditions of the country potter, realizing that good craftsmanship will always be recognized and appreciated.

A HIVE OF INDUSTRY
(above) The industrial potteries helped bring about the decline of the small country pottery, by cheaply mass-producing every type of domestic ware: storage jars, salt 'kits' and cooking pots and pans, as well as garden crocks and fine white table ware. The Staffordshire Potteries developed the craft of press-moulding, using moulds made from biscuit-fired clay. Flatware and holloware pressers draped or forced the plastic clay into the moulds, a process which required much less skill and energy than throwing. The filled moulds were then carted off by young lads to the drying stove.

The Glass-maker's Craft

By melting natural materials like sand (silica) and seaweed potash, the early glass-makers created an extraordinary substance which could be blown into bubbles and manipulated into almost any shape.

The sand dunes and the glass-house seem at first to have little in common, but the glass-works relies on the dunes for its raw materials: the sand forms the main raw ingredient of the glass, and the ashes of washed-up seaweed provide vital potash to make the molten glass more pliable and workable. Small amounts of lime are also added to combat fragility, but usually impurities in the other components satisfy this requirement. Only one more element is vital – fuel to create the intense heat that is needed to melt the ingredients together.

Surprisingly, though, glass also occurs naturally as a result of volcanic activity, and primitive people fashioned knives and arrow-heads from these deposits. Early vessels were even made by carving solid blocks of glass. However, the properties that make glass such a versatile material can only really be exploited when the glass is warmed and thus made plastic. The first people to accomplish this were the Egyptians: 3500 years ago they learned that a core of sand could be coated with layers of molten glass to form a vessel. Once the coating cooled, the sand filling could be easily removed.

This technique was extremely crude and limited, and use of glass only really took off when the Syrians had the idea of blowing air

REVIVING ANCIENT SKILLS
With the end of the Roman occupation of Britain, the glass-blowing skills that produced this fine mould-blown bottle (right) were forgotten. But by the Middle Ages glass-making had been revived in Britain as a small-scale craft, with individuals setting up works in forest clearings (far right) – where there was a ready supply of wood for fuel.

INDUSTRIAL PRODUCTION
By the 17th century, glass-making had become an industrial art. This atmospheric painting, dating from the early 19th century, shows the casting of plate glass at the Ravenhead Works, St Helens (left).

into hot glass to make thin-walled bubbles, around 200 years BC. The Romans learned glass-working from the Syrians, and soon became masters, spreading the technology to all the nations they colonized. In Britain, they established a glass-works in south-west Lancashire. However, with the Roman withdrawal, glass-making in Europe declined rapidly and until 1200 AD, few surviving examples of European glass came anywhere near the quality of Roman and Egyptian glass.

Fortunately, the Crusades took Europeans back to the Middle East where, in the tenth century, glass-making was enjoying a revival.

Venice soon became the glass-making centre of Europe and Venetian craftsmen introduced many new processes that revolutionized glass manufacture. One of these, of particular importance, was the addition of a decolourizer such as manganese, or 'glass-maker's soap', to remove the characteristic green tint caused by iron impurities in the raw materials. The resultant glass was neutral in colour (though actually grey or pale brown, not water white) and was known as 'cristallo'.

Meanwhile, in medieval Britain, glass-making had reached nothing like the same level of sophistication. The industry was concentrated in the south of the country, principally in Surrey and Sussex, where there was ample timber for fuel, and deposits of sand as a raw material. The chief centre was Chiddingford in Surrey, where land was granted to Laurence the glass-maker in 1226.

Laurence was probably making 'forest glass'

– a crude, green product, made from sand and the ashes of seaweed or bracken. He would have used techniques and tools that a modern craft glass-maker would instantly recognize, but his ingredients were gathered exclusively from the countryside. Sand came either from the dunes or from locally-dug deposits – it had to be washed clean before use. The seaweed or bracken likewise was carefully gathered, then dried in the sun and burned. Washing the ashes produced an impure potash solution, and evaporation concentrated this into powder form.

This work all took place in forest clearings: Laurence would have built his glass-works at the top of a small hillock in the woods to provide a better draught for the furnace. The glass-house was a simple structure, either made entirely of timber, or else a lean-to with a single masonry wall. The furnace probably resembled a beehive, and measured some 15 feet across. It was arranged in tiers, with a single hole for tending the fire near the base, and a couple of shelves inside, running round the perimeter.

CULLET AND FRIT

The temperature within the furnace was not uniform, and this suited the glass-maker's needs: the raw ingredients, including chunks of waste glass from earlier melts (called 'cullet') were first heated gently on the upper shelf to drive off any moisture, then stirred together for a day and night to create a homogenous mixture called the 'frit'. When cool, the sandy mixture was broken into lumps and transferred to pre-heated fireclay pots, which were waiting on the lower shelf of the furnace.

Once the ingredients had melted together, Laurence dipped the end of the blowing-iron (a metal tube about five feet long) into the crucible. Turning the blowing-iron, he gathered a lump of glass, resting the tube on an iron bracket or 'tower' to take the weight. Removing the lump from the furnace, Laurence rolled it back and forth along the 'marver' – a polished iron or marble block. Rolling formed the glass into a

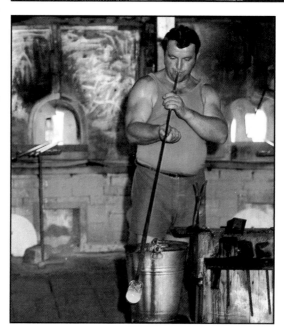

'paraison' – a shape that would expand when air was blown through the blowing-iron.

Blowing simply created bubbles of glass like goldfish bowls, not useful objects, so Laurence shaped his vessels using other tools. The most important was the pontil, a solid iron rod, which stuck to the hot glass when pressed against it, and was removed by touching the hot glass with a damp rod, then 'cracking off' – striking the pontil so that the work dropped gently from the end.

Laurence was probably fairly inexpert in the use of this primitive tool: his drinking glasses lacked flat bases, so wine once poured had to be drunk at one draught. His descendants, though,

BLOWING-IRON
(above left) Using a blowing-iron is hot and heavy work. Throughout the shaping process, the glass has to be reheated in the furnace.

CROWN GLASS
(above) Window glass used to be made by spreading the bubble of molten glass into a circular sheet with the pontil. A bull's eye or 'crown' remained in the middle (where the pontil had been attached).

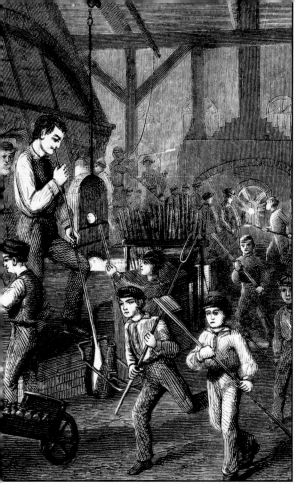

malleable. Once the work was complete, Laurence cracked it off and carried it to an annealing furnace to cool slowly – rapid cooling created stresses that would shatter the glass.

Glass manufacture in the Weald proceeded in this way for generations: the descendants of Laurence the glass-maker continued developing his skills, and began working in teams called 'chairs', which sped up production. A chair consisted of three men and a boy. The master glass-blower was called the gaffer or workman, and he had two assistants – the servitor, who was the first assistant, and a footmaker or second assistant, who made feet for stemmed glasses. The boy's job was to take finished goods away for annealing.

The early history of the industry is sketchy, but we do know that the glass-works in this area supplied glass for Westminster Abbey in 1240, and that the descendants of Laurence sold white glass for chapels in Windsor and Westminster in the 1350s. By the middle of the 16th century, however, the manufacture of window glass in Britain had all but died out.

The 16th century, however, was a time of great change. European glass-makers began to visit Britain, and the continental influence spread

CRYSTAL CLEAR
(far left) For centuries, Venetian craftsmen dominated the glass-making field. As well as refining the skills and introducing many new processes, they invented 'cristallo' – a delicate, colourless glass, which used quartz pebbles, soda ash, barilla, and manganese as a decolourizer. This beautiful crystal vase, produced on the island of Murano (the traditional stronghold of Venetian glass manufacture), dates from the 1800s.

GLASS-HOUSE CONE
The early industrial glass-houses were cone-shaped, with the various departments arranged around the central furnace. This print of the interior of Aston Flint Glass-Works (left) shows the hive of industry inside.

SPECIAL TOOLS
(right) The glass-maker employed a variety of specially shaped tools (in addition to the blowing-iron and pontil). The hot glass was seized in pincers (4) and cut with steel shears (1). Parrot-nosed shears (2) were used to cut rods of glass. Pucellas (3) were the main shaping tools, while the battle-dore (11) was used to flatten the glass. The footboard (9) was a special device for forming the feet of wine glasses.

handled the pontil with greater dexterity, joining the pieces of glass together with it, twisting and pressing the glass bubble to vary the shape of the work. The only other tools the early glass-makers used were shears of various sizes for cutting the soft glass, and 'pucellas' – looking like giant sugar tongs – which served to widen the bowls of drinking glasses, and for other shaping work.

Some of the shaping did not require tools at all. Laurence could use gravity and centrifugal force to mould the glowing lump on the pontil or the blowing-iron. Throughout the shaping process, the glass was constantly returned to the mouth of the furnace for re-heating to keep it

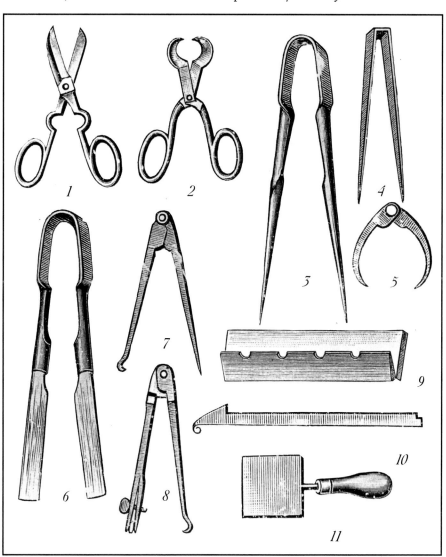

rapidly through the country, bringing with it new techniques, and the foreign names which we now use to describe many of the glass-making tools. The foreigners, however, were not popular. Despite considerable pressure, they were reluctant to share their skills with local people, and they depleted the forests that had covered much of the country.

The foreign glass-makers competed for wood with the ship-building and iron-founding industries, and eventually, in 1615, James I called a halt to the felling, forcing the industry to turn to coal as a fuel. The effect on glass-making was dramatic, transforming an essentially rural craft into an urban industry.

THE VENETIAN INFLUENCE

Glass-making had undergone a transformation, in technique and geography, and in style, too. The traditional forest glass was a heavy, thick material that did not lend itself to fine work or highly elaborate decoration. The Venetian/cristallo influence, on the other hand, was felt most strongly in London. When glass-making moved to the coal producing areas the two styles gradually intermingled, bringing a home-grown feel to the Venetian-influenced product.

Other changes in style were more organized. In the 17th century, a major influence on the appearance of British glass was the Worshipful Company of Glass Sellers. The company exerted a somewhat utilitarian pressure on the producers, demanding plain, strong glass that was suitable for everyday use. To this end, the company commissioned George Ravencroft to experiment with materials and techniques, and his discovery of tough transparent lead crystal, imposed a new, less extravagant style.

The major influence on style in the 18th century was taxation. Glass was taxed by weight in 1745, so drinking vessels became smaller. To compensate for the consequent loss of grandeur, glass-makers reverted to more elaborate decoration, often using white glass which was not taxed until 1777.

The evolution of modern glass-making owes less to stylistic changes than to the development of mass-production techniques. The most important of these was the regenerative furnace, which recycled flue gases to greatly speed melting. Glass flowed through the furnace continuously, and could therefore be made much more cheaply than in a craft-based batch-by-batch kiln.

New techniques of moulding revolutionized the manufacture of glass vessels: standard-shaped bottle bodies had been made for centuries by blowing glass into iron moulds, but to complete the bottle, the neck had to be made separately and welded into place. The split-mould, introduced in 1821, allowed glass-workers to blow the whole bottle in one piece and by 1800 there were 15 glass-works in Bristol alone, making millions of bottles for wine and beer.

The cost of window glass was slashed by the industrialization of broad-glass manufacture. Broad glass had been introduced from Europe in the 16th century, and was made by supporting the bubble of glass with the pontil at a point directly opposite the blowing-iron. In this way, the glass-maker created a cylinder which he could cut open and lay flat to form a sheet. The most spectacular use of cylinder glass was the Crystal Palace, built to house the Great Exhibition of 1851. To highlight their virtuoso performance, the Victorian builders constructed this extraordinary glass-house around a fully grown tree; the irony of this feat would probably not have been lost on Laurence the glass-maker, who spent his life working in a glass-house enclosed by trees.

CRYSTAL PALACE
(above) Crystal Palace, the home of the Great Exhibition of 1851, was a triumph for Britain's glass manufacturers. The prestigious contract was won by Chance Brothers of Smethwick, who used the traditional cylinder method to produce a staggering total of 299,655 panes. The team of glass-makers blew the molten glass into cylindrical forms and then, by swinging the bubbles in deep trenches to elongate them, managed to create cylinders of up to six feet long. The cylinders were then split open and flattened out in a kiln to form sheets of window glass.

The Silversmith

Gold and copper were the first metals to be worked by man, but the working of the dazzling white silver came third. However, its beauty and rarity have always made it precious and valuable.

Official recognition of Christianity by the Edict of Milan in 313 AD was of prime importance to silversmithing in Europe. Supplying silver ornaments and decorations to churches was the main task for the next 1000 years for goldsmiths: for no one worked exclusively with silver, and it was the goldsmith who made silverware as well.

As early as the eight and ninth centuries, English silver was much in demand. Numerous papal orders for English plate have been found. The reputation of English silversmiths rested with two historic figures – Alfred the Great (849-901), who improved the standard of the English craft by importing talented silversmiths from abroad, and the monk Dunstan (924-988), a silversmith who later became Archbishop of Canterbury.

Many monks combined a craft with their religious devotion and Dunstan not only produced chalices, crosses and censers for his own abbey, he also worked on secular plate, little of which survives. After his death, Dunstan was canonized and became the patron, protector and founder of the goldsmiths of London and all England. His effigy in silver gilt has long graced Goldsmiths' Hall in London and the date mark added to London hallmarks in 1478 is changed every year on May 19, St Dunstan's Day.

As well as being melted down to be recast, historic silverware in England has suffered the vicissitudes of history. Much ecclesiastical silver fell into the hands of the Norman conquerors. More was given towards the ransom of Richard I. And in 1338, Edward III borrowed vast amounts from cathedrals and abbeys, claiming that he would replace everything he melted down. Henry VIII also financed his excesses on ecclesiastical silver and the dissolution of the monasteries helped supply his needs.

Henry VIII was also an avid collector of new pieces at a time when the use of silver was expanding rapidly. Production in the silver mines of Germany and Central Europe expanded throughout the 16th century and the Spanish began to bring increasing quantities of silver and gold from South America. The nobility and wealthy followed the trend, spending lavishly on plate and jewels. Cardinal Wolsey had a collection that matched the King's, with

FIT FOR A KING
A sign of luxury and cultured heritage, opulent silverware at a formal, lavish banquet (above right) would have been obligatory, while the main table may have had the more prestigious gold plate.

MONKEY SALT
Fanciful salt cellars, such as the Monkey Salt (left) of New College, Oxford, were considered a mark of status.

enough gold and silver to fill 30 wagons.

One of the most important early domestic uses of silver was in making salt-cellars. These were often massive and made splendid centrepieces on the lord of the manor's table. Etiquette manuals of the fifth and sixth centuries seated guests in order of rank, relative to the salt. An inventory of the plate of Edward 1II in the 14th century listed several hundred salts of various types. Sir John Fastolf had eight large salts – one weighing five ounces (142g) – and the Earl of Oxford had 16 large and four small salts.

Medieval inventories and wills describe salts of intriguing shapes and decoration. Animals were popular, especially elephants, lions, dogs

CLASSICAL INSTRUMENTS
The silversmith's tools (shown, right, along with the silver parts of a flute) have remained virtually unchanged since silver was first worked.

closer to France, many Huguenot craftsmen came to the Channel Islands, bolstering the native craft there.

With the Restoration in 1660, the reinstated nobility craved renewed luxury, but this fashion was emulated right down the social strata. The use of silver tankards, basins, cups and bowls, even by innkeepers, encouraged an outburst of robberies which brought in an act forbidding the public exposure to all wrought plate except spoons.

SILVER FURNITURE

At this time, the wine cistern became fashionable, making huge table centrepieces. The Duke of Rutland had one which was 4 feet (1.2m) long, 18 inches (450cm) high and 3000 ounces (85kg) in weight. And in the Hermitage Museum in Leningrad, there is a wine cistern made in London in 1734, which is 5½ feet (1.6m) long and weighs 8000 ounces (228kg). Even furniture was made from silver: an inventory of royal silver made in 1721 lists a suite of furniture made of solid silver weighing 7306 ounces (207kg).

Today, because of its abundance, silver is worth only around one twentieth the price of gold; the bulk of silver production goes into the

PATRON SAINT OF SILVERSMITHS
The archbishop of Canterbury, St Dunstan (left, tweeking a cheeky devil with a pair of tongs for working silver) was himself a silversmith.

and dragons. Oxford's New College's Monkey Salt, made around 1500, has a decorated circular pedestal, with feet in the shape of wild men seated on cushions. On top of that is a larger cushion with a chimpanzee on it who holds a gilt-mounted crystal bowl of salt on its head.

Small spoons were also made in silver and began to find their way into the home in the 14th century. Edward VI had a fine selection of spoons, some of which were a New Year's gift to the sovereign. Spoons were a coveted status symbol and this was the origin of the expression 'born with a silver spoon in one's mouth'.

In the 16th century, the silver tankard with a hinged cover, thumbpiece and scrolled handle came in from Germany and Scandinavia. Tazzas – or silver standing dishes – were also made, along with the silver candlestick.

During the Civil War (1642-52) much ecclesiastical and secular silver was melted down again, but the Restoration and the influx of Huguenot craftsmen from France heralded a new and prolific period of production. Being

A RARE SURVIVOR
The principal use of silver in Europe was initially for church ornaments. Though most of the ecclesiastical silver in Britain was melted down, this fine Celtic chalice (above) remains a testament to the superb craftsmanship of old.

manufacture of electronic components and the making of photographic film. Some small countries still use it in their coinage, but in the early 1970s, the United States became the last major nation to eliminate silver from all its coins.

Silver occurs in a number of naturally occurring minerals often in association with deposits of gold, lead, copper and zinc. The Romans separated silver from the ore by heating it in a furnace. This method was used through the Middle

A REFINED ART
Most silver is extracted from silver compounds. The Romans refined the metal in a furnace – a method used through the Middle Ages (left).

The craft of the silversmith is an ancient one and little has changed over the centuries. Most of the techniques involved had been discovered by 2000 BC. And most of the tools found in, say, an 18th-century silversmith's workshop would be largely familiar to both a modern craftsman and a medieval one.

The typical silversmith's shop was run by a master goldsmith who had served his seven-year apprenticeship in the trade and had been accepted as a freeman by the Goldsmiths' Company. He would be assisted by a journeyman, another qualified goldsmith who did not have his own shop, and one or two apprentices.

The silversmith would make a drawing of the article he was going to make – say a coffee pot – and show it to the potential customer. They would discuss the amount of silver to be used and the price. The customer would often hand over old silver which would be weighed and the value deducted from the final bill.

The old silver was melted down with any new silver required. The resulting ingot was hammered into a pancake shape with a heavy two-handed sledgehammer. Lighter hammers were used to beat the silver out into a thinner sheet. This tiresome business was taken over by the rolling machine in the late 18th century.

Ages. But in the 19th century, the 'patio' process was perfected in Mexico. This involved grinding silver ore with salts, water and mercury to make an amalgam. The mercury was later driven off by heating, leaving the pure metal. The mercury was recovered by condensation.

These days, most silver is produced as a by-product in the refining of other metals. But pure ores are processed by the cyanide process. The ore is pulverized and leached with dilute sodium cyanide. The resulting sodium-silver complexes are soluble in water. The mixture is washed and filtered and the solids discarded. The precious metal is then precipitated from the solution with fine zinc dust, filtered off, melted down and cast into bars.

Pure silver is too soft for normal use so it is alloyed with another metal to make it harder. Copper is the alloying metal used in making silverware. English silver adhered to the sterling standard for over seven centuries. The proportions of sterling silver are 11 ounces 2 pennyweight (345g) of silver to 18 pennyweights (28g) of copper in troy weight, where 1 troy ounce is equal to 20 pennyweights. This is a ratio of 12.33 to 1.

HALLMARKS OF QUALITY
Read from left to right are the marks of the maker; the quality: sterling silver; the assay office: London; and the date: 1979.

SHAPING THE SILVER
Once the flat piece of silver is worked into its basic shape, more detailed shaping can take place. On a spinning lathe (left) the silver object is fitted on to a wooden mould and while both rotate, the silver is forced into shape against the mould with a tool held in place against a stop. Alternatively, the silver can be 'raised' or 'domed' (below) by being beaten with a 'raising' or 'doming' hammer against a wooden former.

directly on to the solder, which melts and flows around the joint. Surplus solder is polished off on a lathe.

The spout is cast in two halves that must be soldered together before it is fixed to the pot. The strainer is made by drilling a flat piece of silver with a bow drill. The lid is attached by a hinge made from tubular silver, which is soldered on to the body along with sockets for the handle. This would usually be made from wood as a silver handle would become too hot to handle once the pot was filled.

DECORATION

The pot is then decorated. This can be done in a variety of different ways but basically, decoration falls into three different groups – applied, where the decoration is made separately and soldered on, as in filigree work; embossed, where the body metal is hammered or punched; and engraved, where the metal is cut or incised.

The silversmith puts the maker's punch mark on it, even if it had been made entirely by the

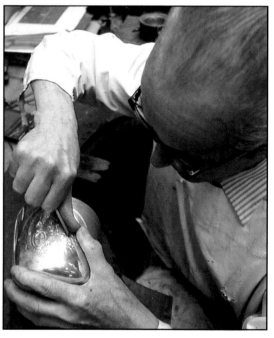

When the goldsmith judged that the sheet had been beaten out to the right thickness, he marked out the shape of the object on it – perhaps a circle for the body of a coffee pot – with a pair of heavy dividers. The excess plate was trimmed off with heavy shears. The circular sheet was then held over a concave section of wood and hammered into a dish shape over the hole.

Constant hammering makes the metal brittle and liable to crack. This is overcome by annealing. The silver is placed in a pan and heated until it glows a dull cherry red, then quenched in a tub of water. The annealing process lets the crystal structure adjust to the new shape of the metal and makes it soft and workable again. It is repeated several times during the working.

The 'sinking' of the circle of silver is followed by 'raising'. The dish-shaped circle is worked over a cast-iron 'raising stake'. The edge, which will become the rim of the pot, is hammered down to thicken it. And the pot is raised on a series of thinner stakes until it reaches its final shape. This process takes about a day.

The hammer-marked surface is then flattened smooth enough to polish with a heavy flat-faced hammer. While the master is raising the body, the journeyman would be casting the spout, handle sockets, foot and the finial for the lid. These are soldered to the body.

The cast pieces are clamped to the body with silver wire, then small pieces of silver alloyed with brass – or these days, zinc – are placed along the join. The silversmith uses a long thin pipe to blow the flame from a charcoal lamp

FILIGREE, EMBOSSED AND ENGRAVED SILVER
Among the many ways of decorating a silver object are filigree and embossing (above) and engraving (right). In filigree, fine silver wires are coiled or twisted into patterns and attached to each other and the base by soldering. Embossing involves hammering or punching the plate, usually with a symmetrical pattern. In engraving, a design first marked on the silver by a sharp tool is then scored deeper with a 'graver' which makes the pattern glitter as it catches the light; a shallower and broader cut can be made with a 'scorper'.

journeyman. At the assay office, minute scrapings are taken from each part of the pot and analysed to make sure that the whole pot is made to sterling silver standard. If it is, the piece is 'touched' with the hallmarks of the assay office and returned to the maker. The item is then polished using ground pumice and oil, then, less abrasive Tripoli powder or Trent sand, and finally, jeweller's rouge.

Little has changed in silversmithing over the years. These days electricity is used to power rollers and lathe, rather than steam or man power. But most of the silversmith's craft is still done by hand. However, recent fluctuations in the price of silver, due to speculation in the metal markets, have inflicted on the traditional silversmith many of the problems of the modern day world.

Traditional Cheesemaking

Names such as Double Gloucester, Sage Derby and Devon Garland reflect a tradition of cheesemaking in Britain dating back to the days when each farm made its own distinctive cheese.

Milk and its products have been staple foods for thousands of years. Long before the Romans arrived in Britain, cows, sheep and goats were exploited for their milk. Much of the milk was drunk, either fresh, or sour (since keeping it cool was difficult) and eaten as curds and whey. Liquid milk did not stay fresh long though, particularly in summer, while in winter milk output often fell as the grazing deteriorated. But long ago it was discovered that by turning milk into a solid cheese, with a heavy salting, this valuable food could be stored for long periods. And a successful cheesemaking season might make all the difference between starvation and survival in the hard winter months when food was short.

In the early days, cheese was made simply by allowing milk to sour and draining the resulting curds in rush baskets or perforated pottery containers. The curds were then salted and sometimes smoked or flavoured with herbs. Later it was discovered that by adding the juices of certain plants such as thistles, teasel flowers and ladies' bedstraw (known later as the cheese-rennet herb), the milk could be made to curdle more readily.

RENNET

These soft curd cheeses did not keep well, however. It was the providential discovery of a new coagulent, rennet – an enzyme produced by the stomach-lining, or vell, of a young milk-fed animal – which enabled cheesemakers to produce hard cheeses which would last, and even improve with age. Thereafter, cheesemakers kept bits of the stomach lining of sheep in the dairy ready to dip in the milk.

In medieval times, cheesemaking was a local and domestic affair and cheesemakers used whatever milk came to hand, whether it be cow's, ewe's or goat's. Cheese provided for the needs of the manorial household and was often used as payment in kind to peasants and shepherds.

Some of the finest cheeses of the time were those made by the monks of the Yorkshire dales, who had come over to Britain in the wake of the Norman conquest, bringing with them long-established French cheesemaking traditions. They made moist, mellow ewe's milk cheeses which blued in the cool cellars of abbeys like Jervaulx and Bolton. They taught their cheesemaking skills to their tenants who, after the Dissolution of the Monasteries (1530s), carried on the tradition to make what later became famous as Wensleydale, Swaledale and Cotherstone cheeses.

By the end of the 16th century, cows had become the main milch animals, displacing sheep and goats in most areas. At the same time, major social and economic changes were taking place in the countryside. The redistribution of land after the Dissolution led to an increasing number of smaller farms, and the yeoman farmer and small landowner became the driving force behind an

DAIRY MAIDS
(left) The dairy was traditionally the province of women, and it was dairy maids who made both cheese and butter – besides looking after the ducks and chickens and helping with the winnowing of the wheat after the harvest. For centuries, they made cheese using skills learned at their mothers' knees rather than following any standardized recipes and so cheese would vary enormously from farm to farm.

expanding rural economy. Towns, too, were growing, providing a hungry market for the farmer's produce. Increasing numbers of livestock produced huge numbers of cheeses which were often bought from the farmer by merchants called cheese factors at specialist cheese fairs like Weyhill, Yarm, Bridgewater and St Giles Hill, and resold to distant clients in London and the larger towns.

CHEDDAR

It was around this time that William Camden wrote of Cheddar's 'excellent, prodigious cheeses...of delicate taste'; and Elizabeth I's attendant, Lord Paulet, complained of Cheddars being 'of such great esteem at court that they are bespoken before they are made'. Cheddars

provided an early example of co-operative cheese-making; the milk of several small farms would be pooled to make one huge cheese, as much as 120lb in weight if the yield were large enough.

Cheshire cheese had been known since Roman times, and was the only cheese mentioned by name in the Domesday Book, but in the 16th and 17th centuries its reputation was enhanced by accolades from many writers including Samuel Pepys and Dr Johnson.

Other cheese fared less well. Kentish cheese was said to be 'the very worst'. Essex cheese was 'harder than the devil'. Of Suffolk cheese it was said that 'hunger will break through stone walls and anything except a Suffolk cheese.' Another flinty cheese was Dorset's Blue Vinney, which according to the locals made an

CHEESES OF BRITAIN
(above) The tradition of cheesemaking in Britain has produced a rich variety of cheeses, each with its own distinctive texture and flavour – smooth, strongly-flavoured farmhouse Cheddars, creamy Double Gloucesters, piquant Stiltons and many more besides. These traditional farmhouse cheeses look – and taste – completely different from the factory-made cheeses that go by the same name. For connoisseurs, there is simply no comparison.

THE CHEESE 'MAKE' ROOM
*Many large farms had
a room next to the milking
parlour specially set aside
for making cheese. Although
methods varied considerably
from place to place, typically
the milk would be heated
over a fire in a huge copper
vat before rennet was
added to separate it into
curds and whey. Once the
whey had been drained off,
the curds would be broken
up and placed in a mould
for pressing – here, the
dairy boy is piling rocks
onto a board to press the
cheese. It could then be
salted and left to mature
in cool, humid conditions.
The whole process was less
than hygienic, but it was
often the very 'impurities'
which gave a cheese its
character.*

admirable substitute for a cartwheel.

By the end of the 18th century, most of the classic British regional cheeses had become established: Cheshire, Cheddar, the Dales cheeses, Leicester, Lancashire and Gloucester – which came in two varieties, single, made from one 'meal' or milking, and double, made from two. Single Gloucester was eaten locally by the farmer and his hands, especially at haymaking time (it was often known as Hay cheese), but the fame of the rich, creamy Double Gloucester spread far and wide, and bargeloads of cheeses, at that time painted brilliant red, were despatched from Lechlade to London.

Scotland and Wales also had their cheeses. Crowdie, Scottish 'porridge' cheese, was an ancient type of curd cheese. Then there was oatmeal-encrusted Caboc, first made in the 15th century by a daughter of Macdonald of the Isles, and Orkney cheese, served at funeral feasts. The most celebrated was Dunlop, a more recent invention of Barbara Gilmour, an Ayrshire farmer's wife. In Wales there was, among others, a soft creamy square cheese from Newport and later, in the early 1800s, Caerphilly, whose moist freshness made it a particular favourite of miners working at the coal-face.

Improved methods of animal husbandry contributed a great deal to the higher quality of cheesemaking in the 18th century. Whereas in earlier times animals had usually been milked in the fields and the milk brought back in open pails to the dairy, it became the practice to bring the animals in for milking, thus reducing the chance of contamination. New and cleaner dairies were built of stone with tiled or flagged floors on the north side of the farmhouse, so that they could be kept cool, sweet and fresh.

Later, in the 19th century, came the pioneering work of men like Joseph Harding, who studied his wife's methods of making Cheddar and published his observations with missionary zeal. He recommended strict hygiene and temperature control in the dairy and better training for cheesemakers. Generations of cheesemakers, including his own seven daughters, heeded his advice. The methods Harding advocated became, with some later refinements, the accepted procedure for making farmhouse Cheddar until well into the 20th century, and similar principles were applied to other cheeses.

CHEESEMAKING

To make cheese, milk is curdled, then the curds are cut, drained, moulded, pressed and left to ripen; but there can be variations at each stage which account for the huge range of cheese which can be made.

The composition of the milk itself is a vital consideration. As well as the type of animal, cow, ewe or goat, the precise breed is important: Shorthorns were always the breed favoured by traditional Cheddar makers. Double Gloucester was made (some still is) from the milk of the ancient and beautiful breed of Gloucester cattle, now almost extinct. Caerphilly was made from the milk of Herefords. The pasturage was also important. Lush flowery pastures produced better cheeses – summer milk was best of all. Then again, the milk could come from the morning milking, or the richer evening milking or a mixture of the two, and it could be skimmed or partly skimmed or unskimmed. Each cheese type depended on a unique combination of all these factors.

Fresh milk was put straight in a large copper vat or, more recently, a double-walled tank. There it was warmed up and allowed to 'ripen' awhile ready for coagulation. Dyes might be added to colour the cheese at this stage – originally a variety of herbs, but since the 18th century a South American vegetable dye called annatto.

After five hours or so, the rennet was added, and in due course – about 1-1½ hours – the milk became one huge mass of junket. For hard cheeses, the mixture was then scalded to firm up the curd particles and the whey was drained off through a tap or bailed out by hand. Hard cheeses like Cheddar were drained much more than crumbly, 'open' cheeses like Caerphilly and Wensleydale. Finally, the curds were allowed to settle on the bottom of the vat, where they were turned and pressed into matted blocks, or 'pitched' and then sliced. To ensure the drained curds were thoroughly smooth and even they were torn to pieces by hand or, later, milled. Then they were packed into drum or wheel-shaped moulds, or 'chessets', of varying sizes, made either of elm wood or metal.

The next stage for many cheeses was the pressing. First the dairymaid hand-pressed the cheese, bearing down with all her weight. For this task, it was a great advantage to be broad and buxom – hence the old Cheshire saying, 'the bigger the dairymaid the better the cheese'. Then the cheese was wrapped, remoulded and placed in the cheese press for anything from a few hours to several days. They had to be turned each day, and regularly dipped in brine or rubbed with salt. Later it became more usual to dry-salt the curds either before or after they were milled, though the makers of some cheese, such as Caerphilly, continue to brine their cheeses even today.

Finally, the cheeses were taken to the cheese store, where they were ripened for a few months to several years. It was during this stage that the blueing of a blue-veined cheese would take

CHEESE PRESS
For good hard cheese, the curds had to be properly pressed in the mould. Originally, cheesemakers simply piled on heavy stones. But from the end of the 18th century they began to use iron screw presses.

TRADITIONAL CHEESEMAKING
Like a growing band of farmers nowadays, the Martells of Dymock prefer to make their cheese, Single Gloucester, in the old way. Their only concession to modern technology is the big aluminium lined vat with motorized blades to break up the curds. The sequence shows (from left to right): breaking the newly solidified curds; scalding the curds and whey; cutting and turning the drained curds; filling the mould with milled curds; and pressing.

others did much to revolutionize the haphazard, hit-and-miss procedures of early cheesemakers. But they also brought with them the seeds of the eventual decline of traditional cheesemaking. The methods he advocated for farmhouse producers were also adopted for factory production, especially in America, and traditional cheesemakers could not compete with the vast quantities of cheap Cheddar churned out by the factories.

FACTORY CHEESE

The spread of factory production involved the mixing of milk from several herds to make cheeses in bulk, a process made acceptable only by pasteurization, introduced in the late 1800s and almost universal in British dairies by the 1950s. Pasteurization involves heating the milk briefly to 72°C and rapidly cooling it to destroy disease-bearing organisms. Unfortunately, along with the germs, it removed much of the innate character of the milk.

In spite of the obstacles, though, traditional cheesemaking persisted in many areas until World War 2 when food regulations dealt a severe blow. Milk was commandeered for the liquid market, cheesemaking was centralized in large creameries, and the making of cheese with a short shelf life – such as Caerphilly and all the soft cheeses like York and Cambridge – was forbidden. After the war the number of farmhouse cheesemakers had dwindled to 126.

THE WAY AHEAD

However, this tiny band proved unexpectedly tenacious, and, in the 1980s, they and their descendants became the spearhead of a quiet revolution in British cheesemaking. Rebelling against factory-made, anonymous, vacuum-wrapped blocks, cheesemakers are returning to traditional methods, making cheeses from the unpasteurized milk of a single herd; reintroducing extinct cheeses, like Swaledale and Single Gloucester and Lancashire Cream Slice; and inventing delectable new ones which display all the inventiveness and glorious variety of traditional British cheeses.

THE CHEESE FAIR
(above) The traditional place for farmers and dairy maids to sell their cheese was at the cheese fair. There, they were completely at the mercy of the cheese factor, who would wander around picking and choosing cheeses to sell in London and other cities at vastly inflated prices. Cheesemakers also had to rely on the factor for supplies of the annatto dye.

THE HOME OF STILTON?
(right) Stilton cheese got its name from the Bell Inn in Stilton where this much-prized cheese was sold to travellers on the Great North Road – the cheese was actually made in the Vale of Belvoir. Even in the 18th century, it was expensive because it was hard to make. As an exasperated dairy maid complained, 'Except that they make no noise, they be more trouble than babies'.

place. This could be a chancy affair, and cheesemakers tried to encourage the process in various ways. The makers of Blue Vinney, for example, would hang mouldy leather harnesses or saddles or old leather boots in the cheese store while their cheese were maturing, or they would dip these objects in the milk prior to rennetting – a process not entirely dissimilar from the modern practice of adding the mould culture (*Penicillium roquefortii*) to the milk at the same point.

The improvements wrought by Harding and

Hives of Industry

For their precious stores of beeswax and honey, bees have been pursued by man for many centuries; successively hunted down and cruelly exploited, they are nowadays nurtured by the humane skills of modern beekeepers.

British beekeeping probably began in the Bronze Age, some 3000 years ago, when bees were prized more for their wax – essential to bronze-casting – than their honey. Before that, ancient peoples would simply have scavenged woodlands for wild honeybee nests and then robbed them of their combs. Eventually they learned that if they left some of the brood comb intact, the colony would survive to provide another honey harvest. But exploiting colonies in the wild left them prey to other marauders – human and animal – so the next step was to bring them nearer to home, often inside a hollow log; other logs were set up nearby and swarms encouraged to move in by smearing honey round the entrance holes. Later, dome-shaped hives, woven from willow and plastered with clay or cow-dung, took the place of logs.

The Romans, during their occupation of Britain, encouraged beekeeping. They needed wax for seals, candles and writing tablets, and they used honey extensively in cooking as a sweetener, a seasoning and a preservative for fruit, vegetables and meat. It was also valued for cosmetic and medicinal purposes: Roman legionaries carried it in their packs as a dressing for wounds – its antibiotic properties have since been scientifically confirmed.

During the thousand years from Saxon time to the Reformation beekeeping prospered, the main impetus being the spread of Christianity which created an enormous demand for church candles. It was not unusual to have 50 candles burning on the high altar at Mass, while a Pascal candle, for Easter use, might weigh 200lb or more (requiring the labours of 20,000 bees for about a year to produce enough wax). Ecclesiastical regulations stipulated that the candle be 100 per cent beeswax, partly because mutton-fat tallow 'smoked and stunk' and partly because the Church attached mystical symbolism to bees and their products.

Since civilization began, honey, wax and bees have been invested with sacred significance. Greeks and Romans considered the bee and its output miraculous and accorded honey and candles a special role in religious rituals. Early Christians continued this tradition. A medieval Welsh document states that 'the origin of bees is from Paradise … therefore the Mass cannot be

IN PRAISE OF BEES
(left) Man has been fascinated by bees since ancient times, impressed by their industry, as in this 16th-century print, and intrigued by the mysteries of their breeding habits.

HEATHER HONEY
(right) Many beekeepers prize heather honey above all others. Actually obtained from ling, a wild heather, it has a distinctive aroma and flavour, and a thick gel-like texture.

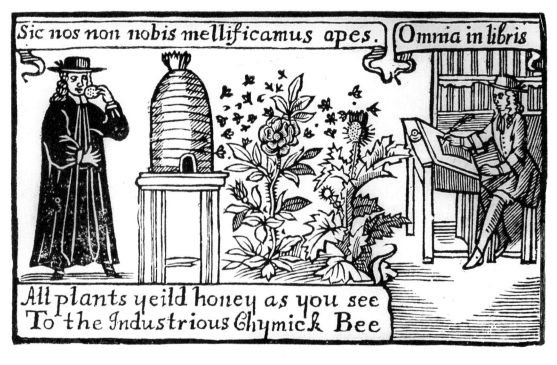

Sic nos non nobis mellificamus apes. Omnia in libris

All plants yeild honey as you see
To the Industrious Chymick Bee

said without the wax'; and in the early Middle Ages eating honey was part of the baptismal ceremony. Misunderstanding their reproductive habits, the Church also presented bees as a model of chastity: candles became symbols of Christ, born of a virgin mother.

Wax chandlery, as a specialist occupation, emerged in the 13th century, but until then candles were made by monks and servants: every monastery, abbey and estate had its bee colony – apiary. Beekeeping serfs and cottagers paid rents and tithes in wax, and legacies of hives to a church for beeswax production were not uncommon. In the houses of the nobility, beeswax candles were used for lighting and for time-keeping: six candles, each marked at 20-minute intervals, covered the day. Ordinary people had

PROTECTING THE HIVES *(above) In Britain's erratic climate, the traditional straw hives, or 'skeps', had to be carefully sheltered against the weather. They were often thatched to keep out the rain, and placed, as diarist John Evelyn suggested, 'against the South sun, a little declining from the East, otherwise the Bees will fly out too early and be subject to the mischief of cold Dews'.*

to make do with tallow candles or rushlights.

The huge production of wax was matched by the output of honey. Most of it was fermented into mead and similar beverages. Mead is the world's oldest alcoholic drink – much older than wine or beer. Other honey-based drinks included pyment, a spiced blend of honey and white wine; clare was the red wine version and both were Chaucer's favoured drinks. Elizabeth I preferred metheglin, which was mead flavoured with herbs and spices; fruit meads included cyser (made with apples) and morat (from mulberries).

Throughout the Middle Ages, honey also served as the standard sweetener. Sugar had been imported since the First Crusade but it was prohibitively expensive – more than 20 times the price of honey in the 1300s. Both honey and wax served as popular cures and ointments for ills ranging from coughs to consumption. So beekeepers helped preserve life; but they were also, on occasion, called on to help destroy it. In medieval warfare, armies would hurl occupied hives at each other to force a surrender.

The Reformation brought an abrupt end to this heyday of beekeeping: altar candles were outlawed, wax effigies banned and bequests for chapel lights burning in perpetuity forbidden; the monasteries were closed and their apiaries run down. By the 1700s, honey also had fallen from favour: sugar, now much cheaper, replaced it as a sweetener, and imported French wines and home-produced beer were ousting mead.

SKEPS AND BOLES

In all this time beekeeping methods had changed little since their Bronze Age beginnings. The hives – wickerwork or straw skeps – stood off the ground on stools. An entrance hole was usually cut through the stool top rather than in the skep, where it might weaken the whole structure. Inside, crosswise sticks provided support for comb-building. From the 1400s onwards, many were kept in recesses called boles, specially built into house and garden walls.

The beekeeper's year began in late spring, the swarming season, and reached its climax in September with the honey harvest. Swarms were needed to colonize hives left empty after the winter. When a keeper spotted a swarm, he laid claim to it by 'tanging', banging a metal pan; the noise was also supposed to frighten the bees into settling, making it easier to capture them inside a skep.

Around Michaelmas (29 September), the beekeeper inspected his colonies, deciding which ones to keep for the following year and from which ones he should take the honey – this meant destroying them. The choice was made by weight: the heaviest hives, evidently well-stocked, were taken for honey; so too were the lightest as their food stores were clearly too meagre to last the winter. Medium-weight hives

REPLACING THE SUPER
(below) As the colony expands, extra honey chambers known as 'supers' are stacked on top of the brood chamber. This helps prevent swarming, and enables the honey to be harvested without disturbing the bees. Until the development of modern hives like this one, there were innumerable attempts to solve the problem of keeping bees without killing them. The ones shown here (below left) were exhibited at the Great Exhibition in 1851.

Neighbour's Cottage, Observatory, and other Beehives.

THE WBC HIVE
Invented by William Broughton Carr in 1884, the WBC hive became immensely popular with British keepers, but is now largely superseded by the less picturesque box-like National hive. This one (right) is a modern version of the WBC, with a deep brood chamber, one honey super with frames, and one shallow super containing sections specially designed for comb honey.

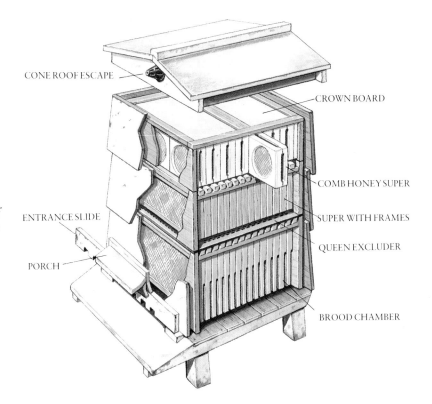

CONE ROOF ESCAPE

CROWN BOARD

COMB HONEY SUPER

SUPER WITH FRAMES

QUEEN EXCLUDER

ENTRANCE SLIDE

PORCH

BROOD CHAMBER

BEEKEEPING GADGETS
The Victorian passion for inventions also extended to beekeeping:

Honey filter

Honey press

Wax melter

Smoker

were spared and their colonies given extra nourishment to help them survive the cold months.

The first stage of honey extraction involved killing off the bees. This was done by setting the skep over a shallow pit containing papers or rags which had been impregnated with sulphur; the bees, suffocated by the fumes, tumbled dead into the pit. The honeycomb was then cut out and, still warm from the hive, was crushed – together with pollen, brood and maybe a few bee corpses as well – and strained through a long linen honey-poke.

HUMANITY TO BEES

An alternative system was designed to save the bees – as one West Country housewife wrote, 'it do grieve me to kill the poor things, being such a waste of good bees …' – this consisted of inverting the full skep and putting an empty one on top. Drumming on the lower hive persuaded the bees to move upwards; but it was not as foolproof as sulphuring.

Nevertheless, from the 17th century onward, the annual slaughter of bees caused concern, partly for economic reasons and partly for humanitarian ones – some beekeepers covered their faces with black crepe, as at funerals. The feeling was expressed in the Never-Kill-A-Bee movement of the early 1800s, culminating in the publication of Thomas Nutt's *Humanity to Honey Bees* in 1832.

The problem of comb extraction was not the only disadvantage of skeps: their rigid enclosed form made it difficult to examine colonies and impossible to control them. In the search for a solution all kinds of hive designs appeared. Several featured lift-out frames designed to hold honeycombs; but these were only partially successful because the frames became fixed to the hive walls with comb or stick propolis (resinous substances from plant buds collected by bees for use as a natural cement in hive maintenance).

The breakthrough came in 1851 when the Reverend Lorenzo Lorraine Langstroth, an amateur beekeeper from Pennsylvania, discovered the 'bee space' – a gap up to ¼ inch wide, enough for a bee to pass through but too wide to become clogged with propolis and too narrow for comb construction. Langstroth's own design, the movable-frame hive, incorporated the bee space between the frames themselves, thus ensuring problem-free removal. As a result, it became possible to gather honeycombs easily and to monitor the colony. All the hives still in use, including Langstroth's, are based on the same principles.

The Langstroth hive revolutionized beekeeping and stimulated other indispensable inventions. First, the 'foundation', a wax sheet, reinforced with wire, which fits into the frame. Embossed with the hexagonal cell pattern, it is used by the bees as a basis for comb building. This was followed by the centrifugal extractor which spins honey out of the cells leaving the framed comb more or less intact for re-use, and by the queen excluder, a grid penetrable by worker bees but not by the queen, to separate the brood from the honey chambers. Next came the bellows smoker which subdues the bees without asphyxiating them; and last, the bee escape, a valve-like spring set into a screen, which allows the bees to pass through it in one direction only, from the supers down into the brood chamber, or up and out of the hive, thus making it possible to evacuate the honey chambers prior to collection.

There have been further refinements but these six inventions remain the basis of modern beekeeping. Essentially, they enable the bee-keeper to manipulate the colony so that it produces a huge surplus of honey, enough to provide a harvest and winter food for the bees. Under normal circumstances, if the colony becomes overcrowded the bees will swarm, and take off to pastures new. The beekeeper aims to prevent this by shutting off the queen with an excluder and by increasing the hive's size with extra honey chambers – the supers – superimposed one by one on the brood chamber; the colony remains intact with a full force of foragers to build up the honey reserves.

THE BEEKEEPER'S YEAR

The modern beekeeper's year begins in early spring. As winter pulls back, the awakening hives are checked, their bottom boards cleaned and sugar syrup for any colony in need of emergency rations provided. In late spring swarming is a major preoccupation. Any swarms that occur must be gathered – not without difficulty or even danger – using a long pole and swarm box and later hived.

Warm weather and blossoming plants create ideal conditions for the honeyflow, a quiet time for the beekeeper but one of frenzied activity for the bees. As the first super begins to fill another is added, then another, and possibly even a fourth in well-favoured sites. By the end of July, it is time to start gathering the honey. A cool billow of smoke calms the bees while an escape screen is inserted under and maybe over the top super. One or two days later, the bees will have evacuated the super and the keeper can safely carry off the golden bounty. The process continues through the summer until mid-September, when the last and largest harvest may yield as much as 100lb.

Before the cold weather sets in, the bees are given another feed of sugar syrup, the hives are

CANDLEMAKING
Candles are an important part of the rituals of the Catholic Church to this day, and beeswax is still the preferred material.

"Hullo Jack! got a prize from school?"
"Yes Dad - teacher asked,'What is it so wonderful that bees make?'
I wrote down'Wax'for Mansion Polish'remembering what a lovely
polish it gives to our floors and furniture. All the other boys said 'Honey'"

MANSION POLISH
FOR STAINED OR PARQUET FLOORS & FURNITURE
POLISHES AND PRESERVES LINOLEUM
'Dark Mansion' is specially made for dark Oak and all dark woods
In tins 6d, 10½d & 1/9. Large family tin 3/- containing 2 lbs. nett
THE CHISWICK POLISH CO. LTD. CHISWICK. W.4.

inspected and, if necessary, made sound, then the bees are left undisturbed for at least five months, from 1 November to 1 April.

Although modern science can help beekeepers with such things as queen-breeding and pest control, beekeeping still depends largely on human skill, the bees themselves – as wild today as when primitive man hunted them down in the forest – and the weather. Britain's erratic climate makes it unsuitable for commercial beekeeping, and most of the 42,000 beekeepers are small-scale producers, motivated as much by devotion to their bees as by hope of monetary gain. Beekeeping remains a vital tradition, retaining much of its age-old fascination. The Guild of Wax Chandlers still gives thanks with its old grace, 'For thy creature the Bee, The Wax and the Honey, We thank thee, O Lord'.

VERSATILE BEESWAX
Man has found innumerable uses for beeswax, from the bronze-casting of ancient metal workers to the more prosaic modern furniture polishes. It was an ingredient of medicinal ointments and cosmetic creams; it coated the embalming shrouds of Persian kings; it provided the notepaper for Roman scribes and the seals for their legal documents. It was even modelled into the effigies of sorcerers and witches, and the lifelike tableaux of Madame Tussaud.

MUTUAL BENEFITS
Orchards are favourite locations for beehives, since there are reciprocal benefits for the fruit grower and the beekeeper. The bees feed on the nectar in the blossoming trees, and are in turn almost entirely responsible for their pollination.

Fine Irish Linen

Until the 1950s, flax flourished in Ireland's moist climate and
rich, loamy soil. Now, with experiments underway into modern techniques
of processing the plant fibre, the crop may soon be grown again.

Linen is one of nature's most miraculous fabrics, a hard-wearing material, with a natural degree of water-proofing, a fine, silky texture and a crisp coolness to the touch. Historically, it is also one of the earliest textiles known to man. For thousands of years it was the everyday garb of peasants and priests, nomads and emperors; it clothed the Egyptian Pharaohs in life and wrapped their mummified remains on their final journey. Flax was being cultivated in Egypt for its fine silky fibres, as well as its oil-bearing seed, as long as 4000 years ago. The growing and harvesting of the flax plant and the extraordinarily laborious process by which the threads are extracted from the stems, then spun and woven into cloth, are clearly depicted in Egyptian wall paintings; and the tools and techniques used in what has been described as 'the long agony of flax' remained virtually unchanged until the late 1700s.

FLAX IN ANCIENT BRITAIN

The Romans, too, were enthusiastic promoters of flax-growing and linen manufacture. Although linen had been traded in Britain by Phoenician merchants around 1000 BC, it was the Romans who introduced it here as an agricultural crop. They even established a linen-making factory at Winchester. Flax flourished in the temperate equable climate of north-western Europe. The moist spring breezes and warm summer temperatures were ideal for producing longer, more lustrous fibres, and by the beginning of the 19th century the most important flax-growing areas in Europe were northern France, Belgium and Northern Ireland.

In medieval times, in Ireland as in the rest of the British Isles, flax was an occasional crop on many farms. It could be dressed, spun and woven in the slow winter months and provided clothing for the farmer's family and household, as well as valuable winter feed for his animals. Even so, the native cloth tended to be rather heavy and coarse; the finest linens, favoured by the wealthy, still had to be imported.

From the late Middle Ages, wool and then cotton began to replace linen as the cheap, everyday all-purpose cloth. Flax-growing, always arduous and labour-intensive, became uneconomical, and in England, at least, the

FLAX IN FLOWER
(above) In summers gone by, the flax fields of Ireland were filled with a sea of elegant green stems, crowned with pale blue flowers. The seed was sown densely, so that the stems (from which the textile fibre is extracted) would grow straight and tall as they strained towards the light. At this stage, the plant would yield fine, though delicate fibres, but once the stems had yellowed – in late July or mid-August – the fibres produced would be supple, yet strong.

linen industry began to rely on imported flax and yarn. In Ireland, however, from the late 1600s onwards, the flax and linen industry expanded dramatically, especially in the north, in the counties of Antrim, Armagh, Tyrone, Down and Londonderry. One reason was the new demand for flax from English spinners and weavers; another was that the embryonic Irish woollen industry had been stifled by embargoes which prevented exports to anywhere but England and Wales. The energy and investment which might otherwise have gone into wool went into the cultivation of flax instead.

Deliberate efforts were made to improve the quality of the cloth by introducing experts from France and Belgium to teach the Irish spinners and weavers their superior skills. One such expert was Louis Crommelin, a Huguenot refugee from religious persecution in France. As well as providing asylum, the English Treasury paid him a salary for his efforts and interest on his investment. Ireland's reputation for fine

'BOGGING'
(left) Separating the fibres from the woody bark and tissue of the plant was one of the muckiest parts of the yarn-making process. Known as 'retting' (or 'bogging' in Northern Ireland) it involved submerging the flax bundles in pools of water ('lint-holes'), created by damming rivers for the purpose. The bundles would be steeped for up to two weeks, until the stems had rotted and decomposed. Then, with the stench of rotting flax and stagnant water in the air, the men would wade into the slimy pools and lift the bundles onto the bank.

HARVESTING THE CROP
For centuries, flax was harvested by hand, an arduous and often back-breaking process. The plant was never cut, but pulled up by the roots, to ensure the longest lengths of fibre. In recent years, harvesting machinery (below) has been developed in Belgium to take much of the pain and effort out of the job. This pulling machine channels the plants into a 'pulling unit', which grips the stems and yanks the plants vertically out of the ground.

linen was gradually established, and at the same time, various administrative measures were enacted to stimulate demand – for example, a requirement that linen hatbands and scarves must be worn at funerals. Finally, in 1696, the duty on Irish linen entering England was abolished, making it for the first time cheaper than its rival products from the Continent.

At the beginning of the 18th century, Ireland was one of the poorest, most backward areas of Europe, and the flax and linen industries provided the only alternative for most country folk to scratching a meagre living from the soil. Farmers gladly gave over what land they had to flax, often to the detriment of other forms of agriculture: 'linen country' became synonymous with poor husbandry.

In the early days, the linen industry was entirely domestic, with farmer-weavers and their families responsible for the whole process. The flax was planted in April, but the farmer had first to decide whether he was planting for seed

weighted down with heavy stones to keep them submerged, and steeped for 10 to 14 days. For the last week or so of that period the foul stench of rotting flax which emanated from the stagnant lint-holes pervaded the countryside for miles around.

The disgusting job of removing the flax from the lint-holes fell to the men. Occasionally, the water was run off first, but it was thought preferable to lift the bundles out beforehand, and this involved wading thigh-high in the slimy waters. After being drained on the bank for a short time, the flax was taken off to the 'spread' fields – closely mown, sheltered meadows – where it was left to dry for up to two weeks to await the first stage in the flax-dressing process, the 'scutching'.

When linen manufacture was still a cottage industry, the women were the scutchers. First, they would pound the dried flax stems with wooden mallets called 'beetles', to pulverize the woody tissues. Then, anchoring one end of the bundle in a slot cut in a vertical wooden pillar –

or for fibre. For seed he would scatter the grain, but for fibre it had to be sown thickly so that the stems, growing closely together, would be tall and straight, with as little branching as possible. The harvesting, too, would take place at different times. For fibre he would wait until the brilliant pale-blue flowers had been replaced by the roughcast pods packed with seed. Then, before the seeds were fully ripe, and when the clear green stalks had begun to yellow, he would pull the plants up by the roots.

The bundles of flax were then handed to the 'ripplers' – often the wife and daughters of the family – who removed the seed bolls by passing the stems through a 'ripple' – a large, comb-like gadget with iron teeth. They then tied the flax into small bundles known as 'beets', and took them off to the flax dams, or lint-holes, for 'retting'. The seed bolls were dried and used to make cattle cake, nutritious winter fodder, or pressed to produce linseed oil.

A MUCKY PROCESS

By universal agreement, retting was the most disagreeable stage in the whole laborious process. The object was to rot down the hard woody stems, dissolving the gummy substances which bind the fibres and stalks together. There were two methods: dew-retting and water-retting. Dew-retting involved spreading the flax bundles in a thin layer on an open field for several weeks, and was widely used in Europe. In Northern Ireland, however, the heavier rainfall made it impractical, and water-retting was the usual method.

First, the farmer would excavate a series of pools, known as lint-holes or bogs, alongside the river, damming them so that he could control the flow of water. The bundles of flax were placed in the lint-holes in a single layer and covered with rushes and straw, then

WOMEN'S WORK
(above) The expansion of the linen industry in 18th-century Ireland created a huge demand for the spinning skills of country women, and provided them with a valuable source of extra income. This engraving shows a cottage industry in County Down, with a woman boiling yarn in the background and another operating a 'clock' reel (which recorded the number of times the reel turned and enabled the yardage to be calculated). The two other women work at treadle wheels, drafting fibres from their distaffs.

HANDLOOM WEAVERS
*(right) Traditionally, once
the yarn had been spun by
the womenfolk, it was woven
into linen cloth by the male
handloom weavers. The most
important products of their
labours, from the Middle
Ages onwards, were table
cloths and napkins, often
with intricate borders and
decorative motifs. In 1804,
a French silk weaver, Joseph
Marie Jacquard, invented a
loom with a mechanism
which improved the lines of
the patterns and the texture
and fineness of the weave.
Here, a top-grade weaver
from Waringstown,
Northern Ireland, makes
fine-woven damask napkins
on a Jacquard loom.*

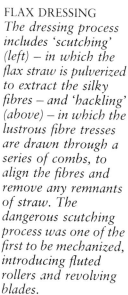

FLAX DRESSING
*The dressing process
includes 'scutching'
(left) – in which the
flax straw is pulverized
to extract the silky
fibres – and 'hackling'
(above) – in which the
lustrous fibre tresses
are drawn through a
series of combs, to
align the fibres and
remove any remnants
of straw. The
dangerous scutching
process was one of the
first to be mechanized,
introducing fluted
rollers and revolving
blades.*

the scutching stock – and using a broad sabre-like wooden blade, they would strike the stems in a slicing motion to extract the fibres.

After scutching, the flax was 'hackled' to comb and align the long smooth fibres – the 'line' – and separate them from the short coarse fibres – the 'tow' – which would ultimately be used for such things as stuffing mattresses and for sacking. The hackles were a series of boards implanted with successively finer clusters of vertical pins or 'tines', through which the flax fibres were drawn. Finally, the flax was wound onto a distaff or into loose hanks ready for spinning.

Traditionally, spinning was the province of the women and girls, and weaving of the men. Early spinners used a distaff and spindle, but by the mid-1700s these were superseded by the flax or treadle wheel, later known as the Dutch wheel, which could also be used for spinning

wool. The handloom weavers were independent craftsmen whose wealth and status were somewhat higher than those of other tenant farmers. Independent in spirit also, the handloom weavers were often at the forefront of radical movements, and led the rebellion of 1798.

In the early days, the linen was also bleached and finished by the weaver, who would boil it in buttermilk and spread it out in the meadow for the sunlight to finish the job. Often the brown (unbleached) linen was bought from the weaver by the draper, who took over the bleaching process. The bleached linen was then taken to the Linen Hall in Dublin to be sold to English and other traders, until in 1783 the White Linen Hall in Belfast was built. Brown linen was sold at the Brown Linen Hall in Lisburn.

The depression which followed the end of the Napoleonic wars hit Northern Ireland particularly hard, since it coincided with a decline in

women found relief from the choking dust. The hackling rooms too were dirty, disagreeable and dangerous, and in the wet spinning rooms the heat and humidity, which protected the brittle flax fibres, was another constant source of complaint. And the walls and floors of the weaving factories were soaked in condensation.

Conditions have vastly improved and linen manufacture is still a major industry in Northern Ireland; but it now relies on imported flax as it has not been grown there commercially since the mid-1950s. In the last ten years, experiments were carried out in an attempt to develop a new process to replace retting and improve the viability of the crop. Water-retting is now uneconomic and dew-retting is impractical in the North although success-ful in the South. However, the new process, which involved a type of chemical desiccation of the flax stems, did not prove commercially successful, and the experiment had to be abandoned. So the glorious sight of fields of flax in full bloom, a rippling sea of elegant green stems crowned with brilliant blue flowers, once common in the Irish country-side, has now sadly become a thing of the past.

the rural linen industry. Competition from cheap cotton textiles led to reduced demand and falling prices, and accelerated moves towards mechanization. Mill yarn was cheaper than handspun yarn and the invention of the wet spinning process in 1825 meant that even the finest linens could be spun by machine. By the 1850s, domestic rural hand-spinning had almost totally disappeared.

Handloom weaving lasted another 20 years or so, until the advent of the power loom. But the position of weavers deteriorated. Already in the late 1700s many weavers had become financially dependent on middle-men, often drapers or the owners of bleach works, who would supply them with yarn and buy back the products. By the 1830s, like the spinners, many had moved to the towns and become the employees of Belfast manufacturers working for piece rates. The weavers of fine white linens like cambric and damask fared better. Their skills were special-ized and less easy to mechanize, and in such areas handloom weaving survived into the 20th century.

The industrialization of flax dressing and linen manufacture was almost entirely complete by the late 1800s, and in contrast to the gentler pace of the rural industry, produced working conditions which appalled contemporary factory inspectors. The scutching mills were especially notorious: 'illbuilt, illkept, unhealthy sheds packed with dangerous machinery', in which many scutchers lost their thumbs. The atmo-sphere, 'one thick constant cloud of dust and fine particles of straw and flax', also caused comment, though some inspectors were more perturbed by the moral dangers posed by the draughts of whiskey in which the men and

THE LINEN INDUSTRY
(above) Although linen is still a major industry in Northern Ireland – catering for a large tourist market as well as home and export demand – the flax is now imported from European countries like Holland and Belgium. In the mid-1950s, flax growing became commercially unviable in Northern Ireland.

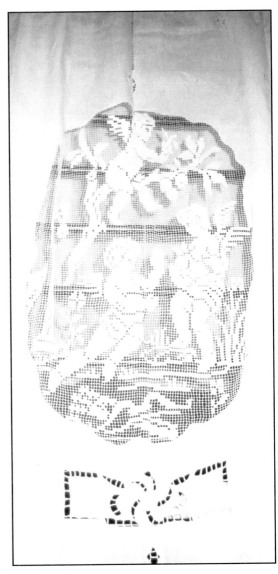

WHITE LINEN
(right) The true colour of linen is greyish or brownish, and the cool, crisp white, which we associate with the finest linens, has always been achieved by bleaching. In the past, the cloth was boiled in buttermilk and bleached in the open air, in sunlit meadows. Nowadays, the cloth is boiled in an alkali solution, and treated with bleaching agents and acids.

Natural Dyeing

Locked away in the leaves and roots of plants that grow in the field corner and hedgerows are the raw materials that our ancestors once released to colour their fabrics.

Fallow land didn't grow enough rye to feed the farmer's family, but those awkward and hard-to-work field margins enclosed by undisturbed hedgerows nevertheless made life brighter in other ways. Locked in the leaves and roots of the weeds that grew here were the blue, green and red dyes that were used to colour many medieval garments; and the lichen that covered the piles of stones cleared from nearby fields yielded the subtle yellows and browns destined for tweeds and woollens.

The desire for ornament is as ancient as civilization itself, and the impulse to dye fabric has a lot in common with the urge to paint faces with mud, draw on cave walls and to trace a pattern in pale clay on a dark pot. These things, however, are different to dyeing in one important respect: they rely on a pigment, a suspension of naturally coloured particles, with an adhesive agent to 'glue' the colour on to a surface. Dyes are quite different in action: it is best to think of them as 'potential', not actual, colours in solution. They are potential colours because most dyes only impart permanent, or fast, colours when used with a fixing medium, called a mordant. Dyes are also potential colours because many substances produce completely different colours under different conditions.

Early British dyers had to be content with a relatively muted range of colours compared to the range that came with the discovery of mordanting, for they had to use 'substantive' dyes – those dyes that give permanent colours without a mordant. Lichens produce substantive dyes, for example, and release warm but dullish colours, such as ochres and browns.

The process of mordant dyeing probably came to Britain with the Romans, who in turn learned the art in Egypt where bright dyes had long been used to colour mummy fabrics. With the fall of the Roman Empire, mordant dyeing declined here and it seems not to have been

A MODERN DYE PLANT
(right) Dye production today shows little evidence of its roots in the field corner: dyestuffs are very much the preserve of the chemist, rather than the herbalist. Here, a rows of tubs called coracles holds fabric dye in the form of filter cake. The damp dye has been discharged into the tubs from filter presses, seen on the left of the picture, and will soon be moved to a computerized spray-drying plant which removes the last of the solvents used in processing. Milling, blending and packing follow. The rich, brilliant colour of the dye in the tubs shown here would have been unheard of in medieval England.

17TH-CENTURY DYEING
'The business of a dyer is laborious and chilly; the workmen are constantly dabbling in water, hot and cold.' The engraving above reiterates this contemporary description: in the foreground, a dyer tends to the dye vat, while his colleagues behind wash fabric in a river.

import of indigo. It dyes wool green in the dye vat, and turns blue on exposure to the air. It was known to the Ancient Britons, but they used it not to dye fabric – instead they smeared it on their bodies as war-paint before going into battle. Wild woad is not a particularly common plant so cultivation probably started quite early. The plant produces four useful crops per year, but the leaves from which the dye is made had to be processed carefully before they could be used. The first stage was to dry the leaves, then grind them into a paste in a woad mill. Then the paste was rolled into balls which were kept under cover for 14 days. The balls were ground once more and fermented for several weeks before being mixed together and made into blue 'cakes'. The dye was extracted by soaking the cakes in water, and mixing with lime-water.

Weld was an important dye plant for three reasons: it was very productive, yielding a lot of dye for a small weight of plant; unlike woad, it needed no special treatment before use as a dye; and it could be easily cultivated, whereas certain other dye-plants did not respond to cultivation. Weld – which was also known as Dyers Greenweed or Dyers Rocket – grew on waste land or poor pastures. The dyer pulled the whole plant in July when it flowered, discarded the root and dried the remainder, then boiled the plant in water. Mordanted with alum and cream of tartar, weld dyed wool a yellow colour, and was used to tint the robes of vestal virgins. It was frequently mixed with woad to produce a green colour.

Madder grew widely as a wild plant, but was hard to cultivate in Britain. Only the root was collected: it had to be peeled, heated and powdered before it could be used. Wild madder gave rose pink, not red, but cultivated madder imported from France and Holland yielded reds and browns. It had another curious property besides the ability to colour fibres: the juice of the stem curdles milk, and the plant was used in cheese-making.

Lichens all yield warm colours – browns, reds and yellows, but the types that were collected and the way each was used varied. Crottle, also known as staneraw or scrottyie, gave an

revived until many centuries later. The earliest recorded reference to British mordant dyeing is in the writings of William of Malmesbury in the 11th century.

DYE-PLANTS

Early home dyers experimented with a huge range of plants that would impart colour to fabric. Gradually, a few were found that gave better, brighter and more permanent colours.

Woad is probably the best known dye-plant and was the only European blue dye until the

THE DYER'S APPRENTICE *(right) The principles of dyeing changed little for many centuries. This early-14th century picture shows a simple winch over which the apprentice dyer has draped two bolts of fabric. Turning the winch wound the fabric through the vat of hot dye, so that all parts of the cloth were dyed the same colour.*

SAFFLOWER
Carthamus tinctorius

BRASILWOOD
Cæsalpinia crista

THE WOAD MILL (*right and below*) Making woad dye began with crushing. This was done in a curiously-shaped building, where horse-drawn rollers pulped plants spread on a circular track. The rollers weighed over a ton – and there might be as many as 24 in the roller house. The work was so heavy that the horses had to be rested hourly.

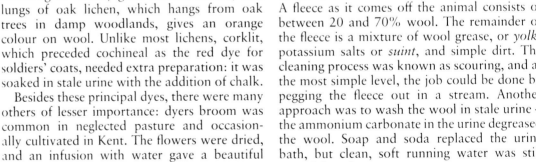

the yellow stigmas of a crocus. Saffron would have been impossibly expensive to harvest without large supplies of cheap labour: 60,000 stigmas were needed for one pound of saffron, and each acre of ground produced only 24lb of dried stigma. Both saffron and madder were used as colouring matter for other things besides fabric: Saffron was widely used as a food-dye, and madder to colour hair.

THE DYEING PROCESS

Dyeing lent itself to craft-based work, because no special equipment and tools are needed – a large cauldron and a fire were to be found in most households. Details of the process varied from place to place, but the principles were the same everywhere. The first stage was always to clean the fibre, which until the introduction of cotton in the 13th century was generally wool. A fleece as it comes off the animal consists of between 20 and 70% wool. The remainder of the fleece is a mixture of wool grease, or *yolk*; potassium salts or *suint*, and simple dirt. The cleaning process was known as scouring, and at the most simple level, the job could be done by pegging the fleece out in a stream. Another approach was to wash the wool in stale urine – the ammonium carbonate in the urine degreased the wool. Soap and soda replaced the urine bath, but clean, soft running water was still essential to the process.

Washing and other dyeing processes con-

orange-brown colour; black scrottle (called Kenderig in Wales) gave reddish-brown; and lungs of oak lichen, which hangs from oak trees in damp woodlands, gives an orange colour on wool. Unlike most lichens, corklit, which preceded cochineal as the red dye for soldiers' coats, needed extra preparation: it was soaked in stale urine with the addition of chalk.

Besides these principal dyes, there were many others of lesser importance: dyers broom was common in neglected pasture and occasionally cultivated in Kent. The flowers were dried, and an infusion with water gave a beautiful yellow dye.

Saffron is well known, and is made from

Plate XIV.

J. Bishop

LOGWOOD
Hæmatoxylon campechianum.

71. Safflower Plant. 72. A Cake Safflower. 73. Indigo Plant. 74. Block of Indigo. 75. Gamboge Tree

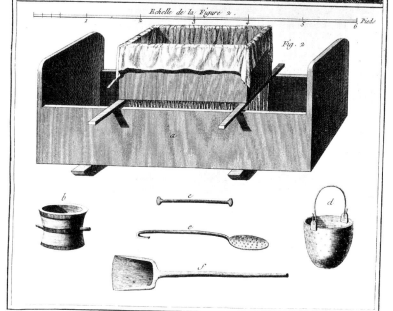

WOAD
Isatis tinctoria.

MAKING YELLOW DYE
(left) *In contrast with the complex processing needed to create blue dye from woad, extracting yellow from safflower, or 'bastard saffron' was easy. The plants were pulverized, and stirred in troughs of warm water. The job was a filthy one and the tanks slippery, so the workers supported their weight on ropes suspended from the ceiling. At lower left are some of the tools used in extracting the dye.*

HERBACEOUS BORDER
(border) *Of the plants shown here, the most widely used in England were woad, weld, madder, and safflower, yielding blue, yellow, red and yellow respectively. Weld, though, was commonly used in combination with woad, to make a green colour, earning the plant the nickname 'dyer's greenweed'. Some of the other plants were imported to Britain, displacing traditional British dye-plants – brazilwood, indigo and logwood all fall into this category. These three plants produced superior reds, blues and blacks, and their import was strongly resisted by home dye producers.*

WELD
Reseda luteola.

sumed a lot of water. In all, a fleece required 50-100 times its own weight in water, so when dyeing began to be industrialized, the dye-works were invariably sited close to rivers.

After washing, the wool was usually boiled with the mordant, then dipped in the dye vat, though the processes were often performed in the reverse order. Leaves and roots of plants were long used as mordants, and alum has a long history; iron and tin compounds also have mordant properties. The twin processes of mordanting and dyeing were called 'stuffing and saddening' and this contemporary account gives a vivid description of the process: *To dye Madder Red.* 'Take three Pounds of Allom,

Two Pounds and half of white Tartar, a quarter of a pound of Foenugreek, two Quarts of Wheat Bran, boil all in the Copper, then put in the Stuff and let it boil two hours and a half, after which take it out, cool it very well, and hang it out for one Night; then to dye it, take seven Pounds of Madder, an Ounce and half of Aqua Fortis, a Pint of Wheat Bran, put them into the Copper, stir them well about, and when the Stuff hath been well rinced in the Dye, then wind it very swift upon a Roller, and tumble it about the Copper for an Hour at least, taking Care that the Fire keep it boiling hot; after which take it out and rince it.'

By this method, dyeing a fleece in a copper

ADDER
tinctorum.

FUSTIC
Maclura tinctoria.

SUMACH
Rhus cotinus

THE BOYS IN BLUE
Natural dyes rapidly fell into disuse with the invention of synthetic substitutes in the 19th century, but vegetable and animal dyestuffs continued to be used for certain specialized applications. Military and police uniforms are two examples: as late as 1945, the bright scarlet tunic of the British soldier's dress uniform was dyed using cochineal, and a mixture of woad and indigo was similarly used to dye policemens' uniforms (above) long after an acceptable blue had been chemically synthesized.

WILLIAM PERKIN
(right) We owe the bright hues of today's fabrics to the discoveries of Victorian chemist William Henry Perkin. He manufactured the first artificial dye – a purple colour – in London in 1856, and his work stimulated a flurry of research activity. Within just a few years, chemists in Britain and Europe had developed the basic forms of many of the artificial dyestuffs that we still use today. The colouring compound present in madder was produced artificially in 1881, and synthetic indigo was marketed in 1894.

was a relatively simple matter, but a bolt of cloth was quite a different proposition. Unless the mordant and dye saturated the fabric evenly, blotchiness would result. To spread the colour evenly, the dyer had to keep the fabric moving in the vat, and this was done using a fluted or slatted roller at one side of the vat, and a guide roller at the other side. Winding on the 'winch' pulled the length of fabric through the vat so that every part of the cloth was evenly coloured.

The edges of a strip of wet fabric have a tendency to curl inwards towards the centre, and one of the most unpleasant tasks in the dye-works was that of the broadsman. His job was to run his fingers under the selvedge or 'list' to turn it out as the fabric emerged from the vat of boiling dye.

Though wool was the first British fibre, and always the most abundant, the dyer dealt with other fibres that required different treatments. Raw silk was boiled to remove the gum that coats the fibre; to prevent the threads from tangling, the silk was enclosed in a bag. The dyeing stage proceeded as with wool, but the mordant and dye vats were usually kept cooler.

Flax was retted before dyeing – in Ireland this was done in stagnant pools, but in continental Europe retting usually took place in running water which produces a whiter fibre. After retting the flax was often bleached: it was soaked then spread out on grass and kept wet for three days. The three-day cycle was repeated for three weeks.

Cotton was not woven into cloth in England until the 17th century and the fibre needed special preparation before dyeing. The process is similar to tanning – the cotton was boiled with astringents such as tannic acid, gall nuts, sumach, or myrobalams.

During and after the 15th century, dyeing expanded and began to assume semi-industrial levels. Around this time explorers were returning home to Europe with newly discovered dye-

stuffs, like indigo, cochineal (made from crushed insects), brazilwood and logwood. These materials dramatically extended the range of dye colours, but they also demanded new processes in their application. Indigo, for example, is only soluble in water in the presence of a reducing agent, but in these conditions the fabric is dyed yellow, not blue; only when air reaches the dye does the indigo colour appear.

The new dyes were not universally accepted though. In particular, the woad dyers resisted the new blues – even claiming it damaged the cloth, or was dangerous.

WILLIAM HENRY PERKIN

Traditional methods of dyeing continued more or less unchanged until the mid 19th century. But, in 1856, the after-hours tinkerings of a humble laboratory assistant lit the fuse on a time bomb that would transform dyeing in just a few years. William Henry Perkin, an assistant to Professor Hofmann at the Royal College of Chemistry, produced a sticky brown mess – aniline – during unsuccessful experiments in the synthesis of quinine. Purified with alcohol, aniline created a brightly coloured powder, and further experiment led to the first artificial purple dye. Perkin called this dye Mauveine, patented the process, and a year later began large-scale manufacture.

Perkins' discovery coincided with the explosive growth of organic chemistry, which deals especially with the aromatic chains of hydrocarbons which themselves were the starting points for dye manufacture. Very soon, workers in all parts of the world were frenziedly researching dye synthesis. By the turn of the 20th century a millenium of tradition had been swept aside and the infant modern dye industry was producing many of the startlingly brilliant hues that we take for granted today.

Making Lace

Once bobbin and needlepoint lace graced the dress of every courtier in Europe. With changing fashions, however, lacemaking declined, although it has now been revived as a rewarding hobby.

Valenciennes, Reticella, Point de Venice, Hollie Point, Carrickmacross – the elegant names of different kinds of lace evoke visions of the stiff ostentatious ruffs worn in the reign of Elizabeth I or the delicate, frothy cravats of the 18th century, both familiar to us from portraits past. Indeed, the story of lace is inextricably bound up with the story of fashionable society over four centuries. It was created specifically in response to the demands of fashion and it remained consistently in the forefront of fashion, only to be finally discarded in the 20th century – inevitably, a victim of fashion.

Compared to other textiles such as weaving and knitting, lace is very modern. Ancient 'lace', discovered in archaeological excavations, has been found, on closer examination, to be no more than intricate embroidery from which the background fabric has simply rotted away. Up until the first half of the 16th century, lace did not exist. Yet only a few years later, between 1560 and 1580, it was firmly established in society, its popularity spreading from court to court throughout most of Europe.

The change in fashion which led directly to the development of lace was in itself fairly insignificant, even humble – it became fashionable to show your underwear. At the end of the 15th century, small areas of white linen smocks and shirts were exposed at the neck and cuffs, and through slashed oversleeves. The next step was to decorate the plain fabric, with seed pearls, tiny beads, delicate braids or embroidery. At first coloured embroidery in simple running stitch was used, then white embroidery found favour which called for more textured effects to reveal the delicate contrast of light and shade. Taking this to its logical extreme, parts of the background fabric were eventually removed altogether, either cut away in 'cutwork' embroidery or pulled out as individual threads in drawn and pulled threadwork. Yet another tradition, dating back to the late medieval period, was knotted net, called 'lacis', technically related more to embroidery.

None of these forms of decoration led directly to the development of lace as a technique, but they are important because they set the scene from which lace was to emerge – literally out of thin air! At this point the history of lace divides because, quite separately, two different techniques evolved almost at the same time. It

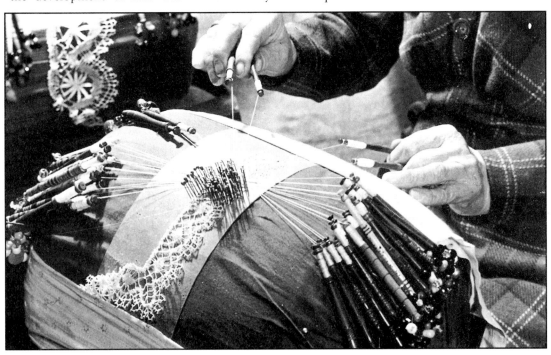

BOBBIN LACE
(left) Bobbin, or pillow, lace is traditionally made by using a tightly stuffed pillow and an array of bobbins wound with fine thread. Firstly, a parchment pattern is attached to the pillow and perforated to hold pins, which will serve as a pattern guide. Then, the threads, which are secured to the bobbins at one end (to preserve their tension), are attached to the pins at the head of the pattern. The lace is then magically created by swiftly manipulating the bobbins in pairs. For a normal piece of lace, up to 200 bobbins are needed, but an elaborate piece of work can use as many as 1000.

was only much later that they were brought together under the one term 'lace', by which we know them today.

The most important of the two techniques in the 16th century was needlepoint lace. Cutwork and drawn thread work had opened up increasingly large spaces in the linen which cried out to be filled, rather than the background fabric just being embroidered. The name first coined for this new technique was *punto in aria* ('stitches in the air').

Meanwhile, a very different tradition was giving rise to the second technique – bobbin lace. The various techniques of plaiting, braiding, fringing and macramé (collectively called *passementerie*) all predate lace. Significantly, they introduced the concept of working with loose threads, using fingers or bobbins instead of needles.

Needle, or needlepoint, lace is worked following a design drawn on parchment. First, guide threads are used to mark the outline of the pattern, then thousands of minute buttonhole stitches are built up around them. Italy was the original centre of production, especially Venice, and the lace industry was closely linked to the convents of the Catholic Church.

The first needlepoint laces – Reticella and *punto in aria* – were geometric, still acknowledging the horizontal/vertical grid of the linen fabric from which they had evolved. This was the time of the Elizabethan ruffs, worn by both men and women, denounced by Philip Stubbes in *An Anatomie of Abuses* (1583): 'the great and monsterous Ruffes . . . whereof some be a quarter of a yard deepe, yea, some more . . . some with purled lace so cloied, and other geugawes so pestered, as the Ruffe is the least part of itself.' As much as 25 yards (23 metres) of fine lace were needed to edge one ruff.

Once the full freedom of the new technique

DELICATE MASTERY
(above) *Vermeer's famous painting beautifully captures the rapt concentration of the lacemaker at work. Quietly bending over her lace pillow, so that she can see in the poor light, she produces the most delicate work – deftly moving the bobbins and twisting the flax threads.*

THE QUEEN OF LACES
(right) *Needlepoint lace is based on a series of intricate loops and buttonhole stitches, and is much more difficult to make than bobbin lace. It was a favourite with court society because it was very finely made – and could only be acquired at great expense.*

point lace, ousting embroidery and lacis.

By the first quarter of the 17th century, the reign of James I, the ruff was obsolete; men were wearing their hair in long, natural curls and wide, flat collars were considered more becoming, made of relatively cheaper soft Dutch or Flemish bobbin lace.

In the same way that all the varieties of needlepoint lace have a common denominator, the buttonhole stitch, so bobbin (or pillow) lace is identified by its use of bobbins as weights to pull the threads taut while they are twisted and plaited. The design is first 'pricked' on to parchment by outlining it with pinholes, then pins are stuck through the holes into a 'pillow', usually stuffed with straw like a bolster. The pins hold the threads in place as the lace is worked.

At first, bobbin lace was still closely linked with the *passementerie* from which it had evolved, especially braiding. The first bobbin laces were richly coloured, worked in silk and metal threads. Hardwick Hall in Derbyshire has bed curtains and table carpets in silver and gold threads; cheaper copper lace was used for costumes in masques and theatrical entertainments. As time progressed, the heavy metal braids and laces became more delicate, but they were still 'a major extravagance in an age of extravagance', James I excelling Elizabeth I in the display of his court.

At this period, bobbin lace was more often called 'bone' lace. Queen Elizabeth I's wardrobe accounts list a New Year's gift of 'a petticoat of cloth of gold stayned black and white, with a bone lace of gold and spangles, like the wayves

was realized, designs became less geometric and more natural. Individual motifs such as flowers were worked separately, and then linked by 'brides' (or bridges) of thread or by a background mesh called a *reseau*. From the beginning, needlepoint lace was seen as a suitable occupation for 'Gentlewomen for to pass away their time in vertuous exercises', as a pattern book published in 1591 promised its readers. Pattern books had followed the development of printing as a way of reaching the newly created market of the leisured bourgeoisie, and were increasingly dominated by designs for needle-

COSTLY DISPLAY
*(above) James I's
courtiers were
renowned for the
extravagance of their
dress. Costly gold and
silver bobbin lace was
hung with highly
ostentatious
'spangles', and men
wore small fortunes
on their shoe roses
and knee sashes.*

LACE PATTERN
(left) This Bedfordshire parchment pattern for bobbin lace dates from the second half of the 19th century. The holes for the pins which held the stitches in place were made with a lacemaker's 'pricker'.

BOBBINS
(below) Lacemakers' bobbins are today as much collectors' items as the lace itself. Made of wood or bone, they were weighted by a ring, or 'spangle' of glass beads. Many were elaborately decorated, bound with fine brass wire or inlaid with pewter. As popular tokens of affection, they were often inscribed with names, dates and love vows or religious quotations.

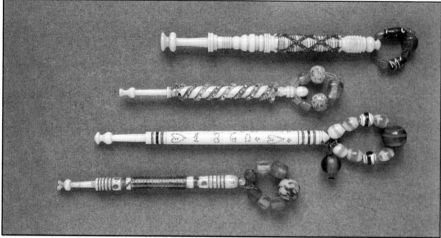

of the sea'. Shakespeare in *Twelfth Night* talks of: 'The spinsters and knitters in the sun, And the free maids that weave their threads with bone.' Bone lace has been taken to mean using sheeps' trotters as bobbins, but these would have been very heavy, especially in a complex design which might call for 300 bobbins at once. In Devon, however, we know that lacemakers used pared fishbones instead of expensive brass pins, and chicken bones were also sometimes used.

The early bobbin laces had solid geometric designs, imitating the early needlepoint laces which they continued to copy, gradually adapting to garlands, wreaths and stylized fruit and flowers in flowing contours. Although there was some overlap, needlepoint lacemaking was generally centred on Venice and southern Europe, while bobbin lace was centred on Flanders and northern Europe. This region produced the exceptionally fine flax thread used until the 19th century when cheaper cotton thread took over the market.

Bobbin lace was introduced to England in the 16th century by Flemish refugees, and became concentrated in the Midlands and round Honiton in Devon. Louis XIV's persecution of the Huguenots in France brought a further influx of refugees, greatly improving the quality of English lace in the 18th century.

LACE AND SOCIETY

At the end of the 16th century, when lace first evolved, Europe was experiencing a great expansion of trade. This created new wealth, and there was more demand for luxury goods than ever before.

Lace was soon recognized as being more valuable than jewels and silk because of the painstaking labour involved in producing even a few inches. Charles I spent £1000 in 1625 on his personal lace and linen, a vast amount in

IMITATION NEEDLEPOINT
(left) This portrait of 'Elizabeth of England' shows James I's daughter in an apron trimmed with bobbin lace (designed to look like geometric needlepoint) with insertions of 'lacis' – a fine knotted net.

LACE SCHOOLS
(right) In the 19th century, lace schools were established, where pauper children from the age of four or five were taught basic lacemaking skills and paid a small wage – while the lace was sold to 'contribute to their upkeep'. The regime was harsh, with some older children expected to work a 15-hour day.

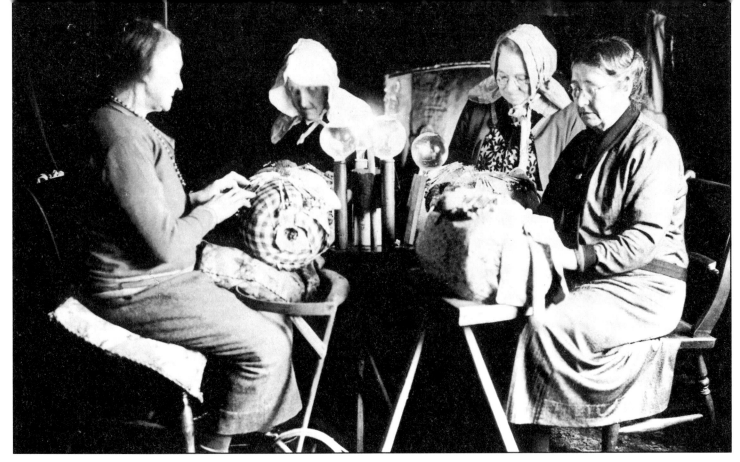

LACEMAKING GROUPS
(top) The older lacemakers often gathered at each other's houses, for companionship and economy. As one visitor wrote, 'they have tea together several days a week, so as to save boiling the kettle at each house'. In winter, they sat working by candlelight, with 'dicky pots' (above) under their skirts. These were small earthenware pots which were filled with glowing cinders – soot and dust from an open fire would have soiled their spotless white lace.

those days. Meanwhile, lacemakers were condemned to work in cowsheds, where the moist, warm atmosphere kept the flax thread supple. As many as 1200 bobbins might be needed to make a wide flounce which would increase by only an inch a day.

In an attempt to protect the English lace industry, imports of foreign lace were banned in 1635 and again in 1662, but all this did was promote smuggling; coffins were a favourite hiding-place. Lace handkerchiefs and fans became easy pickings for thieves, and by the 18th century lace had become so valuable that the police requested ladies to sit in their carriages with their backs to the horses, to prevent thieves slitting open the leather back of the carriage and stealing their 'heads', or wigs, to which lace lappets were attached. 18th-century fashion in lace called for even greater expenditure than under the Stuarts; frills and flounces were everywhere, and there were even special lace ruffles called *engageants* designed to fit the elbow. Soldiers went into battle wearing lace with their armour, and it was court etiquette to die in a lace-trimmed nightcap and be buried in the finest linen.

Then, quite suddenly, the great age of lace came to a bloody end with the French Revolution of 1789. Fashion veered round to simple, unadorned muslin gowns, and extravagance was frowned upon; the guillotine was a chilling reminder of what could happen to the aristocracy if they flaunted their wealth too openly. Lace, once so desirable, was now cast out to servants as frivolous and worthless.

Lace enjoyed a revival in the 19th century with the establishment of lace schools – in many cases, a deliberate attempt to find employment for pauper children. Conditions in

these schools were, to say the least, unhealthy; children were crowded into small cottages with insufficient light to work by, and consumption was common. Even small children were expected to work four to five hours a day, chanting 'lace tells' – or rhymes – to ease the tedium, and young women worked 12-15 hours.

After they left school, lacemakers would often work together in one cottage, for company and warmth. The finished lace was sold to a dealer, usually either the local draper or a travelling agent. The poor lacemakers were often at the mercy of the dealers, who insisted that they buy other goods in part payment for their work.

The Industrial Revolution dealt the final blow to the handmade lace industry. The first development was a simple machine net which was embroidered by hand to imitate lace, but by the 1840s Nottingham factories were producing patterned lace which was virtually indistinguishable from the real thing. Queen Victoria commissioned Honiton lace for her wedding gown and her children's christening robe, but by then it was difficult to find enough lacemakers left to do the work. She also favoured Newport lace, a superior machine product from Newport on the Isle of Wight, made by a firm called Freeman and Nunn. In 1833 they were granted a patent for 'blonde' lace, using silk thread, which at the time was very fashionable.

The Edwardians brought a taste for lace into the 20th century, but this disappeared with the austerity years of the First World War. Recently, however, handmade lace has become increasingly popular as an activity, with numerous devotees, and many scholars researching its history. Lacemaking continues today as a beautiful and intricate skill, with a complex and fascinating tradition behind it.

Hand-made Paper

**Though superseded by mechanization, the ancient craft of hand-making
paper is still alive in a handful of mills, which produce quality
paper for fine books, for artists and calligraphers.**

Originating in China around 100 AD, the craft of paper-making spread slowly across the world, arriving in Europe via Spain and Italy in the 12th century. By 1476 when hand-written books were superseded by mechanically printed books the demand for paper increased dramatically.

In Britain, the first white paper mill of which there is a record was Sele Mill, near Hertford, which operated briefly in the 1490s. But it was with the opening of John Spilmann's mill at Dartford, Kent, in 1588, that the British paper industry really began. John Spilmann, formerly one of Queen Elizabeth I's jewellers, was knighted by James I during a visit to the mill in 1605.

Two factors accounted for the initial slow growth of paper-making. First, paper-makers guarded the secrets of their craft jealously and, second, the raw material, linen rag, was in short supply. Other rags, or indeed any coarse fibrous material like rope or sailcloth could be used for the manufacture of browns – paper for wrapping – but until the introduction of bleaching agents in the 18th century, only white linen or cotton would suffice for the making of fine white paper.

The first job at a mill was to sort, cut and wash the rags, discarding buttons and hooks. The rags were then piled up, damped down and left to rot. The next step was to break down the rags further, softening them into fibrous strands with water-driven hammers.

The resulting soup of fibre and water, known as 'stuff', was then transferred from the circular stuff-chest to a rectangular vat. The stuff — kept lukewarm by a stove, and agitated with a pole, or 'potching stick' was sieved on moulds and formed into paper, by a craftsman known as the vatman.

VATMAN, COUCHER AND LAYER

The vatman's skill lies in the making of sheet after sheet of paper, identical in size, thickness and quality. It was his responsibility to ensure that the stuff was mixed to the correct proportions – about 3 to 5 per cent fibre. Each sheet of paper was formed on a mould, a rectangular wooden frame across which were stretched fine bronze or copper wires, 25 or 35 to the inch. These were supported by thicker wires running

at right angles. A mould was used in combination with a deckle, another wooden frame that fitted over the mould to form a shallow tray.

Holding mould and deckle together, the vatman dipped one of the long edges into the stuff and drew it towards him. As he drew it he levelled the mould so that it was covered with an even layer of the stuff of the right thickness for the type of paper being made. His dexterity and deftness of movement as well as his instinctive knowledge of the amount of stuff needed for each sheet was critical. Giving it a light shake to spread the fibres, he then lifted the mould from the vat. As the water drained off, the fibres bonded together to form the sheet.

The vatman then slid the mould to the second craftsman, the coucher, removing the deckle as he did so. Each vatman had a pair of moulds so that he could be forming another sheet while the coucher removed the first one from the mould.

Gripping one of the long edges of the mould, the coucher placed the other edge on a layer of

SIZING PAPER
*(right) After drying, a sheet
of paper has a rough
absorbent surface. If it is
being prepared to take ink, it
has to be sized to limit its
absorbency. This is done by
dipping each sheet in a
mixture called gelatinous
size.*

PAPER SHEETS
*(below) Individual sheets of
newly made paper are hung
to dry over cow or horse hair
ropes in drying lofts at the
paper mill. Unlike hempen
ropes, cow or horse hair
ropes do not absorb water
and, therefore, do not
leave a waterline mark on
the paper.*

felt placed on a plank at a convenient working height. With an even, rolling motion he laid the sheet on the felt and lifted off the mould. The mould was then slid back to the vatman, and the coucher would flip another felt on top of the sheet before reaching for the second mould which by now would be sliding towards him. A vatman and a coucher working together built up a rhythm of movement that allowed them to produce a sheet every ten seconds or so. The felt acted as a buffer and a drying agent between sheets which at this stage were wet and delicate and called waterleaf.

Once the coucher had built up a pile of about 144 interleaved felts and sheets (6 quires of 24 sheets) he capped it with a pilch, half-a-dozen old felts sewn together. He and the vatman then took this bundle of felts and sheets to the wooden-screw press to squeeze out water from the paper.

The third craftsman, the layer, removed the bundle from the press, and separated the felts from the paper. Next, the paper was taken to be air-dried on lines strung across the drying loft.

Unless it is simply used as blotting paper, paper for writing on has to be sized, so that it will take ink. Gelatine for size was made by boiling up the waste products of tanners, curriers, glovers and parchment-makers. The sheets of paper were dipped in the size, pressed to remove the excess, dried under heat, then taken to the salle, or finishing room, where they were smoothed and trimmed, if required. For a smooth, fine finish, the sheets were interleaved with plates of zinc and pressed, sometimes under heat. The final task was to grade the papers as good, damaged (retree), outsides (less perfect paper from the top and bottom quires of a ream – the top and bottom 24 sheets) and rejects, called brokes. The paper was counted into reams (originally 480 sheets, or twenty quires), and wrapped for delivery. The whole process, from rags to finished work, could take three months.

THE GROWING INDUSTRY

Paper mills of the 17th and 18th centuries were often small, sometimes part of a group of other mills all sharing the same head of water, and often owned by the same proprietor. Only the larger mills employed vatmen, couchers and layers full-time. Paper-makers who had served

BEFORE PAPER
(above) Before the craft of paper-making spread to Europe, books were hand-written and illustrated, usually by monks, on parchment, made from animal skins.

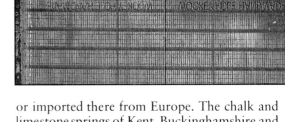

or imported there from Europe. The chalk and limestone springs of Kent, Buckinghamshire and Hertfordshire were perfect for fine paper, and the infant industry grew around them.

In the 18th century the industry began to grow faster. Industrial changes and an ever-expanding population increased the demand for all kinds of paper, especially browns. The quality of white paper improved greatly, largely due to the efforts of Messrs James Whatman, Senior and Junior, at their Turkey Mill near Maidstone. It was they who introduced moulds of woven mesh, instead of parallel laid mesh which was unsuitable for the finest work. At Maidstone they also produced the largest size of single sheet, the Antiquarian, $52\frac{1}{2}$ inches by $31\frac{3}{4}$ inches.

Increased demand brought with it a need to produce more paper faster and in the 18th century several mills had introduced the new Dutch machines, Hollanders, which beat and broke up rags in a faster and more intensive way.

The next leap forward came at the beginning

THE VATMAN
(below) A skilled craftsman, the vatman knows just how much 'stuff' to scoop on to the mould.

RAGS INTO PULP
(above) Cotton rags were prepared for use in paper-making by women rag sorters.

their seven-year apprenticeship were awarded a Card of Freedom, and became journeymen, moving from mill to mill in search of work. As well as the three craftsmen, one or two journey-men were employed to work on the press, to look after the beating engine and to finish the paper. A number of women and children worked in the hot and dusty rag room, or in the salle.

As the industry grew, albeit slowly, paper mills took over sites from other mills; not every site was suitable, however. As well as water to drive the engines, they needed water for the stuff, and in the case of white paper this meant well or spring water, pure and clean. Because a free flow of air was needed through the drying loft, mills could not be sited in deep valleys.

Another important consideration was a ready source of rags and a market for the paper. London was by far the largest consumer of paper, and was also the most concentrated source of rags, generated by its own population

WATERMARK

Watermarks – visible when a sheet of paper is held up to the light – are impressions left by wire designs sewn on to the wires of the mould (left). When the paper is formed its texture is slightly altered over the spot where the design is placed and this leaves a permanent mark. Some watermarks name the mill, others the paper size.

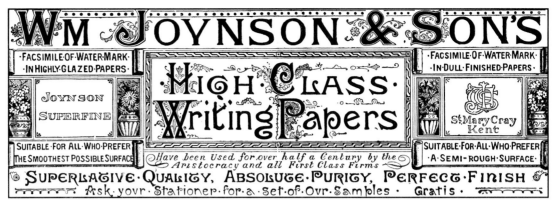

of the 19th century. A French clerk, Nicholas-Louis Robert, made a prototype paper-making machine. Receiving little encouragement in France, he brought a model to England where his cause was taken up by two stationers, the Fourdrinier brothers, and an engineer, Bryan Donkin.

The principle of the Fourdrinier machine, as it came to be known, was an endless belt of mesh. At the 'wet end' of the machine, stuff was sprayed on to the belt; it was shaken as it moved along and transformed into paper. Still moving along the machine it was transferred to felt where it was pressed, then reeled in, still wet, to be taken off, unreeled, cut and loft-dried.

The main limit on machine production was the supply of rags. Then, in 1856 Thomas Routledge, an Oxfordshire papermaker, produced a satisfactory printing paper from esparto, a wild grass from the Mediterranean. Other paper makers followed his lead, and soon large-scale manufacture began. The manufacture of paper from wood pulped either by grinding or made by chemical treatment followed in the 1880s.

Today a few hand paper-making mills are still in existence. One of these, at Wookey Hole in Somerset, maintains the old techniques and provides a living link stretching back nearly 2000 years to Imperial China.

HIGH CLASS PAPER
(above) By the mid 19th century a number of innovative and enterprising paper-makers existed. One of them, William Joynson, built up a considerable reputation at his St Mary Cray mill in Kent. In 1842 he employed 120 hands: by 1865 there were 630 people in the mill's employ, turning out 25 tons of fine paper per week.

MECHANIZATION
(left) The craft of paper-making was revolutionized by the 19th-century arrival of paper-making machines. Work on a machine brought to England by a Frenchman, Nicholas-Louis Robert, was financed by Henry and Sealy Fourdrinier. Today, modified versions of the Fourdrinier machine are universal. Here, (below) at the Bowater-Scott Corporation, soft tissue paper is coming off a forming roll machine on to a gigantic parent reel, prior to being converted into the 1½ million rolls of tissue made daily by the company.

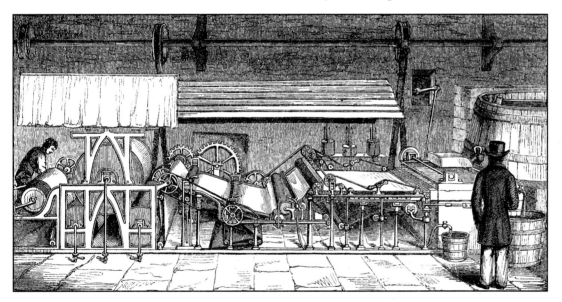

Modified Fourdrinier machines still operate today. They can generate enormous amounts of paper at speed, cut and dried. For a time, hand and machine methods of paper-making continued side by side but Fourdrinier machines soon took over the bulk of the work. In 1805, the peak year for hand-made paper, 16,500 tons were made in 760 vats around the country. In 1860, though 4000 tons of paper was hand-produced, machines accounted for 96,000 tons. At all except the highest grades, Fourdrinier machines produced a better quality product, and those mills carrying on the hand-made tradition concentrated more and more on paper for drawing, for watercolours, for legal documents, stocks and bonds, tracing and banknotes.

The Bookbinder's Craft

Although cloth-covered hard-backs are now mass produced, the traditional craft of leather bookbinding is still very much alive, fulfilling the continuing demand for handsome, durable books.

A hand-bound book has a simple perfection that its modern factory-made counterpart cannot hope to match. A beautiful binding is the perfect foil to a fine text, and Samuel Pepys was moved to comment that he added books to his substantial library 'as much for the sake of the binding' as for the words within! Perhaps the most surprising aspect of craft bookbinding is its continuity – the traditions of bookbinding form an unbroken thread, running right back to the first books.

The earliest books, in the sense that we use the word today, were a fusion of two ideas. The concept of a hinged collection of flat sheets was a Roman one, but Roman writing tablets were made not of a flexible material like paper, but of thick, rigid, waxed wooden panels hinged together to form a diptych or triptych (a 'book' of two or three leaves). The other component of the book is paper or its equivalent such as papyrus or parchment (vellum). Papyrus appeared about 5000 years ago and parchment began to replace it around 200 AD, but in antiquity the conventional method of creating long documents was to fix sheets together in the form of a long roll or scroll.

The first recognizable books were made of sheets of papyrus, and later parchment, bound between sturdy wooden panels. The roll did not disappear immediately, but was considered by the emergent Christian community as a pagan form, and eventually the more acceptable and 'Godly' book replaced it.

EARLY EXTRAVAGANCE

Since all early books were hand-written and often lavishly and painstakingly illuminated – with intricate initial letters and brightly-coloured miniatures – they were very valuable items, and strictly the province of the rich and the clergy. Early English bindings were relatively simple, but gradually decoration began to appear on the grained oak or beech covers. Texts that were to be carried around – perhaps by itinerant holy men – were still kept fairly plain because of the risk from highwaymen, but books for churches and abbeys were often extravagantly decorated, with gold, silver, silk or velvet and precious stones. The earliest recorded English binding dates from the seventh century.

By the time of the Norman Conquest, the book had evolved into a form that bears a clearer resemblance to today's volumes, but it was still a heavy, unwieldy object. However, over the next four centuries or so, bookbinding was gradually refined, especially in decoration. At the monastic centres of York, Gloucester, London, Durham and Winchester, the monks stamped animal signs and emblems into the deerskin coverings, and by the 12th century, embossed metal dies began to be used. These were heated, then pressed into the wet leather to leave a raised mark rather like a cameo; the heat also subtly coloured the leather.

This technique, called blind stamping, was later elaborated by decorating the pattern with gold leaf. Gold tooling, as it was called, was probably brought to Britain by a Frenchman, Thomas Bethelet, who sold and printed books for Henry VIII from 1530 to 1555. On the more elaborate bindings, gold leaf was also applied to the page edges.

From simple stamped patterns, decoration developed – some would say degenerated – with the use of wheeled tools carrying a pattern on the rim, which were pressed into the leather, and with panel stamping. The latter technique involved forcing a large metal plate carrying a pattern into the leather, so enabling the whole cover to be embossed in one piece.

Books were still jealously guarded, and in many libraries were chained down to prevent theft. Real changes in the pattern of bookbinding and book ownership had to wait until the middle of the 15th century, with the large-scale introduction from continental Europe of paper, and printing with movable type. Paper was very much lighter and thinner than parchment, so books became smaller; and the replacement by printing of laborious hand-copying made books much cheaper and more widespread. This in turn led to less lavish decoration on the cover – a cheaper book did not warrant a fancy binding.

By 1476, when William Caxton began printing in England, all the basic processes of craft bookbinding had evolved and were to continue more or less unchanged – except in details of finish, style and decoration – until mechanization

HAND-WRITTEN BOOKS
(below) In the days before printing, the monasteries assumed the task of copying books out by hand. Many monks spent their days laboriously writing out histories and religious works. They bound their elegant texts between oak or beech boards and, later, evolved the art of leather-binding.

in the first part of the 19th century made the bookbinding craft virtually obsolete.

In the 17th century, the bookbinder often worked on a volume from start to finish. The master craftsman (women usually worked on sewing operations) typically operated from the ground floor of his house, and was helped by an unpaid apprentice who lodged with the family upstairs. Work probably started at first light, and continued until sunset – a guttering candle was considered too much of a fire risk.

Industrialization affected only books destined for mass consumption, and some smaller traditional book binderies continue to operate today. This continuity makes a visit to a bindery a rare treat: unlike many craft workshops where lost skills are revived, the bindery is both a slice of craft history and a living, profit-making place of work. And, with modern innovations – such as new hingeing structures, new sewing equipment and new and imaginative bookbinding materials – the craft continues to evolve.

A hand-made book looks simple, but it is actually a remarkably complex work of engineering. Every material used in the binding has to be carefully chosen, thoroughly prepared, and meticulously worked. For example, adhesives must be sufficiently strong to hold the books together, but not brittle, or they will crack with age and use. The threads that fix the pages in place must be pulled to just the right tension:

PRECIOUS POSSESSIONS
The heavy bindings of early medieval books were often lavishly decorated with hand-worked gold or silver, silk and velvet, and even precious stones and exquisite cloisonné enamels (above right). Inside, the vellum pages were adorned with brightly-coloured miniatures and delicate marginal decoration (right). Even the more modestly bound volumes were of such value that they were beyond the means of ordinary people. Indeed, until the 15th century, only the wealthy could afford to own a Bible. The great monastic libraries carefully guarded their precious volumes, and some of the finest collections – like that of Hereford Cathedral (above) – were chained down to prevent theft.

too slack or too tight and the pages will either tear from the binding, or not open flat.

The binder's first task is to fold the printed sheets of the book and gather them together so that the pages run in the correct sequence. The folded sheets, now called sections, are next stacked in a pile to make the complete book in loose-leaf form. At the top and bottom of the pile, the binder puts 'end-papers'; these are tough paper sheets, often beautifully hand-marbled, that secure the first and last sections to the boards that form the binding. The binder carefully slides the pile into a simple wooden frame, across which are strung a series of stout cords, which the binder will later fix tightly on to the boards. In this way, all the components of the book are held securely but flexibly together along the spine.

The binder's needle passes in and out of the folded edge of each section in turn, passing around the cords, so that each and every page is secured to cords at several points along the spine. Cut free from the frame, the sewn sections already begin to take on the shape of a book, although the page edges are still rough and untrimmed. 'Glueing-up' further increases the likeness: the binder brushes a gelatin-based glue along the folded and sewn edges to fill the gaps between the sections and strengthen the spine.

At this stage, folding and sewing have considerably increased the thickness of the book at the spine, so the binder now 'rounds and backs' the volume. He uses a hammer to tap the sections into a concave shape, so that the folded and sewn edges protrude further at the middle of the book than at the endparts. To solve the problem of the thickening at the spine, the binder clamps the book in a form of wooden vice, and hammers the sections outwards in a fan shape at the spine. The front and back

UNDER PRESSURE
(below) Once the book covers have been glued, the books are compressed for several hours.

TRADITIONAL BOOKBINDING
(above and far right) This sequence shows some of the main processes of craft bookbinding. One of the most important stages is the sewing of the sections (using a sewing frame), which ensures the strength and sturdiness of the book. The page edges are then trimmed with a guillotine or 'plough' and, later, the leather is cut to size for the cover. Finally, the leather binding is embossed with gold-leaf.

sections fold over almost at 90°, forming a neat recess ready to receive the boards. A vellum head and tailband is then sewn on to the stitching at the top and bottom of the spine, using silk or cotton thread. This provides the book with extra resilience for the forthcoming rigours of the library shelf.

The binder has already prepared the boards, by cutting them to size, lining them on both sides with strong paper, and piercing holes for the cords. He now threads the cords through the punched holes, then frays and hammers the loose end of the cords flat, using paste to hold them to the boards.

To trim the page edges flat, the binder moves the book to a large wooden frame called a 'lying-in press'. A wooden clamp holds the book inside the frame, adjacent to a horizontal rail, along which runs a 'plough'. This is a bit like a woodworking plane in that it carries a razor-sharp blade which slices off paper from the book edge, shaving by shaving. The binder is left with a perfectly flat edge which is smooth enough for gilding.

All that is needed now to complete the book is a cover. A quarter-binding covers just the book's spine in leather, with cloth or paper protecting the rest of the cover; half binding additionally covers the four corners of the boards. A full binding, though, provides the most protection, since it wraps the entire book in leather. The binder cuts the leather to fit the boards and spine, then shaves the edges of the hide so that they will lie flat on the inside of the boards. Flour or rice paste holds the leather cover to the spine and to the boards, and the book is left overnight between wooden boards while the paste sets. Finally, the end-papers are pasted down on to the boards to cover the edges of the leather, and the book is left under pressure for several hours.

Details of binding methods have changed and evolved through the centuries in response to fashion, to new ideas from the continent, and to the availability of new materials. The traditional style of binding described above is now known as 'flexible' binding, because the spine is quite literally flexible. When the book is opened, the shape of the spine magically changes from convex in section to concave.

This style of binding puts a lot of stress on the paper. Traditional hand-made paper could take the stress, but flimsy machine-made paper, which was invented around 1800, tore when bound in this way. To solve the problem, bookbinders cut grooves in the paper to recess the cords. There was also an ulterior motive for introducing sunken cords: books could be made very much more cheaply by this method, because

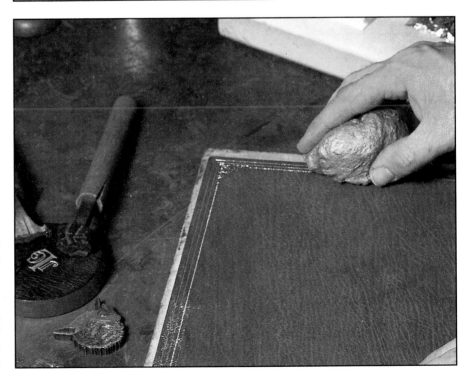

FACTORY PRODUCTION *(above) In the 19th century, hard-back books were mass-produced in large binderies. The women folded the sheets and sewed the sections in sewing frames, while the men 'rounded and backed' the spines, using round hammers. Here the women are using three – as opposed to the usual five – sewing cords, so cutting down on sewing time and saving on costs.*

FRESH IDEAS *(right) Modern bookbinders have pioneered new creative techniques and the use of imaginative new materials. Philip Smith's* Lord of the Rings *boasts spattered endpapers – made by applying waterproof inks on damp paper (which are washed off when almost dry) – and an abalone shell inlay in the centre of the 'eye'.*

sewing time was reduced by up to 80 per cent. Once the cords had been hidden, binders succumbed to the temptation to cut down on the number of cords, in order to bring down costs still further. To disguise the inferior quality of their books, they constructed fake cords on the spine of the book, and introduced a hollow back from a tube of paper, so that the book could be covered in a fabric instead of leather.

Books bound in this way wore badly, partly because in a sunken-cord binding the leather is pared away at the hinge so that the book opens and closes easily. As a result, the library style of binding evolved, to meet the demand for more durable books. These books have a groove between the edge of the boards and the spine itself, so that heavier leather can be used – making a stronger 'hinge'. The book was additionally sewn onto durable linen tapes, instead of hemp cord, and other features added further reinforcement.

Machine production of books in the 19th century led to the cased binding. Here the binding was made separately from the rest of the book, and the sections – ready-sewn on tapes – were pasted into the cover. This technique made mass production possible, and virtually all books are now sold in cased bindings. Nevertheless, a cased book is not really suitable for hard wear, and if you have a volume you use regularly – such as a road atlas or a business directory – you'll probably find that within a year of daily use the cover and pages have parted company.

A book damaged in this way is not totally beyond repair. A traditional bookbinder can break the book up for you, and reconstruct it using traditional hand-binding methods. The rebinding will probably cost you as much as a new cased book, but it will last a lifetime of daily use.

The Village Smithy

Before the Industrial Revolution, no rural community could exist without a smithy. The blacksmith shod horses and manufactured and repaired many of the necessities of farming and domestic life.

For many centuries the smithy was the hub of village life. There, in the glow of the forge, their faces lit red by showers of bright sparks in the murky gloom, people waiting for work to be done met those who were simply waiting; gossip and parish news were exchanged to the measured beat of hammer on anvil and the hissing of steam. It was especially popular in winter when the fires were roaring.

In medieval times there was at least one smithy in every village. It would often be sited in the centre of the village, usually, strategically, at crossroads. The smithy was, in effect, a miniature factory, turning out all manner of domestic utensils, agricultural equipment and craftsmen's tools, from ploughshares to cooking pots, billhooks to boot scrapers.

MEN OF IRON

Blacksmiths were among the earliest independent craftsmen, their own master; they contracted to do jobs rather than work hours – though the hours they did work were long and arduous. A blacksmith had to acquire a formidable array of skills, and be physically immensely strong – like Longfellow's 'mighty man . . . With large and sinewy hands; And the muscles of his brawny arms Are strong as iron bands'. He might have other jobs to do, as well as smithing. The job of village barber often fell to the smith, and many were not above a spot of dentistry. He was sought out as an advisor or oracle, and he could conduct a form of marriage over his anvil. Partly this was a testament to his status in the community, and partly it was in deference to his seemingly magical mastery of fire and iron.

The process of extracting iron from the ground and shaping it into tools and weapons is about 4000 years old. All the metals previously worked by man were soft enough to be worked cold – copper, tin, silver, gold. The shaping of iron, however, required great heat, and once cooled it was harder than any other metal.

The first British blacksmiths – so-called because iron was known as blackmetal – were itinerant, going from manor to manor, and often smelting their own iron. Their favourite material was always wrought iron, 99.9 per cent pure iron, resistant to corrosion and easily shaped when hot. (This has now largely been superseded by mild steel.) With the introduction of the blast furnace in the 15th century, the production of iron was stepped up and taken out of the hands of the smiths and monasteries to become an industry in its own right. The smith set up his own workshop, bought his iron from the ironmaster and concentrated on what his skill could make of it.

The blacksmith rarely worked alone. Most supported one or two labourers, apprentices and a mate, who, apart from undertaking the simpler jobs at the smith's direction, worked the bellows, wielded the hammers and helped to look after the horses.

HOME REPAIRS
(left) The development of gas welding meant that farmers could repair their own tools and equipment, thus removing a major source of employment for the traditional blacksmith.

HAMMER AND TONGS
(above) Hammers and tongs were the smith's most useful tools. They were operated virtually as extensions of his hands. The full-length, spark-proof leather apron has been the uniform of the blacksmith for centuries. Sometimes the bottom edge would be fringed, and he would use it to sweep debris off the anvil.

The hearth, or forge, was the heart of the smithy. Usually square and brick-built, the hearth contained the fire and raised it to a height where work could be switched from it to the anvil and back with the minimum of lifting. Above the forge, a tapering cowl, built of brick or sheet iron, collected the smoke and fumes and led them up to the chimney. In front of the forge, often built into it, was a cast-iron water trough, or bosh, used for cooling the work or quenching tools that got too hot. A rail on which the smith kept his array of tongs was fixed to the forge at a handy height.

Raising the fire's temperature sufficiently to enable iron to be worked requires a forced draught. From the earliest time this was provided by a bellows, which could be as much as six feet across. The bellows produced a draught on

IN THE HEAT OF THE FORGE
Even in medieval times the forge was a busy place. Apart from the smith and his customers, there might be an apprentice, and an assistant to operate the bellows.

235

ARMS AND ARMOUR

One of the main functions of early smiths was to provide the vast range and variety of armoury which was a commonplace of medieval warfare. Helmets, visors, breastplates, chain-mail, spears, halberds, maces, daggers, shields and swords were all fashioned by the versatile blacksmith.

TOOLS OF THE TRADE

The blacksmith was a toolmaker for himself as well as for others, and the extent of his home-made armoury was vast. Apart from bulky items like the anvil, swage block and vices, the village smithy would display a formidable array of hammers, tongs, rasps, files and drills to cover everything from decorative ironwork to repairing reaper-binders.

both the up and down strokes, delivering it through a cast-iron tube called a tuyere to the heart of the fire. They were operated by a handle projecting out over the forge at around shoulder height, either by the smith himself, or by a labourer or apprentice or compliant passer-by.

However, it was skilled work, as pumping too vigorously or too lazily could prove disastrous. Heat iron too fast and it becomes brittle; heat it too slowly and it melts and burns. Wrought iron can be worked at a wide range of temperatures, but within that range are narrower bands at which the iron becomes particularly suitable for specific tasks. Judging these 'heats' by eye, and managing them, is one of the smith's most indispensable skills.

Heats are known not by numbers of degrees but by nicknames based on the colour and appearance of the metal. Snowball heat, beyond which iron melts, makes the metal white hot and spongy. At this heat two pieces of metal can be fused by hammering. Below this are the welding heats – Full, Light and Slippery – which are most often used. Next comes Bright Red, Cherry Red and Dull Red which are used for shaping metal and for flattening, smoothing and finishing. Then there is Black Heat just enough to make the iron glow faintly in deep shadow. Lowest of all is Warm Heat, where the metal is wafted through the fire rather than held in it, until it is just too hot to hold. This heat is used for setting up springs.

THE ANVIL

Next to the forge, the most important part of the smith's equipment was the anvil, where all the hot metal was worked. Early anvils varied in design from square to torpedo-shaped. As they evolved, one model, the London pattern, square at one end and conical at the other, prevailed.

Near the square heel are two holes. Holes are punched over the circular 'pritchel hole' using a punch called a pritchel. This, and the square swage hole, also takes the shanks of tools, holding them steady while the hot metal is hammered over them.

Most of the work is done on the face, which is covered with a welded plate of hard, blister steel to withstand heavy hammering. Between the face and the pointed 'bick' is a small ledge, the table, softer than the face. This is used when iron is chiselled cold, as a cold chisel's edge would be damaged by a hard steel surface. The

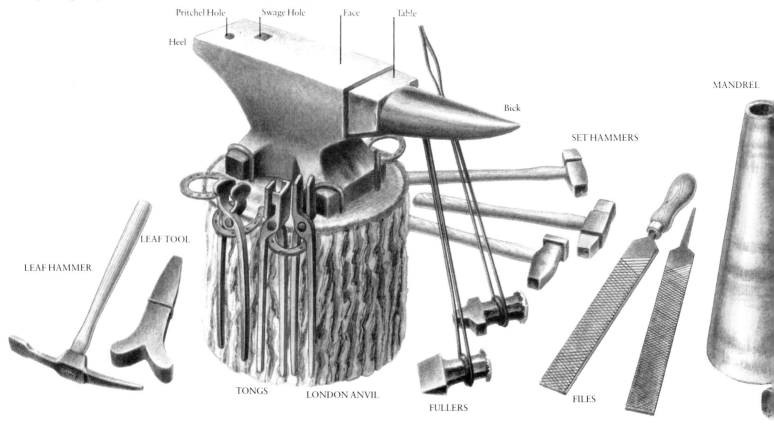

LEAF HAMMER

LEAF TOOL

Pritchel Hole   Swage Hole   Face   Table

Heel

Bick

MANDREL

SET HAMMERS

TONGS   LONDON ANVIL

FULLERS

FILES

main purpose of the bick is to curve metal for horseshoes or forge links for chains.

The anvil was raised to working height on a massive block of wood, usually elm, that was embedded in the brick, stone or beaten earth of the smithy floor. The block served as a shock absorber and gave some spring to the hammer. The recoil of a hammer from a well-set anvil took much of the effort out of lifting it.

The basic tools of the smith's trade were hammers and tongs. He usually wielded a double-headed ball-peen hammer weighing a

SWAGE BLOCK

BALL-PEEN HAMMER

SWAGE   ANVIL SWAGE

SLEDGE HAMMER

WOMEN AT WAR
(left) In wartime women have often taken on tasks that were previously reserved for men. When necessary, even the physically demanding job of blacksmithing was carried on by women.

couple of pounds. For small and medium-sized jobs he used this directly on the hot metal, but for heavier forging he simply tapped the metal to indicate to his assistant the target for the blows of a heavy striking hammer or sledge. The smith tapped and the striker struck in easy counterpoint.

Just as the hammer was an extension of the smith's right hand, so the tongs with which he held and manipulated the work were an extension of his left. He might have 50 or more pairs of tongs, varying in the size and shape of their jaws.

There could be hundreds of other tools, each designed to ease the task of cutting, shaping, smoothing and finishing the metal. Sets were wedge-shaped cutting tools. Fullers were rounded so that they indented rather than cut. When a piece of metal needed to be lengthened, it was fullered across its width several times so that it became wavy, then the waves were smoothed out with a flatter – a tool with a broad flat edge that was hit from above with a sledge.

A variety of swages enabled the smith to mould rods of iron into a particular size or shape. Larger pieces were formed in the swage block, a piece of cast-iron pierced and indented with slots, holes and grooves. Rigidly mounted when in use, it was effectively an auxiliary anvil. Another essential tool was the mandrel

HOT METAL
(top and above) The smith's skill lay to a great extent in manipulating the fire, bosh and bellows to produce precisely the degree of heat required for a specific task. He judges the heat by eye, watching for fine gradations of colour from a dull, dark glow, through blood red, to gold, to the fierce glare of white heat.

used for truing up hoops and rings.

Some techniques allowed metal to be formed with the hammer and tongs only. Two pieces can be joined by vigorous hammering at snowball heat, while a bar can be made thicker and shorter by 'upsetting' it. One end of the bar is heated, then it is held upright, hot end on the anvil, and struck up and down on the face. If the bar is to be reduced, it is subjected to 'drawing down'. Hammered on all four sides to keep its shape, it takes several heats as the smith works along the bar.

A hard cutting edge could be given or restored to a tool by tempering. Wrought iron is hardened by rapid heating and cooling. To temper a blade, it is first heated, then the edge is quenched in the bosh. The smith watches the colours as the rest of the blade cools more slowly, and quenches that at the critical moment. The hard edge can then be ground for sharpness.

To begin with it was the violence of the

WROUGHT IRON
In the centuries before the Industrial Revolution, iron was the raw material for thousands of objects in everyday use – on the farm, on the battlefield, and in houses, churches and castles. All these were individually crafted by hand, often by the village blacksmith. Some smiths specialized in decorative work, embellishing simple functional items, like gates and hinges, with elegant scrolls and extravagant curlicues.

FIRE IRONS
(below) A cottage kitchen would house many products of the smith's skills – the fire basket in the hearth, and all the paraphernalia of tripods and trivets, spits, kettle irons, cauldrons and griddles.

society around him which provided a market for the blacksmith's skills. The end products of his labours tended to be weapons and armoury, for the local squire and his dwelling; the tradition of decorative ironwork and grilles grew out of the need to secure buildings. The wrought iron gate is a direct descendant of the portcullis.

As time went on, and iron became more readily available, the smith found himself making and repairing a huge variety of products. For the farmer there were ploughshares and hoes, shovels and scythes. For the cottager there were candle holders, cauldrons, locks and hinges, fire irons, even toys for the children. He made the tools for the thatcher and mason, carpenter and coach builder. One of his most frequent tasks was to provide the metal tyres for vast wagon wheels. He also shod horses. In an age utterly dependent on horses for power and transport, this latter function spawned a specialized type of blacksmithing, farriery; although most general

smiths could shoe horses also.

The Industrial Revolution was the beginning of an inexorable decline for the village smithy. Tools and utensils became mass-produced and horse-power gave way to steam. Just before and during World War 2, the introduction of tractors on to British farms cut the horse population by half and made the British blacksmith largely redundant.

Faced with a drop in demand for their services, some smithies became garages, others specialized in decorative ironwork. Farriers took to the road, and other smiths found employment in larger concerns like foundries and quarries. Even where the hearth was still alight, there was change. Electric fans replaced bellows, electric drills and grinders the hand-held kind. The skills of the blacksmith are still practised in some places, but the traditional village smithy, meeting-place, hive of industry, universal repair-shop and bespoke manufactory is no more.

The Farrier

The old-time farrier used to shoe horses in the heat and noise of the smithy; but his modern-day counterpart has largely taken to the road, travelling with a supply of ready-forged shoes.

ROMAN STYLE
(above) The Romans used fancy 'hipposandals' to protect the horse's hoofs on stony ground. A plate of metal with side-clips, and spurs or rings at the front and back, was tied on to the hoof with leather thongs – rather like a stylish Roman sandal. This hipposandal, in the Hull Museum collection, is a particularly unwieldy example, weighing 23½oz.

THE VICTORIAN FARRIER
(left) Landseer's atmospheric painting shows a nervous bay mare being shod in the stable. The farrier is using the hot shoe to burn a slight impression in the insensitive horn of the hoof, to make sure that the shoe fits tightly. He is wearing the traditional leather apron, which is split between the thighs, so that he can grip the horse's hoof firmly in his lap. The fringe of the apron was used to brush the scraps of metal off the anvil, which mingle with the hoof shavings littering the floor.

MAKING A SHOE
(right) This red-hot shoe is being hammered into shape on the anvil. Lying on the side is a punch, which will be used to make the nail-holes, and a rasp for finishing off the edges. The farrier's tool-box lies on the ground, behind a three-legged stand for the horse's hoof. This is often referred to as the 'lazy blacksmith', as most old-time farriers believed that the horse's foot should always rest in the lap, never mind the discomfort.

A heavy horse standing patiently in the flickering light of a forge; the acrid tang of the grey-white smoke that billows up from a hoof when it comes into contact with hot metal; the hiss of the hot shoe as it is quenched in the bosh; the bubbling of the bellows and the ringing of the hammers – few things are more evocative of Britain's recent rural past than the shoeing of horses, or farriery. In one image is combined the engine of rural Britain – the horse, and the sweltering workshop, the smithy.

The craft of the farrier does not have the antiquity of that of the blacksmith. The Romans shod their horses with bulky 'hipposandals', iron cups tied to the hoof with leather thongs (rather like fashionable sandals), but these were very temporary and often inefficient. If a stone worked its way inside the hipposandal the horse would quickly be lamed. The nailed-on horseshoe seems to have been a 'Romano-British' or 'Celtic' invention and dates from sometime during the Roman occupation.

THE HORSE'S HOOF

A horse's hoof grows very much like a human fingernail, but at the rate of an inch a month. In the wild, natural wear and tear usually keeps the horny outer covering of the hoof at a comfortable length, but when the horse has to walk hard roads, or carry heavy loads, it can be worn down too far and eventually make the horse lame. The same principle applies to all hoofed animals, many of whom were shod. Donkeys and mules take a light U-shaped shoe, quite like a horseshoe, but cloven-footed animals like cattle take double shoes. Cattle were shod in the days when they were used as draught animals, or just before embarking on a long drove to market. The arduous journey from Scotland to the English markets along uneven tracks and

roads would otherwise have left them lame.

The oldest horseshoes which have survived are wavy-rimmed, with large, punched nail-holes. The nails themselves were massive, with domed heads; the horse, in effect, walked on the protruding nailheads.

The next development was a tapering, flat-headed nail that wore down with the shoe while keeping its grip. The shoes were grooved, or fullered, all around the bottom, so that the nail-heads could be sunk further beneath the surface of the shoe. However, these smooth shoes gave a poor grip on cobbles or paving, especially in wet weather. To stop them slipping, heavy horses working docks or cobbled yards were shod with shoes that had the ends (at the heel) bent over to form heavy 'calkins'.

One hundred and fifty yeas ago, the basic

HOT-SHOEING
(above) When hot-shoeing the horse, the farrier holds the shoe by a punch, lodged in one of the nail-holes. As the smoke billows up from the scorching hoof, he checks the fit and makes any minor adjustments.

THE BLACKSMITH'S FORGE
(below) In the past, the farrier worked in the smithy, shoeing horses in the heat of the forge. The giant horse-shoe door of this smithy in Northumberland boldly advertises his trade.

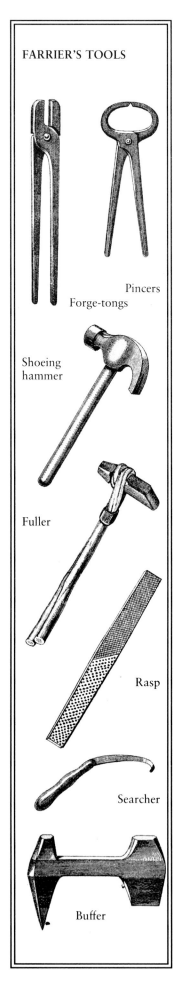

FARRIER'S TOOLS

Pincers

Forge-tongs

Shoeing hammer

Fuller

Rasp

Searcher

Buffer

modern design was achieved with the introduction of the toe-clip, a triangular lug that slopes upward and back from the centre of the shoe to grip and support the front of the hoof. These horseshoes, however, protect the hoof so well that they have to be changed regularly: this is because the hoof is not subject to normal wear and tear and if its growth is not checked the frog – the fleshy part of the foot – does not come into contact with the ground and the horse again finds difficulty walking. If this is neglected, the muscles in the foot waste away and the horse is permanently lamed. A heavy farm horse needs a pedicure and new shoes every three months or so; a hunter or town horse requires them every month; and a race-horse perhaps as often as once a week.

A farrier must have a thorough knowledge of horses, and not just their limbs and feet. He must study the anatomy of the whole animal to gain an understanding of its posture and balance and so be sure of fitting the right shoe. Working with such a large, nervous and potentially dangerous beast, he also has to be something of an animal psychologist. And in the days before vets, farriers were horse-doctors, too, and today they collaborate with vets in diagnosing problems and, where possible, producing special surgical shoes to correct them. The modern farrier must pass examinations in all these areas, as well as learning the art of shoeing. Though there have always been specialist farriers, in the past much farriery work was undertaken by the general blacksmith.

TOOLS OF THE TRADE

In every smithy there was a farrier's box – split-level, open-sided, and measuring about eighteen inches long by ten inches wide and ten inches deep. In it were kept all the tools of the craft, tools that were used for no other purpose. There was a hammer with a V-shaped claw; a pair of pincers: a pair of clippers with sharp overlapping jaws; a paring-knife, razor-sharp and hooked over at the end; a tool shaped like a flat elongated 'H' with an edge on the underside of the bar, known as a buffer; and a collection of rasps, files and nails of various sizes. All of these tools, including the specially-shaped nails, would have been made in the smithy itself.

Horseshoe nails are unlike any others. Rectangular in section, they taper to a point from a flat wedged top, curving slightly so that they can follow the natural curve of the hoof – which is no more than a quarter to half an inch thick. The nails expand when driven in to give a tight grip. Big draught-horses take a three-inch nail while racehorses make do with less than two inches. The farrier always kept a good supply on hand, ready-forged; industrial mass-production of horseshoe nails began only in the 19th century.

In the past, horses would always have been brought to the smithy to be shod. A population of two hundred horses could keep a farrier

CUEING AN OX
(above) Other animals, besides horses, were shod by the farrier, including heavy working oxen. Because cattle have cloven hooves, the farrier had to make double shoes (known as 'cues') which were crescent-shaped with a clip. The cueing itself required considerable strength and a cattle-rancher's skills. The beast would be lassooed with a rope, which would be pulled tight as it drooped towards the ground, drawing the ox's legs together and causing the animal to fall.

more or less permanently employed, and horses were sufficiently plentiful to support local farriers in every village. The mate, or 'doorman' would check the horses while the farrier began to forge the shoes. His initial task was to remove the old shoes and check for signs of wear on the hoof which might indicate problems to come. First of all, he knocked off the points of the nails where they emerged on the top of the hoof with a buffer. Then, gripping the shoe with a large pair of pincers, he carefully eased it away from the hoof, pulling the nails with it. A tap of the hammer knocked the shoe back down leaving the heads of the nails standing proud ready to be removed by the pincers. Old shoes were kept as a pattern for further shoeing of the same horse, or returned to the scrap pile to be melted down and remade.

The exposed hoof was cleaned with a paring knife, then gradually cut down and levelled

THE FARRIER'S ART
*(right) This sequence
illustrates five major
stages of shoeing a
horse. First of all, the
farrier removes the
old shoe with a large
pair of pincers. Then
he cleans the hoof and
files it level, ready for
taking the new shoe.
Having prepared a
shoe and made sure
the fit is correct, he
next hammers in the
nails – an extremely
skilled operation, for
driving one in at the
wrong angle can lame
the horse for life.
Then, using the claw
of the hammer, he
bends or 'clinches' the
ends of the nails over
the hoof. Finally, the
hoof is filed flush with
the new shoe, and the
farrier moves on to
the next leg.*

with knife and clippers. At this stage, the farrier usually had four strips of metal ready for the shoes; most preferred to make a pair at a time, so that one shoe was worked while the other was taking heat. Unless they were to be bent over to make calkins, the ends of the bars were rounded off in a tool called a heel cropper, placed in the swage hole of the anvil.

At the first heat, the metal bar was bent over into a boomerang shape. With a second burst of heat, it took on the more familiar horseshoe curve. Any twists it acquired in this process were then hammered out, and the shoe was heated again and formed into an exact shape over the bick or beak of the anvil. Next the shoe was brought to red heat and six to ten nail-holes were punched into it; these were finished over the pritchel or punching hole.

The last step was to make the toe-clip. This was teased out with a special wedge-faced hammer called a catshead, and bent up at a right-angle. The edges of the finished shoe were then chamfered so that the horse did not damage itself when trotting.

Shoeing always began with the left front leg, and continued anti-clockwise. The farrier would tap the leg he wanted, and then slide his hand down it; the horse's reflex response was to lift the leg ready for shoeing. Holding the hot shoe by a punch placed in one of the nail-holes, and positioning it with the toe-clip, the farrier now 'seated' the shoe, checking the fit through the clouds of billowing smoke.

Putting the horse's hoof down on a metal tripod called a farrier's stand, or 'lazy black-smith', he then returned to the forge with the shoe to make the final adjustments. It was then left to cool until the other three had been made and fitted, and only then was it finally nailed on. As the hoof is so thin, there is very little margin for error, and a nail driven into the quick can ruin a horse for life; the horse will also lash out and possibly permanently injure the hapless farrier.

Cradling the horse's foot in his lap between his split leather apron, and using his own knees as an anvil, the farrier hammered in the nails until they emerged an inch or so above the shoe. The ends of the nails were twisted with the claw of the hammer and then knocked over to grip the outside of the hoof and secure the nail; this is called 'clinching'.

Shoeing nine or ten horses made for a long day's work, and an exhausting one. Horses always lean heavily when their feet are picked up, and plough horses can weigh up to a ton. Continually working with the back and knees bent, braced against the weight of a leaning horse could be crippling, and there were a host of other occupational injuries.

A smithy was an alarming place for a horse, full of heat, smoke and noise; shoeing itself, though painless, could certainly unnerve a first-time visitor, though most horses soon became accustomed to it. First-timers were often brought in with an older, calmer horse to settle

and stand, a portable anvil and a small electric-powered forge, most of his shoeing was and is still done cold.

Working away from the stink and racket of the forge, the modern travelling farrier has the advantage of calmer horses to deal with, but the disadvantage of having to improvise to fit a shoe, especially on an unfamiliar horse. For his regulars, he will carry shoes shaped to fit, but for others he must cold-hammer or bend one of his spares. Horses today are shod with mild steel rather than wrought iron; racehorses take shoes made of the lighter aluminium. Race-horses are always cold-shod, and standard shoes can be bought in various sizes; from three and a half to four inches for ponies, and twice that size for heavy horses.

THE PROFESSIONALS

Since the Registration Act of 1976, farriers have had to be registered with the Farriers' Registration Council; new entrants to the trade can only be registered after four years' training and passing the examinations for the diploma of The Worshipful Company of Farriers. Farriery is no longer a rustic craft, and has now, to a large extent, been divorced from the smithy. Thirty-odd new farriers qualify each year, and enter a craft that is scientific and professional in its outlook.

Farriery is a growing trade once more. Heavy horses are making a comeback, but it is in the leisure-riding boom that the farrier is finding new work. The Police and the Army keep their own farriers, too. But the largest source of farriery work is in the racing world. Centres like Newmarket, Epsom and Lambourne main-tain horse populations in their thousands, en-suring that the farrier is always in demand.

HEAVY WORK
(above) Shoeing a horse can be punishing work: for when a horse lifts its hoof, it tends to lean heavily, and a big shire horse can weigh up to a ton. Working with his body braced against the horse's weight, and with his back and knees continually bent, the farrier can find the task liter-ally back-breaking. Doubled up, and concentrating on the intricacies of fitting a new shoe, he can physically only manage ten heavy cart-horses a day.

HORSE-SHOE HOARD
(right) Oakham Castle in Leicestershire has an extra-ordinary collection of horse-shoes. The estate was once owned by an inspector of far-riers, who demanded a horse-shoe from every visiting peer.

them down. If all else failed, the spooked horse would have its legs fettered and be shod in an undignified position – flat on its back. Apart from the dangers of being kicked, shoeing smiths also had to contend with cuts from unclinched nails and having their feet stepped on. When, to this catalogue, is added the hazard of hot metal spattering on to unprotected arms, it can be appreciated what desperately punishing work shoeing horses could be.

At least until World War 1, however, there was no shortage of farriers or customers. Horses were ubiquitous in town and country, working on farms, in the docks, on the canals and in the city streets; they pulled ploughs, drays, delivery vans, milk wagons, barges and lighters, buses and coaches. But the drastic falls in the working horse population in the 1920s and 30s, in the face of the challenge of the tractor, car and lorry, altered the working pattern of the farrier irrevocably.

In many cases the farrier took to the road, visiting the few horses that were left, scattered about a much larger catchment area than he had been used to. Travelling in a van with a supply of ready-forged shoes, his farrier's box

244

The Wheelwright

With skill and knowledge handed from father to son, the rural wheelwright combined the strengths of ash, oak and elm to make the carts, wagons and wheels once so common in the countryside.

The harvest wagon rolling home from field to farmstead, laden with sheaves of corn and drawn by two heavy draught horses is one of the most evocative images of the countryside of old. It also represents the acme of achievement in the ancient country craft of wheelwrighting – the making of carts, wagons and wooden wagon wheels.

The techniques of wheelwrighting have changed very little over the centuries – indeed, since the craft began about 6000 years ago in Mesopotamia the single revolutionary change was the replacement, in the 18th century BC, of the solid wheel of antiquity by the wheel with spokes. More recent developments have largely been confined to the refinement of the wheelwright's tools, with the advent of mechanization, rather than major changes to the craft itself.

The craft probably reached its peak in Britain during the 150 years or so following the mid to late 18th century, when advances in agriculture led to higher yields of crops from the land, which in turn prompted the development

of the large four-wheeled wagon. Prior to this lighter, smaller two-wheeled carts were commonly used on the land.

The making of cart and wagon bodies was ostensibly the task of the wainwright, but the wheelwright was capable of making the complete wagon from start to finish and his job included that of the wainwright.

With a market of only a dozen or so farmers, a miller, a carrier and possibly a timber dealer, the scope for work on carts and wagons was limited. So, to supplement his income, the wheelwright often took on general carpentry and joinery work and he was, as often as not, the village coffin-maker too.

GENERAL REPAIRS

Spring was often the busiest time of year for the village wheelwright. It was then that farmers preparing for the spring cultivation and sowing pulled their carts and wagons out of the sheds, only to find defects which should have been attended to in the autumn. So, rattling and

COUNTRY CART
(left) Before they were superseded by large four-wheeled wagons, light horse- or oxen-drawn two-wheeled carts were the commonest form of wheeled transport in rural areas.

creaking, the carts and wagons would be persuaded down to the wheelwright's shop where urgent requests would be made for new floorboards, repairs to tailgates, attention to the wheels or a new coat of paint and varnish.

The wheelwright's shop was then a hive of activity. Travelling tradesmen played their part in the busy round. There was usually a sawpit where itinerant sawyers worked, sawing the trees, which the wheelwright had bought, into planks or blocks for hubs. The blacksmith and a 'liner' the man who decorated the bodies of finished vehicles, also found work in the wheelwright's shop from time to time.

For a few weeks the wheelwright would be

working all hours trying to satisfy the demand for his skills. Repairs usually were the mainstay of his income, since craftsman-made wagons were constructed to last a lifetime, and most farmers saw to it that they did.

In a market town things were very different for the wheelwright. As well as the passing trade which he might win from nearby farms there was nearly always work to be done for the town tradesmen. Millers, brewers, agricultural merchants, bakers, furniture stores and coal merchants – all needed carts, wagons and delivery vans.

In many instances the skills, expertise and experience of the craft were passed from

WHEEL POWER
(above) Until the decline in the late 19th century of the horse as the main means of transport, the craft of wheelwrighting had a vital place in rural community life. The village wheelwright, sometimes known as the wainwright, produced the farm carts and wagons so vital for carrying people and their produce to and from home, farm and market.

SHAPING THE HUB
(above) Centre-piece of the wheel, the hub block, usually of solid elm, was turned on a large, hand-driven lathe. The wheelwright cut it to shape with a hand-held chisel, recessing both ends to take the axle assembly.

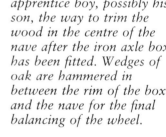

generation to generation in family concerns. If not a member of a wheelwrighting family, young apprentices would be taken on for a period of at least seven years. Even then they might have to serve a few more years under the supervision of the wheelwright before they could set up shop on their own, or even be considered experienced enough to 'have a free hand'.

MAKING A WHEEL

A wheel has three main components: the central hub or nave, a number of spokes and a rim made up of curved sections called felloes (pronounced 'fellies').

The hub, from 12 to 17 inches in diameter and usually up to 18 inches long, was made from a solid block of wood. Invariably this was elm, which was unlikely to split when spokes were hammered in, nor would it shatter when subjected to the strains of use. The wheelwright bought standing timber for hubs, as well as for the other work he did. He was prepared to travel miles visiting the woods and plantations to inspect the trees before buying. For hubs he

THE APPRENTICE
(above) The wheelwright demonstrates to his apprentice boy, possibly his son, the way to trim the wood in the centre of the nave after the iron axle box has been fitted. Wedges of oak are hammered in between the rim of the box and the nave for the final balancing of the wheel.

THE WHEEL
Fitting together snugly, each separate part of the wheel is made from material strong enough to take the stresses and strains imposed by the loaded wagon and poor rural roads. The nave of elm, the spokes of oak and the felloes of ash are bound in place by the iron tyre. For extra strength and to counterbalance the sideways thrust of a wagon, rural wheelwrights sometimes 'dished' the wheels (left): the spokes were set into the hub at angles to create the dish shape.

PARTS OF A WHEEL

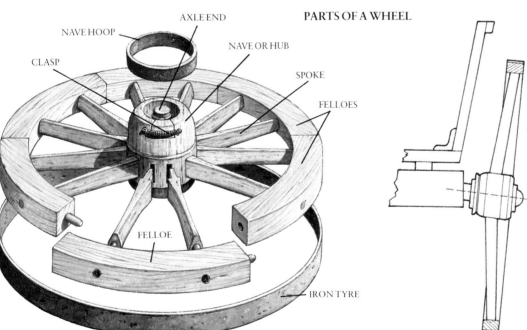

AXLE END
NAVE HOOP
CLASP
NAVE OR HUB
SPOKE
FELLOES
FELLOE
IRON TYRE

chose straight winter-felled trees. These would be sawn into appropriate lengths and stored to season for up to ten years before use.

When he came to work the timber, the wheelwright first stripped off the bark, then hewed it roughly to shape, using a small axe or adze. Final shaping was done with the hub mounted on a special lathe. The lathe was massively built, with a bed up to 12ft long, so that it could take the longest shafts and axles the wheelwright might turn, as well as the large diameter wheel hubs. The most striking feature of the lathe was the large driving wheel – about six feet in diameter. Power to turn the lathe was provided by one workman, most likely an apprentice or junior, who hand-cranked the driving wheel – hence its huge size to help give momentum to the turning of large, heavy chunks of wood. Not all wheelwrights possessed such lathes, and those without shaped the hub while it was clamped in a large vice. Using a small paring knife he could turn out hubs as smooth as those turned on lathes – though it took much

MEASURING THE RIM
(above right) Using a traveller, a tracing wheel, the wheelwright checked the size of the old iron tyre to be replaced on a newly repaired wheel. Starting at a marked point on the wheel rim, the traveller, marked with chalk, was wheeled around the old tyre and the number of revolutions counted. The traveller was then pushed the same number of revolutions along a strip of iron to give the exact length to make the tyre.

THE WHEELWRIGHT'S SHOP
(below) Springtime was the busiest time of year for the wheelwright when farmers brought him their carts and wheels to repair.

longer. After turning, the next job was to trim the hub ends to shape, a job of some delicacy, since an end cut out of round or off dead centre could upset the whole alignment of the wheel.

Next, the hub was set on a morticing cradle, a low stool with wedges to hold the block steady while the holes or mortices for the spokes were marked with a pair of compasses and cut.

If a wheel was to be dished (made concave) the mortices in the hub had to be cut at angles, carefully gauged so that all the spokes would be evenly set into them. Dishing was a characteristic feature of the wheels of farm carts and wagons. A complicated practise, dishing strengthened the wheel, and counteracted the sideways movement of the wagon caused by the pulling of four-legged animals. The tyring of a wheel with hot iron, which contracts as it cools, also helped make the wheel concave.

PUTTING A SPOKE IN

The spokes were made from pieces of cleft oak. Sawn wood was unsatisfactory for this purpose because sawing involves cutting through the grain – the natural line of maximum strength within the wood. Cleaving, on the other hand, splits the wood along its grain and preserves the natural strength of the timber. The oak pieces were shaped first, roughly, with an axe, then finely pared with a draw-knife and spokeshave and a hollow-bladed plane known as a jarvis. Part of the wheelwright's skill was his ability to make a set of spokes identical in shape and weight.

To insert the spokes, the hub was placed securely in a vice and the spokes driven into the mortices by blows from a massive 14lb sledgehammer. The felloes, the curved sections which make up the rim, were usually designed to take two spokes each. Made of ash wood, springy and tough enough to stand the strains that a wheel rim has to take, they were cut using wooden felloe patterns and smoothed to the right shape with an adze and a jack plane.

Placing the spoked wheel on a stand and

TYRING THE WHEEL
(right) The iron tyre was
forged by the blacksmith
either at his own smithy or at
the wheelwright's tyring pit.
The iron was heated over a
circular fire until red-hot.
Then, grasped firmly with
iron tongs, it was taken to
the tyring platform. It was
lowered carefully over the
wheel until it touched the
rim. Then, in a burst of
activity, all hands set about
hammering and levering it
into position. As it cooled the
iron contracted to bind the
wheel. To hasten the cooling
and stop the wheel burning,
the iron was quenched with
water.

BOW WAGON
(below) Curved, slatted and
over-hanging edge-boards,
high enough to clear the back
wheels of the wagon, are
typical of the Oxfordshire
bow wagon. The sinuous
edge boards could also
support additional loads of
hay or straw. This type of
wagon with its waisted body,
which allowed a greater
front-wheel lock, was
particularly suitable for use
in hilly countryside.

using a giant wooden compass, the wheelwright then marked each felloe with the position of the holes where the spokes were to fit. He cut these holes with a chisel, then, using a spoke cramp, knocked the felloes on to the spoke ends. The felloes were made to abut at a slight angle and were joined to each other by dowels, ensuring a close fit. Next, the wheelwright bored a hole in the centre of the hub to take the iron box where the wheel turned on the axle.

IRON TYRING

The next stage, the making and fixing of either the iron tyre or iron strakes, on to the rim of the wheel, was the task of the blacksmith. The iron tyre served a dual purpose: first, it protected the wooden rim from damage by rocks and stones, thus promoting durability; and

second, it helped bind the whole structure tightly together.

Some wheelwrights had tyre pits and all the necessary equipment for tyring on their premises. In these circumstances the village blacksmiths would do the work at the wheelwright's shop. Otherwise the wheel would be taken down to the blacksmith's shop, usually nearby. The smith heated a strip of iron of precisely the right length and forged it into a continuous circular band. This was then heated up to expand it and while hot dropped over the rim of the wheel. The heat made the wheel catch fire – which would be quickly doused by all hands. As the tyre cooled it contracted sharply to bind the wheel firmly, and, if the design demanded, dished it.

If strakes (separate curved lengths of iron) were fitted, the process was similar, except that forged strakes were nailed into the felloes.

THE END OF THE ROAD

The late 19th century ushered in many changes in working techniques. Factory methods of production were applied to the manufacture of wagons and by the 1860s firms were producing simple yet uniformly constructed wagons. The village wheelwright had to adjust to the competition and before long was also making simple plank-sided carts. He could buy standard fittings for these carts from the factories, as well as cheap ready-made wheels, many imported from America. By 1914 it was rare to see the traditional 'box' and 'bow' construction wagons being made in a wheelwright's shop.

Although some wheelwrights remained in business well into the 1950s the decline of the horse as the main mode of transport and power eventually killed off the craft as a living feature of the countryside. Today, although the wheelwright is in demand still in some areas for work on ceremonial carriages, gun carriages, dray carts and for restoration work, the traditional craft has all but gone.

Saddle Making

Providing protection for the horse's back and security for the rider's seat, the saddle is a masterpiece in leather created by craftsmen using skills handed down over generations.

The bond between horse and rider has always been the stuff of romance, not just in the English shires, but as far away as the Wild West, Arabia and Japan. But this legendary partnership was largely made so successful because of a padded leather go-between, the saddle. The saddle not only makes riding more comfortable for both rider and horse, it also helps make sure that the two do not unintentionally part company. The shape, dimensions and construction of the saddle are largely dictated by these aims, but other factors influence saddle design too: the shape of the horse, the size and weight of the rider and the riding style are the main influences, though fashion has also played a part.

The saddler's craft is one of the oldest, though early saddles were much simpler than those used today. The Parthenon frieze in Greece shows horsemen sitting on pads of soft material placed over the horse's back and secured by straps, and similar saddles were probably used wherever the horse had been domesticated. An early variation on this elementary pad saddle was some simple means of redistributing the rider's weight. Typically, this consisted of rolls of straw placed each side of the animal's spine. A leather cover for the saddle was also a natural development, because it was more durable and comfortable than a folded blanket.

The forerunner of the modern saddle though, was probably developed by the Mongols – nomad warriors of the Steppes – in the fourth century. By bridging the horse's back with a rigid wooden framework, or 'tree', they made a saddle that was comfortable enough for the horse to wear, and stable enough for the warrior to ride in, all day. Since the Mongols, developments to the saddle have been evolutionary rather than revolutionary.

THE MODERN SADDLE

All saddles have certain shared characteristics, but their size and shape vary from one design to another. The principal structural component of the saddle is the tree: this is the wood and spring-steel skeleton around which the rest of the saddle is built. The tree takes the rider's weight, and directs the downward force on to the parts of the horse's back where pressure is most comfortable and least likely to cause injury. This essentially means taking the weight off the spine and transferring it to areas a little way down the horse's sides, where layers of muscle provide a cushioning effect. If you stand behind a saddled horse, you will see that the tree lifts the saddle completely clear of the

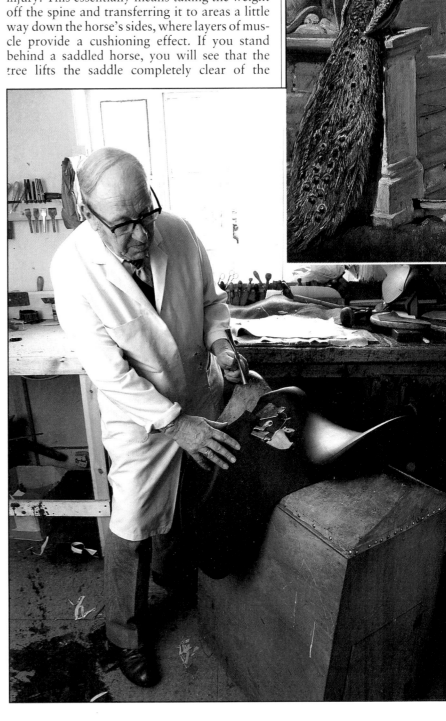

TWO TYPES OF SADDLES
The saddle not only provides a comfortable seat for the rider, it also protects the horse's spine. Through the ages and in various cultures, several types of saddle have evolved. The most commonly used is the 'general purpose' saddle, as seen on the white horse; it is also sometimes known as the 'English' saddle. The brown horse sports a side saddle mainly associated with women riding in skirts, though men have been known to use it too. The side saddle is, in fact, a more secure seat than a 'man's' saddle as the prominent pommels enable the riders to lock their legs in position. It originated as a pack saddle with the rider crooking a leg over the prominent pommel, or 'horn' used for tying loads to.

THE VERSATILE SADDLER
With increased interest in horse riding, the saddler's ancient trade has been revived (left). Before the advent of the 'horseless carriage', when horses were used not just by farmers, but by all businesses, from baker's to undertaker's, most towns boasted several saddleries. The saddler's trade ranged from making saddles and harnesses to a diverse variety of items from boots to hedging gloves. For a while after the motor car replaced the horse, even parts of this new mode of transport were catered for by the saddler. Straps for securing goods and spare tyres, clutches and gaiters for springs were made of leather. Though demand for the saddler's varied services is today much reduced, he still provides the essential connection between horse and rider.

horse's spine along its whole length and you should be able to see light at the other end of the gap.

If the wooden tree was the only thing between rider and horse, both would soon begin to feel the pinch. So the other components of the saddle provide cushioning for the rider's bottom and the horse's back.

THE TOP AND PANEL

A saddle is constructed in two sections: the upper half, which is simply called the top, takes care of the rider's comfort; the lower half, or panel, is responsible for keeping the horse happy. Around the lower edge of the saddle, the top and panel are separate from each other and flap around quite freely when the saddle is lifted from the horse's back. The two parts are stitched tightly together around the tree directly beneath where the rider sits.

Besides these three principal components, there are anchorage points on the tree to support the stirrups, and on the panel to attach the girth straps that hold the saddle firmly but comfortably on the horse's back. Additional flaps, straps and rings protect horse and rider from the chafing effect of buckles, hold luggage and accessories and help keep the different bits of saddle in the right place relative to each other.

Before making a saddle, the bespoke saddler starts by measuring up the rider, and possibly the horse, to determine the ideal fit. Some saddlers used strips of lead to take a profile of the horse's back as a pattern for the tree, but within broad limits, it is possible to make a saddle that fits a wide range of horses, so, often, only the rider is measured.

The business of manufacture proper starts with the tree. This consists of two arched pieces of wood joined by side-members and often reinforced with steel strips. The front arch is known as the 'pommel'; the back one, the 'cantle'; the extensions of the arches beyond the joins with the horizontal bars are known as 'points'. The saddler stretches pieces of webbing lengthways across the open areas of the tree to provide a form of springing for the rider, using steel tacks at the front and back to hold the webbing in place. An extra layer of leather covers the tack heads at points where they are liable to rust and cause staining. Over the web goes a layer of scrim – open weave cotton fabric – and on top of this, a covering of serge.

Between them the scrim and the serge form a kind of pocket, which the saddler stuffs with unspun wool using a long-handled tool to push the wool around between the serge and scrim, and a variety of rollers and other blunt instru-

MEASURING THE TREE
The tree is covered with cloth (above) and measured for the leather which will go on top to form the seat.

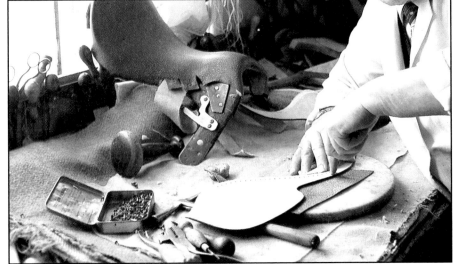

ments to manipulate the stuffing from outside the emerging saddle.

Once the stuffing is complete, a loosely-tacked pigskin cover goes over the serge, and the approximate shape of the seat begins to appear. The saddler now cuts the sides of the seat – the skirts – from the pigskin, and traces out the line where the skirts must be sewn on to the seat itself. When this is done, the seat comes off the tree, ready for sewing.

Beneath each skirt the saddler sews a further flap of leather called a 'back'. This is necessary because the skirts and seat are attached directly to the tree only at the front and rear. Around the sides of the saddle the skirts hang down loosely, and it is the backs beneath that stretch the other components tightly across the tree. The seat, backs and skirts are all sewn on to a paper-thin strip of leather, followed along its length. In this way, the seams joining the skirts to the seat lie absolutely flat and do not chafe the rider's legs.

CUTTING THE FLAPS

Once the skirts are sewn to the seat, the saddler cuts the flaps. These are the sections of the saddle that hang from the skirts to protect the rider's legs from the horse's sweat. The basic dimensions of the flaps are determined by three measurements taken from the rider: the overall leg-length fixes the total length of the flap; the stir-

rup length determines how far below the front arch of the saddle, the pommel, the saddler should cut the leading edge of the flap; and how far forward the flap extends depends on the rider's crotch to knee measurement. Though these three distances approximately fix the size of the flap, a good saddler cuts the flap free-hand, without recourse to a pattern.

With the flaps sewn on to the skirts, the saddler looks to the comfort of the horse, and makes the panel. The processes involved here are similar to those used in making the top, except that the 'pocket' to be stuffed with wool is made entirely from leather. The outside of the pocket – the panel lining – has a layer of scrim bonded to it to prevent the hide from stretching in use. The layer that touches the horse's back is not

CUTTING OUT THE SKIRT
Once the seat has been covered, the saddler maps out the skirt on a piece of leather using a template of paper or card (above). Standard templates are used for off the peg saddles, but special ones would be made for a bespoke saddle.

FIXING ON THE FLAPS
The flaps, once lined and stuffed for the knee and thigh rolls, are tacked on to the tree (right) positioned by guide marks made earlier.

ILLUSTRIOUS ANCESTOR
The precursor to the modern saddle (left) was invented by the Mongols when they fashioned the saddle tree.

treated in this way, and will in time conform to the horse's anatomy. A couple of pockets sewn into the panel will carry the points of the tree when the saddle is finally assembled.

The saddler sews the panel inside out, fixing leather piping between the two layers of hide all the way around the edge to prevent creasing. Once the panel has been turned, a row of stitches creates a pocket at the front and back, and when stuffed with wool, these two pockets will form the thigh and knee rolls. These are raised sections that will eventually go behind and in front of the rider's legs, to make it easier to stay in the saddle while riding. Different types of riding demand bigger or smaller thigh and knee rolls: when jumping, for example, a rider needs as much support as possible, so the two rolls are large, and are supplemented by an extra piece

ILLUSTRIOUS ANCESTOR
The precursor to the modern saddle (left) was invented by the Mongols when they fashioned the saddle tree.

STUFFING THE SADDLE
Only very small amounts of wool are pushed in at a time through a chink, making stuffing one of the most difficult parts of saddle making.

of padding called a false roll, which is stitched on top of the panel. However, thick thigh and knee rolls insulate the rider from the horse, making control more difficult, and for dressage riding, where the horse must sense every twitch of the rider's legs, thigh and knee rolls are almost vestigial.

FINAL ASSEMBLY

With the lower part stuffed, the saddler now brings together the panel and the top, sliding the points of the tree into the pockets on the panel lining. Once everything has been assembled, the stuffing goes into the upper part of the panel, and the saddle can be stitched together and buckle guards, girth straps and stirrup straps added to complete the picture.

The saddler needs to acquire a considerable degree of skill and judgement in selecting mate-

SADDLE STITCH
Hand sewing takes years to master. Stitches pulled too high are called 'dead men'.

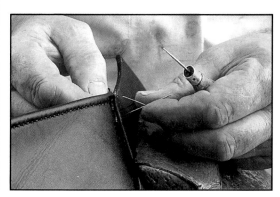

SPECIAL SADDLES
*Different types of riding
require different saddles. For
show jumping (above), the
rider sits well forward, so
the flaps and panel are
designed to provide extra
support for the thighs and
knees which bear most of the
rider's weight. In dressage
(right), the rider wants the
closest possible contact with
the horse and to be able to
move easily in the seat. The
flaps are, therefore, straight,
long and narrow and the
seat is deep and well
balanced. A racing saddle
(below), can weigh as little as
8 oz (225g) and uses a
specially light tree. Pockets
in the saddle are sometimes
filled with weights to satisfy
handicap rules.*

tightly into every corner of the pocket: even a small ball of compressed wool is enough to cause a sore on the horse's back. To make matters more difficult, this highly-skilled process is usually carried out through a narrow slit cut in the serge or hide – a bit like wallpapering the entrance-hall of a house by reaching in through the letterbox.

The organic nature of all the materials with which the saddler works makes the job still more skilled: webbing must be 'fired' to eliminate stretch before it is nailed to the tree; leather stretches and shrinks as it gets damp and dries out, so for many of the fitting processes, the hide is kept wet.

A TRUE HANDICRAFT

Even in its heyday, saddle-making remained a hand craft, with only the very simplest of stitching done by machine. Saddle-making tasks did become compartmentalized, though, with the less-skilled work farmed out to home workers, usually women. A major centre for this kind of piecework was Walsall, though the association is now preserved only in the name of the local football team, the 'Saddlers'.

The invention of the internal combustion engine sounded the death-knell for large-scale saddle-making, and the industry began a rapid decline. Saddlers turned to other forms of leather-work to supplement their shrinking market. Some made and repaired leather drive-belts for machinery; others moved into sports and fancy goods such as patent-leather collars for shirts or special harnesses for injured animals.

Demand for the saddler's traditional skills never totally disappeared, though, and with the increase in riding for leisure and pleasure, business began to improve once again. And though many of Britain's saddles are now imported, most medium-sized shire towns still boast at least one workshop where you can see a skilled saddler deftly stitching away, surrounded by aromatic chestnut hides, bales of fluffy white wool, and rolls of soft grey serge.

rials, cutting, stuffing and sewing. Most of the components are made from scratch, including the waxed thread, which is made from twisted strands of hemp and flax. Different parts of the saddle require different thicknesses of thread, so the saddler's apprentice spent the early days of his training learning this basic craft. Sewing is another essential skill. Hand-sewing is the rule, even today, for most parts of the saddle, and the saddler uses an awl to make the individual holes for each stitch on the saddle, marking positions beforehand using a serrated punch or toothed wheel. The primary tool for much of the cutting work is a razor-sharp crescent-shaped knife, though this is supplemented by a small straight knife for fine trimming.

Perhaps the most difficult skill to acquire, though, is the stuffing of the various parts of the saddle. The wool must be pushed evenly and

LIVING OFF THE RIVER AND SEA

A Mill by the Stream

Watermills were once working buildings, harnessing the power of fast flowing rivers to grind corn harvested in nearby fields. Now mostly still, they remain potent reminders of a vanished way of life.

The soft splash and clack of the turning millwheel and the steady rumble of the meshing gears have been familiar country sounds since the earliest days of British village life. But earlier this century, the watermill seemed doomed to disappear from Britain. While a few deserted mills were being converted into private houses, many were falling into such disrepair that demolition was inevitable. Now, with the renewed interest in conserving the countryside, a number of mills have been put back into working order and once again are grinding flour for local bakeries.

Many of these mills stand on sites first used in Saxon times when our villages were originally established, but the buildings and their functions have changed repeatedly over the centuries. Mills could be adapted for a variety of purposes – to provide power for fulling wool (pounding woven cloth in water to make it expand and thicken), driving hammers and bellows for forging iron, or turning grindstones to make gunpowder. Flour milling was the most widespread of these uses, but although the number of corn mills increased during the Industrial Revolution because of the surge in demand for flour, by the end of the 19th century many were in decline.

THE MILLER'S YEAR

Although it was often built some distance from the village, the flour mill played a central role in the life of the community. Year in, year out, farmers and peasants would cart their corn to the miller to be ground between the great millstones. The chains in the hoist tower would rattle into action, hauling the sacks of corn up to the top floor, where the millhands would swing them inside and stow them in huge bins. A day or two later, the flour would be ready for collection – less one sixteenth, the miller's share.

Constant maintenance was needed to keep the machinery going and the watermill provided work for many local craftsmen. Carpenters,

CONSTABLE'S MILL
Flatford Mill (left) in Suffolk once belonged to the family of artist John Constable and was the inspiration for one of his most famous paintings. The scene is as peaceful and idyllic now as in 1817 when he painted it.

joiners and builders were needed to replace and repair broken or worn out parts; woodcutters would supply timber; blacksmiths would provide iron fittings and sack-hoist chains; and leather workers would make all kinds of straps. The millwheel itself needed regular attention for exposure to the extremes of weather and constant immersion in water rotted and warped the wood.

Most mills were built from materials available locally, although the best grindstones were imported from the Peak District or from France. Each mill followed the local style of building, whether it used stone, brick or half-timbering. Only the weatherboard style of many 18th- and 19th-century mills is truly widespread, reflecting the demand for

rapid construction at a time when the Agricultural Revolution was boosting wheat production.

Like the mill building, the machinery also tended to be made from local materials. The wheels and shafts were commonly of oak, while the 'floats,' or paddles, were elm and the cogs generally apple or some other hardwood such as beech or hornbeam. The wooden pins or 'trenails' holding things in place were often holly. Iron was rarely used, and only for parts subject to exceptionally heavy wear, such as the axle pins.

Each mill was designed specifically for its own river conditions. There are countless variations on the basic vertical wheel, usually adapted to suit the flow of water. In lowland areas, where the course

AN ANCIENT SITE
The site of Houghton Mill, on the Ouse near Huntingdon, was originally owned by the Abbey of Ramsey, and mills have stood there for centuries. When the present mill was last worked commercially in the 1930s, it boasted three massive wheels. These have now been removed but the machinery inside is perfectly preserved.

259

WEIR

LEAT

ACCESS ROAD

SLUICE GATE

SACK HOIST

MILL WHEEL

DIRECTING THE FLOW

Where the natural flow of water generated insufficient power to drive a wheel, the river could be diverted. Weirs would raise the water level, and so increase the pressure, and artificial channels or 'leats', would direct the stream on to the mill wheel. By opening and closing the sluice gates the miller could control the flow of water as he pleased.

of the river is almost flat, 'undershot' wheels are common; these simply dip into the water and are driven round by the force of the current alone. Where the river course is steep, however, much more efficient 'overshot' and 'breastshot' wheels could be used; these depend on the weight of water falling on the floats to turn the wheel. With overshot wheels, the water is channelled over the top of the wheel to fall on the downstream side, turning it forwards. In breastshot wheels, the water is shot on to the wheel at roughly the two o'clock position and turns it backwards – though there is considerable variation.

But the biggest challenge to the millwright's skill was ensuring a steady supply of power to the wheel, by producing a constant flow of water regardless of fluctuations in the river level. On a

well chosen site, the natural fall of the river or stream can produce sufficient power to drive the wheel. The water is channelled through a sluice gate on to the wheel; by raising and lowering the gate, the power can be increased or shut down. Where the flow is too weak or erratic, however, an embankment is built up on either side of the stream above the mill to create a millpond. With judicious use of sluices to control the flow of water in and out of the millpond, the miller can ensure a constant supply of stored power.

It was the loss of control over the very driving force of the wheel that almost silenced the watermills of Britain. For, with the improvements in land drainage made during the 19th century, many rivers became unstable. Worse still, water levels everywhere began to fall. For as town populations grew, water was increasingly diverted for domestic consumption, making the supply to mills even less dependable. Despite improvements in design, few wheels were still turning by the 1930s.

IN THE MILLPOND

Although watermills are no longer a focus of economic life their effect on the local environment and its wildlife remains significant. Because the millpond is usually maintained at a steady depth, it provides an exceptionally stable habitat for flora and fauna. Around the pond, willow trees and waterside plants flourish. In summer the air may be filled with the fragrant scent of meadowsweet and late in June the graceful blooms of purple loosestrife and the delicate pink flowers of great willowherb may decorate the banks.

Down on the water margin, the poker-like reedmace, common reeds and various sedges thrive, offering shelter to insects, frogs and small

THE MILL MACHINERY
The corn was ground between two huge stones – the lower one stationary, the upper one rotating – with a paper thin gap between them. The miller fed the grain down the central shaft through a barrow-like hopper (below left) and the flour was expelled outwards along radiating furrows (below right). The stones were levelled and the furrows cut with great precision, using a tool known as a mill bill (right) made of hardened steel. This might be done by the miller himself or by a specialist stone dresser.

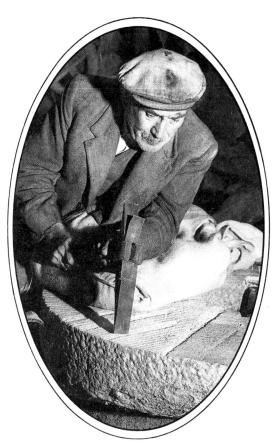

birds such as the dabchick or little grebe, which can often be seen bobbing and splashing in the water. The pond itself provides a home for all kinds of insects and fish, from tiny minnows to carp, tench and chub. A lone pike may grow to enormous size in the deep, almost still waters of the millpond, while the millrace has traditionally provided the miller with a feast of eels.

In turn the fish and insect life of the pond, attracts many different bird species – aquatic birds such as the mute swan and various types of ducks and moorhens, and land-based birds such as kingfishers. Around the pond, sedge warblers and reed buntings may make their nests amongst the grass and many other birds may visit. And in the old millhouse, a barn owl may nest, coming out at night to prey on voles that live around the pond.

Rushwork

The graceful, slender rushes swaying in the wind along our marshes and riverbanks have long been exploited for a surprisingly wide range of applications.

Testament to the erstwhile importance of the humble rush in everyday life, the custom of rushbearing still survives in some of our country churches. In centuries past, rushes were strewn on the cold stone or earth floors of dwellings, rich and poor alike, as a rudimentary form of carpeting. The gentry added a little straw and 'nose herbs', such as mint and sage. As this rough and ready carpeting was renewed only two or three times a year, the nose herbs must have been a welcome addition; the philosopher Erasmus condemned rushes soiled with spilt food and grease as a major source of infection and plague. Sometimes, the rushes were plaited or woven together to make a kind of rush matting.

Fresh rushes were also strewn on church floors before religious festivals and saints' days – especially when these fell during the summer months. In this way, bearing the rushes to church developed into gala occasions, reaching a peak in the early 19th century. Rushcarts were the centre of a procession of brass bands and Morris dancers, with as many as ten carts in one procession, each hauled by a team of men or decorated horses. The green rushes were piled skilfully in a pyramid or mitre shape, and held in place with flower-woven rush ropes. Patriotic slogans and ostentatious displays of silver added a less religious note, and by the Victorian era, rushbearings were frowned on for their rowdiness – often ending in an all-out fight between rival bands of rushcarters.

In some churches, rushes were plaited into elaborate 'bearings' which were carried in procession to the church and left there as a decoration. William Wordsworth and John Ruskin patronized such a ceremony at Grasmere in Cumbria, marked by a special rushbearing hymn and a distribution of gingerbread to the children of the parish. In other parts of the country, the tradition is upheld in 'Rush Sunday' services and 'rush sermons'.

In districts where rushes were abundant they also had a wide variety of other practical uses: they were used instead of candles as a cheap form of lighting. The rush stalks were peeled, except for two supporting strips, revealing the white pith, which was then dipped repeatedly into melted fat or tallow. Forty inches (1m) of 'rush dip' would burn for about two hours, and the celebrated naturalist Gilbert White wrote in one of his letters, 'An experienced old housekeeper assured me that 1½ pounds of rushes completely supplied his family the year round'.

Rushes were also essential to the cooper, or barrel maker. The wooden staves shrink if the barrel is left empty, so the best and thickest rushes were set aside for packing tightly into the joints; the absorbent pith swells when the barrel is filled, sealing the gap. Another function of the versatile rush was to make lightweight horse collars for young colts, to get them accustomed to the heavier collars. Rushes and sand were once used to scour armour ready for battle and for cleaning pewter tableware.

Rush is also the oldest thatch, older than straw, used especially for haystacks in the West country. The squat circular stacks were built over a frame with great care and precision. A stout stake was driven into the top of the stack and the thatcher attached twisted rush ropes crossing from one side to the other, dividing the stack into quarters. Starting again at the stake, he then wove more rushes round the stack like a spider's web until he reached the bottom. Rush is extremely strong and a comparatively thin layer will fend off the heaviest rain.

CRADLES AND CHAIRS

A century ago in England, cradles were commonly made of soft plaited rush, and every farmworker carried his tools and lunch in a 'flag' basket – the leaves of many water plants, including the yellow flag iris, were also used.

Chair seaters, working rush (or cane) out on the streets, were once a common sight. A comfortable rush seat is still the only complement to a sturdy English ladder back chair. Medium-sized rushes are best for chair seats, used two at a time, knotted together with the butt end of one to the tip end of the other to make an even thickness along the whole length. The rushworker ties these two rushes to the frame of the chair and then twists them together to make a single strand. It is a simple technique

THE RUSH GATHERER

Rushes are gathered around June by a fenman, sometimes, as here, from a flat-bottomed boat (above). He cuts them close to the water, where they are strongest, with a fagging hook, trying to keep the 5-10 foot lengths straight. The cut rushes are tied in bundles and stood to dry against wooden racks on the river bank for about three weeks. Recalling an ancient ritual when the rushes carpeting a church floor were renewed, young choristers carry 'bearings' — plaited rush decorations (left). Basketwork is one of the most ancient forms of rushcraft (right). The one on the left uses plaiting and the other mainly check weave.

yet it takes practice to do evenly and firmly. As the work progresses, the seat is padded out with waste rush, to thicken it.

Because rush seating requires much less physical strength than willow basketwork, rush seats were traditionally seen as women's work. The women were known as 'matters'; the expression that you 'could smell a matter a mile off' referred to the dust, a powdery mould which developed on the stored rushes, which gave off a terrible smell when they were dampened with water before working.

WORKING WITH RUSH

About thirty different varieties of rush grow in Britain, varying in shades of green and gold and in length. The rushes found in the Norfolk Broads are firm and hard, while the rushes native to the shallow rivers of Bedfordshire, Huntingdonshire and Northamptonshire are more delicate and a softer green. The variety used most in traditional rushwork is *Scirpus lacustris,* the true bulrush, which grows 4-10 feet (1.2-3m) tall, tapering gracefully towards the tip. It is harvested when a tuft of brown plumes show that it is in flower.

Around Midsummer's Day, in late June and early July, the fenman's flat-bottomed boat was once a familiar sight, gliding noiselessly down shallow rivers and marshes for the annual rush-harvesting. Using a short-bladed sickle, the rushman's fagging hook, the rush gatherer stoops to sever the rushes close to the roots, the thickest and strongest part of the plant and the best for weaving. Great care has to be taken not

to bend and break the slender stems, and often the rushes are floated ashore to avoid lifting them out of the water.

The rush harvester rotates his wild crop like any farmer, cutting in alternate years and allowing the plants to rest for a season. A wet summer ruins the harvest, making it so late that the rushes have matured past their best and become tough and brittle.

The cut stems have to be thoroughly dried, otherwise they easily go mouldy and lose their beautiful soft green colour, which matures gradually to an equally soft brown. Ideally, they are left to dry naturally in a cool shed or barn, out of strong sunlight which would accelerate fading. The rushes are then gathered together in bundles, called 'bolts', and stored indoors; they are too hard to be used immediately.

Compared to other stems used for weaving, such as willow, rush is a delicate material, brittle when dry but soft and pliable when damp. 'Plain' lengths were used for chair seating, lightweight baskets and tablemats, while plaited rushes, which were stronger and thicker, were commonly used for floor matting, hassocks, horsecollars and housemaids' kneelers and heavy workmen's baskets.

The rushworker first sorts the rushes in the 'bolt' putting the thickest stems aside for heavier work. The dried rushes must be moistened to make them pliable for weaving but they must not be allowed to get too damp, otherwise the finished work will shrink too much and end up looking loose. The rush stalks are doused in rainwater (or left out in a shower) and then

RELATED PURSUITS
Like rushes, straw, too, can be plaited and formed into domestic articles. In the 19th century, a flourishing cottage industry employed women and children (above). Such was the demand that complaints arose that straw plaiting 'makes the poor saucy and no servants can be procured where this manufacture establishes itself'.

wrapped in a thick blanket or a piece of felt until the following day. Immediately before starting work, each stalk is wiped with a wet cloth, cleaning and dampening it in one movement and also expelling the air inside the stem. The rushworker learns with experience to know when the rushes are in the ideal condition for weaving: silky and smooth, like soft suede or velvet ribbon.

Rushes are so sensitive to humidity that a rushworker would never work in a frost or an east wind, or sit near a fire or in hot sun. Warm, moist, muggy weather is perfect. Finished rush seats and matting needed an occasional 'bath' to keep them from drying out: too wet, and they can go mouldy.

The rushworker's tools are very elementary. The only tool of the trade is a rush threading needle with a flat eye and a wooden handle. Other equipment is usually to hand: scissors, string (for sewing plaits together) and a mallet

WEAVES WITHIN WEAVES
One of the simplest objects to weave from rush is a table mat (right). A centre of check or tabby weave is encircled by pairing or coupling, where slightly twisted rushes are worked in pairs. Two of the mats have their 'spokes' left free as fringes while the one in the centre has them worked into a finished edge.

(used for gently hammering mats flat while the rushes are still damp).

To make a basket, the rushworker first cuts 'spokes' from the stouter 'butt' (bottom) end of the rush stems, and uses these to weave the base of the basket, continuing the sides with the weaker parts of the plant. The two main weaving patterns, on which all the others are based, are check weave (one over, one under) and pairing weave (similar to plaiting). These are used together in different variations. Openwork designs, called 'fitch' or 'fitching', add extra interest to decorative work. Flowerpots or wooden blocks are used to shape the basket while it is being worked, and also while the rushes are drying and shrinking. When the basket is completely dry, it is taken off the block and plaited or twisted handles are added.

BEE HIVE
Once a common country sight, rush bee skeps (hives) were made by tying coils of rush into a domed basket shape. The ties are made of split bramble, which is trimmed and shaved to make it pliable (top left). To make the skep, the first coil is formed around a peg (left), and then built up with successive coils. Each coil is 'stitched' to the one below with the bramble tie which is guided through by a goose bone awl (below left).

Catching Eels

Creatures of mystery and superstition, eels have been an important source of food for thousands of years, and eels are caught today using techniques little changed since the Dark Ages.

The teeming millions of eels that swim Britain's lakes and ponds, rivers and streams have been a rich source of nutritious, high calorie food for thousands of years. Nowadays, they have all but disappeared from our diets, but in ancient times they received all the veneration due to such an important source of food – mixed with certain suspicions and superstitions about their nature.

The ancient Greeks treated eels as a delicacy; the ancient Egyptians treated them as gods. The Romans, on the other hand, felt there was something a little distasteful about them – perhaps because they roamed the city's rather dubious sewers. And Jews are forbidden them under Levitical law for, being without scales, they are considered unclean. The fact that eels do actually have scales – small and deeply embedded in their skins – is typical of the mystery that has surrounded eels and eel catching through the ages.

Because eels have no visible reproductive organs and because no one has ever seen them spawning, their regeneration was long the source of endless superstition and speculation. They were born of the entrails of the earth, said one ancient; they sprang naturally from the mud, claimed another (Aristotle). The Roman author Pliny the Elder believed they rubbed themselves on rocks and their scrapings came to life, while the 16th century chemist Jan Van Helmond said they were born of the dew drops of May and suggested a recipe for making them: 'Cut up two turfs covered with May-dew, and lay one upon the other, the grassy side inwards, and then expose them to the heat of the sun; in a few hours there will spring from them an infinite quantity of eels.'

Even the rigorously scientific Isaac Newton believed they regenerated spontaneously. Right into Victorian times children chopped up horsehair and kept it in jars of water in the hope they would turn into eels. It was not until 1922 that it was proved they spawned deep in the Sargasso Sea in the Southern Atlantic.

With such a blend of superstition to guide them, it is surprising that eel-catchers ever managed to perfect their techniques. Yet most methods of catching eels have changed little over the centuries since the Venerable Bede, the famous Saxon chronicler, noted the success of Britain's eel-fisheries in the 7th century.

There are essentially two ways of catching eels: trapping and catching. 'Silver' eels – the eel when its belly turns silver and it swims down river on its way back to the spawning ground – are usually caught in fixed traps which operate at night when the eels are running.

EELS BY THE MILL

At one time, every mill, weir and water meadow had its trap, and the eels caught in the trap were the perks – or more often the wages – of the man responsible for controlling the sluice, a job which entailed working unsocial hours when water levels rose or dropped during the night. Even quite recently, the taking of eels was part of a river keeper's wages.

The fixed traps used by old mills usually consisted of an inclined grating between two walls of brick, stone or timber in the sluice. The bottom end lay in the water beneath a hatch, and the top end flattened out on to a horizontal grating. When the hatch was raised, the water rushing through swept the eels up the slope on to the grating, where they were left stranded as the water drained away. From the grating, the eels wriggled into a trough, from where they were driven into a keep tank.

Many of these traps have continued to work long after the mill to which they were attached had fallen derelict. One ancient mill-race eel trap still in use is at Charlton on the River Avon south of Salisbury.

On slower waters, such as mill wastes, and on broad creeks and rivers, eel-trappers often constructed a row of shuttlecock-shaped basketwork traps like lobster pots; called 'eel-bucks'. These were winched down into the water in the evening and up again, full of wriggling eels, the following morning. These traps, now usually made of steel, were elaborately constructed from wickerwork, and often lasted many decades.

Simpler traps, consisting of brushwood inter-

WINDING UP THE EEL-BUCK
(right) Up until the 1920s, eels were still caught on the upper reaches of the Thames in basketwork traps called eel-bucks, suspended on wooden frames across the river.

Eel-catchers on the Norfolk Broads often lived on the water for months on end, in floating huts built over a punt (left). From there, they went out every day with their fyke-nets which they dragged along the bottom to catch the eels. Broadsmen would also catch eels with gruesome four-pronged barbed spears (below) thrust into the mud. These were banned many years ago.

Hungry Customer. "'Taint Bad."
Chef. "Glad you Like it; for, to Tell yer the Truth, a'though I've been a Makin' o' this Soup for Fifteen Year, I ain't never Tasted it Myself!!"

COCKNEY CHARACTER
(above) Eel-sellers were a familar sight on London's streets for centuries and, in the Victorian era, the jolly cockney eel soup and pie-man became a favourite target for caricaturists.

woven between posts driven into the river bed and arranged so as to guide eels into narrow gaps covered by nets, may have been in use for 300 years or more. Remains of wickerwork traps of this type found near where the Lower Bann river enters Lough Neagh in Northern Ireland may date back to 1000 years BC. Further up the Bann at Toome, a net trap originally built by medieval monks 500 years ago is still in use, unchanged but for the replacement of rotten timbers. The silver eels caught in these traps are believed to be the best in the world.

Almost as old, perhaps, is 'fyke-netting'. Fyke nets are rather like anglers' keep nets, but they have two wings at the mouth of the net to guide the eel in. For centuries, eel-fishermen on the broads and rivers of eastern England would drift slowly over the water in their punts and lay their fyke nets on the bottom to catch brown eels – mature eels – before they head back down river to spawn.

Besides these fyke nets, the Norfolk Broadmen used to catch eels with 'bobs' or 'babs'. The bob was made by threading lobworms and strands of wool or worsted on to a length of twine and then tying it all up in a bundle on the end of a pole, rather like a mop. This bundle was lowered into the water and slowly bobbed up and down on the bottom. According to the Victorian author Lady Colin Campbell, 'The eel's teeth get entangled in the worsted as soon as he attempts to take the bab, and he can then be lifted out of the water into the boat, if the angler be in one, or else allowed to drop off the line into a pail, which the angler puts on the bank at a convenient distance from his standing place.'

Much more dramatic, and barbaric, was spearing with an eel comb, now banned. These were broad forks with barbed prongs on a long handle, which the eel catcher would thrust sharply into the mud when he spotted the telltale bubbles rising from an eel. On the Irish

MAKING BUCKS
(above) In spring, before the eel runs started, eel-catchers and their families would make basketwork eel-buck traps ready for summer.

SNIGGLING FOR EELS
(below) Sniggling, poking the bait into the eel's feeding hole, was once a popular pastime.

loughs, eel-men would rise early on summer mornings, when the sun sparkled on the lake, to go 'sun-spearing' from a boat. 'Standing up in the bows and, if alone, using his spear to propel the boat gently along, he steals over the crystal waters of the lough. Presently, he sees the gleam of the 'silver' eel as he lies quietly at length on the sandy bottom. The spearer takes aim; there is a sudden splitting of the atmosphere, and either eel comes up writhing on the 12 close-set teeth of the sun-spear, or the spearer has taken a header into the water.'

STITCHERING AND SNIGGLING

More sporting, but thoroughly unreliable, was 'stitchering', a technique favoured on the Hampshire drainage ditches in which eels once abounded. Using only a worn-out sickle attached to a 12-foot long pole, the stitcherer would try to thrust the sickle under the eel and then flip it on to the bank and into a waiting bag. The stitcherer was lucky to catch any eels – and equally lucky to avoid slicing someone's ear off with a wild hoist.

Only a little more successful was 'sniggling', which meant thrusting bait on a stick into an eel's hiding hole. This was surprisingly popular among people who caught eels as a hobby.

Nowadays, sportsmen prefer to catch eels with rod and line, and professional eel-catchers catch them using long lines with traces and baited hooks laid across a river bed or the floor of a lake. This technique has been used on Lough Neagh for many centuries, and the Lough

MEDIEVAL NET TRAPS
(above and above left) These simple wickerwork net eel traps on Ulster's River Bann, originally built by medieval monks, have remained almost unchanged for five centuries.

Neagh eel-fisheries remain the largest in Europe, involving 200 or more open boats, each with a crew of two.

There has always been a ready market for eels. Way back in the 12th century, Thomas à Becket (the archbishop murdered in Canterbury Cathedral) expended 'the large sum of one hundred shillings in a dish of eels' when travelling in France. And through the centuries, both rich and poor alike have appreciated eels.

For many years, the London market was supplied mainly from Holland, and the trade was considered so important that Queen Elizabeth I gave Dutch 'skoots' free mooring when they landed their cargo of eels. The eel-pieman was a familiar sight on London streets. But from the mid 18th century on, the upper and middle classes began to lose their taste for eels, and by the Victorian era, jellied eels and 'eel pie, mash and liquor' had become classic East End cockney fare alone. Eel-fisheries, both in England and abroad, began to disappear.

In recent years, however, continental Europeans have acquired a taste for smoked eels, and English eel-fisheries are coming to life again to meet the demand, using refined equipment and materials, but the same traditional techniques that they have used for centuries.

Harvesting the Sea

From countless rocky coves, bays and inlets, and storm-lashed
harbours around the British coast, fishermen have for centuries defied the
elements to bring the bounteous harvest of the sea safely to shore.

Fish from the sea has always been a significant part of the British diet. Nowhere in
these islands is far from the coast, and the
encircling waters are rich in both demersal – or
bottom-feeding – fish, such as cod and haddock,
and pelagic – or mid-water – shoal fish like
mackerel and herring. Traces of fishing activity
from as early as 30,000 years BC have been
discovered. Harpoons tipped with flint, antler
and bone, and lines and traps were probably all
in use. Later hunter-fishermen, up to 2000 years
BC, used hooks and basketwork traps and
hand-operated drag nets.

Medieval fishing was dominated by the
herring. The herring spawns all around the
coast of Britain at a variety of times throughout
the year, so that there was always good herring
fishing to be had somewhere. In certain seasons
they flooded close inshore, cramming inlets,
shallows and even harbours to such an extent
that they could be scooped out of the water
with anything that came to hand. In the open

sea the shoals can be gigantic – the name
'herring' means army. A shoal of herring
measured in 1877 was 118 feet deep and covered
an area the size of central London.

The traditional herring fisherman took the
fish by drift net at night as they rose towards the
surface to feed on plankton. The drift net hangs
like a curtain in a line or curve, at a depth
dictated by the floats on its upper rope and
sometimes also by weights on its lower rope.
The drift net is not anchored, but fastened to
floating buoys, or to the boat itself, drifting
along with tide and current. The herrings were
caught by their gills – as the net's alternative
name, 'gill net' suggests – the mesh size ensuring
that only the larger, more mature fish were taken.

From the earliest times, British fishermen
faced competition from those of other countries.
Fishermen from Flanders and Normandy were
using east coast ports long before 1066. Grimsby
is named after a Danish entrepreneur called
Grim, who sold his catches there 1000 years

FOLLOWING THE HERRING
(left) Great Yarmouth, on the
east coast, was already a
major fishing port in the
early Middle Ages. Its
Herring Fair, at which
millions of the salted fish
were bought and sold,
lasted a full 40 days. It
was chartered in 1270,
though it had been going
long before that, and
continued to be held
annually for the next
500 years.

ago. The most serious threat came from the Dutch, whose herring 'busses' were forerunners of the modern factory ship. They weighed up to 100 tons, had crews of 15 men or more, and developed a method of gutting and salting down the herrings as they were hauled aboard. By the 15th century they had wrested the major part of the North Sea herring fisheries from their British counterparts.

LONG-LINING

Second to herring in importance to medieval fishermen was cod, also ideal for salting and a mainstay of the export trade – the herring were mostly eaten locally, especially on the innumerable 'fast' days of the Christian calendar. Until the advent of legalized trawling in the 17th century, cod were caught largely by long-lining, whereby thousands of baited hooks were fastened by means of five-foot traces or 'snoods'

at six-foot intervals to the long-line. One end of this was anchored and buoyed. Long-lining was also the ideal way to catch other bottom-feeding fish, such as haddock and halibut. Its great disadvantage, however, was that the bait had to be set and the fish removed from each hook by hand. Even so, cod were caught by long-lining in many regions long after the intro-duction of trawling.

Cod and halibut are cold-water fish. They spawn in the North Sea, but migrate at maturity to the cold seas off the Norwegian coast and west through Icelandic waters and on to New-foundland. The impetus for British fishermen to brave the treacherous seas in relatively flimsy boats in the wake of these migrations, pursuing them into distant and unfamiliar seas, was their losing battle with the Dutch herring boats. Increasingly, British deep-water boats headed out into the Atlantic resigned to being away

IN STORM-TOSSED SEAS *(above) Fishing has always been a perilous calling, with the sea at once the fisherman's friend and his greatest enemy. Like the crew of this Hebridean fishing boat, he must brave ferocious gales and mountainous seas to bring in the catch.*

FISHING NETS

There are three main net designs. Drift nets have been used to take pelagic fish since medieval times. The otter trawl net came into its own in the late 1800s, with the advent of the powerful steam-driven boats needed to haul its immense weight along the sea bed. The purse-seine net is a modern development of the traditional seine-net used in shallow waters by Cornish pilchard fishermen, among others. It encloses the entire fish population of a huge area of sea. Theoretically, the mesh size allows immature fish to escape. In practice they are trapped by the bodies of larger fish clogging the net.

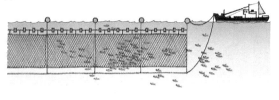

DRIFT NET

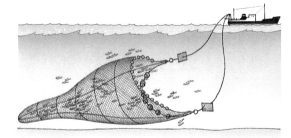

TRAWL NET

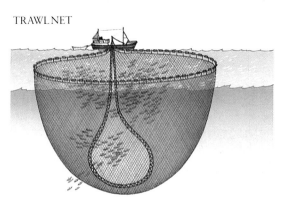

PURSE-SEINE NET

from home for sometimes months at a time. Iceland was the farthest limit for most of them, though some may have fished the rich waters of the Newfoundland Banks as early as the 15th century, before their major rivals for cod, the Portuguese.

The long-distance fisheries demanded larger, better boats, but small local boats continued to fish from ports and harbours all around the coast, their design often unchanged for centuries. Shetland yoals were square-rigged, clinker-built boats directly descended from the Viking boats of the 7th century. The four-oared version was used to fish for cod and ling. In the late 1700s, as the inshore grounds began to fail, the Shetlanders were drawn further offshore and the sixerne was developed – this was a yoal with six oars, which would make two trips a week, staying out at sea for two nights on each occasion.

West Country fishermen used two-masted luggers, which could be winched up on to steep shingle beaches when threatened by breaking seas. For centuries pilchards by the million were caught and cured there, especially in Cornwall. Entire shoals were encircled with huge seine nets and dragged in from the shallows. Special lookouts, called huers, kept watch from huer's

PROCESSING THE CATCH
(left) Traditionally, herring were preserved by salting them. Because they deteriorate rapidly, the herring had to be processed immediately after landing. In season, thousands of women would be employed – often from far afield like these Scottish women at Great Yarmouth – in gutting and packing the fish in barrels between layers of salt.

THE END OF AN ERA
Britain's fisheries were once the province of small-boat fishermen from hundreds of close-knit fishing communities dotting the coastline from the tip of Cornwall to the icy northern shores. But many are now being squeezed out by a combination of industrialized fishing and low fish stocks. Countless coastal villages, small ports and harbours are now in decline, with tourism and the seasonal holiday trade for some the only alternative.

huts on headlands and other vantage points to raise the alarm when the dark shadow which heralded the pilchard shoal could be seen in the inshore waters. Eventually, during World War 1, the great pilchard shoals stopped appearing in the seining areas, and the industry died out.

A 'WONDROUS DEVICE'

Trawling first made an appearance in the 14th century, but it was subsequently banned after complaints by estuary fishermen that the new 'wondrous device' took immature as well as mature fish, and destroyed breeding grounds. Trawling was legalized in the 17th century and a new type of fishing boat was developed which reached the peak of efficient sailing design in the Brixham trawler of the late 1700s. This was one of the most powerful fishing boats for its size ever built, and it became the model upon which the great trawler fleets of the east coast were based, following the discovery of the well-stocked fishing grounds of the North Sea.

The first trawl nets were beam trawls. The trawl is a conical bag of net towed behind the boat by two long ropes or 'warps'. The cod end

is the pocket at the end of the net where the fish are concentrated. The mouth of the beam trawl was kept open by a heavy wooden beam, weighted so that it worked along the sea bed, disturbing the feeding fish from the bottom, where the trawl scooped them into its depths. In early trawlers the trawl had to be hauled in hand over hand. The men stood at a low rail on the boat's stern, grabbing handfuls of net as the boat rocked from side to side. It was perilous, body-numbing work.

Later trawlers used the otter trawl. Instead of a beam to hold the mouth of the net open, two 'otter boards' – specially designed wooden panels angled so they are forced apart by water pressure as the rig is towed along – were fitted to the sides of the net. The otter trawl is more efficient than a beam trawl, but needs a more powerful boat to tow it; so it came into its own only after the development of steam power in the 19th century.

PURSE-SEINING
(above) By the time the 'purse' has been hauled aloft the fish are mostly dead from suffocation.

THE PILCHARDS ARRIVE
(below) Every year towards the end of summer, enormous pilchard shoals would strike the Cornish coast – at first a little to the east of St Ives – where they would be caught in huge numbers by local seine-fishermen. On one occasion, 30 million were taken at St Ives in a single hour.

Increasingly, new technology came to dominate the British fishing industry. The capital costs involved in buying the new, larger, more powerful boats and advanced gear and tackle were prohibitive for the traditional self-employed fisherman of Britain's close-knit fishing communities. Ports such as Aberdeen, Hull, Grimsby and Fleetwood became urban industrial communities. The men worked on the wharves and the boats, while the women were employed in the processing industries. The inshore fishermen watched helplessly while the trawlers scraped the bottom of their barrel, and the shoals of herring and mackerel dwindled. A living which had often been precarious, and hazardous, became even more uncertain.

THE COMING OF THE RAILWAY
(above) The railway made inland markets accessible to coastal fisheries, facilitating a huge expansion in the industry.

CORNISH MACKEREL
Some of the catch is still landed locally (above right), but the bulk of it disappears into the bowels of Soviet and other foreign factory ships waiting offshore (below) to buy it up for processing.

The dramatic change in scale of the industry was made inevitable by the expansion of the railway system in the late 1800s, bringing speedy communication between remote fishing ports and inland towns. At the same time the availability of machine-made ice meant that the fish could be delivered fresh to the many new fish markets which were opening up all over the country. In 1877 25,000 tons of ice were imported from Norway into Hull, one of the great North Sea trawling stations, for the sole purpose of packing fish.

DWINDLING FISH STOCKS

Concentrated 'industrial' fishing has had severe consequences for traditional fishermen, but also for fishing stocks, and for Britain's relationships with other countries. With the increasing range of the new trawlers came the intensification of that international rivalry for fish stocks which culminated in the 'cod wars' of the 20th century in the North Atlantic. The North Sea herring grounds had been the focus of similar conflict for centuries, but in the 1960s a new threat appeared in the form of the Norwegian purse-seine fleet.

The purse-seine net is laid in a wide circle around the shoal, resembling a vast underwater colander of netting. When the power winches bring in the draw-rope, the 'purse' closes up, entrapping everything within it. The effect on herring stocks was devastating and eventually, in the wake of ineffective conservation measures, a complete ban on herring fishing was imposed in the late 1970s.

British fishermen are now leaving the sea in droves. Those that remain are being forced to 'poach' in one another's home waters, with Scottish seiners cleaning out mackerel stocks that Cornish-men still line-fish for on a far smaller scale. The hazards of the open sea remain the same as ever they were, but the rewards, like the fish, are dwindling.

'Alive, Alive, Oh'

**Oysters and shellfish may now be considered a
gourmet's delight. But once, they were cheap and
plentiful and very much the poor-man's food.**

The stooping figure of the shellfish gatherer
is the marine equivalent of the hill-farmer
– eking out an existence from the most
marginal of food resources. Carrying a basket
and a spade, or perhaps a bent piece of wire,
the shellfish harvester was delving into the mud
and rock pools of our beaches long before his
(or, more often, her) fellows first set out in
crude boats to fish in the sea itself.

To the prehistoric Briton, shellfish were just a
convenient and abundant food-source – a back-
up in case the crop failed. But to the invading
Romans, shellfish were a delicacy. The conditions around our coasts ideally suited the oyster,
in particular, and Sallust, writing in 50 BC, put
it succinctly in a rather back-handed compli-
ment, 'Poor, Britons…there is some good in
them after all – they produce an oyster.'

PRE-PACKAGED

Highly nutritious, edible molluscs are incredibly
abundant and even today, their food potential
is far from fully exploited. Recent estimates
suggest that a reasonably productive estuary
could yield almost one ton per 2½ acres of
cockles and mussels every year, and that using
farming methods, mussel beds could provide
50-100 times as much food as the equivalent
area of grazing land.

Harvesting molluscs is simple and safe com-

A FAIR CATCH
*(below) In long worsted
stockings over trouser legs
jammed into heavy sewer
boots and thick Guernsey
jumpers clamped tight on
top, the three-man crew of a
Whitstable oyster-catching
smack was allowed to fish
only for its share of fixed
orders telegrammed through
from London. Organized in a
most democratic co-operative,
they shared the profits as
allotted by an elected jury.*

pared to sea-fishing. Though relatively few species of shellfish are eaten today (the list was much longer in the past and included several varieties now used only as bait by sea anglers), the methods of gathering them remain substantially unchanged.

The easiest shellfish to collect are those that live on the surface among the rocks of the foreshore. These include mussels and periwinkles as well as some species no longer popular for the table – such as limpets. Harvesting is simply a matter of plucking up the shells or prising them free of the rocks.

Several other types of shellfish live on or below the surface of estuary mud, and a little more ingenuity was required for their capture. Cockles and razor shells are easily alarmed and are capable of quickly burying themselves. Cockles can even spring across the mud to escape a predator. One traditional way to catch these lively bivalves was to drag a dredge or a hoop from a barrel through the mud to bring the shells to the surface.

Most other species of edible mollusc live on the sea bottom in deeper water, and these were traditionally brought to the surface by dredging. Oysters, whelks and scallops are the best-known of this group which also includes oxhorn cockles or 'Torbay noses' – another species of shellfish that was once considered a delicacy, but is now neglected.

TRADITIONAL HARVESTING METHODS

In times of relative prosperity or in the wealthy coastal areas, the job of collecting mussels, winkles and limpets would be delegated to children, or at best, casual labourers: the fish were so abundant and simple to harvest that the price they fetched was low – if there was a market at all – and the work was therefore not worthy of the effort of grown men. In 1863, Exeter mussels fetched eight shillings a sack – each sack holding some 80 pints. Periwinkles were cheaper still: Oban winkles cost just six pence a bushel (16 pints). Limpets were not even sold commercially, but were knocked or

OYSTER DREDGING
(below) Except for the benefit of industrial technology, which has provided sophisticated hydraulic-powered winches, oysters are still dredged from the bottom of the sea very much as they were a century ago. Once hauled up, they are cleaned, sorted and brought back to the beds for further cultivation until they reach a viable commercial size.

AND SO TO BED
(above) Britain's oyster gatherers have now introduced the Pacific oyster (Crassostrea) for large-scale cultivation. Though it cannot spawn in our colder waters, it grows very well when cultivated from seed in oyster beds. Housed in convenient plastic containers, which allow water to circulate through, it will be ready for marketing in 18 months or two years. Commercial hatchers provide the baby seeds which are grown in Scotland, Devon, Wales and Norfolk, and production is fast overtaking that of native species.

prised off the rocks and eaten raw, or else strewn on the ground and covered in burning straw to be cooked on the spot.

At other times, though, winkles and mussels were very much a cash crop that was exploited by the coastal population. Mussels gathered on the Northumberland coast were stored between the tides in 'mussel gardens' – rings of stones enclosing small pools – to await buyers. There are also records of mussels being used for their protective action in Bridport, Devon, where the local corporation attached them to the submerged parts of the bridge to deflect the heavy tide. But even when these shellfish were being traded regularly, they usually remained a foodstuff of the poor.

PLENTY OF MUSSEL
(right) Mussels are one of the easiest of shellfish to gather. As with other bivalves – except the oyster – they are now not as abundantly harvested as before. Once, they were extremely popular – literally, tons were brought in at a time – and traded all over Europe. Though coastal populations depended on them for their livelihood, in Britain they remained principally a cheap form of nourishment for the poor.

Dredging could yield an almost inconceivable quantity of cockles and razor shells on a productive beach. Of Barra on the shores of the Western Isles, it was said that every tide brought so many cockles that scores of horseloads could be removed from the beach. Local people were many times saved from starvation only by turning to the cockle as their staple diet, and inhabitants of areas where the shells were plentiful – such as the Gower Peninsula – have in the past lived on cockles for up to nine months of the year.

COMBING THE DEPTHS

Dredging required a measure of physical strength that was beyond the ability of children, so this task was women's work in many parts of Britain. However, juvenile ingenuity was sometimes as productive as brute force. Razor shells were lured to the surface by sprinkling salt on

FISHING FOR COMPLIMENTS
Coyly entitled, 'Limpets' the century-old photograph (above) captures the cheekiness of two limpet-gatherers. Limpets cling tenaciously to rocks and need a sharp knock to be dislodged.

THE SHRIMPER
(right) This pretty shrimper with her net poses daintily within the leather-bound pages of an elegant volume on the many different occupations of the British Isles.

SHRIMPER.

the hole left in the mud. The salt irritated the mollusc, which then pushed itself from the mud into easy reach. Another technique was to creep up and spear the opened shell with a barbed, sharpened piece of wire. Razor shells caught in this way were taken to towns, such as Tenby, and were also popular in Rye, the Channel Islands and in Faroe.

GOOGAWNS AND CUCKOO SHELLS

Whelks have always been abundant and the wealth of dialect names – conch, buckie, stingwinkle, googawns and cuckoo shells – suggests that they have been fished in virtually every coastal area. The commonest name is derived from the Anglo-Saxon, *weolc,* meaning 'that which gives purple dye' – actually a property of the dog-whelk, a near relation.

The whelk, however, was not universally popular: lobster fishermen even considered them as pests, since they took the bait from the lobster pots. In areas where they were thought to be worthwhile quarry, though, fishermen used wicker baskets similar to lobster pots to catch the whelk. A piece of rotting offal inside the basket was enough to entice the shellfish in.

Like the whelk, the scallop has numerous aliases. In Cornwall, the fish were called frills or queens, and in Dorset, squinns. A haul of scallops was often simply a welcome byproduct of a trawling expedition, rather than the principal motive of the trip: fishermen

believed that the shells were most easily taken after a fall of snow.

The oyster, of course, is the king of shellfish, and the fact that it was the first to be farmed is some indication of the importance attached to it. Usually, the oyster 'farms' were developments or extensions of existing natural oyster beds, rather than artificially established areas that had not been previously occupied by oysters. Farming consisted of seeding with young oysters, tending the growing shells, removing mud, debris, dead oysters and predators, and harvesting the adults ready for the table.

Rearing an oyster for the table takes about four years, and although the local oysters produced numbers of young, most of this 'spat' drifted with the tide, and could not be guaranteed to attach itself to the oyster bed where it originated. There was, therefore, a considerable trade in 'brood' – tiny oysters little bigger than pin-heads.

CHILD'S PLAY
(above) Before mass industrialization and attendant social reforms brought better conditions for the majority of the populace, gathering molluscs such as mussels and periwinkles was often delegated to children when the adults were occupied with worthier and more laborious tasks.

ONE WOMAN AND HER DONKEY
(left) As late as 1954, cockles were gathered in the early morning light by women sifting through the sands. Shellfish-collecting was back-breaking work – mostly confined to women and children. Women, such as Lizzie Davies, shown here, earned a precarious living, for even a full donkey-load would fetch a mere 25 shillings (£1.25).

Trade in brood occurred not only between different parts of Britain, but also with the Continent. Nevertheless, native British species, spawned and raised locally, have always been considered superior to transplanted shells.

SHARE AND SHARE ALIKE

Whitstable was fairly typical of the oyster fishing grounds around the country. In the mid-19th century, a co-operative company ran the square miles of oyster beds, and the hereditary shareholders had grown wealthy from the proceeds of the desirable molluscs.

A contemporary account paints a vivid picture of the oyster fishing trade in its heyday: 'A primitive and curious joint-stock company it is; a joint-stock company whose shares are unknown upon the Stock Exchange, because they are never in any market except Billingsgate market... The free-dredger is thoroughly independent, not given to touch his hat to lord or squire; and if he does pay any mark of

'WICTORIAN WICTUALS' (above right) Oysters were plentiful and infra dig in Dickens' London. Travelling through Whitechapel, Sam Weller remarked to Mr Pickwick, 'Blessed if I don't think that ven a man's wery poor, he rushes out ... and eats oysters in reg'lar desperation.'

READY AND WAITING (above) Proud railmen pose at Whitstable with a valuable cargo. Efficient railways meant a quicker and fresher supply of oysters.

respect to the Duke of Cumberland, it is only at the sign of the dredgers' public house, where the profit of the free company of oyster fishers are divided and paid. At 21 he comes into his full birthright... with all the claims and privileges that belong to the free-fishing state... If a free-dredger dies without male issue, then his share becomes engulfed in the common stock but his widow receives a certain reduced payment out of each day's fishing profits, up to the time of her death. The aged, infirm, and super-annuated, about one-fifth, are provided for in the same way, as well as those who are compelled, by temporary illness, to stop on shore. The dredging for the London market... is regulated by the two salesmen who represent that happy fishing-ground in the market of Lower-Thames Street... The telegram received

from these agents direct the number of bushels that are to be caught on each fishing day.'

Because of its antiquity, a tremendous amount of folklore is associated with oyster cultivation. According to one persistent legend, the Cockenzie fishermen kept up a wild and monotonous song all the time they were dredging, which they claimed charmed the oysters into the dredges. However, attempts to record the words failed as no verse was ever repeated. Oystermen would also turn back if a pig crossed their path while walking to work, and they thought it bad luck if a group of them were counted while standing or walking. The popular 'rule' about eating oysters only when there is an 'r' in the month is not solely for health reasons: the oysters spawn in the summer months so this voluntarily imposed closed season helps to preserve stocks.

RISE AND FALL

Transporting shellfish over long distances became very much faster with the introduction of the steam train and steamboat during the last century; and commercial refrigeration systems meant that the fish arrived fresher. Unfortunately, this led to overfishing of many of Britains most famous shellfish areas in order to satisfy the demand in major cities. Increasing pollution from sewage and toxic industrial wastes either destroyed some of the shellfish beds or made their fish inedible. And widespread sea dumping of high explosives after the last war also damaged stocks.

These changes have led to steep price increases in shellfish — especially scallops and oysters — so that, ironically, these once abundant and lowly foods are now viewed very much as a luxury: a far cry from Dickensian days when Sam Weller told Mr Pickwick, 'It's a wery remarkable circumstance, sir...that poverty and oysters always seem to go together.'

Lobster Fishing

Armed with a vast store of local knowledge and inherited fishermen's lore, the lobstermen, in their tiny cobles and curraghs, set their home-made traps each day in summer along the rocky bed of Britain's inshore waters.

Lobstering with pot and creel is part of the traditional picture of life in fishing villages up and down the British coast. No quayside seems complete without a stack of pots waiting to be loaded aboard a fleet of small boats moored alongside, and the vision of these attractive inshore craft working slowly along the pot line on a balmy summer morning has tempted many a deskbound landlubber into what appears to be an idyllic way to earn a living.

Lobsters are found abundantly in British waters, especially on rocky seabeds around the coast of Scotland and the Scottish Islands, the north-east coast of England, the West Country, Wales and the south coast between Portland Bill and Dungeness. Traditionally, catching lobsters has been an inshore summer occupation, though none the less hard work for that. Rolling about in cockleshell boats among rocks and cliffs, heaving cumbersome tackle in and out of the swell, would be especially dangerous in winter gales, but it is not this that makes

lobstering a summer trade. The explanation lies with the feeding habits of the common British lobster.

Lobsters do not forage for solid food until the water temperature has reached around 50°F (10°C). While the sea is colder than this, they feed almost exclusively on tiny planktonic organisms – which cannot be used to bait a pot. The precise limits of the season vary in different parts of the country, but it generally falls between the end of April and the beginning of October. In the old days, fishermen relied on natural signs to tell them when the time was right – in Wales, for example, they did not consider setting their pots until the corn was in ear.

One of the continuing attractions of lobster fishing is the scale of the operation. It has not yet succumbed to the large diesel boats and clattering gear of much of today's commercial fishing industry. The two- or three-man crew of a small boat still relies on the traditional skills of their forebears – an accumulated store of local knowledge concerning the formation of the seabed, tides and currents, and, not least, the life style and eccentricities of the lobster itself.

LOBSTER LORE

Several creatures classed as lobsters are found around the British coasts. The small Norway lobster is trawled in Scotland and the North-east, and ends up on the fishmonger's slab as scampi or Dublin Bay prawns. The spiny squat lobster, or crayfish, and the long-clawed squat lobster can be found at low tide, sheltering under rocks and boulders. These are generally too small for commercial interest, though are sometimes eaten locally. But the best known is the smart blue species with threatening claws – the common lobster. This is the one for which the fishermen set their strings of pots in summer.

Like oysters, the common lobster was once eaten by rich and poor alike, but its current dizzy price reflects its increasing rarity. It grows slowly: a modest seven-incher can take as many years to reach that length. Its maximum life-span is thought to be about 30 years, and by that time it might just have equalled the largest recorded size of a lobster caught in British waters – 14lb 8oz, caught in 1967 by a skin-

PLAITING THE WITHIES *(far left) Traditional lobster pots are made by local fishermen – usually from willow. It takes about two hours for a skilled man to weave the willow withies into a robust pot that will last for several years.*

diver off the Pembrokeshire coast, preserved and now displayed in the local pub at Amroth. The size of lobsters is, however, the stuff of legends, and historical writings tell of the landing of monstrous beasts such as the lobster found in the Orkneys in the 16th century, whose gigantic claws could crush a man to death.

The average size of lobsters marketed in Britain is 11½in. from 'beak' to tail, weighing in at around 1½lb. Lower size limitations vary according to local byelaws, but many lobstermen mark out nine inches on the gunwale of their boats with copper nails, returning smaller specimens to the sea.

The lobsterman's success depends on his pots and his skill in baiting and placing them. Until the mid 19th century, the use of hoop nets, known as 'trunks', was a common method of catching lobsters, and they are still in use on parts of the Suffolk and Essex coast, but the traditional lobster pot and creel have certainly been favoured by British lobstermen for the last 150 years or more.

There are several pot designs and all rely on the same principle of trapping the lobsters — that is, the pot allows the creatures to enter easily in search of the bait, but make it very difficult for them to get out again. The Cornish

WELSH POTS
(above) Small boats like the coble, which could be launched from the beach, were the typical craft of traditional lobstermen. Up to a dozen pots could be stowed aboard, just enough to be handled by two men. This fisherman, at St Brides, Pembrokeshire, in 1936, is breaking up pieces of stone to weight his pots.

PROSPECT OF WHITBY
The Yorkshire coast was, and still is, one of the main centres of lobster fishing in Britain, though, as elsewhere, it was not a full-time job, even in season. Most lobstermen had other work, sometimes in fishing but often in local factories or farms, and nowadays in the tourist industry.

LIFTING THE POTS
(below) Today many lobstermen lift their pots with mechanical haulers, which means that lobster can now be fished in much deeper waters than when the job was done entirely by hand.

pot, used throughout the West Country, is the well-known wickerwork inkwell or beehive shape. It has a circular base about two feet across, a domed body, and a single funnel-shaped entrance. Made locally from green willow, the pot is begun from the top, unlike most baskets. The funnel, or neck, is completed first, then the willow wands – the withies – are bent over to shape the body. The base is made separately and woven on. Spare willow rods, known as skivers, are pushed through the body and neck for hanging the bait inside the pot.

The North Welsh pot is similar to the Cornish pot but is spherical rather than hive shaped and made of alder, a tough wood heavier than water. The creel, used along the east coast and in Scotland, has a flat base of wooden slats and a rounded netted section. There are usually two entrances, one at each end on opposite sides. The parlour pot is a larger version of the east-coast creel. It also has two entrances, but incorporates a separate compartment, the parlour, reached from the main part by a tapering tunnel. In its attempts to escape, the lobster retreats to the parlour, leaving room, and sometimes bait, for more lobsters. Parlour pots can be left down for days, whereas the standard sized pot, ideally, needs to be lifted every day.

A FATAL ATTRACTION

All types of pot have to be heavily weighted to sink them, secure them against strong currents and keep them upright. Concrete is a favourite ballast as it can be moulded flat. Some Connemara fishermen inlay the concrete with mirror glass – there is some evidence that lobsters are attracted by brightly-coloured or shiny objects as well as smell.

Many modern pots are of plastic or metal construction, though some old-timers will not use them, claiming that the pots 'sing' under-

small boat with two crew. The ideal fishing ground is a rocky seabed, full of the kind of holes and crevices in which lobsters typically find shelter. The pots are attached to a substantial rope, at either end of which is an anchor of some sort, often a rock. The fleet of pots is set out preferably in the direction of the tide, so that the current helps keep the pots clear of the lead rope. The fleet is usually left down overnight – lobsters are nocturnal creatures – but sometimes they are lifted twice a day, once in the early morning and again at midday.

The catch must be taken from the pot with extreme care as the lobster's powerful pincers can inflict a nasty wound or break a finger. One is blunt, for crushing, and the other is sharp, for tearing. The fishermen slip strong rubber bands, or sections of bicycle inner tube, over the claws, or tie them with tarred string. In the old days, the lobsters would be sold locally or packed in straw in wooden boxes and sent by road or rail to Billingsgate. Now they are such an expensive delicacy that many go direct to hotels and restaurants, or are shipped to the continent.

COMMERCIAL PRESSURES

The luxury value of lobster now threatens to alter the character of lobster fishing. As the inshore waters are steadily overfished, the lobsters are pursued further into deeper water. Raising the heavy pot lines needed for such depths is impossible without mechanical gear and the traditional small boats – flat-sterned cobles and tarred curraghs – cannot take the gear. The lobsterman who combines his fishing in the summer with carrying tourists on trips around the bay, and goes after the herring or mackerel in the winter, is being replaced by larger scale commercial operations. If this continues, the loss of the pot-men, with their gardens stacked with creels, their bright little boats, and their slow summery workpace, will be immeasurable.

water and scare off the lobsters. Folding pots are also used – and can be conveniently stowed aboard a small boat – though, again, the traditionalists shake their heads, insisting that a pot should be rigid and 'lie quiet'.

Bait lore is also hotly debated. High on some lists is skinned, gutted, sun-dried cormorant flesh. Others favour the heads of salmon, bass and mullet. Herring and mackerel are considered best if left to go off for a few days. Gurnard is used fresh or salted.

The pots are usually set out in a string, or fleet, of a dozen or so – a manageable load for a

THE FISHING FLEET
(far left) Pots are sometimes set individually, but more often they are worked in strings or fleets. The number of pots in a fleet varies from about a dozen for a small boat to up to 500 on a 50-footer, though no more than 70 would be strung together. They are attached at intervals along a main rope with a buoyed anchor at each end.

POT AND CREEL
The two major types of lobster trap are the round inkwell pot and the half-cylinder creel, but there are many regional variations on each one, including the parlour pot shown here. The traditional materials – wicker, netting, cane, hazel – are being replaced by plastic, wire mesh and expanded metal.

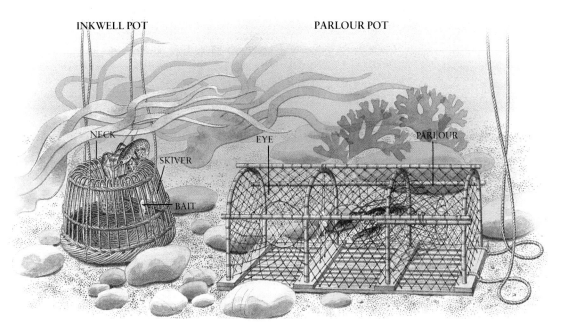

INKWELL POT   PARLOUR POT

NECK

SKIVER

BAIT

EYE

PARLOUR

Fish and Meat Smoking

Now regarded as something of a delicacy, salted or smoked fish and meat were once common fare, as salting and smoking were the only known ways of preserving the seasonal harvests from land and sea.

Before the discovery of salt, the prehistoric Briton had a problem: how to preserve abundant summer catches of fish and meat for the leaner winter months ahead? The first solution was to wind dry them. If the wind was strong enough, thinly-sliced strips of flesh could be brought to the point of desiccation before they began to putrefy. But this process was too dependent on the weather and the results tough and chewy and more like leather than meat. Smoking was the next technique to be developed, possibly discovered by people who had tried to hasten the wind drying process by hanging their fish and meat close to a fire.

But wood or peat smoke did much more than simply dry the meat: it introduced the preservative formaldehyde into the flesh. Furthermore, it warded off insects which kept the meat maggot-free and, as a bonus, gave it a new flavour.

Smoking also allowed for the curing of a great deal more flesh in one go. So when whales were stranded, their carcases would be stripped of skin and blubber and the massive quantities of flesh would be smoked and saved for winter.

A CRAVING FOR SALT

As agriculture spread throughout Europe from the Middle East, the new cereal diet created a craving for salt. Salt not only brought out the flavour of bland cereals, it was also vital for health. And it was a useful preservative for meat and fish. It dried out flesh quickly by osmosis – the salt sucked the moisture out of the tissue.

At about the same time as salt was first used in Britain, the climate began to change. The weather became colder and wetter and not unlike that of today. In the humid air, wind drying became a slower and more risky business. Mould and bacteria would often spoil the flesh before it had been completely dried by the wind. When the Romans invaded Britain, they brought with them salt-pickled Mediterranean fish. But these were rare delicacies and the local fish-salting industry continued to thrive.

In both Celtic and Saxon Britain, salt tubs were common kitchen items. Sides of pork and hams were usually stored in them, but salted oxen are also listed among Anglo-Saxon food rents. Bacon fat and lard were used for cooking

DRYING IN THE WIND
Since micro-organisms cannot grow on dry materials, one of the simplest and earliest methods of preserving fish is to dehydrate it in the open air. In wind-swept areas, such as along much of the Scottish coast, the catch was laid out (above) or hung out (right) to dry just like the washing. Today the catch is flash frozen in refrigeration units on board the trawler long before it is brought ashore.

HEAVY SMOKING

The value of smoking food was probably first discovered accidentally as fires were used simply to hasten the drying of hung food. Herrings were soaked in brine and then hung on racks in tall smokehouses where fires of hardwood burned. The fish would be rotated to ensure even treatment. Today, fish is smoked less for preservation than for the distinctive flavour. The fish are hung in brick kilns, and the racks alternated by the 'night-smoker' (above), an operation decidedly more sedate than the dare-devilry of the Victorian smokehouse (left).

for chewing. It was then eaten with mustard or butter.

Initially, herring were salted in heaps on the foreshore without even being gutted. But by the 14th century, they were gutted first, then soaked for 14 or 15 hours in brine before being packed in barrels between layers of salt. The practice of smoking herring started in the late 13th century. The fish were first soaked in brine, then hung in tall chimneys for many hours before being barrelled.

As fishermen ventured further from the shore they had to take salt with them to preserve their catch. English sailors would set off in February or March and fish in Icelandic waters. There, they would salt the fish on board and dry it before storing it. Not all the fish was dried first though. Some would be barrelled with salt and left to pickle, either to be sold that way or dried and salted later.

SEASONAL SLAUGHTER

In medieval Britain, seal was still eaten and in the remote northern islands, it was salted with the ashes of burnt seaweed as late as the 17th century. From the medieval era until the improvement of farming techniques which would allow livestock to be wintered, the majority of farm animals were traditionally slaughtered in the autumn to save on winter feed. It was then that people would eat their last 'green meat'.

Salt demand would then be at a maximum. Fortunately, the coastal seawater evaporation pools, or salterns, worked most efficiently in summer when they were aided by natural evaporation in the warm weather. But salt was still expensive, so generally only plump carcases — usually pork and beef — were salted. Mutton was invariably too scraggy, besides, sheep could usually overwinter without any extra feed unless the weather was particularly severe.

The sides of pork or beef would be dry- or wet-salted — that is, salted in brine. The salted

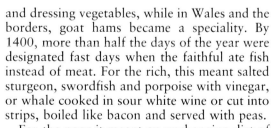

and dressing vegetables, while in Wales and the borders, goat hams became a speciality. By 1400, more than half the days of the year were designated fast days when the faithful ate fish instead of meat. For the rich, this meant salted sturgeon, swordfish and porpoise with vinegar, or whale cooked in sour white wine or cut into strips, boiled like bacon and served with peas.

For the poor it meant an unchanging diet of salted herrings. A 15th century school book records just how unpleasant this was: 'Thou will not believe how weary I am of fish, and how much I desire that flesh were come in again, for I have ate none other by salt fish this Lent, and it hath engendered so much phlegm within me that it stoppeth my pipes that I can neither speak or breathe.'

The alternative was worse — it was stockfish that had to be beaten with a hammer for an hour and soaked in warm water for two hours before cooking simply to make it supple enough

CANNED, SEALED AND DELIVERED

With the introduction of canning (above), the mass smoking and salting of food fell into decline. Canning was first developed in France, with food sealed in jars and then heated. But it was not until the work of Pasteur that the process was understood – the bacteria trapped inside were killed by the heat, while new bacteria could not invade through the seal. Canning not only preserves food, it also makes it more transportable in large quantities – one of the reasons why it was invented in the first place: to keep the French military well supplied.

PACKED IN SALT

Salt, liberally thrown over gutted fish (right), draws out moisture from the tissues by osmosis. This prevents the growth of mould and bacteria and delays decomposition.

pork would often spend weeks suspended over a fire or hung high up in the chimney until it acquired a rich smoky flavour and sheen.

Beef smoked this way was not held in high esteem among physicians. 'Matinmas beef, which is called 'hanged beef' in the roof of the smoky house, is not laudable; it may fill the belly and cause a man to drink, but it is evil for the stone, and evil of digestion, and maketh no good juice,' says one text book.

Bacon was served with veal to celebrate the end of Lent and rashers of salted bacon fried with eggs were a 'usual dish toward Shrovetide'.

In the Middle Ages, as now, physicians looked on this as an unwholesome food.

By the reign of Elizabeth I, the roads had been improved and fresh fish could be transported quickly from the ports. The salt tax of 1643 encouraged this process. It remained until 1825 and during that time fishermen found that it was often more profitable to throw back fish that would not keep until it got to market.

Although for a time, salt-fish mongers ran in competition with wet-fish mongers, salt fish and meat soon became the food of the poor. It became increasingly unpopular, but it remained the only effective way to provision an army or the ships of the Elizabethan adventurers who set out on their voyages of discovery.

NEW METHODS

In the 17th century, potted meats and fish became the fashion, often served as a lighter second course. And at the end of the 18th century, an employee of the East India company suggested transporting fish by packing it in ice. He had seen fish carried in snow in China. Soon ice-houses were being built on the principal salmon rivers and London was receiving its regular consignments of fresh Scottish salmon.

The death knell of the mass salting and smoking industry came with the advent of canning. It was invented by the French chef, confectioner and distiller, Nicholas Appert in 1809, after the French Directory offered a prize of 12,000 francs for the first effective method of preserving food for army and navy. He sealed the food in jars and heated them for a certain length of time, and provided the jars were not opened, it was

CURING HERRING
Once caught, herring were pickled in brine. They were then layered tightly with salt in barrels (above).

ARBROATH SMOKIES
Modern preservation techniques have superseded smoking as a means of preserving fish. However, certain smoked fish, such as the smoked haddock known as Arbroath Smokies, though produced humbly (above right) in Arbroath, Scotland, is much appreciated by discerning palates.

PICKLED PORK
Meat preservation was an early necessity when large numbers of animals were slaughtered each year before winter, due to insufficient feed. Sides of beef or pork were marinated and then smoked. Here (below right), home cured bacon in brine is basted with a mixture of treacle, vinegar and beer.

found that the food remained fresh.

No one knew how it worked, though, and it was another fifty years before Louis Pasteur explained why the food treated this way did not spoil – the heat killed the bacteria present in the food and the sealing jar prevented other bacteria from entering it.

MECHANICAL REFRIGERATION

A method of freezing food was patented in Britain as early as 1842 – the food was immersed in ice and brine. But it was not until mechanical refrigeration was introduced that it became commerically viable, though it came into use by accident. In 1880, a cargo of meat coming from

Australia to Britain under refrigeration accidentally froze. The results were so good that the method was quickly adopted for other long distance shipments.

Flash freezing is now more commonly used. Rapid freezing helps prevent the build up of large ice crystals which destroy the cell structure and, hence, the texture of some foods.

Until the advent of the home refrigerator in the 1950s, however, smoking, salting and pickling were still common methods of preserving small quantities of foodstuffs in the country areas of Britain.

Bacon is still salted and smoked in very much the traditional way. It is soaked in brine made with salt and saltpetre for 21 days, then smoked over hickory or oak chips for up to 60 days. But most fish these days are only mildly smoked simply to enhance their flavour, rather than to preserve them.

Fish smoked today are normally soaked in an 80 per cent brine solution for 20 or 30 minutes, then stretched on 'tenter hooks' protruding from 'tenter sticks' – both terms from the textile industry. They are then smoked in brick-built kilns over oak, or occasionally pine, for six to 18 hours. The kiln operator or 'nightsmoker' takes the bottom fish out first when he judges them to be done, and moves the other ones down. This process is known as 'stripping' the kiln.

Smoking foodstuffs has had something of a revival recently as bland mass-produced foods slowly give way to gourmet products. Although it is no longer necessary to smoke fish to preserve it, smoked salmon is as popular as ever though the modern, mild smoked salmon cannot be compared with the dry, salty salmon that was eaten in the 17th and 18th century – but then neither can its price.

The Coracle Makers

Drifting silently downstream in their waterproofed wickerwork boats, the coracle men of West Wales, fishing in pairs for fat salmon and sewin, may be the last to use these primitive river craft.

From the ancient weathered hills of central Wales run swift pure rivers. The most picturesque is probably the Teifi, with its rushing rapids and eddying pools, willow-lined banks and deep rocky gorges. As long ago as the 12th century the chronicler Giraldus Cambrensis reported its reputation for providing the finest salmon in the whole of Wales.

Giraldus also described the boats used to catch the fish; they were roughly triangular and constructed of twigs and hides. Clearly these were coracles, representatives of a design that has persisted from prehistory to the present day, a primitive craft without keel or rudder that has never been bettered for working on shallow, rocky rivers.

The use of coracles long predates any written record of them. The Welsh romance, the *Mabinogion*, written down in the 13th century but depicting an oral tradition stretching back into the Dark Ages, has several references to them. It describes the great bard Taliesin himself as having been set adrift in one at birth, to be rescued from the sea near Aberystwyth.

LEATHER CRAFT

Other scattered references show both Henry V and Edward III taking 'leather boats' with them on their expeditions to France. But a surer testament to the longevity of the coracle tradition is the variety of forms that have survived into more recent times, evidence of strong local traditions slowly evolving types particularly suited to the materials at hand and the nature of the river, its depth and speed.

A coracle is basically a waterproof basket, an open lattice covered with some impermeable material. It is light enough for one man to carry on his back, draws only two or three inches and is very manoeuvrable, able to twist and turn, to shoot rapids or thread channels better than a canoe. It can be paddled one-handed, leaving the other hand free for a net or rod and line. Part of its lasting appeal was that everyone could make his own.

Despite local variations in shape and materials, the methods of construction are broadly similar. Poles are cut from pollarded willows in the autumn and winter when the sap is not running.

HOMEMADE BOATS
Coracles have many advantages for the salmon fishermen of the fast-flowing Teifi (above and right). They are quick, cheap and easy to make and, despite their unsafe appearance, are astonishingly stable in these shallow, rocky streams. Conveniently, a coracle can also be carried home by its owner, using the strap set into the seat.

These are cloven with a billhook, shaped into laths with drawknife and spokeshave, then made pliable by soaking in very hot water.

The framework of the coracle is laid out on the ground. Seven laths, spaced four to five inches apart, form the long axis, and others are woven through at right angles. Sometimes the structure is strengthened by placing two or more laths diagonally. The middle of the lattice – which forms the bottom of the boat – is then weighted down with rocks or held firm by forked pegs driven into the ground to straddle the crossing points. The ends of the laths are bent up to form the sides of the craft, and secured temporarily with twine.

Traditionally, the gunwale is made of plaited withies of hazel. Their bark is peeled off and they too are soaked to make them pliable. Three rows are plaited together, and worked all round the top of the frame, binding the laths tightly together and giving the coracle its final

shape. The seat, usually a plank of deal, is then fitted to complete the frame, and the whole is creosoted before the covering or 'hide' is put on.

Up to the 17th century, the hide was exactly that, the complete skin of a horse or cow, worked with lard, tallow-cake or butter. This limited the size of a vessel and added considerably to its weight. Eventually animal skins were replaced with tarred flannel and later unbleached calico, which is still used.

The calico, about five yards of it, is stretched over the frame, lapped, and secured with twine or wire. It is then waterproofed by painting it with a mixture of around six pounds of pitch, lard, and half a pint of linseed oil. The oil and lard prevent brittleness and stop the pitch from flaking off.

A carrying strap, long enough for the coracle to be slung around the shoulders, is fixed to the seat. This may be made of leather, plaited hazel or rope.

A coracle thus built will, with care, last

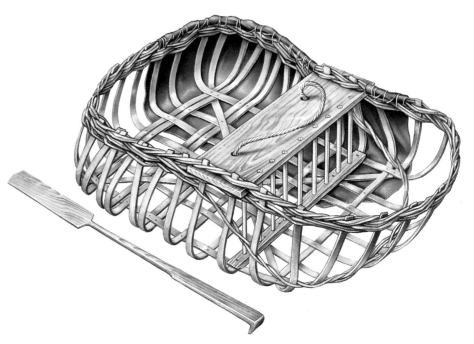

FLOATING BASKET
(above) Basically waterproof baskets, coracles are woven from laths of pliable hazel or willow that grow along the river banks.

IRISH CURRAGHS
(left and below) The keel-less, cloth-covered curraghs of Ireland are often classed with coracles; but they are sea-going craft, ones that carried the Irish monks and saints on their missionary voyages, and today fish along the wild Atlantic coast. Curraghs have a conventional boat shape, with a pointed prow and squared bow, and are made to be carried and rowed by more than one person.

several years. Small tears in the fabric can be patched over with tarred cloth, or the whole frame can be recovered. But coracles are so quick and cheap to make that they are often as easy to replace as to repair. Old ones are generally burnt, the combination of wood, cloth and pitch making for a good blaze.

Local circumstances sometimes dictated other materials. At Bewdley on the lower Severn, for example, where willow was scarce, cleft oak was used for the laths and old sailcloth for the hide. In other areas sawn ash was used for laths and, shaped into hoops, for the gunwales.

Although once probably widespread throughout Britain, the coracle survived in recent times only in Wales and the Welsh Marches, where their use was sustained for the most part by salmon fishing. Centres of the industry in south-west Wales were the Teifi, Tywi and the Taf. Coracle fishing – though not necessarily for salmon and sea-trout – also took place on the Usk and Monnow in the South, the Dyfi, Conwy and especially the Dee in the North, and on the Severn from Worcester to Welshpool.

THE DEADLY CNOCER

Coracle fishermen work in pairs, usually at night. Each man takes one end of the rope to which the net is attached by rings. Keeping as close to their respective banks as possible, paddling with the free hand, they ghost slowly downstream. As soon as the fish hits the net the fishermen spring into action. The net bunches up, enmeshing the catch, which is then hauled in and immediately despatched with a club called a cnocer or – since it administers the last rites – a priest. It is important that this is swiftly accomplished as a large salmon is a formidable thing to have thrashing around in a relatively flimsy craft.

Netting has declined this century as it was seen by other anglers to be too effective. To

CASTING THEIR NETS
The fishermen use two nets joined top and bottom. One, the armouring, has a wide mesh, while the other, the lint, is much finer. They are attached by rings to a horsehair rope that will neither stretch nor sink. The fish slip through the armouring and hit the lint.

preserve fish stocks, nets were licensed, and the number of licences offered was continually cut. Netting is now entirely prohibited on the Severn, though at the turn of the century the rivers supported three major centres, at Shrewsbury, Ironbridge and Bewdley. Use of coracles here, though, was never so specialized as it became on the Welsh rivers, and as a result a type of coracle that probably predates other surviving types remains in use.

Here coracles are much more rounded and symmetrical. They are less stable than the fishing types, but though unsuitable for salmon netting, they have a more general usage. The Severn Gorge is deep and there are few bridges between Ironbridge and Arley, so Severnsiders habitually used coracles to cross the river. Most families had one, hanging outside the cottage door or in a handy tree when not in use.

CATCHING RABBITS

Coracles were also useful when the river was in flood, for retrieving articles that had floated away, or for catching rabbits stranded by the rising waters on high ground or the tops of hedgerows. Lower down the river, at Bewdley, similar coracles were also used as ferries – passengers stood behind the seat, clinging to the paddler and each other – and for angling, laying lines, and setting out eel traps.

These bowl-shaped craft have the same shape as the only surviving Scottish example, a 200-year-old, much-decayed museum-piece that once worked the River Spey in Morayshire. This was constructed entirely of wickerwork and was used for crossing the river, though in its last years it was employed in guiding downstream rafts of timber cut in the Highlands for the coastal sawmills.

Fishing coracles can be put to other uses. At Cenarth, the sheep are washed before shearing each spring by being thrown into the pool formed there by the Teifi. Coracle men are still employed on the river, making sure that none escape downstream or otherwise come to harm.

The art of coracle making is also kept alive by the Welsh people's unremitting defence of their culture, and in the sport of coracle racing. The first recorded race took place near Welshpool in 1798, and annual festivals are still held on the Teifi in July at Cenarth, and in August at Cilgerran in the dark gorge below the castle.

A LIVING TRADITION
Coracles are still very much in use on Welsh rivers, especially around long-standing centres like Cilgerran and Cenarth.

The Craft of Boat Building

Boat-building is one of the oldest of all traditional British crafts, and small wooden boats today may be built using skills refined and honed over more than 4000 years.

The graceful wooden-hulled steamers that ply Britain's larger upland lakes belong to a tradition of small-boatbuilding that dates back to the primitive dug-outs of prehistoric times, hewn from a single tree-trunk with fire and axe. One such canoé, found in Dumfriesshire, is 4000 years old, but they were almost certainly made long before this. By 2000 BC, boatbuilders were beginning to make boats by joining together planks of timber, for dug-outs were heavy and limited in size by the tree-trunks available.

The earliest plank-built boats in Britain were made of overlapping oak planks, sewn together with yew and willow bindings and waterproofed with moss. But it was soon realized much stronger boats could be made by laying the planks over a wooden frame. Frame-built boats probably emerged in about the third century BC.

At first, timber-framed boats were 'clinker' built – that is, the planks or 'strakes' were overlapped, making it much easier to ensure a watertight join. Usually, the planks would be attached to the frame by driving a wooden peg through the plank and into the frame, and fastening it in place with an iron nail. To make sure the iron nail never slipped, the protruding end would be 'clenched' – turned back into the wood like a staple. Boat nails are still clenched even today, usually using a metal bar or 'dolly' to turn them back.

EMERGING TRADITIONS

Before long, however – perhaps even at the same time – an alternative to clinker building began to emerge. This is 'carvel' building, in which the planks are laid edge-to-edge and a watertight seal is ensured by caulking. The planks were all keyed together by wooden tenons set in to slots in the edge of each plank, and then secured by trenails (wooden dowels) driven through the plank into the tenon.

These two traditions, clinker and carvel building, continue right to this day. But the Dark Ages brought a crucial outside influence to bear on clinker building in Britain: the longboats of the Vikings and other raiders from across the North Sea.

The Viking boats had a central keel, and a stem at either end, and the planking was laid over a temporary frame to enable the builder to create a large flat belly.

The Viking boats were unusually long for clinker built boats – for it is very difficult to clinker build a large boat and keep it watertight. Even the Viking longboats suffered from problems like fractured keels. The problem is that the structure allows far too much movement. Medieval boatbuilders did attempt to make large clinker boats but soon gave up and turned to carvel building. Consequently, most clinker boats are between 8 and 18 feet in length.

Carvel building required much more time and effort, for each plank had to be very precisely mated, but the final structure was much more solid. So ships and large boats would be carvel-built. For smaller boats and dinghies, where the structure could be a little more flexible and low cost was essential, clinker building was favoured.

CLINKER STYLES

Over the centuries, each stretch of the coast developed its own distinctive type of boat – especially clinker-built boats, which were usually built locally for local use. Small yards carried on traditions of clinker-building over

LAKELAND CRAFT
(below) Sturdy wooden carvel-built lakeland passenger craft and clinker-built rowing skiffs embody a centuries' old tradition of the building of small, robust, yet elegant wooden pleasure and working boats.

(left) Reginald Emery and two of his sons, Chris (top) and Harold, at their Norfolk boatyard completing the 30ft clinker-built whelk boat, William Edward, *which 40 years later still works out of Wells, Norfolk. Like many small boat-builders, they worked by eye — relying on experience, not plans, to create the right shape.*

shortage of harbours, the crabber used at one time to be carried across wide stretches of sand and mudflat by passing the ash oars through opposing oar-ports ('orrocks') and using them as handles.

BUILDING BY CLINKER

Despite the many local variations in style and shape, however, all clinker built boats tended to be constructed in much the same way. Typical of the way clinker-built boats were made is the Shetland fishing boat or 'yoal'.

To build a yoal, the builder needed a long piece of good timber, which would be seasoned in open air. Since Shetland has few trees, the builders would import larch from Sweden or the Baltic; boat-builders elsewhere might use local wood.

For the keel, the builder carefully selected a stretch of timber with as few knots as possible, about the length of the boat and measuring roughly seven inches by three (18 × 8cm). He then secured this to a beam on the floor and marked the position for stem and stern posts. An adze shaped the keel to the builder's own

hundreds of years.

On the Yorkshire coast, for instance, there was the 'coble' (pronounced cobble), with its distinctive oak keel plank or 'ram'. This keel helped to keep the boat stable but was very shallow and sturdy, and allowed the boat to be used in shallow waters and launched from a beach. The coble, which tapered gradually from stern to stem, was steered by a very deep rudder hanging over the stern, but this could be shipped swiftly and easily when the boat entered shallow waters. Short side keels helped protect the bottom of the boat when it was drawn on to the beach. Cobles can still be seen on and around the Yorkshire coast.

Another distinctive local craft is the Sheringham 'crabber' of the Norfolk coast, unchanged in shape and construction since the Middle Ages. As the name implies, they were used for rowing to and from the crab pots, and they were double ended so that they could be rowed in either direction as the pots were hauled up or set. Black with tar below the water-line, the Sheringham crabbers were brilliant red, white and blue paint above the water. Because of the

VIKING INFLUENCE
(right) Today's clinker or lap-strake boats are direct descendants of the shapely longships of the 3rd and 4th century Viking raiders.

particular style, and the sides of the keel were planed flat and cut with grooves to accept the ribs of the boat. The stem and stern posts were cut following a thin wooden template and then shaped with an adze, planed smooth and fixed to the keel.

With the basic frame complete, the builder began to build up the hull, row (or 'run') by row of planks. The first run of rough-hewn larch planks or strakes, known as the 'garboard strakes', were shaped and chamfered and fastened to the keel with copper nails. Remaining runs of strakes were cut according to patterns. To accommodate the sharp curves in the hull shape, all but the first run of strakes had to be made from two or three pieces fastened end to end, or 'scarfed', together. The end pieces of these strakes were softened with hot water before being drilled for fastenings and nailed into position.

Once the second run of strakes was secured short ribs of timber were used to shore up the entire structure and, once the hull planking was complete, sole-bands or lower frames were fitted into the shell, to stop it twisting sideways. The gunwales (the rim of the boat) were usually made of red fir, and had to be softened for a week in the loch to enable them to be bent into shape.

Side bands or frames were also fitted, to which the planking was nailed, as were the three main cross-beams called 'fastibands'. On top of the fastibands were laid the longitudinal stringers which supported the removable thwarts that provided seats for the rowers. Triangular webbing called 'breasthooks' fitted into the stem and stern angles, completing the yoal's strengthening.

With the hull complete, removable floor-boards, called 'tilfers', were cut and fitted into each compartment of the hull shell. Each boat came with two pairs of oars, fastened by rope loops on to iron 'thole' pins protruding from the gunwales. A rudder and rudder hangings were only provided if the boat would be sailed. The only protective coating applied to the timber in the years before World War 1 was Archangel Tar, but, nowadays, polyurethane varnishes

INNER FRAMEWORK
(above) After building up the overlapping strakes to form the hull, the boatwright fits sole-bands to give the boat lateral stiffness.

TOOLS OF THE TRADE
(below left) The tools used by makers of wooden boats have changed little over the centuries. The most important of these is the curved handled adze. To make holes for bolts and wooden pegs, augers – like large corkscrews – of different sizes, were used. If a boat was carvel-built the boatwright would have caulked it to make it watertight. To do this he used a mallet and caulking irons to drive lengths of caulking cotton in between the planks.

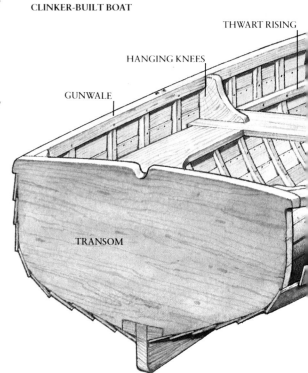

CLINKER-BUILT BOAT

THWART RISING

HANGING KNEES

GUNWALE

TRANSOM

USING THE ADZE
(left) Using a traditional adze with curved wooden handle, the boatwright worked towards himself in a rhythmic manner, taking thin bites of wood off the timber at each swing.

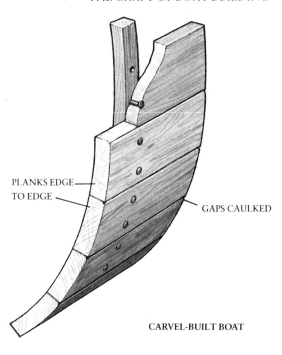

PLANKS EDGE
TO EDGE

GAPS CAULKED

CARVEL-BUILT BOAT

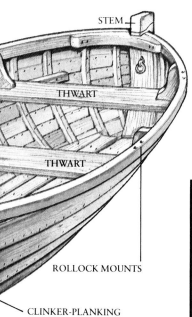

STEM

THWART

THWART

ROLLOCK MOUNTS

CLINKER-PLANKING

REPAIRING A CARVEL BOAT
(above) Many of the 19th-century fishing boats made by the carvel method, with hull planks placed edge to edge, and caulked to make them watertight, are still in use.

and paints are applied to seal the wood.

In Shetland, a few boatbuilders still make yoals this way and, around the coast of Britain, wherever clinker boats are still built, similar age-old techniques are employed.

CARVEL BOATS

200 years ago, virtually all large boats and ships – such as the navy's ships-of-the-line and the famous tea clippers – were carvel built. But the tradition of building small boats by carvelling is much less widespread in Britain than clinker-building, largely because the construction is so elaborate that it was beyond the means of most fishermen. As larger boats were made, more and more with steel hulls, so carvel building began to die out. Nevertheless, carvel boats are

CLINKER-BUILT BOAT
(above) The clinker-built boat was faster and cheaper to make than a carvel boat and its overlapping planking lent it stability in the water. Once the hull strakes were fitted the gunwhales were fitted and the inner ribs firmly fixed. Later the thwarts, stem-ends and floor planking were added.

STARTING POINT
Boatbuilding starts with keel laying. Once made from single lengths of timber, today they are more likely to consist of several different pieces of timber firmly fixed together. The skiff on the left was made following age-old Viking methods. The sweeping line of the overlapping strakes was built up without fixed interior moulds or frames. Using judgement of hand and eye and movable half-moulds to check the width, the boatwright achieves perfect symmetry. For the skiff above a Cumbrian boatyard used fixed frames to shape the boat.

still used to fish for salmon on the River Severn.

The Severn carvel boats are heavy, broad-beamed boats that hold steady in the strong current as the fisherman casts his unwieldy stopnet out over the water. One man can control the boat, sculling with a single oar over the flat stern. They have no keel, for the internal frame is very robust, and they are used only for rowing.

Few boatyards still make carvel boats any more and the Severn boats are almost 100 years old. But, again, where the tradition survives, the techniques are the same as they have been for many centuries.

A carvel built boat is constructed on a mould. The planks are laid around the mould and nailed together through their width, edge to edge. Between each plank edge is a coat of 'luting', a thick, waterproof paint, and one surface edge of each plank is slightly bevelled to give a seating for the caulking.

Caulking material used at one time to be oakum, made from recycled rope strands laboriously picked apart in prisons and workhouses. Later, caulking cotton was used. This soft material, lightly twisted into a thin rope, was soaked before use in pitch, or in linseed oil and varnish.

In the days of wooden ships, the country's boatyards echoed to the steady pounding of the caulkers' mallets as they stripped out old caulking and replaced it with new. The mallet is a short-handled tool with a long, narrow head bound at each end in metal.

The caulker also used a variety of caulking irons, chisel-like implements in a number of sizes according to the width of the seams being dealt with. The caulker held loops of caulking cotton and the driving iron in his left hand, driving it into the seam with steady, even blows of the mallet in his right hand.

It was a skilful job to both feed the loops of cotton and position the iron correctly with one hand. Wrong positioning could cut the cotton strands, and uneven paying out of the cotton could cause a jam which would have to be picked free before starting again from scratch. After the plank seams had been caulked, they were puttied or pitched, sanded smooth, and then painted.

All these traditional techniques, both for carvel and clinker building, are fast disappearing, as modern materials, like glass reinforced plastic, replace wood for hulls. But there still exist many wooden craft dating from the 1950s, when there was a boom in small-boatbuilding and, up and down the country, there are small boatyards keeping alive the old traditions using techniques little changed in centuries.

Sailing Barges

Sailing barges once plied our rivers and coastal waters, laden with bulk cargo like bricks, horse fodder and refuse. Now, the few that survive are used as holiday craft or floating 'museums'.

The sailing barge has only just slipped down-estuary and out into history. Its unmistakable silhouette – long, low hull and towering canvas – is still familiar to us from photographs and paintings. Some can still remember its steady motion: straining against the wind or surging forward on a racing tide to the accompaniment of creaking spars, clattering blocks and the glittering gurgle of bow-cut waves.

Throughout the 19th century and well into the 20th, these purposeful craft plied England's eastern seaboard. Although their tideway beat extended from Newcastle to Newlyn, the 'barge coast' proper, radiating out of London's Thames, comprised Suffolk and Essex to the north, Kent to the south. And it was the geography of this inconstant shore – silting estuaries, shifting sands, pervading marshes and mud-thick creeks – that dictated barge design. Unlike deeper-hulled vessels, the sailing barge, flat-bottomed and drawing only a few feet, could negotiate treacherous shoalwaters and nudge up narrow gutways with easy confidence; while its spreading canvas – ruddy brown through annual dressings with salt water, cod-oil and ochre – snatched every whisper of wind.

BARGE DESIGN

Sailing barges, although built to a similar plan, varied considerably in size and hull shape. The smallest, loading some 30 tons, were about 40 feet long; the largest, two hundred-tonners, measured 90-100 feet overall. To compensate for lack of keel and shallow draught – as little as three feet unloaded – all barges had lee-boards (plank frames fixed to the sides): winched down into the water, these increased resistance underneath the keel and so prevented sideways drift. In terms of canvas, barges originally carried three sails – foresail, mainsail and mizzen – but, by the mid-1800s, were setting topsail and jib (triangular staysail) as well. Instead of a conventional boom, which would have impeded cargo loading and unloading, the mainsail was supported by a diagonal spar or sprit (giving the name spritsail barge or 'sprittie') attached to the mast base. The mast itself stood in a mastcase so that it could be lowered for shooting bridges.

BARGE BUILDERS
(above) This photograph shows the building team of the sailing barge Lillie. *These craftsmen cut the planks, steamed them in hissing steamchests to make them pliable, and then built the vessel from the keel up, using simple tools like a shipwright's adze (curved axe), a hand drill and a caulking mallet.*

SHALLOW WATERS
(right) Sailing barges were designed to nudge up the coast, taking muddy creeks, shifting sands and treacherous shoalwaters in their stride. The hull was flat-bottomed, so that the barge drew very little water and sat easily on the estuary bed at low tide. C. W. Wyllie's painting shows a 'stackie' – lying in the shallows – being loaded with trusses of fresh hay.

Spritties were by far the most common type of barge afloat, but there were also 'stumpies' and 'boomies'. Stumpies were Cockney craft: they covered the industrial Thames and its connecting canals and, since most trips took them upstream and under bridges they never carried a topmast – hence their name. Stumpy traffic was largely involved in taking the capital's rubbish down-river to the estuary marshes then bringing back either building materials from the Medway ports or timber off-loaded from Norwegian steamers. At the other end of the scale, boomies – carrying two hundred tons or more – were large ketch-rigged barges, designed to replace traditional sailing vessels on North Sea routes. Their cargoes included Tyneside coke, Cornish china clay, Channel Island flints, Dutch tiles and mineral water from Remagen, far up the Rhine.

During the 1800s, the focal point for all barge movements was London. With every tide, convoys swept in, laden with bricks, stone, sand and cement – essential construction materials for the rapidly-expanding metropolis. Other spritties, largely from East Anglian ports, supplied the capital's everyday needs: flour, root vegetables, brewing malt and, most importantly, fodder for the horse population. In summer, hundreds of 'stackies', their decks piled high with trusses of hay or straw, sailed daily from farm quays along the Stour, Colne, Crouch and Blackwater; perched on top of each floating haystack, the barge mate used to act as pilot, since the skipper could see nothing from the wheel. Having unloaded at Greenwich, Vauxhall, Lambeth and the Chelsea Omnibus wharf, the barges returned to Essex with loads full of street

manure to lay on the land. A load of muck bought for around nine pounds, would be re-sold to farmers for a profit of three or four pounds.

Cargoes were loaded and unloaded in various ways. Often the barge anchored in shallow water or edged into a creek and waited for low tide; then once it was stranded on the mud bed, horsedrawn carts would draw up alongside. Freights like coal and timber were 'jumped' up a plank, while sand and mud, both required by

THE 'ALDERMAN'
(above) The 'Alderman' *was built in London in 1905 and registered in Harwich. Here, her skipper and mate pose on deck, against a background of sombre London warehouses. The barge's stern boasts some particularly fine and elaborate scrollwork.*

the construction industry, were loaded 'overside': it took four men – normally the skipper, mate and two heavers – two tides to dig out and throw up one hundred tons, enough to fill a medium-size barge. This was literally back-breaking work, as a barge side stood at least five feet high and the wooden shovel, heaped with mud, weighed around 30 pounds; no wonder heavers were paid as much as six shillings a tide. Stone cargoes had to be packed carefully to prevent them shifting in rough seas and puncturing the sides. Grain, too, could bring disaster: a leak, however small, might cause the grain to swell and subsequently burst the vessel's seams.

The growth of barge traffic up and down the coast brought temporary prosperity to many waterside towns and villages. Wharves were erected wherever they were needed, often to serve an industry which has since disappeared – such as the brickworks at Lower Halstow on the Medway, the lime-kiln up Tollesbury Creek off the Blackwater and the gunpowder mills near Harty Ferry on the Swale. Likewise, barge yards, at first concentrated along the Thames, opened up in other parts of the country – notably at Sittingbourne, Faversham and Whitstable and at Ipswich, Harwich and Maldon.

Whether building or repairing, the barge yard

'BOOMIES'
(above) This picture shows the magnificent 'Cock o' the Walk', *lying in Ipswich Docks. Large cutter-rigged barges like this were known as 'boomies', because, instead of a sprit (a diagonal spar supporting the mainsail), they had a boomsprit which extended from the bow. Extra sails were attached to the boom, while the mainsail was attached by hoops to the mast. These stately barges sailed Britain's rivers and coast, but they also made regular Channel crossings carrying cargoes of 200 tons or more.*

'SPRITTIES'
(right) Spritsail rigged barges, known as 'spritties', were the most common and best designed of the sailing barges. Their mainsail was supported by a sprit – usually made of Oregon or pitch pine – which ran diagonally from the base of the mast to the peak of the mainsail. The sprit did away with the need for a main boom, which would have hindered the loading and unloading of cargo.

echoed to a miscellany of sound: rhythmic cutting in the saw pit; hissing steamchest, packed with timber ready for bending; bubbling buckets of pitch; dull thuds of the shipwright's adze shaping a hull plank; and insistent taps from caulking mallets, forcing hemp strands into joints and seams.

The relatively low cost of construction – around six hundred pounds for a 50-ton sprittie in the 1880s – was one factor that helped barges outlast all other commercial sailing vessels. Low operating costs were even more significant: a two-man crew – skipper and mate – could handle any size barge. And the wind was free.

For the crew, home on board was a cosy, but cramped, cabin. Gleaming with varnish, brass and well-washed lino, it contained two bunks (the starboard one traditionally occupied by the skipper) set above benches and lockers, a central table and a galley area with a coal-burning stove. The working day, which often lasted 24 hours, was as multi-faceted as the waters the crew sailed. It could involve navigating the open sea; shooting bridges under oars; inching along reed-lined creeks; replacing spars smashed by dockside cranes; taking a horse-tow through a narrow-cut; lying on the buoys hoping for work; dashing ashore to fetch in water and food; and jostling for cargo at the quayside.

Occasionally, the skipper's wife served as mate, but usually a lad was taken on straight from school. He would aim to become a skipper by his early 20s, by which time he was expected to have acquired a good working knowledge of the 'barge coast' – its tides, winds and hidden hazards – so that he could confidently ship a freight anywhere. Although there were some skipper-owners, most barges – like lorries today – belonged to farmers and industrial companies such as brewers and timber merchants.

Some firms operated sizeable fleets. Eastwoods Brickmakers, based at Conyer and Sittingbourne, had around 60 vessels; many were named after English counties or Greek letters – 'Surrey', 'Durham', 'Alpha', 'Sigma' – and carried the company's name prominently on their sails. The biggest fleet of all – 147 barges in the early 1900s – belonged to Goldsmith's of Grays. Unlike other fleets, their boats did not carry the company's own freight but worked 'by seeking' east coast haulage contractors. Goldsmith barges ranged from squat stumpies, like the 'Wasp', 'Hornet', 'Fly' and 'Bee', to boomies able to load three hundred tons and with names ending in '-ic' such as 'Celtic', 'Runic', 'Doric' and 'Cedric'. (Two, the 'Norvic'

'STUMPIES'
(below) The 'Clyde', *built in 1868, was one of a fleet of 'stumpies' owned by the Grays Chalk Quarries. Stumpy craft were sturdy little barges which were built without topsails, allowing them to pass under bridges and travel further upstream. The* 'Clyde' *plied the industrial Thames, carrying a cargo of chalk which was used for preparing barge beds: level areas where the vessels could lie at low tide. Here, she is seen passing the Broadway Wharf at Limehouse, St Anne's, a familiar sailing landmark.*

END OF AN ERA
(right) The role of the sailing cargo boat was gradually taken over by new forms of transport – articulated lorries and freight trains. This postage stamp contrasts the new railway age with the old days of the picturesque sailing barge.

slump of the early 1920s sounded warning shots. Then came competition from small coasters and, on land, from lorries and railways: ironically, it was the barges who had helped develop the road network by freighting stone and other materials. Finally, many craft laid up during the Second World War never went back into the water.

Yet although numbers dropped dramatically – from over two thousand in 1900 to under two hundred in 1950 – those barges that remained held their own for another ten years or more. Mostly spritties and now fitted with auxiliary engines, they carried cargoes like corn, cement and coal out from London's docks to the country ports. But the end was inevitable: in the 1960s the last two fleets still trading, reduced to two vessels each, were sold off by Paul's and Cranfield's – both Ipswich mill-owners. From further down the Ipswich river, at Pin Mill, a privately-owned sprittie called 'Cambria' sailed on, working the Suffolk and Essex estuaries. In 1970, aged 64, the 'Cambria' retired.

BARGE YACHTS AND 'MUSEUMS'

It was the end of an era, but not of the sailing barge. Today there are some 50 spritties, refitted as barge yachts, cruising the tideways of eastern England. Some are sailed purely for pleasure; many earn their keep by chartering – taking on fee-paying passengers. Every year, 15-20 of them take part in one of the various barge races that are still held at places like Pin Mill, Chatham, the Blackwater and the Swale. Two or three, including the 'Cambria', have been restored and are now open to the public. Ultimately, these 'museum' barges will probably be the last survivors: those still afloat, however well maintained, are unlikely to last more than 150 years – and no new wooden barges have been built since the 1930s.

and 'Cymric', made barge history by sailing out to Argentina.)

Working conditions varied from fleet to fleet: basically 50 per cent of freight earnings went to the owner, with the remainder divided two-to-one between skipper and mate. Some owners refused to pay crews if they were windbound or unable to find a return cargo; but others not only paid fairly but also provided cottages and, ultimately, pensions for their workforce.

Owners, whether skippers or fleet magnates, always added a personal touch to their barges through hull decoration: flamboyant scroll-work on the broad transom, painted rails, colourful bow badges and intricately carved tillers. The designs would incorporate the owner's monogram or company insignia, the vessel's name and, sometimes, its motto. The Ipswich barge, 'Cock o' the Walk', had 'While I live I crow' emblazoned on its stern and on the canvas wheel cover a resplendent cock in full throat.

One fleet owner, forever remembered in the barge world, was William Henry Dodd. Born in 1801, Dodd started life as a ploughboy but then turned to refuse disposal, by barge, and made his fortune. In the 1860s, the Golden Dustman, as he was known, instigated and sponsored sailing barge races with the dual aim of improving barge design and promoting better seamanship; appropriately enough, one of his own barges won the first race in 1863. For one hundred years, working craft – some built specially for the event – took part in these races which were based on the Thames and Medway.

Barges survived longer than any other commercial sailing vessel. Even so, their days were numbered. The Great War and the shipping

UNLOADING AT PUTNEY *(above) At low water, the barge cargo could be unloaded into small horse-drawn carts.*

MUD, GLORIOUS MUD *(below) With London's rapid expansion, building materials were in constant demand. Barges were loaded with mud for the cement works by teams of 'muddies'.*

Rope & Net Making

For hundreds of years, the ropes and nets used by the British navy and the fishing fleet were made by hand by fishermen and their families in the cottages and alleyways of coastal towns.

Rope must have been one of man's earliest inventions. The first hunters and fishermen needed ropes and lines to climb trees, fish in deep water, moor rafts and dugouts. The domestication of animals such as horses and cattle required tethers and leads; and the land uses of rope would also have included tying poles and joists in building construction and binding tools to their handles. The development of shipping in the Ancient World provided the earliest positive evidence of rope and net making, in wall paintings and in the discovery of papyrus ropes in Egyptian tombs.

The first cords and ropes were strips and plaits of grasses, reeds and animal hides and hair. Experience showed that the long fibres of certain plants, like the nettle, flax and hemp, could be made into stronger binders by bunching and twisting them. Eventually it was discovered that if several twisted lines were twisted together again, but in the opposite direction, they would lie together in tension. Fastening the loose ends locked in the tension, creating a rope that would not unravel.

MEDIEVAL ROPERY

From these early beginnings, rope making remained virtually unchanged until the Industrial Revolution. It had existed as a trade in Britain since Roman times, but it was the increasing importance of the sailing boat in the Middle Ages which gave impetus to the industry. The Dorset flax mills appear in the Domesday Book, and some of the earliest medieval guilds, such as the Corders of Ropery, were based on the need for miles of rigging in the ever-expanding boat-building yards. Netting, too, developed with the growth of the offshore fishing industry. By the end of the 18th century, in the heyday of sail, whole communities were employed in producing the ropes, cordage and nets that supported merchant shipping, the Navy and the fishing fleet.

Many coastal regions had rope and net makers but the industry became centred on Bridport in Dorset, partly because the moist loam of the area is an ideal soil for growing hemp and flax, the chief raw materials. Hemp – known as 'neckweed' in Dorset – was tied in bundles after harvesting, then immersed in running water for several days to rot the core, and flailed to separate the fibres from the stalk. Finally, the tangled mass of fibres was 'hackled' – usually by women. Handfuls, or 'streaks' of hemp were oiled with whale or linseed oil, then pulled through the tapering steel pins of the hackle board repeatedly, a process similar to carding in spinning. This cleaned and aligned the fibres, removing any remaining stalk or pith.

THE ROPE-WALK

The hackled hemp was spun into yarn along a rope-walk. The spinner wore a thick belt of hemp fibres. He twisted some between his fingers and tied them to a hook attached to a wheel. The wheel was slowly turned by a second person, often a child, while the spinner backed down the rope-walk, feeding out fibres from his supply.

To make a rope, groups of these yarns were twisted together, then three or more of the groups were themselves twisted again. The more yarns in each group, the bulkier the rope would be. The yarns were laid out along the rope-walk

NAVAL CORDAGE
(left) The principal use of ropes was for shipping, especially in the age of sail, when millions of miles of cords and cables went to rig not only the Royal Navy, but also the entire coastal fleet of fishing boats, traders and carriers.

— which was sometimes as much as 1000ft (305m) long. Each group of yarns was attached at one end to one of a series of revolving hooks on the rope jack. At the other end all the yarns were fixed to a single hook, which also rotated, on a mobile trolley known as a 'traveller'. At first, the single hook would be fixed in position, and a grooved top was inserted at the same end to separate the groups of yarn, which were twisted as the handle of the rope jack was turned – this caused the traveller to move slowly towards the rope jack. When the twist was judged to be sufficiently tight – usually when the yarns had shrunk to about a quarter of their original length – the traveller was fixed in position, the single hook released and the top pushed by the rope maker slowly towards the rope jack. Behind him, the rope would make itself, twisting the groups together in the opposite direction to their own twist. Such a rope is described as 'hawser-laid'. Three hawser-laid ropes can be twisted together to make exceptionally thick 'cable-laid' ropes, such as those used for anchor cables.

GRIMSBY TRAWLERS
(above) The huge trawl nets used in the herring fisheries off the east coast of England in the 1930s were still knotted by hand using natural fibres, but in vast net factories in Grimsby rather than the domestic setting of the earlier cottage industry.

STURDY HEMP
(right) Hemp was the favourite material for ropes, being tough, long-lasting and cheap. Manila rope, also ideal for marine uses, was more expensive than hemp. Other fibres included sisal, jute and coir – made from coconut fibres and used mostly for mooring ropes.

SPLICING THE MAINBRACE

In the late 18th and early 19th centuries, much of the huge mileage of rope and cordage being produced on the rope-walks of Britain went to meet the demands of the type of rigging carried by large sailing ships of the time. Ships such as the *Victory*, Nelson's flagship at Trafalgar, carried over 100 guns, and some 15 miles (25km) of rigging. This varied from small-gauge line to the immense anchor cable, which was of hemp, 24in (61cm) in circumference and 100 fathoms (600ft, 180m) long. The spars, yard-arms and sails of the great ships were enmeshed and supported by a complex spider's web of tarred hemp. Each shroud, stay and brace had its own name and particular function. The mainbrace, for example, supported the mainmast. Such was the girth of this great cable that splicing it to secure the end was a labour of Herculean proportions, and one that warranted the issue of a special ration of rum on its completion – hence the tippler's expression 'splice the mainbrace'.

Rope-walks existed inland as well as on the coast, and one of the most spectacular was in the mouth of the Peak Cavern at Castleton, Derbyshire. The villagers could carry on working there whatever the weather. Country rope makers produced a range of goods, from lightly twisted garden twine to beautifully woven one-piece headstalls for horses.

In Bridport and other rope-making towns the industry was often a family affair. Some of the Bridport houses had their own rope-walks in long narrow gardens. Other rope-walks were in the alleys and streets of the town. While the man of the house twisted up ropes with the help of his children, the women might well be

HACKLING THE HEMP
The coarse tangle of natural hemp fibres must be cleaned, carefully sorted and aligned before they can be spun. In a modern rope-making factory such as the one in the naval dockyard at Chatham (above), this 'hackling' is done by enormous machines. In the traditional rope maker's cottages in Bridport, it was women's work.

SPINNING A YARN
The basic yarn of rope making was spun from a group of hackled fibres by a 'spinster' who twisted them between his fingers.

manufacturing nets from their own twine – Bridport supplied many of the country's nets as well as ropes. The workforce was predominantly women. They also helped with spinning the hemp. At the beginning of the 19th century they were earning about eightpence a day.

NETTING KNOTS

The net maker's tools are simple: shuttle-like needles to hold the twine and spacers, called mesh pins to ensure that the size of the mesh remains constant. Working to a fixed line strung between posts or rings, the net maker began braiding the net by tying a series of clove-hitches, creating a row of loops. To this first row was added subsequent rows of loops using a continuous length of twine, knotting with sheet bends, and working from left to right and right to left in succession, to produce a diamond mesh. As each loop was made, the needle of twine was passed once round the mesh pin. Some net makers were capable of braiding 40 knots per minute. By increasing or decreasing the number of loops in a row, by varying the mesh size, adding gussets and using a variety of twines, net makers could braid a wide variety of net shapes, sizes and types. But their most important customers were fishermen.

Drift nets are straightforward long nets weighted at the bottom and floated at the top, usually with cork floats. They are also known as gill nets, as the fish are caught by the gills in the meshes. Sometimes long-nets are staked out in estuaries so that they either trap fish as they swim in on the tide, or catch them on the ebb. Salmon are sometimes fished in this way. Herring and mackerel nets are made in three 'rands', or strips. Each year the bottom rand, which gets most wear, is removed, and a new rand added to the top of the net.

ROPE-WALKS AND
ROPE MAKERS
*(below and right) According
to some calculations, a
traditional rope maker
would have walked the
rope-walk the equivalent
of an entire circuit of
the earth during a lifetime's
work.*

TRAVELLER

TOP

ROPE JACK

The trammel is considered one of the most difficult to make. It consists of a long net with three layers – two large-mesh nets sandwiching a third one of finer mesh. As fish strike the net, they push through the first wide mesh into the loosely hung fine net, which is forced through the wide mesh on the far side, forming a pocket which holds the fish securely.

A trawl net is made in the form of a deep, tapering bag. It is hauled behind the trawler by lines to a bar which holds the mouth of the bag open.

NURTURING THE NETS

Traditionally, nets are tanned to preserve them. Oak bark was a main source of tannin for this purpose, though the bark of other trees, such as elm, birch and pine, was also used. The bark was powdered and boiled in water, and the nets were passed slowly through this liquid, then left to drain for several days. As the nets became paler with use, they would be re-tanned, to a deep russet brown.

Carefully looked after, nets could last for years. Conscientious fishermen would regularly repair them, wash them and dry them out after use. The same tools and techniques were used for repair and rebraiding as for making the nets. Sometimes the nets were draped on poles at the harbourside for repair and drying. On some parts of the coast, especially in the south and east, there are specially built net-houses – fishermen's lofts built very tall on a narrow base. They are usually made of wood, faced with tarred clapboard or planking. The extra-tall lower room is used for hanging nets.

Nets were made for other purposes apart from fishing. Gamekeepers – and poachers – needed nets for catching animals and birds: purse nets for rabbit warrens and long-nets for

staking across fields. Other nets included hay nets for horses, vegetable nets for carrying produce to market and fruit nets for protecting orchards against birds. Trapping nets were dyed to disguise them. Green dye came from green wheat chopped and boiled. A pale strawy yellow came from celandines. Russet came from a decoction of logwood chips.

ARTIFICIAL FIBRES

These days certain small oddly shaped nets, such as those for billiard table pockets, and some special ropes, such as bell-pulls, are made by hand from natural fibres, but for the most part, nets and ropes are made by machine using artificial fibres – polythene, polyethylene and polypropylene. These have some advantages: they are exceptionally strong and resistant to rot; but they have a tendency to stretch and may deteriorate in bright sunlight and their resistance to rotting means that nets lost at sea remain a permanent hazard to marine fish and mammals. For trapping game, for example, nets made from artificial fibres are also unsuitable, since they do not take up the camouflaging smells of the earth and undergrowth as organic fibres do. The last visible wielders of the netting needle and mesh pin, however, must be the small-boat fishermen, who can often be seen at work with impressive dexterity, in the shelter of the harbour wall, for whatever the fibre, dogfish still wreck nets, and nets must still be repaired.

NET HOUSES
The natural fibres used by traditional net makers, though strong and resistant to sunlight and heat, were prone to rot if left to lie wet for lengthy periods. Drying some of the huge trawl and drift nets could be a problem, so special drying sheds were built on some parts of the coast, notably at Hastings (above). In other places, such as Wester Ross in Scotland (above left), the nets would simply be draped over poles in the open air.

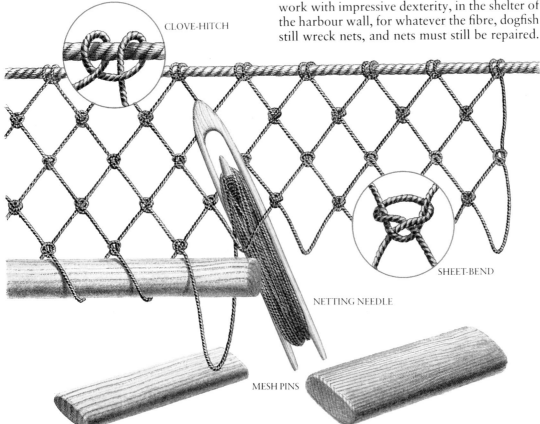

CLOVE-HITCH

SHEET-BEND

NETTING NEEDLE

MESH PINS

NETTING
The net maker's tools were very simple. The needle was made of wood or bone. These and the mesh pins which gauged the size of the loop were available in a range of sizes for different types of net.

The Sailmakers

For thousands of years, the skill of the sailmaker in cutting, shaping and finishing canvas has provided seamen with the sails they need to harness the power of the wind.

The sailmaker who created the means to snare the wind and coax it into service, was once seen as something of a magician, controlling a force believed to be of supernatural origin. In more recent times, however, the sailmaker's fortunes have been based on commercial rather than superstitious considerations, waxing and waning with the empires of Western Europe whose vast fleets – both naval and merchant – plied the seven seas in search of power and glory. Nowadays, sailmakers tailor their craft to suit the demands of the growing fleet of sporting and pleasure boats that use windpower through choice, rather than need.

Despite the huge variety in sail shape and size, all sails work in two basic ways. Held square on to the wind, a simple sail acts like a bag, containing the force of the wind and so causing it to push the vessel along. Most sails are a little more sophisticated, however. Curving naturally and by design, a sail as it fills with wind takes on the shape of an aerofoil which forces the air flowing around the convex side to travel faster than that which passes over the convex side. The result is a drop in air pressure in front of the sail and a suction effect which pulls the vessel forward. Early, square-rigged ships tended to rely most on the push of the wind, while later fore-and-aft rigged vessels could exploit the pull of the wind which enabled them to sail much closer to the wind.

SQUARE RIGS

In a square-rigged ship, the square sail hangs from a spar or yard in front of the mast. It is relatively free of the rigging that supports the mast and at right-angles to the keel. The sail can be turned on its yard to starboard (right) or port (left) a certain distance before it fouls the rigging. This means the boat can be sailed to one or other side of the direction of an on-coming wind. Sailing boats zig-zag along such courses or tacks if there is no wind behind them or to the side of them. Because at a certain point

CUTTY SARK
The Cutty Sark (left) was commissioned in 1869 as a tea clipper. From 1885 to 1895 she carried wool from Sydney to London, consistently making the fastest runs of all clippers on this route. Her speed was a tribute to the skill of captain and crew in handling the ship's 32,000 square feet of sail.

the square rig is fouled by the rigging, it is not a good rig to sail directly into the prevailing wind.

In the early days of square-rigged sails the sail was simply designed to catch the wind. Some, particularly topsails, high on the masts, were therefore cut in such a way as to encourage a buxom billowing.

The square rig was the ideal rig for larger ships on long runs. Long sea voyages were usually planned to take maximum advantage of trade winds which blow reliably in a largely constant direction. The square rig flourished and survived from Viking times, throughout the Middle Ages, into the era of the 19th century clippers and beyond. In fact some of the last working sailing ships in Britain were the square-rigged stately Humber Keels, which carried their cargoes along river estuaries and canals. They had barge-like hulls, and a single mast on which were set square mainsails and square topsails above.

The largest square sails ever made in Britain were for HM battleship Temeraire, completed

SAILMAKER'S LOFT
(above) With space enough to spread the canvas out, sailmakers work together to produce a suit of sails. Although today's sailmakers use modern materials and some modern tools, the basic skills they employ have changed little over the centuries.

The company of many large-crewed ships would most certainly include a sailmaker. Apart from making and mending the sails he would make other canvas items, such as rigger's bags (to be hoisted to repair sites), canvas buckets and even canvas clothing. Other members of the crew, particularly the riggers, would be expected to carry out workmanlike running repairs to sails while under way.

SAILMAKER'S PALM
(below) Using the tough built-up eye of the roping palm, the sailmaker pushes the needle through the canvas to set in the ropes.

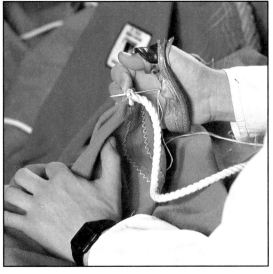

in 1877 and immortalized in the popular painting by Turner. The mainsail was suspended from a yard 115 feet long, and contained 5100 square feet of canvas, weighing two tons. The total sail area of the ship was a staggering 25,000 square feet. The Cutty Sark, most famous of the clippers, boasted 34 sails, carrying 32,000 square feet, or three-quarters of an acre of canvas.

FORE-AND-AFT RIGS

In fore-and-aft rigs, the line of the sails is roughly in line with the length of the boat. The mainsail is fastened so that one edge is always forwards, and one edge to the rear. Although adjustments are possible, they are slightly difficult to make because they are fixed inside the standing rig.

However, fore-and-aft rigs are more efficient than square sails at making way in the face of the wind. The fore-and-aft rig is also highly suitable for smaller craft which work in crowded waters, inshore, and have to carry out speedy manoeuvres, sometimes heading close into the wind.

SAILORS AND SAILMAKERS

Over the years experience taught sailors and sailmakers that some sails worked better than others. Sailmakers sought to create ideal curves in the sails by the way they cut the lines of the flax strips. They also learned how to create the strongest possible sails by assembling the strips in certain patterns so that the straining points were equally distributed around the sail.

CUTTING A SAIL
(above) Cloth is laid out on the smooth varnished floor of the sail loft. It is either pinned to templates or chalk shapes on the floor and cut into the required shapes. Once the pieces are stitched together, the edges are trimmed and then reinforced to withstand the wear and tear of daily use.

A FULL SUIT OF SAILS
Hanging from the mizzen (1), main (2) and foremasts (3), sails are called into service depending on the strength and direction of the wind. When sailing into headwinds fore- and aft-sails (4-9) do most of the work; the topsails (10-12), staysails (13-16) and the jigger (17) give easier control and balance. Lighter weather sails, like the fore topmast stay sail (9), and the inner, outer and flying jib sails (18-20) were useful when the wind dropped. In moderate conditions all the sails had a part to play.

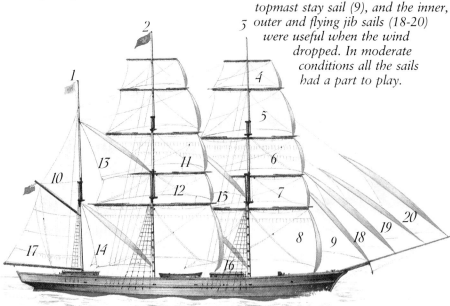

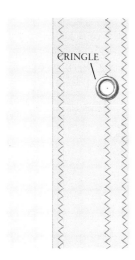

SAIL PROFILE
(right) The leading edge or luff is attached to the mast. The bottom edge or foot is either loose-footed or attached to a spar called a boom. The rear edge or leech is strengthened with battens. The sail is kept in place by ropes passed through holes at head, clew and tack. These are reinforced with metal rings or cringles (left).

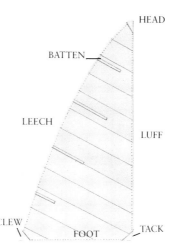

In general, however, sailmakers worked from the shore. They became established wherever there was a large demand for sails – at naval centres, in fishing communities, and in the great trading ports.

THE SAILMAKER'S LOFT

Sails for ships of war, merchantmen and carriers, as well as for the larger fishing vessels were huge. To make them, a sailmaker needed plenty of space in which to work, a flat floor and a certain amount of peace and quiet in order to handle quickly and accurately huge amounts of fabric.

From these needs evolved the sailmaker's loft. Usually situated on an upper storey, the

ON THE BENCH
(below left) Each sailmaker works from a wooden bench with his own set of knives, mallets, needles, fids, and beeswax to hand.

TRADITIONAL TOOLS
(below) Although modern sailmakers may use computers to make their calculations and power tools for sewing, many of their tools have remained the same for centuries.

became the standard sail material until the introduction of heavy cottons and synthetic materials.

The flax-canvas used by the Royal Navy from the early 17th century onwards came in bolts of fabric 40 yards long and 24 inches wide. The heaviest quality, used for major sails, or courses, was known as No. 1. This weighed 46lbs to the bolt. No. 2 weighed three pounds less per bolt and so on, down to No. 8 which weighed 25lb to the bolt. An extra heavy quality, known as No. 00, was used for the sails of ships which went round Cape Horn and had to endure the ferocious weather of the southern oceans.

SAILMAKING TOOLS

A sailmaker's tools are surprisingly few and simple. Most important are the sailmaker's palms. These are wide bands of stitched leather and rawhide that fit around the hand, with a reinforced hole for the thumb, and built-up 'eye', containing a disc of white metal pitted with indentations. This is positioned over the fleshy part of the palm at the base of the thumb and used to press hard upon the heads of the needles to drive them through the thick canvas.

There are two sorts of palm used in sailmaking. One, the seaming palm, has an eye with small indentations, to accommodate the heads of finer needles used in sewing seams in light canvasses and for putting in patches and 'tablings', which are reinforcing strips sewn

loft had a carefully laid floor, which had to be kept clean and smooth. Here a number of workers could be accommodated to cut and assemble the sails from the bolts of cloth laid out and pinned to templates or to chalk shapes drawn on the loft floor. Working together in this way sailmakers could pool their experience and produce sails of uniform design with predictable performance.

At first sails were made from wool but this was not a satisfactory material. It stretched out of shape and did not have a surface texture necessary for efficient sailing. Flax-canvas

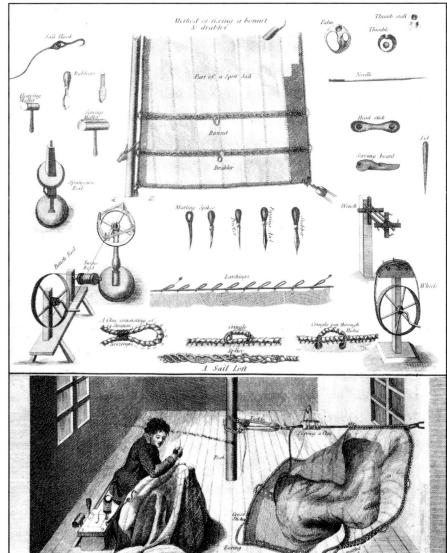

(right) Although no longer called on to make acres of sail for individual sailing ships like the 19th century clippers, sailmakers today are still very much in demand to make the bright, modern sails for the flotillas of leisure and sports boats which now exist. But rather than the traditional canvas modern sails are generally made of light and durable synthetic materials such as terylene and polyester.

SETTING SAIL
Sail enthusiasts today are able to experience first hand the rigours of life on a tall ship. Numerous old ships have been restored or replicas built. The crew above are manning the yards, the spars from which the sails hang. Once unfurled, the sails will billow in the wind, taking the ship forward on its course or tack.

along the edge of a sail.

The second, the roping palm is a more robust tool. Its eye has larger indentations, to take the large needles used to set ropes into the edges of sails, and to make the various eyes and loops which must be built into sail ropes. These enable the sail to be fastened to spars and masts, and hauled up and down. The roping palm also has an extra piece of tough reinforcement around the thumbhole so that tough material can be stitched without breaking the needle.

To flatten any stitches which stand proud, and for pressing the sailcloth, the sailmaker once used a seam-rubber, a shaped piece of hardwood, often box, with a blunt chisel head and a pad at the other end, sometimes in the form of a Turk's head knot.

To hold the material under tension in exactly the right place the sailmaker uses a sailhook or bench-hook. This is a finely pointed hook with a long shank mounted on a swivel to which is attached a strong lanyard about six feet in length. To make holes in the cloth and to open up the rope loops or cringles, before inserting into them the brass or other metal eyes (thimbles) he uses tapered and pointed pieces of polished hardwood, known as fids. Fids are also used for separating the strands of a rope so that it can be spliced when the sail is rigged.

The sailmaker usually cuts his cloth with a knife, which has a 'sheepsfoot' profile, and a thick V-section blade which is kept razor sharp.

Sailmaker's needles are quite unlike other sewing needles. Triangular in cross-section, with rounded edges, they force a passage-way between the threads of a fabric, rather than through them. They come in a variety of sizes, and are chosen according to the thickness of canvas being sewn.

The thread used varies from linen thread to spun polyester. Linen and cotton threads and twines are usually bees-waxed before used with a block of bees-wax on the sailmaker's bench. He also keeps a wide assortment of the metal fittings which go into a sail, such as thimbles, fasteners, and slides all of which were traditionally sewn in. Today a modern sailmaker may use crimping tools and punches to inset them.

MODERN MATERIALS

The canvas and cotton sails of the old wooden boats are becoming rare. Modern sail materials include Terylene, a synthetic fibre much stronger than cotton and almost impervious to water. Nylon has too much stretch in it for most sails except for the enormous and spectacular spinnakers which are used by racing yachts for extra pull when the wind is behind or abeam, and not too strong. Many racing yachts now use sails made from heavily resinated, hard finished fabrics. High stress sails, designed to cope with heavy weather, such as the storm trysail that can replace a bermudian mainsail in high winds, are more likely to be made of heavy quality but soft-finished polyester sailcloth.

New materials have inevitably brought with them new techniques and skills. Sail cut and angle is now calculated by computer where once guesswork would have sufficed. But the traditional craft of sailmaking remains very much alive, not only in keeping many fine examples of our maritime heritage in perfect order, but also in providing the sails for the huge fleet of pleasure craft which now throng our waters.

INDEX

Museum: 14(b).
Nick Birch: 37, 38(c), 40(t).
Anthony Blake Photo Library: 287(tr), 289(tr).
Blue Circle Industries: 304(b).
Bodleian Library, Oxford: 32(bl), 142(c), 213(br), 225(b); MS Bodley 264 f.84 235(br); John Johnson Collection 34(c).
Janet & Colin Bord: 65(b), 102(b).
Bowater-Scott Ltd.: 227(b).
Bridgeman Art Library: 22(c), 70(bl), 76(br), 151(tr), 177(tr), 208(tl), 221(c); John Bethell 161(b), 169(cl); Bibliothèque Nationale, Paris 236(t); Bristol Museum & Art Gallery 'A View from the Park Place' by S. Jackson 142(b); Bury Art Gallery 42–43(t); Christie's 184(tl), 'A Coastal Scene' by William Wyllie 300–301(b); 'Banquet for the Prince Regent, 1814' by George Clint 188–189(t); Department of the Environment 150–151(b); Guildhall Art Gallery 'Looking Towards Glen Coe from Rannock Moor' by Thomas Miles Richardson Jnr 64, 186; Oscar & Peter Johnson Ltd. 'Horses and Dogs' by John Emms 252–253(t); 'The Hop Garden' by Cecil Gordon Lawson 84(t); Musée Condé, Chantilly 10(br); Musée Condé, Chantilly/ Lauros-Giraudon 127; 'Outside the Inn' by David Monies 85(c); Musée du Louvre, Paris 'The Lace Maker' by Jan Vermeer 218–219(t); Private Collections 'Rebuilding of Southill' by G. Garrard 144(b), 'Girl and Bee Hives' by L.L. Pocock 200–201(t); Temple Newsham House, Leeds 'Portrait of Elizabeth of England' by Paul van Somer 220(br); Whitbread Collection 'Mr. Whitbread's Wharf' by George Garrard 82–83(t); Wolverhampton Art Gallery 'The Timber Wagon' by J.F. Herring 112–113(t), 'Down the Dregs' by John Seymour Lucas 82(b).
British Library: 78(bc).
Britain on View: 290(tc), 293(b).
H.P. Bulmer Ltd.: 'The Cider Press' by Henry Ziegler 92(t).
Jim Burke: 132(bc).
Ed Buziak: 146(bc), 250(b).
Bill Carcary: 78(tl).
Celtic Picture Agency: 66(tl), 66–67(t), 67(bl).
Cephas Picture Library: 77(b), 79(cr), 126(tr), 243(r), 296(bl); Frank B. Higham 255(tr).
John Charity: 296–297(t).
Chestnut Country Crafts, Stilton: 198(b).
The Clayton Aniline Co. Ltd.: 212(bc).
John Cleare 100(bc).
Bruce Coleman Ltd.: Nicholas Devore 50–51(t); Colin Molyneux 234–235(t); Jonathan Wright 270–271.
County Museum, Truro, Cornwall: 273(b).
The Courage Shire Horse Centre: 244(t).
Crafts Council: 125(br); Chris Chapman 122–123, 126(tl); George Wright 125(tr).
Andrea Cringean: 59(br).
Crown Copyright: 124(tl); Shetland Archives 53(b).
Daily Telegraph Colour Library: GEG Germany 284(b); John Marmaras 292(b); Christine Pearcey 309(bl); P. Thurston 237(cr).
John Darling: 128(br).
Adrian Davies: 119(b), 120(br).
Eric Edwards: 277(cl,br).
Robert Estall: 194–195(t), 204(br).
E.T. Archive: 278(l); Bibliothèque Nationale, Paris 9(br).
Mary Evans Picture Library: 28(bl), 42(c),

54–55(t), 86(t), 122(b), 124(br), 179(tr), 180, 198(tl), 204(t), 262–263(t), 267(br).
Exeter Maritime Museum: 298(b).
Paul Felix: 45(tl), 91(bc), 97(c,b), 110(b), 145(b), 146(t,c), 147, 162(tl), 171, 179(c,cr,bc,br), 181, 197(c,b), 204(bl), 224(b), 226(tr,b), 249(t), 251, 297(tc), 299, 308(tr), 311, 314(tl,tr), 315(cl), 317.
Fine Art Photographic Library: 109(tl), 124–125(t), 264(t), 279(tr); Anon 'Haymakers' 32–33(t); Carl Fisher 'View of Rye' 28–29(b); Myles Birket Foster 'Hop Pickers' 14–15(t), 'Near Hindhead' 246(b), 'Sheep Feeding' 38(b); L. Papaluca 'The Cutty Sark' 312(b).
Forestry Commission, Edinburgh: 112(cl), 114(t).
Derek Forss: 100–101(b), 168–169(b).
Fotomas Index: 26(b), 68(t).
Garland Collection: The Old Shop, Bignor, Sussex 154–155(t).
Garnar Booth plc: 74(b).
S.A. Gibson: 214(tr).
Giraudon: Bibl. Ecole des Beaux-Arts 166.
Glasgow Art Gallery & Museum: Thomas Faed 'The Last of the Clan' 49(t).
Ronald Goodearl: 174–175(t).
Goodlad & Goodlad: 55(bl).
Guildhall Library, City of London: 164(t).
Peter Haas: 154(b).
Sonia Halliday: 27(br).
Richard Harris: 23(b).
The Harris Tweed Association: 58–59(t), 61(br).
Hereford Library: 30(b).
John Heseltine: 261(bl,br).
David Higgs: 292(c).
Highlands and Islands Development Board: 114(b).
J. Hinks & Son, Appledore: 296(bc).
Michael Holford: 149(t,b), 183(tl), 192(tl), 229(tr,cr), 254(tr).
Hull Museums: 240(tr).
Hulton Deutsch Collection: 10(bl), 12(b), 28(cr), 34(t), 36(t), 44(t), 46(b), 51(tr), 96(br), 97(tl), 98(t), 132–133, 141(b), 142–143, 144–145(t), 151(c), 176–177(b), 183(tr), 190(tl), 194(bl), 200(b), 202(bl), 211, 225(t), 226(tl), 233, 237(cl), 239, 266–267(t,b), 270(bl), 274(tl), 284(t), 295(b), 306–307(t).
Impact: Mark Cator 20(b); Pamela Toler 158(cr).
International Linen Promotion: 207(b), 208–209(b), 210(tl,br).
G. Jackson & Sons Ltd: 160(b).
Lamberhurst Vineyards: 80(bl).
Andrew Lawson: 189(b).
Leeds City Art Galleries: John St Helier Lander 'H.R.H. The Prince of Wales' 54(tl).
Leicestershire Museums: 244(b).
Stewart Lindford: 175(br).
By permission of the Council of the Linnean Society of London: 214–215(border).
Littlethorpe Potteries: 178–179(c).
London Assay Office: P.V.A. Johnson 191(bc).
London Regional Transport: 303(br).
J.E. Manners: 51(c,b).
The Mansell Collection: 14–15(b), 16(c), 35(t,b), 45(tr), 62(t), 68(c), 73(tr), 86(b), 95(br), 110–111(t), 113(b), 118(t), 129(br), 130(br), 134(t), 178(tl), 196, 208–209(c), 212–213, 214(tl), 216(t), 227(t,c), 228(br), 248(tr), 267(cr), 268–269(b), 272(bl), 278–279(t), 280(t), 288–289(t), 290–291.

Marshall Cavendish: 252(br), 254(c), 255(bl,br); Ray Duns 24; Melvin Grey 263(br), 265(tr); courtesy of F. Sangorski & G. Sutcliffe Ld. 230(tr), 231.

S. & O. Mathews: 7, 13, 16–17(b), 25, 29(t), 31, 32(br), 36(c), 43(b), 47, 79(tr), 81, 93, 98(b), 105, 115, 121, 129(cr), 152(b), 155, 158(t), 165, 172(bc), 199, 234(b), 238(tl), 245, 257, 275, 281, 282(bl), 285(t).

Metropolitan Police: 135(b).

Colin Molyneux: 88(bc).

Museum & Art Gallery Stoke-on-Trent: 178(c).

Museum of Cider, Hereford: 90(tr), 91(r), 92(b).

Museum of English Rural Life, Reading: 8–9(t), 11(tr), 18(b), 20–21(t), 29(bc), 30(t), 34(cl), 69, 72(tl), 75, 84(c), 91(tl), 112(b), 116–117, 123(br), 125(bc), 135(tr), 139(t), 140(t), 148(bl,br), 153, 177(br), 197(tr), 203(r), 218(b), 222(t), 242–243, 248(tl), 249(b), 250(t), 254(tl), 264–265(b), 265(c,b), 289(b), 308(cl); Richard Whitmore, BBC 246–247.

Museum of Leathercraft/Northampton Museums & Art Gallery: 70–71(t), 71(b).

The National Library of Wales: 65(t).

National Maritime Museum: 300(t), 302(t), 315(br).

National Monument Record: 303(c), 304(t).

National Museum of Ireland: 190(b).

National Museum of Wales (Welsh Folk Museum): 67(br), 76–77(t), 78–79(t), 134(b), 282–283.

National Portrait Gallery, London: 216(br).

The National Trust: Horst Kolo 163(t).

Natural Image: Robin Fletcher 116(b), 201(bl).

Nature Photographers: S.C. Bisserot 310(tl); Andrew Cleave 104(t); Christopher Grey-Wilson 118(c); J.A. Hancock 103(br); E.A. Janes 102(tl), 103(c); C.K. Mylne 104(c); Paul Sterry 104(br).

NHPA: Bain & Cambridge 109(ctr); Stephen Dalton 202(br), 205; E.A. Janes 237(tr); S.& O. Mathews 156(tc); Roger Tidman 157(b).

North Norfolk News: Collection J. Emery 294–295(t).

Oxford City Library: 44–45(b), 268(tl).

Oxford Scientific Films: Graham J. Wren 108(tl).

Oxfordshire County Library: 90–91(b).

Period Mouldings Ltd.: 164(b).

The Photo Source: 12(t).

Pilkington Glass Museum: 182–183(b).

Poppyland Photos: 298(t).

Press Association: 261(tr).

Press-Tige Pictures Ltd.: 162(tr,cr).

Ranger's House, Blackheath: Edward Sackville, 4th Earl of Dorset by William Larkin 220(tl).

Mike Roberts: 256(c).

Ann Ronan Picture Library: 83(br), 84–85(b), 184–185(t), 191(t), 217, 221(b), 223, 230(bl), 232(t), 287(tl), 288(tl).

Royal Brierley: 187.

Royal Photographic Society: 136(t).

Glyn Satterley: 48, 50(b), 60(cl), 61(tc), 62(cl).

The Science Museum, London: 214(c).

The School of Scottish Studies: 58(b), 60–61(b).

Scottish Ethnological Archive, Royal Museum of Scotland: 60(t), 138–139(c), 140(c), 286(c), 286–287(b).

Scottish Tourist Board: 57, 63.

Seaphot Ltd: Planet Earth Pictures: John Lythgoe 273(tl); J. & G. Lythgoe 307(br).

Shepherd's Boatyard, Windermere: 297(c,cr,bc).

Shetland Museum and Library: 53(t).

Shetland Tourist Organization: 56(b).

Brian Shuel: 192(cr).

The Slide File: 141(tl).

Edwin Smith: 163(c).

Philip Smith: 232(bc).

Sam Smiths, Tadworth Brewery: 99.

Sotheby's: 167(bl).

Spectrum Colour Library: 18(t), 55(br), 136(b), 145(c), 202(t), 238(cr), 241(tc,tr), 302–303(b), 316(t,c).

Frank Spooner Pictures: 274(b).

S.S.B.R. courtesy J. Harden: 301(t).

Suffolk Record Office, Ipswich: 16(t), 150–151(t).

Charles Tait: 288(b).

The Tate Gallery, London: 'Shoeing' by Sir Edward Landseer 240(l).

Robert Thompson's Craftsmen Ltd.: 167(tr), 169(tr), 170(t).

Three Choirs Vineyard: 80(br).

Topham Picture Library: 11(bl), 17(t), 26–27(t), 41, 44(bl), 46(t), 55(tr), 72–73(t), 101(t), 104(bl), 112(c), 128(t,c,bc), 130(tl), 157(cr), 170(b), 172–173, 174–175(b), 258(bl), 279(c), 312–313.

Trustees of the Victoria & Albert Museum: 74(t).

Bobby Tulloch: 52, 54(b), 56(t).

Ulster Folk and Transport Museum: 206–207(t), 209(t).

Victoria & Albert Museum: 167(bc), 168(t,bl), 219(b), 221(tl).

Wales Tourist Board: 293(t).

Chris Walton: 191(c,br).

The Wardens and Scholars of New College, Oxford: 188(c).

John Watney: 49(c), 160–161(t), 238(b), 268–269(t), 269(t), 305.

The Weald and Downland Open Air Museum: 163(b).

Douglas West Collection: 276, 280(c).

Whitbread: 87.

Derek G. Widdicombe: 19, 102(tr), 294(br).

Wildlife Matters: Dr. John Feltwell 158(b).

Woodmansterne Ltd.: Clive Friend 228–229(t).

Wootton Vineyard: 78(br).

The Worshipful Company of Goldsmiths: 193.

Jon Wyand: 40(b), 85(t), 139(br), 140(br), 141(tr inset), 156(tr); Holmes Hall Tanneries 72(b), 73(b).

Zefa: 184(c), 306(b); Bob Croxford 274(tr): G. Marche 94(b).

Artwork credits

Russell Barnett: 39.

Brian Delf: 96(l), 103(tr), 108(tr), 236–237(b), 260, 272(tl), 285(b), 309(t), 310(b).

Pavel Kostal: 38(t), 174(bl).

Norman Lacey: 292(tr).

Peter Sarson: 22(t).

Peter Sarson & Tony Bryan: 10(t), 11(tl), 129(tl), 156(l), 157(t), 203(t), 248(b), 297(tr), 314(br), 315(tl).